SECOND EDITION

Records Management

A Collegiate Course in Filing Systems and Procedures

MINA M. JOHNSON, Ph.D.
Professor of Office Administration
Department of Data Systems and Quantitative Methods
School of Business
San Francisco State University

NORMAN F. KALLAUS, Ph.D.
Chairman, Business Education
The University of Iowa

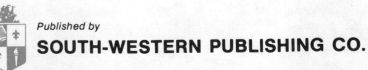

Published by

K67   **SOUTH-WESTERN PUBLISHING CO.**

CINCINNATI   WEST CHICAGO, ILL.   DALLAS   PELHAM MANOR, N.Y.
PALO ALTO, CALIF.   BRIGHTON, ENGLAND

PREFACE

Records Management is written for you—the student and the professional worker—who want and need to know the principles underlying the effective management of records. As a text and as a reference book, it combines technical aspects of records technique with sound principles of management that extend far beyond the day-to-day activities in the office.

In this revision of the original textbook, special emphasis is given to the systems approach to records management along with updating of information and terminology. Illustrations and examples from modern records systems are included for clarification and instruction. Many of the end-of-the-chapter activities require visiting of records installations to get first-hand knowledge that will strengthen and add new meaning to the contents of the chapters.

As a text, *Records Management* furnishes guidelines for students who need an understanding of the field of records management. Included are the criteria by which records are created, stored, retrieved, retained, and disposed of; procedures for the operation and control of manual and automated storage systems; clear-cut rules for alphabetic indexing, the foundation of records storage methods; principles for the selection of records personnel, equipment, and supplies; thought-provoking review and discussion questions and learning projects that teach decision making; and up-to-date illustrations included as teaching aids, not merely to enhance the pages. The text is designed for college, junior college, and private business school usage.

As a reference book, *Records Management* is valuable to those who need to refresh their memories concerning storage, retention, transfer, and disposition of records; it is a guide for those who create records; it provides a comprehensive look at the entire scope of records management; it gives executives an insight into the responsibilities of records management personnel; it is of special importance to those who direct the operation of records storage and retrieval activities at any level of office work; it contains information of benefit

iii

to teachers in the storage of their own materials; and, because of the alphabetic filing rules contained herein, it can be used successfully in any storage situation.

The text is divided into four parts, containing a total of 14 chapters. Part One, "Basic Principles and Procedures of Records Management," includes an explanation of the nature of records management and the history of business records. It describes systems and methods of correspondence storage and gives terminology to enable the reader to understand the text. Intensive coverage is given to the alphabetic method of filing and to cross-referencing; and retrieval procedures are explained in detail.

Part Two, "Numeric, Geographic, and Subject Methods of Records Storage," presents a detailed description of these three methods of storing and retrieving cards and correspondence. Part Three, "Methods and Systems for Storing and Retrieving Special Records," includes information on the filing of cards and visible records, the storage and control of noncorrespondence and unconventional records, and an explanation of coding, storing, and retrieving automated records.

Part Four, "Managing the Records System," includes discussion of the records cycle from creation through disposal, a detailed chapter on the procurement and use of equipment and supplies, and a capstone chapter on the organization and operation of a records management program.

Within the book mention is made of well-known manufacturers of filing equipment and supplies and of professional associations which offer guidance and direction in records management. An extensive list of these firms and organizations is contained in the Teacher's Manual which accompanies this text. A comprehensive glossary of terms is also included in the Manual.

Accompanying *Records Management* is a practice set entitled *Records Management—Laboratory Materials*. This set consists of 14 realistic assignments: Laboratory Assignments 1, Card Filing—Names of Individuals; 2, Card Filing—Names of Businesses; 3, Card Filing—Other Names; 4, Card Filing—Review; 5, Alphabetic Correspondence Filing—Names of Individuals; 6, Alphabetic Correspondence Filing—Names of Individuals and Businesses; 7, Alphabetic Correspondence Filing and Tickler File Usage; 8, Requisition and Charge-Out Procedures; 9, Numeric Correspondence Filing; 10, Numeric Correspondence Filing—Review; 11, Card Filing—Geographic Method; 12, Geographic Correspondence Filing; 13, Geographic Correspondence Filing—Review; 14, Subject Correspondence

Filing, with an expanded set of correspondence. The text and laboratory materials used together give practice in storage and retrieval under conditions similar to those in an office.

The cooperation of filing equipment and supply manufacturers and of publishers who have furnished illustrations and given permission for use is gratefully acknowledged. And we thank the many representatives who gave time and explanations to the authors in their efforts to keep this edition up to date.

Finally, we as co-authors owe much to our families and friends whose encouragement and understanding can never be measured. The result, we believe, is a readable, instructive, enlightening text for your study of records management.

Mina M. Johnson
Norman F. Kallaus

Comments and suggestions from teachers using this text are welcomed at any time by the authors.

CONTENTS

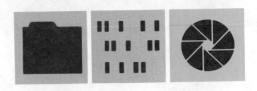

Laboratory Assignments follow Chapters 3, 4, 5, 6, 7, and 8.

PART ONE

BASIC PRINCIPLES
AND PROCEDURES
OF RECORDS STORAGE
AND CONTROL

Chapter 1

Records management and the history of business records

The *management* function, simply stated, consists of setting objectives for an enterprise and then planning for the achievement of those objectives as economically as possible. The study of management has evolved through the years to include many topics important to the successful operation of any firm. A very brief treatment of the development of managerial skill and knowledge would include the scientific management movement—the logic of "efficiency"; the human relations movement—a recognition of employee attitudes; and the information technology movement—an emphasis on the systems approach to solving information problems. *Records management*, which is primarily devoted to the control of an organization's records and papers, constitutes one important area of study in the age of information technology.

SECTION 1. MANAGERIAL NEED FOR RECORDS

Decisions involved with planning, organizing, directing, and controlling the various activities of an enterprise depend on the availability of information. Therefore, timely and accurate data are necessary for management and its employees to perform efficiently. Today it is common to hear the term "data processing" used to describe the collecting, processing, and communication of these data used in businesses. And, with this term, the records management function has emerged—a function which includes all those activities required to manage the records of an organization from their creation to their final disposal.

OVERALL IMPORTANCE OF RECORDS STORAGE

Few people realize that, of all the service activities of an organization, the creation and the storage of business records are the greatest "consumers" of space, salaries, and equipment.

In 1951 the federal government was said to have some 20,000,000 cubic feet of accumulated records, growing at the rate of 1,000,000 cubic feet a year.[1] As of July 1, 1972, the total accumulated federal records in current and storage areas was 29,692,781 cubic feet, over 12,000,000 cubic feet of which was in records storage centers and archives. A comparison of these figures with the ones for 1971 (28.6 million cubic feet) shows governmental records are still growing at the rate of 1 million cubic feet a year in spite of efforts to dispose of and purge unneeded materials![2]

The U. S. Department of Labor reported clerical and kindred workers in the United States in 1950 to be 7,632,000; in 1960, 9,783,000; and in 1972, 14,314,000—17.1 percent of the total number employed. In a twenty-year period, the number of clerical and kindred workers in the United States has almost doubled.[3] Since nearly every clerical worker is concerned with the making, processing, or handling of records, the foregoing figures give an indication of the growth in volume of papers in modern offices.

In 1972, it was estimated that a single file cabinet, taking 76 square feet of space, represents a space expenditure of $48 a year. Thus, the maintenance of a file cabinet in a year would be $180, with the average cost of filing a document being 4 cents. One file drawer can hold up to 4,500 documents.[4]

---

[1] Nona Brown, "Paper Pile-Up," *New York Times Magazine* (December 23, 1951), p. 33.

[2] Information received from National Archives and Records Service, Washington, DC, 11/14/72 through Mr. Harold Elliott of the San Francisco office.

[3] Bureau of Labor Statistics, *Employment and Earnings*, Volume 19, No. 3, September 1972, p. 3.

[4] Miss Gloria Wilkes, Vice President of a national management consulting firm which specializes in paperwork management; frequent adviser to the federal government on its records housing and retrieval problems; and past President of the New York Chapter of the American Records Management Association. "Profit-Eating File Cabinets Must Be Made to Heel," *Iron Age*, April 13, 1972, p. 27.

This expenditure of time, effort, and money is wasted unless records can be produced when they are required for reference; consequently, records must be arranged systematically according to some storage plan and procedure that will make it possible to find papers and other records immediately upon request. Such a plan is called a *filing system,* and the procedures for use of the system are the *steps in filing and finding.* Together, they represent one of the most important phases of office work. Frequently, however, executives give this phase of office operation little attention until the loss of a valuable paper emphasizes the need for a more effective system of records storage and control or for better-trained files supervisors and operators. One record lost, mislaid, or delayed can and often does inconvenience and retard a dozen or more people in their work. All too often a filing cabinet is considered to be merely a piece of furniture

> Where everything's listed,
> From A to Z,
> And everything's lost
> Systematically.[5]

For effective decision making, management needs records of correspondence, credit, employee work history, equipment and other company assets, plans for products and services, procedures and regulations, purchases and sales. To provide this information promptly when needed, records management personnel must be concerned with every detail of the creation, retention, access, storage and disposal of these records. The improper control of records creation, retention of unnecessary records, free access by anyone at any time to the files, no control of records taken from the files, and no plans for disposition of obsolete records or retention of needed ones is poor records management, creates chaos, and wastes a tremendous amount of time and money.

A CAREER IN RECORDS MANAGEMENT

Few office employees are aware of the importance of paper flow in an office. Often, employees fail to realize the importance of training in the principles underlying the classification and arrangement of business records. High school, business school, and college graduates

---

[5] Stephen Schlitzer, "Filing Cabinets," *The Saturday Evening Post* (February 2, 1957), p. 40.

are being hired for initial jobs that include filing as one of their daily duties. They must, therefore, know the fundamentals of filing and records control:

(1) so that they may be able to care properly for records entrusted to them and to produce them promptly when desired;

(2) so that they may know what to expect of others who may file records for them and also may be able to give them helpful guidance; and

(3) because a knowledge of filing techniques develops the ability to analyze, organize, and classify records that come to their desks, enabling them to handle and dispose of the records more intelligently than if they did not have that ability.

Records management is concerned with the life cycle of a record from its creation through processing, checking, maintenance, and protection, to its destruction; detailed discussion of these techniques will be found in later chapters. However, not everyone who studies records management aspires to the position of "records manager"; some will be happy to work in the service areas of filing and information storage and retrieval; others will find their places working with inactive records and providing for safekeeping of valuable records. Others will devote their time to forms management and paperwork flow studies.

Today the information contained in the filed records is the lifeblood of any business. The person who is responsible for the orderly arrangement of those records has one of the most responsible positions in any business office. From a beginning position as a file clerk, an alert, intelligent, well-trained person may rise to the position of records manager. A career in this field is a career on a professional level with an annual salary of $20,000 not unusual.[6]

To have information readily available when needed for decision making and for justification of action taken is the goal of enlightened management. At some future time, organizations may have a records manager instead of a files supervisor, but the demise of small-office filing methods will probably not occur within our lifetimes. Therefore, presenting the principles of proper management of business records as those principles apply to large and small organizations alike is the primary purpose of this text, which concentrates

---

[6] William J. Guy, "A Yardstick for a Successful Career in Records Management," *Records Management Quarterly* (April, 1969), p. 5.

on the storage and retrieval processes in the early pages and leads to the discussion of the entire scope of the records manager in later chapters.

SECTION 2. HISTORY OF BUSINESS RECORDS

EARLY EVIDENCES OF FILING AND RECORDS RETENTION

Filing has existed in one form or another since written history began. Many original tablets, parchments, and manuscripts of great historical value have come down through the ages and are now carefully guarded in museums all over the world. Without some method of preservation, most of these valuable documents would have remained forever unknown, although possession of many of them is the result of chance—record-bearing stones and tablets having been found buried in the loose earth in many places, with no attempt at preservation.

The National Stationery and Office Equipment Association states:

> We don't quite know just how Cleo, the Egyptian file clerk, kept track of her stone tablets, but we do know that ever since there was a written record, filing has been an important business function!
>
> Back in Roman days, records were strung on a thread for safekeeping. Thread is called "Filum" in Latin, hence our modern term, "file." [7]

One of the most common methods used by the ancients for the filing of their papers was that of keeping them in a stone or earthenware vessel. Many bits of historical evidence have been preserved on wax, on stone, on parchment, or upon a receptacle itself. An interesting survival of this custom is the widespread practice of sealing letters, pictures, newspapers, and other memorabilia of the current day in the cornerstone of a new building.

Among the ancients, with their primitive life, written records played a small part compared to the place records hold in present-day law and life. The orderly arrangement of records for the purpose of later reference was of little importance. Gradually there developed the realization of the convenience of keeping together the papers received from one individual or organization, or those bearing upon one subject, or those received on a certain date, or those pertaining to certain localities. Here were the signs of the alphabetic, the

---

[7] *How to Sell Filing Supplies* (Washington, DC: National Stationery and Office Equipment Association, 1957), p. 3.

subject, the chronologic, and the geographic methods of filing, respectively.

FILING FROM THE MIDDLE AGES TO 1900

Spindle file. The spindle, on which papers may be impaled, appeared about the 15th Century.[8] Occasionally firms today still cling

Figure 1-1
Spindle File

to this device for memoranda of temporary importance. In the early days of business, the records of many merchants consisted of two spindles, one of which carried the unpaid bills and the other, the paid bills. When the "paid" spindle became too full, some of the older of the "paid" bills were thrown away. Sometimes when the spike became filled, the papers were removed, a string was substituted, and the papers were tied together in a bundle.[9] This practice may have been the beginning of "disposition and retention" as we know them today!

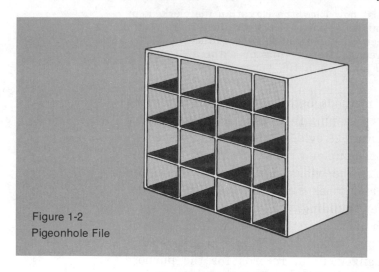

Figure 1-2
Pigeonhole File

Pigeonhole file. Persons who disliked the spindles folded or rolled their papers, wrote the names or subjects on the outside, and placed them in pigeonholes in rolltop desks or in a series of separate box-like openings in a cabinet. When the holes became filled, the papers were tied together (sometimes between boards) and put on a shelf or very often stored in boxes or trunks.[10]

Copybook file. Some of the early-day businesses had their few forms printed with copying ink. The ink used in filling out these

---

[8] *Ibid.*

[9] Coleman L. Maze, *Office Management, A Handbook* (New York: The Ronald Press Company, 1947), p. 584.

[10] Estelle B. Hunter, *Modern Filing Manual* (Rochester: Yawman & Erbe Mfg. Co., 1936), p. 2.

forms also had copying qualities. By means of a *letterpress,* these forms were copied into books on tissue paper before the originals were mailed.[11]

Bellows file. The bellows file, appearing about 1860, closely resembled an accordion or bellows.[12] Each numbered or lettered compartment was convenient but decidedly limited in capacity. In small file departments, the alphabetic bellows file is sometimes used as a sorter today.

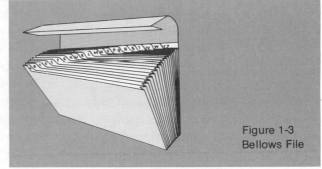

Figure 1-3
Bellows File

Flat file. In 1868, the first attempt was made to file in a cabinet equipped with drawers. Papers were filed one on top of the other, and this arrangement led to the designation *flat file.*[13] At first, each drawer was limited to a single letter of the alphabet. Usage soon showed that some drawers were overfilled (B, C, H, M, S, W), while others (Q, X, Z) were practically empty. In 1875, the *vowel method* of drawer division was adopted, whereby each drawer was divided into five parts; for example, the *B* drawer was divided into *Ba, Be, Bi, Bo,* and *Bu* sections.[14] Although this system divided the material into smaller groups and simplified finding, it did not distribute the material throughout the drawers.

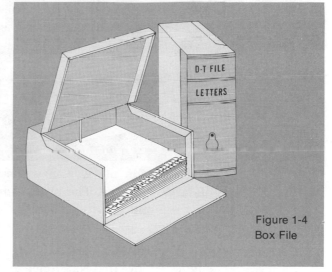

Figure 1-4
Box File

Box file. During 1875, a file box shaped like a book, opening from the side, was invented.[15] Each box contained a set of sheets having extension labels bearing the letters of the alphabet. It is still popular for a limited amount of correspondence, and, especially, for home use.

---

[11] Maze, *op. cit.,* p. 585.

[12] *Filing Equipment Comparisons and Costs* (Youngstown, Ohio: The General Fireproofing Company, 1953), p. H-2.

[13] *Ibid.*

[14] Hunter, *op. cit.,* p. 68.

[15] *Progressive Indexing and Filing* (Buffalo, New York: Library Bureau Division, Remington Rand, Inc., 1942), p. 11.

Alphabet subdivision. During 1875-76, several commercial firms began a careful search for a scientific method of subdividing the alphabet. One of the first attempts was based upon an analysis of the names appearing in the Chicago City Directory. Although this procedure was satisfactory for firms located in Chicago, it did not apply generally throughout the country. It was used, however, until 1880 when indexes compiled from Bradstreet's commercial rating lists were made available. In 1897, an index based on 205,920 names was placed on sale by Cameron, Amberg & Company. By 1906, all the large business houses selling indexing systems had worked out alphabetic subdivisions up to and including 6,000 in number.[16] Today, subdivisions number over 225,000!

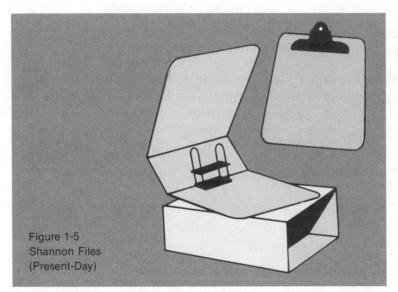

Figure 1-5
Shannon Files
(Present-Day)

Shannon file. Named after its inventor, the Shannon file was originated in 1880 in response to a need for greater security for papers.[17] The Shannon file consisted of a double side-opening arch, mounted on a board with a drawer front on the end. Papers to be filed were first perforated at the upper edge and then placed on the arches according to the system or arrangement being used. The Shannon file was, however, unsuitable for the correspondence of large concerns. The present-day Shannon arch-board files operate on the same principle, but they are designed for temporary filing.

Vertical file. Vertical filing of papers was in all probability first suggested by Dr. Nathaniel S. Rosenau, Secretary of the Charity Organization Society of Buffalo, New York. His long experience with card filing made him believe the same principle might be applied to filing papers (placing them on edge behind guides). He advanced the idea in 1892. The following year several firms demonstrated vertical

---

[16] Hunter, *op. cit.*, p. 68.
[17] *Ibid.*, p. 4.

files at the World's Fair in Chicago. Large crowds gathered before the exhibit; but the general opinion was, "It will never work; you cannot stand papers on edge; and if you leave them loose, they will be lost." Today vertical filing is generally recognized as the best method of caring for the majority of business records! The first files were built of wood in horizontal sections, but about 1900 the first steel vertical files appeared.[18]

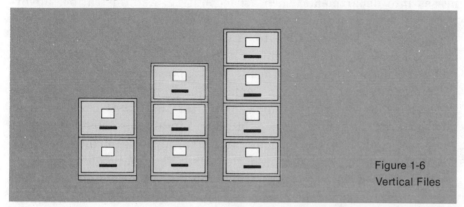

Figure 1-6
Vertical Files

FILING IN THE TWENTIETH CENTURY

Less than a century ago, a businessman placed much emphasis on house and trade secrets that he kept within his head; he kept few records except for those required for legal documentation and protection and for historical interest. With the Industrial Revolution, rapid improvements in production technology, introduction of the factory system, and emergence of the various forms of business ownership, firms grew in size and scope of operations. Competition became keener; finance, production, marketing, and other departments vied for management attention. An awareness of responsibilities to employees and to society in general emerged. The number of external and internal communications burgeoned.

As time went on, more and more correspondence became necessary between those with whom business was done. As the country grew and business expanded, more dependence was placed on the written word than on the spoken word. Clerks who were assigned to various functions of the business retained the papers relating to their particular duties. At this point the first "headaches" from lost papers were experienced.

The dividing of businesses into branches involved additional correspondence. Purchases of the same line of goods could be made in various cities and sections of the country, thus necessitating more

---

[18] *Filing Equipment Comparisons and Costs, op. cit.*, p. H-3.

correspondence. The ease with which records and correspondence could be written with the aid of shorthand and typewriting did much to increase the volume of papers to be handled and stored.

At the turn of the century, large national organizations came into being. Divisional files separated the records on a given subject. With further expansion, progressive firms reorganized their businesses into departments, such as accounting, administration, advertising, production, purchasing, and sales; and the head of each department was responsible for its records. In order to save time, cut costs, and fix responsibility for the whereabouts of all business papers, central filing departments first appeared about 1919.[19]

With the ever-increasing demand for improved records storage methods came a corresponding demand for those who could file and find quickly. The proper storage of papers in an office obviously could not be relegated to the various clerks to be accomplished in their spare moments. Filing became a definite, fixed, and important office vocation, but a vocation with which no one was familiar. Trained stenographers, typists, bookkeepers, and receptionists were available; but no provision had ever been made for similar instruction for filing and records management personnel except by library schools whose work was confined to library methods.

In order to train properly qualified persons for filing duties, early in 1914 the New York School of Filing was founded.[20] Credit is given to Mr. J. M. McCord, who was doing sales work with the Library Bureau Division of Remington Rand, New York City, for starting the first schools. During World War I and for a time thereafter, schools were operated in Boston, Chicago, and Philadelphia. At present, many high schools, business schools, colleges, and universities include instruction in filing and records management in their curricula either as a special course or in connection with other business subjects. There are special schools for file operators with day and evening classes in Boston, Chicago, and New York.

The need for more records management personnel was greatly accelerated by the creation of emergency boards and bureaus during World War I and World War II. Information was produced at an alarming rate; the creation of records was not controlled as little

---

[19] Edna B. Poeppel, "The Role of Records in American Business Administration," *Journal of Business Education* (December, 1944), p. 19.

[20] N. Mae Sawyer, "Teaching of Filing—Remington Rand Materials," *Business Education World* (December, 1952), p. 175.

thought was given to the consequences of storing everything that was produced. This has resulted in an inordinate volume of records of all types being kept unnecessarily in many of today's offices.

The development and perfection of the electronic computer during the last twenty-five years has given impetus to the production of information at an alarming rate. This technological advancement and the advancements that have been made in communication media and methods have brought about a substantial increase in the number of records that are created in a business, have greatly placed new demands on records personnel relative to storage equipment and methods, and have put new emphasis upon the role of records management personnel. Control over the creation, use, and storage of these voluminous and varied records *is* the responsibility of "records management."

For Review and Discussion

1. List several reasons why management needs records.

2. As you think of a beginning office job for yourself, why is it important that you know how to file and manage records, aside from the fact that filing will probably be one of your duties?

3. When a bellows file is used as a sorting device (explained on page 7), frequently one of the sections is too small for the material to be placed in it, while the section next to it just as frequently remains unfilled. How would you solve this problem of unequal distribution so that you could get all of your papers sorted into the file?

4. In planning for the alphabetic subdivisions of a large name file, you must consider the types of names with which you will be working. What differences might you encounter among names to be filed in Minneapolis, San Francisco, and El Paso, Texas?

Learning Projects

1. In the construction of new buildings in or near your area, cornerstones have undoubtedly been laid containing memorabilia of the day (see page 5). Investigate to find out what types of written records were encased in one of these cornerstones for preservation.

2. In your school or local businesses, find examples of current uses of the early filing methods—spindle, pigeonhole, bellows, box, or Shannon files. What is the nature of the material filed by each method?

3. In your area, are there any schools which offer courses of study for the specific purpose of teaching people how to file? If so, get as much information as you can about the courses.

4. On page 2 statistics for clerical and kindred workers are given. What are the most up-to-date figures for clerical and kindred workers in the United States (number of employees, salary scales, industries in which they are employed, etc.)? Give your source. What significance do these figures have in relation to the records of a business?

5. Read an article written within the past 12 months concerning records management or filing. Type a one-page report, or be prepared to give an oral report of not more than 5 minutes. Include a brief summary of the article and your comments about it. Be sure to give your source.

6. Ask your friends and relatives what types of things they file in their offices and their homes and what methods and systems of filing they use. Tabulate their replies.

7. In your library, refer to indexes of business periodicals and choose four articles written within the last five years relating to the emerging importance of records management. Read the articles and then type in your own words a one-page listing of events or circumstances which have occurred within the last decade or so that have caused records management to become as prominent a career as it is now.

Chapter 2

Correspondence storage: terminology, methods, and systems

The five methods of filing, according to the consensus of most authorities, are: alphabetic, geographic, numeric, subject, and chronologic. With the exception of chronologic filing, each of these methods employs alphabetic concepts somewhere in its operation. In essence, therefore, there are really two basic methods of filing—alphabetic and numeric.

Every method of filing has several variations. One method with its variations may be satisfactory for one office but unsatisfactory for another. Each, however, is based upon (1) logical arrangement so that papers may be filed in minimum time, (2) flexibility so that the method can be changed or expanded, and (3) instant accessibility so that a minimum of handling is required to find any desired record.

SECTION 1. TERMINOLOGY OF STORAGE

Filing terminology may be somewhat confusing to one who is not familiar with it. To understand the basic methods of correspondence filing and to be able to analyze the various systems available, those who work with records must have a knowledge of the terms used. The brief definitions given on the following pages are acceptable ones which will help your understanding of records management.

FILING

Filing is the actual placement of materials in a storage container, generally a folder, according to a plan. In a broader sense, it is the process of classifying, coding, arranging, and storing correspondence, cards, papers, and other materials systematically so that they may be located quickly when needed.

FILING MANUAL

A *filing manual* is an instruction book containing detailed information about some or all phases of filing routine (including rules for the methods used). Illustrations of procedure and examples of clerical details, such as folder labeling, typing style, and materials used, are usually included in it.

RETRIEVAL

Retrieval is the term used to mean *finding* information that has been stored in files. Retrieval can consist of physically taking something from the files or of locating the information by machine so that it can be either noted or copied.

TRANSFER

Transfer refers to the plan followed for the systematic removal of materials from the active file to some other file.

RETENTION

Retention denotes the period of time set for keeping a particular record.

DESTRUCTION

Destruction means the elimination of a record.

METHOD

A series of steps for orderly arrangement of records: alphabetic, numeric, geographic, subject, or chronologic, is called a *method*.

The word *system* is reserved for any plan of filing devised by a filing equipment manufacturer. Several alphabetic systems are described in this chapter.

The arrangement of a group of items in A-to-Z sequence is called *alphabetizing*. Some writers refer to this term as *alphabeting*.

The names, initials, and words used in determining the order of filed materials are called *units*. The name *John C. Brown,* for example, has three units: *Brown* is the first, *John* is the second, and *C.* is the third.

Dividers in filing drawers are called *guides,* as information on them serves as a guide to the eye in filing and locating items. A *primary guide* introduces a main division in a file drawer. A *special guide* introduces a special section that falls in the alphabetic range

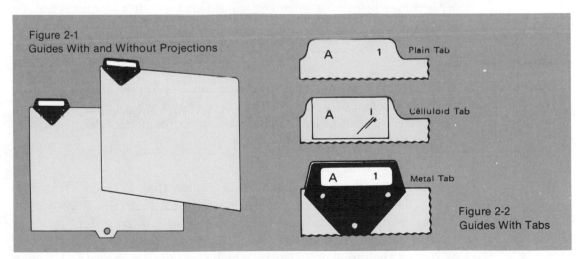

Figure 2-1
Guides With and Without Projections

Plain Tab

Celluloid Tab

Metal Tab

Figure 2-2
Guides With Tabs

of the primary guide it follows (such as a section devoted to a special subject, like "Applications," or a special name group, such as names beginning with the word "General"). An *OUT guide* is a heavy guide that replaces a folder in the file drawer when the folder is temporarily removed. Information on the OUT guide indicates who has the folder, the date it was taken, and related information.

Guides are available in many styles and materials, the most popular material being pressboard. Because of their thickness and rigidity, guides serve to keep the contents of a file from sagging. A guide may have at the bottom edge a small projection that contains a hole through which a rod goes. Guides of this type must be used with equipment that has a trough for the projections and a built-in rod to hold the guides firmly. They cannot, therefore, be removed in error when a folder is taken from the file. (See Figure 2-1 on page 15.)

FOLDER

The container in which papers or materials are kept in a filing cabinet is called a *folder*. Popular materials of which folders are made are manila, kraft, plastic, and pressboard. A *miscellaneous folder* is a folder that contains materials for various correspondents, the materials not having accumulated in sufficient volume to warrant being removed to their own especially labeled folders known as *individual folders*. A *special folder* contains all papers pertaining to one subject (such as applications) or all papers from correspondents with names beginning with the same name (such as "American" or "General").

SCORE

A *score* is an indented or raised line (or series of marks) near the bottom edge of a folder. The score shows where the folder may be refolded once or twice to allow for expansion of the folder contents.

TAB

The portion of a guide or of a folder that extends above the regular height of the folder or guide is called a *tab*. (See Figure 2-2.) It may be in any one of a number of positions from left to right across the top. The material of which a tab is made may be the same as that of the guide or folder of which the tab is a part; the tab may be reinforced with an extra thickness of its own material; or it may be of celluloid, metal, plastic, or any combination thereof. Tabs are sometimes angled for easier reference from above.

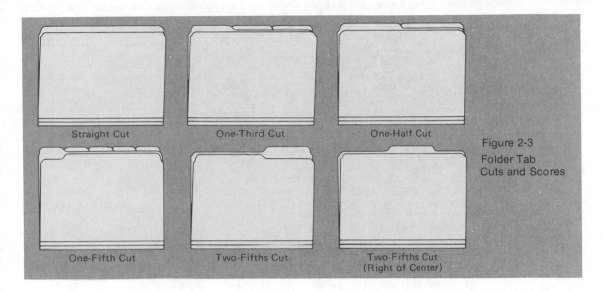

Figure 2-3
Folder Tab
Cuts and Scores

CUT

The tabs on guides and folders are said to be *cut* according to the width of the tabs. A tab that extends across the complete width of a folder is said to be *straight cut*; a tab that is only one-third the width of a folder is known as *one-third cut*. Five *one-fifth-cut* tabs in staggered positions would completely fill the space across the top of a folder. The illustrations in Figure 2-3 show some of the most frequently used cuts.

POSITION

Position refers to the location of a tab at the top of a guide or a folder as seen from left to right. *First position* means that the tab is located at the extreme left edge of the guide or folder; *second position* refers to the location of the tab in the second place from the left edge; and so on. Series of guides and folders may have tabs in staggered positions or straight-line positions. The difference between the terms is illustrated in Figure 2-4 on page 18. *Staggered positions* are used when the tabs on the folders or the guides in a series are in several different positions from left to right according to a set pattern; *straight-line positions* are used when the tabs on all the folders or on all the guides are in one position only; for example, all the tabs in the first position, or all down the middle, or all in some other *one* position.

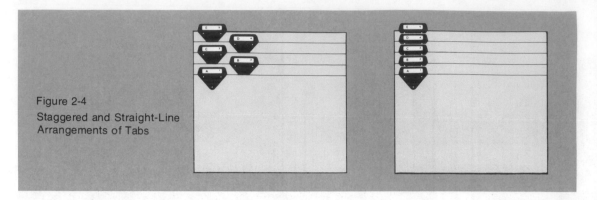

Figure 2-4
Staggered and Straight-Line
Arrangements of Tabs

LABEL

The tab on a folder is often covered with a piece of gummed paper, called a *label,* that identifies the contents of the folder. Insertion of a label or a strip of labels into a typewriter for typing information on the labels is easier than attempting to roll the complete folder into the typewriter in order to type directly on the tab. Labels may be obtained in various colors and styles. In many instances, they aid in proper filing because of color and/or number sequence.

Guides, like folders, have labels on their tabs for identification purposes.

CAPTION

A *caption* is the name, subject, title, number, or other information that appears on the label or the tab of a guide or a folder. Often the two terms "caption" and "label" are used interchangeably. A label or caption is used also on the front of a file drawer to indicate the range of the materials filed in the drawer as an aid to the files operator in locating the proper drawer.

SECTION 2. BASIC METHODS OF FILING CORRESPONDENCE

ALPHABETIC METHOD

The fundamental features of all alphabetic methods of filing are alike in principle: The file is divided into a number of alphabetic sections with a guide for each section (see No. 1 in Figure 2-5). For every guide there is a corresponding miscellaneous folder (see

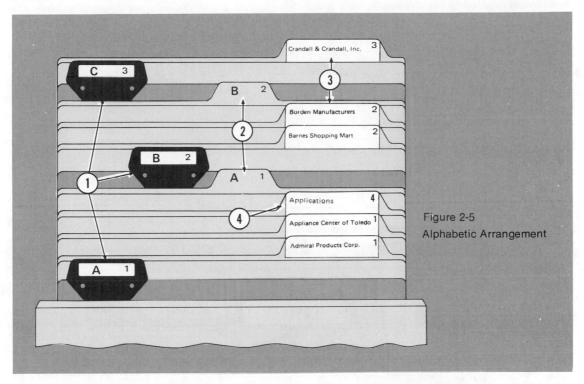

Figure 2-5
Alphabetic Arrangement

No. 2 in Figure 2-5) bearing the same caption as the guide. This folder is the last item in the section designated by the guide; it is preceded by individual folders (see No. 3 in Figure 2-5) and perhaps special folders (see No. 4 in Figure 2-5), which fit into the alphabetic range indicated by the caption on the guide tab.

The miscellaneous folder may occasionally be placed at the front of the section, but this is not the usual arrangement. Special sections of the file may have special guides to call attention to the special folders in the sections.

The captions on tabs may be of two types: letters only or a combination of letters and numbers. (See Figure 2-5.) As a files operator arranges numbers more easily in sequence than he does letters of the alphabet, each guide for an alphabetic division may be numbered as well as lettered, and all folders between one guide and its corresponding miscellaneous folder may bear this same number.

Under the alphabetic arrangement, all material is filed in dictionary order by name. If the first letters of the first units are alike, the second, third, fourth, and succeeding letters and units are used to arrange proper alphabetic sequence.

Additional illustrations of various kinds of alphabetic filing arrangements are shown on the colored inserts preceding Chapter 2.

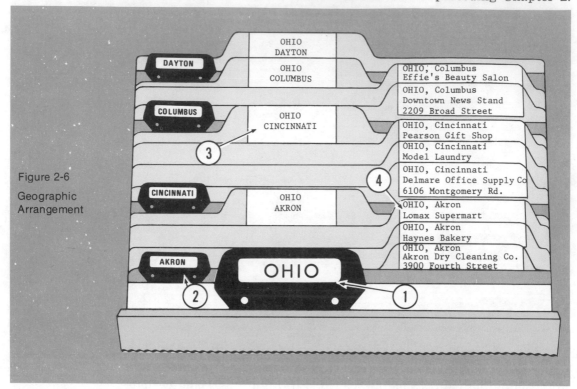

Figure 2-6

Geographic Arrangement

GEOGRAPHIC METHOD

Geographic filing is an alphabetic arrangement based upon the locations or addresses of the correspondents instead of upon their names. Papers are filed alphabetically by the geographical areas (see No. 1 and 2 above) indicated by the guides and folders. Within the miscellaneous folder for each city (see No. 3), the papers are filed alphabetically by the names of the correspondents. Individual folders are used for correspondents who have enough communications to warrant a separate folder. (See No. 4 above.)

Some businesses use, in addition to the geographic file, a supplementary card index, which is arranged alphabetically by names of correspondents. If the geographic location of one correspondent is temporarily forgotten, his name can be located by reference to the supplementary alphabetic card index; and from his name card his address can be determined.

Additional geographic systems are illustrated in Chapter 7, at which time procedures for the geographic method are detailed.

NUMERIC METHOD

In numerical filing records are assigned numbers and indexed in numerical sequence. This method of filing lends itself especially to the filing of serial business records, invoices, and orders. Correspondence may be filed in this manner when it is deemed desirable to use numbers instead of the names of correspondents on folder tabs. (See Figure 2-7.) This method is very useful in businesses where customers' names are kept in confidence or where many people have access to the files and the chance of misfiling is great. People file more easily and quickly by number than by letter.

Equipment for the numeric method includes numbered guides and folders, a book or other means to determine the next number that is available to be assigned to a new correspondent, and a card file arranged alphabetically by correspondents' names. Detailed procedures for the numeric method are contained in Chapter 6, together with explanations of variations and specialized systems.

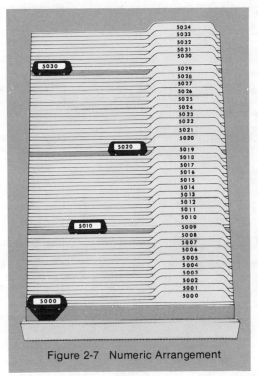

Figure 2-7   Numeric Arrangement

SUBJECT METHOD

Basically, subject filing is the alphabetic arrangement of papers according to the subjects or topics about which the papers are written. (See Figure 2-8, page 22.) Main subjects may be subdivided alphabetically into other subjects. A subject folder has materials within it arranged alphabetically by correspondents' names. Only the most skilled of files operators, familiar with materials to be handled and knowing the firm's operations thoroughly, can do subject filing well.

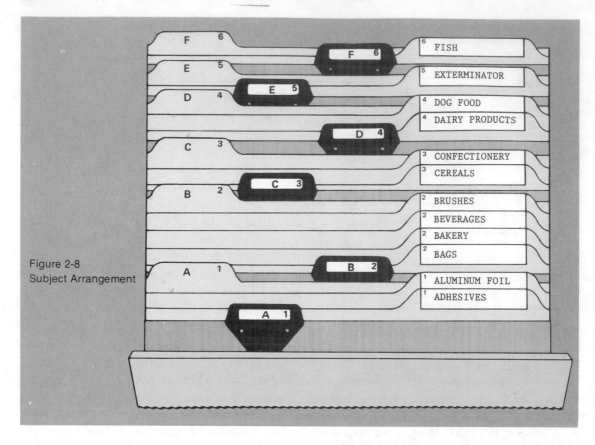

Figure 2-8
Subject Arrangement

Selection of the subject titles to be used as captions and maintaining an up-to-date index of them, easily accessible and constantly used, are important duties included in subject filing. Chapter 8 contains further discussion of this method.

CHRONOLOGIC METHOD

As its name implies, chronologic filing is filing by date. Exact chronologic filing is not well suited to correspondence files because of the need for keeping all the correspondence from, to, and about one individual or organization together. Chronologic filing is often used for daily reports, deposit tickets, freight bills, statements, and order sheets, which may be best stored by date.

Some offices keep a *reading file,* which consists of copies of all daily correspondence filed by date. This file may be circulated so that all executives know what has taken place; a secretary may keep one in her desk for easy access to extra copies of correspondence written

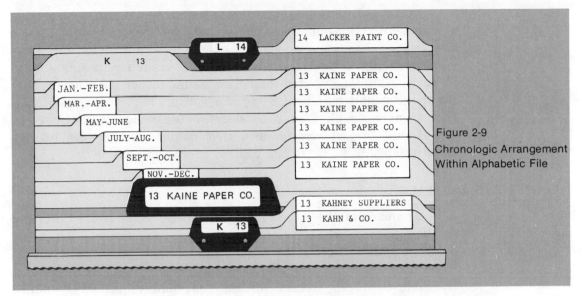

Figure 2-9
Chronologic Arrangement
Within Alphabetic File

within the past few days; a reading file may be the first item in an easily accessible file drawer, to which anyone may refer.

Another form of a chronologic file is the *tickler file*. This is always an arrangement by date. It may be a card file or a file with folders. As the name suggests, it "tickles" the memory by serving as a reminder to someone that something must be taken care of on a certain date. Chapter 5 contains additional explanation of the tickler file.

The chronologic *principle* is followed in all methods of filing as papers are placed in their folders. The top of each sheet is at the left, and the paper with the most recent date is on top of each name group so that anyone who opens a folder can see immediately the very latest piece of correspondence—what has happened most recently. When a folder becomes congested, it may be subdivided into folders with monthly captions on them. Some correspondents' materials are so numerous that monthly folders are necessary for efficient filing. (See Figure 2-9.)

SECTION 3. SPECIALIZED ALPHABETIC FILING SYSTEMS

Many manufacturers have produced trade-named systems, most of which are based on the alphabet but which have certain special devices or characteristics that are intended to speed up filing and finding of material and to provide a double check against misfiling.

Special color schemes may be added to guide and folder tabs; alphabetic notations and numeric symbols may be combined on guide and folder tabs; the arrangement of guides and folders within the file drawer may be varied; provision may be made for special sections of various kinds; a system based on sound rather than on spelling for the first unit may be used (described in Chapter 6); an adaptation of numeric filing may be selected (described in Chapter 6). All of these are special features that manufacturers have inaugurated ostensibly to make the control of records easier.

ILLUSTRATIVE SYSTEMS

A number of these specialized alphabetic systems are described on the following pages. Except for the first four systems, which are illustrated in multicolor, the special systems are taken up in alphabetic order according to name. Each has at least one feature distinctive from all other systems described. Text material should be studied with frequent reference to the illustration to obtain maximum understanding. Special attention should be given to the sequence of items within the file; the descriptions here proceed from left to right across the file drawer but the items mentioned are not necessarily in front-to-back order.

Many other trade-named filing systems are available; the systems described are meant to be representative but certainly not inclusive.

Colorscan System (Sperry Remington, Office Systems and Machines, Sperry Rand Corporation, Blue Bell, Pennsylvania). The Colorscan System uses the instant-recognition-by-color principle (see page A of the colored insert). Primary guides are fifth cut, white and located in first position to signal main alphabetic sections throughout the system. Single name or special name guides are also white and occupy first position (e.g., Rayburn Mfg. Co.); this follows the principle that the most active folders should be located behind the main guide. Nine color-coded action guides are fifth-cut and located in second position. These guides divide primary sections into smaller alphabetic sections and show that a particular color is designated for that section. Individual folders are colored to match the secondary guides behind which they are placed; their tabs are white for easy reference and are double cut in third and fourth positions.

White miscellaneous folders, bearing the same caption as the secondary guides they follow and having a color bar the same as the color of the folders they follow, occupy fifth position. Special guides

A

U to Z

RECORDING X-Ray Company
RAPAPORT Van Marvin
RAMSEY Underwriters

RADIO Wado

REED Thomas

RAPPAPORT Toy Bazaar
RADIO Steel Company
RABHOR Sportswear Inc
RECORD Press
RAW Rubber Engraving Co
RALEIGH Paper Company
RADIANT Quilting Company

RESEARCH Programs

ROVER National Motor Inn
RENDEZVOUS National Originals
RACEWAY National
RAYBURN Mfg Co
RAYBURN Mfg Co Jan -June
RICH Marvin
RAWLINGS Martin
REYNOLDS Manual

RAYBURN Nancy

P-Q-R

National

Rayburn Mfg. Co.

M-N-O

REDDY Kilowatt Inc
RAINBOW Knitting Mills
RABIN John
RADIO Land
RATHSKELLER German American
RAPAPORT Isadore
RADIO Hawaii Inc

RABB George

RAT Fink Room
RAMSET Fastening System
RAHR Export Clinic
RADIANT Dress Company

REED Cuff (&) Associates
RAYTHEON Company
RAHR Clor Clinic
RADIO City

RAWLINGS Albert
RIDDLE Albert
RATHMAN Albert
RADIO Amusement Corp

RABBITT Byron

RABBINECAL Assembly

RAB Alice

REYNOLDS Aluminum Co

RAAB

RAI

RAB

REL

G-H-I

D-E-F

C

R

U to Z

ST

P-Q-R

M-N-O

OUT

JKL

G-H-I

D-E-F

C

A-B

SINGLE NAME

Remington Rand's COLORSCAN SYSTEM

B

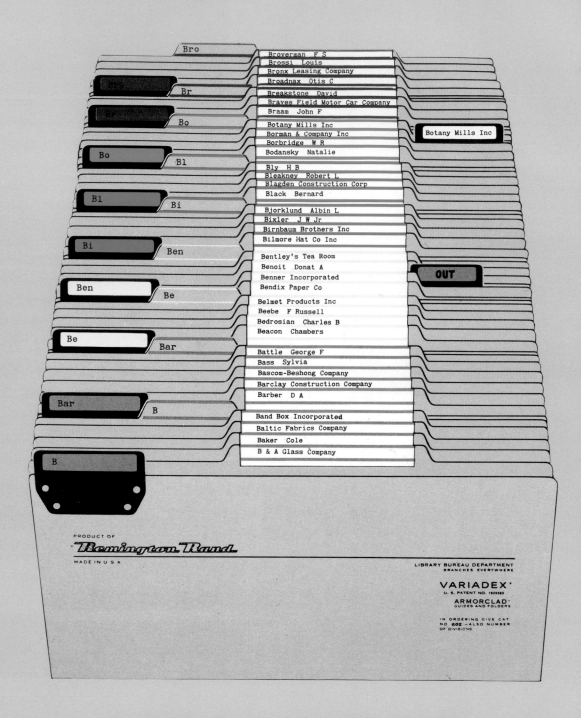

Remington Rand's VARIADEX SYSTEM

C

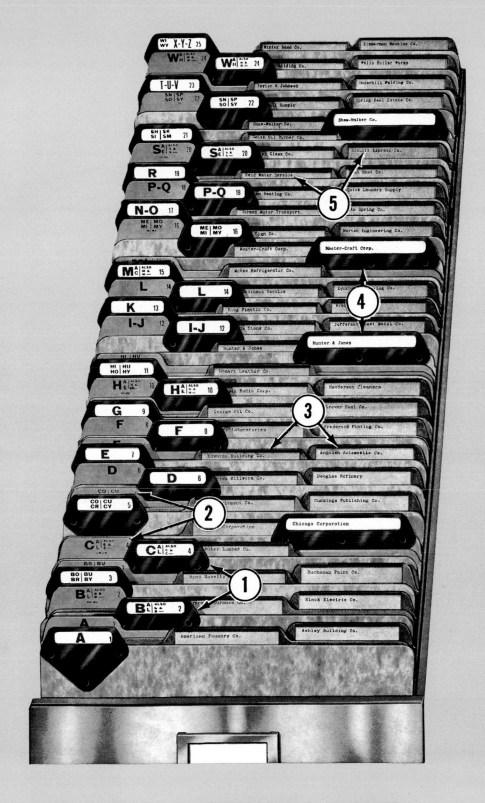

Shaw-Walker's SUPER-IDEAL SYSTEM

D

TAB Products' ALPHA CODE SYSTEM

to lead the eye to frequently used folders appear in second position throughout the drawer.

Folders in this system are not arranged in strict alphabetic order—this is a random arrangement with any name whose first unit begins with "R" being filed within the drawer in an order determined only by the letter of the second unit. If the files operator desired, folder arrangement COULD be in strict alphabetic order. Colorscan is not the true alphabetic arrangement that the following three systems illustrate; it is used here only to show what can be done with color.

Variadex System (Sperry Remington, Office Systems and Machines, Sperry Rand Corporation, Blue Bell, Pennsylvania). The Variadex System (see page B of the colored insert) is an alphabetic arrangement with a definite color scheme that serves as an aid to filing and finding. Within each letter of the alphabet, orange, yellow, green, blue, and violet appear in that order. Alphabetic guides are placed in first position, with second position designated for miscellaneous folders. The third and fourth positions are occupied by individual folders; and special guides for names having a large volume of correspondence or for names of frequent reference are in fifth position. The color of all folder tabs behind any one guide is the same as the color on the tab of the guide.

Color of the tabs is determined by the *second* letter of the first unit. If the second letter is *a, b, c,* or *d,* the color is orange; if the second letter is *e, f, g,* or *h,* the color is yellow; if the second letter is *i, j, k, l, m,* or *n,* the color is green; if the second letter is *o, p,* or *q,* the color is blue; if the second letter is *r, s, t, u, v, w, x, y,* or *z,* the color is violet. For example, the folder for the name *Bane* would have an orange tab; the folder for the name *Bean* would have a yellow tab; the folders for the names *Bine* or *Blane* would have green tabs; the folder for the name *Boone* would have a blue tab; and the folders for the names *Brown, Burns,* or *Byrnes* would have violet tabs. Similarly, the folder for the name *Nasman* would have an orange tab; the folder for the name *Neuman,* a yellow tab; the folder for the name *Nichols,* a green tab; the folder for the name *Nolan,* a blue tab; and the folders for the names *Nugent* or *Nyland,* violet tabs.

Super-Ideal System (Shaw-Walker, Muskegon, Michigan). Alphabetic guides (see No. 1 on page C of the color insert) consecutively numbered, with one-fifth-cut metal tabs, are staggered in first and second positions. Blue miscellaneous folders (No. 2 on page C), with one-fifth-cut tabs numbered to correspond to the guides they follow, are in first position only. Individual name folders (Nos. 3 and 5 on page C) with one-third-cut tabs are staggered in second and third positions. Special name guides (No. 4 on page C) with one-third cut metal tabs are at the right. The notations on some guides and miscellaneous folder tabs are open (*A, D, E, F, G,* for example); multiple-closed notations are used for those letters of the alphabet containing high-frequency combinations (as *B, C, H, M*).

Alpha Code System (TAB Products Company, Palo Alto, California). The Alpha Code system (see page D of the colored inserts) is housed in a shelf-type arrangement instead of in a drawer; the folders bear color-coded labels on their open side instead of across the top, and only the main alphabetic guides are necessary. The long folder tab contains two labels: a 2-color label indicates the FIRST TWO LETTERS of the name by which the folder is filed, and a white label contains the entire name of the correspondent. (See *AN* and *Anderson, Dennis T.* at the top left of the illustration.) "A" is red, "B" and "C" are orange, "D" is green, etc. The first two letters of each folder are easily visible because of the two distinctive colors out of a spectrum of ten, specially formulated so that even colorblind people can read them. Pressboard guides with insertable plastic labelholders are located at the top of the arrangement. Red, yellow, or green vinyl OUT guides with pockets have center tabs and may be secured in any one of seven colors.

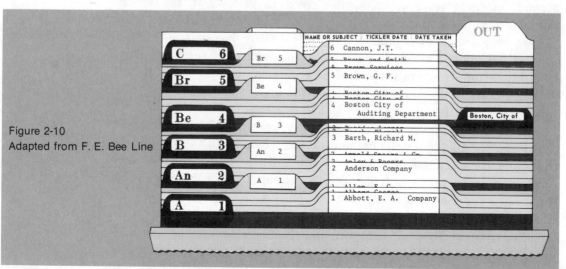

Figure 2-10
Adapted from F. E. Bee Line

F. E. Bee Line Filing System (Filing Equipment Bureau, Boston, Massachusetts). The Bee Line System consists of alphabetic guides consecutively numbered in first position only, salmon-colored miscellaneous folders in second position, individual folders in third and fourth combined positions, special name guides and OUT guides in fifth position. As in other systems with both alphabetic and numeric captions, individual folders and the miscellaneous folder bear the same number as the alphabetic guide behind which they are located.

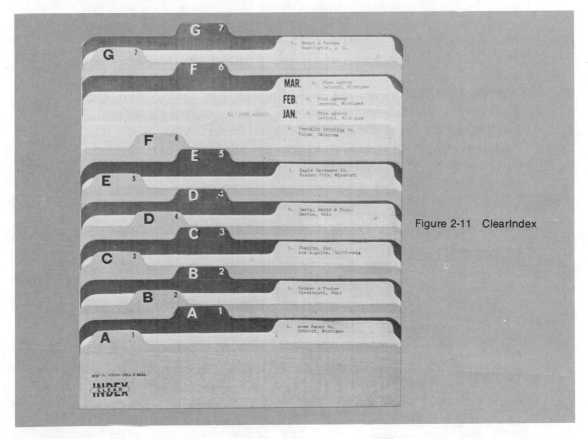

Figure 2-11   ClearIndex

ClearIndex (Globe-Weis Systems Co., Wauseon, Ohio). The ClearIndex system consists of alphabetic guides bearing numbers as well as letters, staggered in the first and second positions. Miscellaneous folders of clear red in third position bear the numbers of the guides preceding them. Auxiliary or special name guides in fourth position are also numbered to correspond to their guides. Individual name folders in fifth and sixth combined positions likewise bear the numbers of the guides behind which they are filed.

Chronologic folders are provided where the bulk of correspondence is great. The use of numbers in addition to letters helps the files operator replace material more easily and quickly than by alphabet only.

"Nual" Alphabet Index or Amfile Index (Amberg File & Index Company, Kankakee, Illinois). The Amfile Index has alphabetic guides with one-fifth-cut tabs consecutively numbered and staggered in third, fourth, and fifth positions (1 A AK, 2 AL AM, etc., in Figure 2-12). Miscellaneous folders have one-fifth-cut tabs and are in first position placed *directly* behind their alphabetic guides. Folders behind the alphabetic guides bear the same numbers as the guides they follow. Individual folders have one-third-cut tabs and are staggered in second and third positions. Special unnumbered name guides, called *Leader Equipment*, are two-fifths-cut and are in first and second combined positions (Arbuckle Brothers). Behind these special guides are placed chronologically labeled folders with wide tabs covering three positions. These folders are staggered to cover combined positions 2, 3, and 4 or positions 3, 4, and 5 across the drawer.

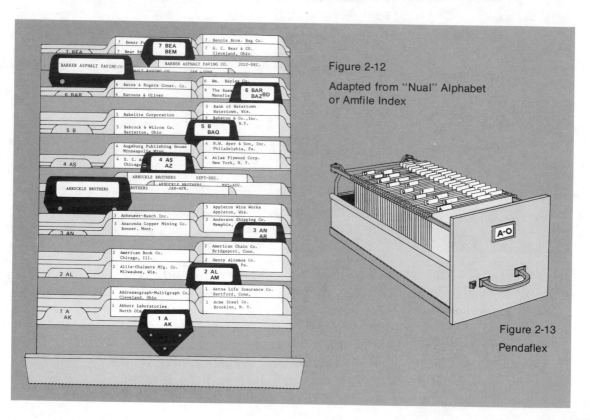

Figure 2-12

Adapted from "Nual" Alphabet or Amfile Index

Figure 2-13

Pendaflex

Pendaflex (Oxford Pendaflex Corporation, Garden City, New York). The important feature of the Pendaflex System is that the file folders hang from steel hanger rods instead of resting on their bottom edge in a drawer. (See Figure 2-13.) The rods slide along horizontal bars at the sides of the drawer. Slightly slanted celluloid tabs on the front edge of the folders are inserted through precut slots along the top edge of the folders. With the folders suspended in the drawer, there is no need for a steel plate of any kind at the front or back of the drawer to keep the folders upright. In Figure 2-13, alphabetic miscellaneous folders that serve as guides are staggered in first and second positions; individual folders are staggered in fourth and fifth positions, leaving the center position open for special features. Tabs are available in second-, third-, fourth-, fifth-, and sixth-cut and in every combination of positions therein.

"I.N.F." is an application of Pendaflex filing. This term refers to *Integrated Name Filing*. All papers relating to a name are filed in the same place, in *one* Pendaflex folder, but with correspondence housed in one interior manila folder, orders housed in another interior manila folder, invoices housed in another, with all the manila folders concerning the one name being held in the one Pendaflex folder tabbed with the name of the correspondent.

Speed Index (Oxford Pendaflex Corporation, Garden City, New York). Special notice should be given to the height of the guides and folders in this system. The main alphabetic guides are numbered consecutively, are made with one-fifth-cut tabs, and are staggered in first and second positions. (See Figure 2-14, page 30.) Their steel tabs and heavy construction afford prolonged life and usage. Individual name folders with one-third-cut tabs are staggered in two positions, second and third. The folder tabs are at a lower level than the guides, to protect them from becoming "dog eared," and are numbered to correspond to the guides they follow. Salmon-colored one-fifth-cut miscellaneous folders have tabs in first position at the lower level of the other folders. Special heavy-duty folders (*Gelatin Products Co.*, for example) for bulky correspondence have steel tabs and red windows; they have one-third-cut tabs in third position at high level for easy reference. Special heading guides (*General*, for example) are one-fifth-cut and tabbed in third position with high tabs for easy visibility. Special chronologic folders for active correspondents (i.e., *General Motors Corp.*) are fifth-cut in combined

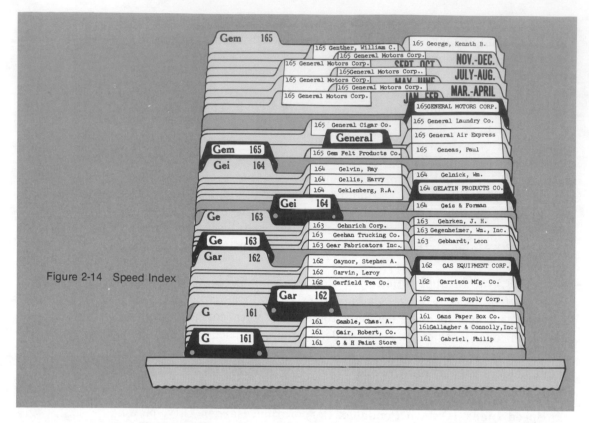

Figure 2-14 Speed Index

positions 2, 3, and 4 or positions 3, 4, and 5. The folders are at the high level behind a special metal-tabbed high-level guide that is third-cut in third position.

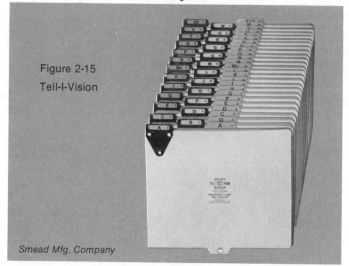

Figure 2-15
Tell-I-Vision

Tell-I-Vision (Smead Manufacturing Co., Hastings, Minnesota). The Smead Tell-I-Vison system consists of consecutively numbered alphabetic guides in alternating first and second positions and miscellaneous folders consecutively numbered in third position. Individual folders would be inserted at the right.

To aid in refiling, guide tabs are blue for odd numbers and orange for even numbers. This system is one of a type widely used in business today.

Ideal Index (Shaw-Walker, Muskegon, Michigan) is another example of this type.

Triple-Check Automatic Index (Sperry Remington, Office Systems and Machines, Sperry Rand Corporation, Blue Bell, Pennsylvania). This system has two sets of one-seventh-cut guides. One set of white guides, each guide bearing a division of the alphabet, is in first position; the guides relate to the first units in names to be filed. In the 30-division set pictured in Figure 2-16, the "A" section begins with the number 10, the "B" section begins with 20, the "BI" section begins with 30, and so on. (The numbering of the guides depends on the total number of guides used to divide the alphabet.) The other set of guides is in second position; these guides relate to the second units in names to be filed, and they divide the material back of each

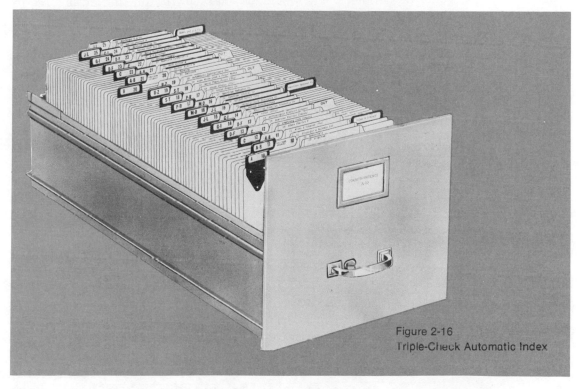

Figure 2-16
Triple-Check Automatic Index

of the first set of guides into nine sections of the alphabet. The labels on the first three guides are tan; on the next three, green; and on the last three, yellow. This pattern is repeated behind each white guide. Miscellaneous folders are in third position and are plain manila tabbed. Individual folders are fifth-cut with tabs in third and fourth combined positions. Miscellaneous and individual folders have the same color line on their labels as the color of the secondary guides they follow. OUT folders and guides are seventh-cut, sixth position. Special name guides are fifth-cut and occupy fifth position.

This system of filing includes both letters of the alphabet and numbers. For example, correspondence pertaining to Charles W. Abrams is marked *12* (*10* for the letter "A" of "Abrams" plus *2*, since "Charles" is in the second subdivision within the "A" section). Correspondence from the Blake Lumber Co. bears the number *25* (*20* for the letter "B" of "Blake" plus *5*, since "Lumber" is in the fifth subdivision of the "B" section). A single name or subject folder is provided in third position at the beginning of each alphabetic section for those correspondents who have only one unit in their names and who are not active enough to warrant a special folder. An example would be "Alden's." It would be marked *10* for the letter "A" of "Alden's." Since there is no other filing unit, no other number can be added.

Filing by this system is by name, then checked by number, and finally checked by color. This is the reason for the name "Triple-Check." Careful study should be given to the illustration of this system.

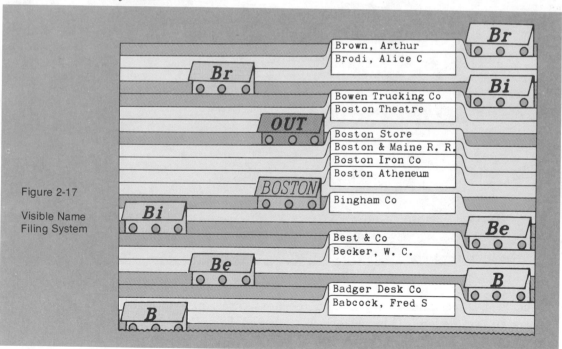

Figure 2-17

Visible Name Filing System

Visible Name Filing System (Remington Rand Office Systems, Victor Safe and Equipment, New York City). This system consists of alphabetic guides with green tabs staggered in first and second positions, special name guides with orange tabs in third position, individual name folders with plain manila or color-bar labeled tabs in fourth and fifth combined positions, yellow miscellaneous folders tabbed in sixth position. Blue-tabbed OUT guides are used in the third position when material is removed from the file. Angled tabs are recommended for all guides, but straight tabs are obtainable.

IMPORTANCE OF CAREFUL SYSTEM SELECTION OR DESIGN

Before an organization can install a filing system or improve an existing filing system, a filing expert or the files supervisor should make a careful study of all the needs of the business and the factors peculiar to it. Among the points he should consider are the following: (1) the nature of the business, that is, whether the business is local, regional, or national in scope; (2) the types and number of records to be filed; (3) the frequency of use of the records; (4) the length of time the records serve a useful purpose and must be kept; and (5) the possibility of the need for expansion of the filing system as it reflects the growth of the business.

The person making the analysis may find that one of the tailor-made systems (with or without slight modification) will be satisfactory. On the other hand, he may find that a special system must be devised so that it will be geared to the needs of the particular office. The utmost care should be exercised in the selection of the system because the system, after it is once installed, will likely be used for a long time.

SECTION 4. IMPORTANCE OF FILING RULES

Regardless of the convenience, cost, colors, or arrangement of the filing system chosen for use, papers can become lost in the files if those who handle the records do not follow the same rules and follow them consistently. All too often filing rules may be handed from person to person by word of mouth instead of by written instruction. At times of sickness, during vacation periods, or when employees leave the firm, chaos may result because no one knows what rules of filing have been followed. The necessity for *written* rules available to all and followed by all is then "brought home."

Filing rules are as important to records control as the multiplication table is to arithmetic. A necessary part of an office manual is the compilation of the filing rules so that records may be stored and retrieved quickly.

**For Review
and
Discussion**

1. What is the difference between a filing system and a filing method?

2. Who should be responsible for compiling a filing manual? Who would use it? Why?

3. If frequent additions of folders or guides (or both) are to be made to the files, would the staggered or straight-line arrangement of tabs be better? Why?

4. What factors should determine the size of cut for a folder?

5. Why are the papers of some correspondents filed in a separate folder exclusively for them while some correspondents' papers are filed alphabetically with other correspondents' papers in a miscellaneous folder? What is the folder for one correspondent exclusively called?

6. Why is filing numerically usually faster than filing alphabetically?

7. Why is chronologic filing not well suited to correspondence filing? Give specific examples in your answer.

8. What might a reading file look like? How is it used? Where can it be kept?

**Learning
Projects**

1. Secure a sample of a manila folder, a kraft folder, a plastic folder, and a pressboard guide. Prepare an informative bulletin board display of interest to the class.

2. Obtain an illustration of an alphabetic filing system not explained in this chapter. Write a clear description of it, including any special features, to be used for bulletin board display.

3. Visit 8 offices of various types—small, medium-sized, large; in industry, government, education, the professions—in your area. Get as much information as you can about filing methods and systems used, such as:
   a. trade names, if any
   b. methods used (alphabetic, geographic, etc.)
   c. use of color
   d. type of filing manual used and its contents
   e. housing of the files—cabinets, drawers, open-shelf, etc.
   f. manual and/or mechanical systems
   g. comments about how the system works—strengths and weaknesses
   h. other information that you believe will be of interest

   After you have gathered the information, write a factual report showing good organization of your materials. Since your survey has been limited, do not draw conclusions; this is an informative report only.

Chapter **3**

Rules for alphabetic filing
and cross-referencing

No one set of filing rules written by textbook authors is followed without variation by every office even though there is general agreement on most of the rules for alphabetic arrangement. Where variation does exist in the procedures for indexing (classifying) and maintaining records, the one procedure to be used in the office must be determined and written as policy so that no deviation from it can be permitted.

In recent years, a tendency to simplify and condense rules for alphabetic arrangement has been prevalent in textbooks and office manuals. This tendency has led to misfiling, for it is the exception to the easily understood rule, the unusual situation, the infrequent problem that cause papers to be filed incorrectly. An attitude of "Oh, we just use the straight alphabet when filing" can result in as many interpretations of what is alphabetic arrangement as there are people making the statement!

Without written instructions, filing procedures deteriorate with time, changes in personnel, and oral explanations. Unless those who maintain the files are consistent in their procedures of storing the papers therein, they will be unable to locate filed material when it is needed. Furthermore, the volume of filed material is constantly increasing; and to remember where every piece has been filed is beyond human ability. Once a paper is filed correctly, it should always be refiled in that same way unless the rule or procedure for filing it is changed and that change has been publicized to all concerned with the files.

Students who learn thoroughly the rules in this textbook should have little difficulty in adjusting to any exceptions that they may meet in the specific offices where they may be employed. Files supervisors who adopt these rules for their offices will find them logical, workable, and comprehensive enough to provide answers to the filing questions that arise.

In this chapter, rules for alphabetic filing are presented with illustrative examples and indexing problems to help the reader understand the application of these rules. The necessity for rules is clearly shown by an attempt to put into alphabetic order the following fifteen names:

1. Sandusky Repair Shop
2. St. Lawrence River Steamship Company
3. Marie St. Claire
4. Sister Marguerite Sinclair
5. Santa Anita Paymasters' Corporation
6. Sampsons' Furniture Shop
7. William F. Sampson
8. Sampson, Small & Sinclair
9. Savery Foods, Inc.
10. S. A. S. Specialties
11. Sav-Well Grocery Store
12. Sir Malcolm St. Claire
13. Second National Bank, Spartanburg, South Carolina
14. Sanitation Department, Muncie, Indiana
15. 7th Street Shoppe

Many questions no doubt occur: Do I consider "St. Lawrence" as one word or as two words? Do I look at "Sister" or at "Sinclair" first? In No. 6 do I use that last "s" in "Sampsons' "? In No. 10 do I use "S. A. S." or "Specialties" or just "S."? In No. 11 do I use "Sav" or "Sav-Well"? Where do I start in No. 12? The need for rules to be used when filing alphabetically should be apparent after an attempt to arrange the preceding list without them.

Alphabetic filing rules easily divide themselves into three groups: those rules pertaining to individuals' names, those rules pertaining to business names (sometimes referred to as "company names" or "firm names"), and those rules pertaining to other names. The illustrative examples accompanying each rule in the three sections of this chapter should be carefully studied, because they clarify the rules. The items for review and discussion following each of the sections make use of each of the rules.

Correct alphabetic arrangement of a list of names or of cards containing names and addresses (even though difficult) is much easier than is most filing of other materials done in an office. When working with correspondence, someone in the office must make a decision as to which name is the important one—the name to be chosen for filing. Is it the letterhead name, the name in the inside address, a name in the body of the item, or the signature? "Someone else" will not always make that decision; the work of the one who files may well include this decision-making responsibility.

In most instances, this decision means scanning the piece of correspondence to become familiar with its contents while mentally determining the name under which it is to be filed (known as *classifying* or *indexing* in filing terminology). This step is followed closely by marking the name, a process known as *coding*. As the examples following the rules in this chapter are studied, indexing will be taking place—mentally determining the first, second, and succeeding units in the names under consideration.

SECTION 1. RULES FOR NAMES OF INDIVIDUALS

1: *Order of Indexing Units*

a. Each part of an individual's name is considered to be a separate indexing unit.

b. An individual's name is transposed so that the surname is shown as the first unit, the given name or initial as the second unit, and the middle name or initial as the third unit.

c. When the surnames of two or more names are alike, filing order is determined by the second units in the names if they are different; if the second as well as the first units are alike, filing order is determined by the third or succeeding units.

d. In all cases, "Nothing goes before something." An initial, therefore, is a unit by itself and precedes a name that begins with the same letter.

Names	Alphabetic Index Order		
	Units: 1	2	3
A. Jane Rose	Rose	A.	Jane
Anna J. Rose	Rose	Anna	J.
Anna Jane Rose	Rose	Anna	Jane
Paul Ross	Ross	Paul	

(Illustrative examples continued on page 38.)

Names	Alphabetic Index Order		
Units:	1	2	3
Paul J. Ross	Ross	Paul	J.
Paul John Ross	Ross	Paul	John
Paul A. Rosse	Rosse	Paul	A.
Paul Andrew Rosse	Rosse	Paul	Andrew
R. Carleton Rossman	Rossman	R.	Carleton
R. D. Rossman	Rossman	R.	D.
Richard Rossman	Rossman	Richard	
Arnold Sadler	Sadler	Arnold	
Arnold A. Sadler	Sadler	Arnold	A.
B. F. Sadler	Sadler	B.	F.
B. K. Sadler	Sadler	B.	K.

Note: In each example an underline indicates the letter of the unit that determines the alphabetic order of the units.

2: *Hyphenated and Compound Individual Names*

Each part of a hyphenated or a compound name, whether a given name or a surname, is considered to be a separate unit. The hyphen is disregarded. In a surname containing either the word "Saint" or the abbreviation "St.," the word "Saint" or the abbreviation in spelled-out form is considered to be the first unit; the word after "Saint" is considered to be the second unit.

Names	Alphabetic Index Order			
Units:	1	2	3	4
Howard St. Claire	Saint	Claire	Howard	
Charles Saint John	Saint	John	Charles	
M. L. Saint-Vickery	Saint-	Vickery	M.	L.
Marie L. Sainte	Sainte	Marie	L.	
Marie-Louise Sainte	Sainte	Marie-	Louise	
Jo-Etta R. Salisbury	Salisbury	Jo-	Etta	R.
Jo-Ellen Salisbury-Jones	Salisbury-	Jones	Jo-	Ellen
Marie San Louis	San	Louis	Marie	
John L. Santa Emma	Santa	Emma	John	L.
Patrick L. Somes	Somes	Patrick	L.	
P. Lawrence Somes-Taylor	Somes-	Taylor	P.	Lawrence
Victor A. Somes	Somes	Victor	A.	
Fred P. Taylor-Trent	Taylor-	Trent	Fred	P.
V. A. Taylor	Taylor	V.	A.	
A. J. Taylor-Voss	Taylor-	Voss	A.	J.
John F. Taylors	Taylors	John	F.	

Note 1: A variation of the rule pertaining to the word "Saint" (and its variations "San" and "Santa") in a surname considers "Saint" (and "San" and "Santa") and the word that follows to be one unit.

Note 2: A variation of the rule pertaining to hyphenated names considers a surname or a given name that contains a hyphen to be one unit. (Drop the hyphen and assume that the letters are continuous.)

If either of these alternate plans were used, the order of the names given above would be different.

3: *Particles* (*Prefixes*)

A particle (or prefix) in a surname is considered to be part of the surname, not a separate indexing unit. Examples of particles are *De, El, Fitz, Il, L', Ia, Las, Ie, Les, Los, Lu, M', Mac, Mc, Me, O', Te, van, vander,* and *von.*

Names	Alphabetic Index Order		
	Units: 1	2	3
Erma Lee Darrett	Darrett	Erma	Lee
Elmer J. D'Arro	D'Arro	Elmer	J.
Perry O. Delaro	Delaro	Perry	O.
Maurice de la Roche	delaRoche	Maurice	
Andrew F. Delaron	Delaron	Andrew	F.
Henry B. Elder	Elder	Henry	B.
Hilda G. El Salvador	ElSalvador	Hilda	G.
A. Walter Elsasser	Elsasser	A.	Walter
Stan K. Il Aban	IlAban	Stan	K.
D. Roy Ilagan	Ilagan	D.	Roy
Norman B. LaLonne	LaLonne	Norman	B.
K. DeWayne Lalor	Lalor	K.	DeWayne
Louise A. La Salle	LaSalle	Louise	A.
Lu-Anne Lasalle	Lasalle	Lu-	Anne
Ben R. Lee	Lee	Ben	R.
Albert O. L'Esperance	L'Esperance	Albert	O.
John J. LeStrange	LeStrange	John	J.
Paul Lee Lumson	Lumson	Paul	Lee
Frances LuNardelli	LuNardelli	Frances	
Clift Lunde	Lunde	Clift	
Ann J. MacCarthy	MacCarthy	Ann	J.
Agnes R. Macey	Macey	Agnes	R.
A. T. McCarthy	McCarthy	A.	T.
Al McCorder-Brugge	McCorder-	Brugge	Al

Note: The application of this rule is not affected by spacing between the prefix and the rest of the surname or by the capitalization of the first letter of the prefix.

4: *Abbreviations*

Abbreviated given names are considered as if they were written in full. When the brief form of a given name (Don, Ed, Jack, Jeff, Ray, Will) is used by an individual in his signature, the brief form is considered as it is spelled by him, since these shortened names are now often used as complete given names.

Names	Alphabetic Index Order		
	Units: 1	2	3
Don Samson Porter	Porter	Don	Samson
Donald P. Porter	Porter	Donald	P.
Sam P. Porter	Porter	Sam	P.
Samson J. Porter	Porter	Samson	J.

(*Illustrative examples continued on page 40.*)

Names		Alphabetic Index Order		
	Units: 1		2	3
Sam'l J. Porter		Porter	Samuel	J.
Will O. Richey		Richey	Will	O.
Wm. O. Richey		Richey	William	O.
Jas. St. Paul		Saint	Paul	James
Jno. St. Paul		Saint	Paul	John
Jos. St. Paul		Saint	Paul	Joseph
Josh St. Paul		Saint	Paul	Josh
Ted L. Stine		Stine	Ted	L.
Theo. E. Stine		Stine	Theodore	E.
Thos. A. Stine		Stine	Thomas	A.
Tim Rod Stine		Stine	Tim	Rod
Tom I. Stine		Stine	Tom	I.

5: *Seniority*

A seniority designation, such as "Junior" and "Senior" or "II (Second)" and "III (Third)," is not considered to be an indexing unit but is used as an identifying element to distinguish between two otherwise identical names.

Names		Alphabetic Index Order			Identifying Element
	Units: 1		2	3	
John Jones, Jr.		Jones	John		(Junior)
John Jones, Sr.		Jones	John		(Senior)
John L. Jones, Jr.		Jones	John	L.	(Junior)
John M. Jones		Jones	John	M.	
John M. Jones, Jr.		Jones	John	M.	(Junior)
John M. Jones, II		Jones	John	M.	(Second)
John M. Jones, Sr.		Jones	John	M.	(Senior)
John M. Jones, III		Jones	John	M.	(Third)
Joseph M. Jones		Jones	Joseph	M.	

Note: A variation of the rule pertaining to seniority designations considers such a designation to be an indexing unit at the end of the name.

6: *Unusual and Foreign Names*

Unusual and foreign personal names are indexed in the usual manner. The last word written is considered to be the surname and therefore the first indexing unit. (This type of name should be cross-referenced in the manner explained on page 45.)

Names		Alphabetic Index Order		
	Units: 1		2	3
George Albert		Albert	George	
Gaetano Balice		Balice	Gaetano	
Ming Casse		Casse	Ming	

(Illustrative examples continued on page 41.)

Names	Units:	Alphabetic Index Order		
		1	2	3
Ettore Dell'Amico		Dell'Amico	Ettore	
Stanley George		George	Stanley	
Tamahido Yukihaka Imoto		Imoto	Tamahido	Yukihaka
Fashe Ishada		Ishada	Fashe	
Larry John		John	Larry	
Harold Lawrence		Lawrence	Harold	
Mun Quah Lum		Lum	Mun	Quah
Wong Soo On		On	Wong	Soo
Milorad Ratokovich		Ratokovich	Milorad	
Wai Cho San		San	Wai	Cho
Wun Ong Shaw		Shaw	Wun	Ong
Kazuo Tsujimato		Tsujimato	Kazuo	
Jurras Ty		Ty	Jurras	
Vrisky Venno		Venno	Vrisky	

7: *Titles and Degrees*

a. *Titles with Complete Names.* A title (military, religious, personal, educational, professional, and the like) is disregarded in indexing if it is followed by a complete name. The title is placed in parentheses after the name so that it will not be omitted from the record. (The tilde appears over the letter "n" in the Spanish title "Señor.")

b. *Titles without Complete Names.* When a title is followed by only one name or by only a given and a middle name, the title is considered to be the first indexing unit.

c. *Degrees.* A degree (for example, *Ed.D., Ph.D., M.D., M.A., D.D.*) is disregarded in indexing but is placed in parentheses after the name.

Names	Units:	Alphabetic Index Order		
		1	2	3
Brother Francis		Brother	Francis	
Francis Brothers		Brothers	Francis	
Father Hanson		Father	Hanson	
The Right Rev. Michael P. Flack		Flack	Michael	P. (The Right Rev.)
Father Thomas L. Flinn		Flinn	Thomas	L. (Father)
Dr. James D. Flynn		Flynn	James	D. (Dr.)
Professor John Flynn		Flynn	John (Professor)	
John D. Flynn		Flynn	John	D.
Major John Flynne		Flynne	John (Major)	
Senator John B. Flynne		Flynne	John	B. (Senator)
Lieut. A. R. Garson		Garson	A.	R. (Lieut.)
A. Roy Garson, Ph.D.		Garson	A.	Roy (Ph.D.)
E. R. Haynes		Haynes	E.	R.
Rev. Howard J. Haynes		Haynes	Howard	J. (Rev.)
Rabbi Marvin Julius Jacobs		Jacobs	Marvin	Julius (Rabbi)

(Illustrative examples continued on page 42.)

Names	Units:	Alphabetic Index Order 1	2	3
Gayle Kane, D.V.M.		Kane	Gayle (D.V.M.)	
Gayle A. Kane		Kane	Gayle	A.
Mrs. Gladys Kane		Kane	Gladys (Mrs.)	
Mme. Carla		Madame	Carla	
Miss Kathy L. Martin		Martin	Kathy	L. (Miss)
Sister Mary Katherine		Sister	Mary	Katherine
Sister Theresa, O.S.F.		Sister	Theresa (O.S.F.)	
Theresa M. Sister, Ed.D.		Sister	Theresa	M. (Ed.D.)
Brother Francis Small		Small	Francis (Brother)	
Sister Theresa Small, O.S.F.		Small	Theresa (Sister, O.S.F.)	
Señor Juan Soriano		Soriano	Juan (Señor)	

Note: In filing names including the religious titles "Father," "Brother," and "Sister," the preceding rule may be disregarded or modified as follows:

(1) If it is considered desirable to group together in a filing system all names bearing the title "Father," all names bearing the title "Brother," and all names bearing the title "Sister," the titles themselves are considered of first importance in indexing regardless of the names that follow them. Names that do not include a surname are indexed in the order written, but names that include one or more given names and a surname are transposed after the title.

(2) If it is considered desirable to set up a separate section for such names in the files, the name or names following such titles are considered of first importance, with the title disregarded, whether there is but one name, two names, or more. Names that do not include a surname are indexed in the order written; names that include one or more given names and a surname are transposed.

(3) With the current practice among those in religious work of using surnames, Rule 7b will become used less and less in these instances.

8: *Identical Names of Individuals*

If all the units in the names of two or more individuals are identical, filing order is determined by addresses, which are used as auxiliary means of indexing rather than as indexing units.

The auxiliary means (or identifying elements) are considered in order as follows: (1) city names, (2) state names if the city names are identical, (3) street names, including the designations "Avenue," "Street," and "Drive," with directions, such as "East" and "West," transposed, and (4) house and building numbers, with the lowest number filed first. (The name of the building is used as an identifying element only when the street name is not known.)

Names	Units:	Alphabetic Index Order 1	2	3	Identifying Elements
Leo G. Sloan, Canton, Ohio		Sloan	Leo	G.	(Canton, Ohio)
Leo G. Sloan, Columbus, Indiana		Sloan	Leo	G.	(Columbus, Ind.)
Leo G. Sloan, Columbus, Mississippi		Sloan	Leo	G.	(Columbus, Miss.)
Leo K. Sloan		Sloan	Leo	K.	
Leo Kent Sloan		Sloan	Leo	Kent	
Leo Kenton Sloan		Sloan	Leo	Kenton	
Leo M. Sloan, Milford, Delaware		Sloan	Leo	M.	(Milford, Del.)

(Illustrative examples continued on page 43.)

Names	Alphabetic Index Order			
Units:	1	2	3	Identifying Elements
Leo M. Sloan, Milford, Ohio 45150	Sloan	Leo	M.	(Milford, Ohio 45150)
Leo O. Sloan 1214 East May Drive, Omaha, Nebraska 68111				
Leo O. Sloan 1214 East May Street, Omaha, Nebraska 68103				
Leo O. Sloan 1100 West May Street, Omaha, Nebraska 68102				
Leo O. Sloan 2717 West May Street, Omaha, Nebraska 68102				
Leo O. Sloan Worley Apartments, Omaha, Nebraska 68110				
Leo O. Sloan 101 Oak Street, Oregon, Illinois 61061				
Leo O. Sloan 12 Newton Turner Drive, Oregon City, Oregon 97045				
Leo O. Sloan 16 Tree Lane, Oregon City, Oregon 97045				

Note: ZIP code numbers are disregarded in indexing.

9: *Names of Married Women*

The legal name of a married woman—her first name, either her middle name or initial or her maiden name, and her husband's last name—is the one considered in filing. If her husband's name is known, a cross-reference should be made to it. (See page 46.)

Names	Alphabetic Index Order		
Units:	1	2	3
Mrs. John J. Anders (Esther Johnson)	Anders	Esther	Johnson (Mrs. John J.)
John J. Anders	Anders	John	J.
Bart L. Anderson	Anderson	Bart	L.
George A. Anderson	Anderson	George	A.
Mrs. George A. Anderson (Janice T.)	Anderson	Janice	T. (Mrs. George A.)
Karen O. Anderson	Anderson	Karen	O.
Mrs. Bart L. Anderson (Louise P.)	Anderson	Louise	P. (Mrs. Bart L.)
Don Anderson-Williams	Anderson-	Williams	Don

10: *Individual's Name Within Another Name*

If an individual's name appears within a business or other name, the individual's name is transposed in the usual manner.

Names	Units:	1	2	3	4	5
				Alphabetic Index Order		
Wm. R. LaDuc Carpet Company		LaDuc	William	R.	Carpet	Company
Helen Larsen Dress Shop		Larsen	Helen	Dress	Shop	
John A. Larson		Larson	John	A.		
John Larson Implements		Larson	John	Implements		
John Joseph Larson		Larson	John	Joseph		
Ray Moore--Don Josten Company		Moore	Ray	Josten	Don	Company
H. P. Rose Book Company		Rose	H.	P.	Book	Company
Ronald St. Francis, Limited		Saint	Francis	Ronald	Limited	
Kenneth St. John Sales Agency		Saint	John	Kenneth	Sales	Agency
Lawrence St. John		Saint	John	Lawrence		
Harry L. Sanders		Sanders	Harry	L.		
Harry L. Sanders Real Estate		Sanders	Harry	L.	Real	Estate
Harry Leon Sanders		Sanders	Harry	Leon		

PREPARING CARDS FOR ALPHABETIC FILING

Many offices keep card files of names and addresses, arranged alphabetically. For maximum efficiency and ease of handling, the cards in a card file should be prepared according to the style selected by the files supervisor or office manager. In general, file cards follow the same pattern. Each card contains the following data:

1. The name of the individual (or business or organization) written or typed in index form just above the line drawn across the card near the top or a uniform space down from the top of an unlined card.
2. The name of the individual and the address of the individual (or business organization) written or typed in the usual envelope form a triple space below the line typed in #1 above.

Uniformity of style in the typing of cards makes the filing and finding of the cards easier. Therefore, the style adopted by the office should be followed consistently. The following method is frequently used in preparing a file card for an individual:

1. The name of the individual should begin three spaces from the left edge of the card and slightly above the horizontal line. The name should be typed in index form with the surname first (if the surname is the first indexing unit), the given name or initial second, and the middle name or initial third. A comma should be used to separate the surname from the other units in the name.

   A title that is not an indexing unit (such as "Dr.") or an identifying element (such as "Jr.") should be typed in parentheses after the last indexing unit on the top line.

   The name at the top of the card may be typed (a) in all capital letters, (b) in a combination of capital and lower-case letters, or (c) with the first unit in all capitals and the following units in a combination of capital and lower-case letters.

2. The title (if known), the name, and the address should be typed a triple space below the name at the top of the card in envelope addressing style.

3. If the name on the file card is assigned a number so that the card can be used in a numeric system, the code number should be typed in the upper right corner of the card as in two of the cards illustrated below.

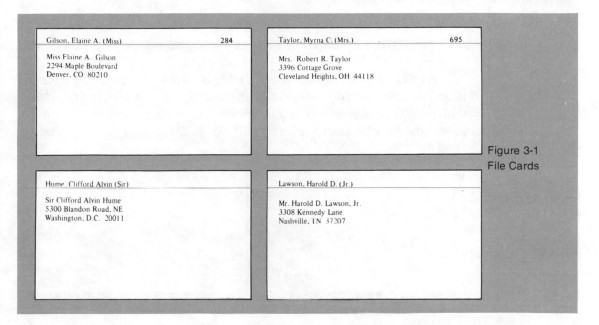

Figure 3-1
File Cards

CROSS-REFERENCING OF INDIVIDUALS' NAMES

Because certain types of names are sometimes thought of and materials bearing them requested in more than one way, it is often desirable, and usually necessary, to prepare an additional record of such a name under a second or a third form. This additional record is called a *cross-reference*. A cross-reference card in a card file shows a name in a form other than that used on the original card, and it indicates the location of the card bearing that name.

Two types of individuals' names that lend themselves to cross-referencing are:

1. Unusual and foreign names
2. Names of married women

Unusual and foreign names. A cross-reference should be made for an unusual or a foreign name in the exact form in which the name is written. Then, if someone recalls the name in transposed order, the files will contain the needed information.

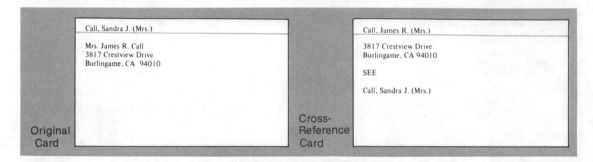

Abdul, Hai (Dr.)		Hai Abdul (Dr.)
Dr. Hai Abdul 414 Park Tower Oakland, CA 94601		414 Park Tower Oakland, CA 94601 SEE Abdul, Hai (Dr.)
Original Card	Cross- Reference Card	

Names of married women. The legal name of a married woman, if known, is used for indexing purposes. If her husband's first name and middle name or initial are known, a cross-reference should be made under it so that a record will be available under both names.

Call, Sandra J. (Mrs.)		Call, James R. (Mrs.)
Mrs. James R. Call 3817 Crestview Drive Burlingame, CA 94010		3817 Crestview Drive Burlingame, CA 94010 SEE Call, Sandra J. (Mrs.)
Original Card	Cross- Reference Card	

If the legal name of a married woman is not known, the records pertaining to her will have to be kept, of course, under her name as she signs it. When her legal name does become known, the records can be changed so that the original record will be under her legal name, and a cross-reference will be under her husband's name.

CODING PROCEDURES FOR CROSS-REFERENCES

Cross-references are coded in the same manner as are original cards and pieces of correspondence. The name on the first line of the cross-reference card or sheet is always the one that is used to determine placement in the file; this name is the one to be indexed and coded. The units in the examples given in the cross-references above are: *Hai*, Unit 1; *Abdul*, Unit 2; and *Call*, Unit 1; *James*, Unit 2; *R*, Unit 3.

In essence, the cross-reference card or sheet is a sign that points the way to the correct filing place of a name. Correspondence is never filed in the cross-reference location. The important point to remember is that the cross-reference tells where the wanted paper is, and the person who is looking for it then goes to that other place in the file to find it.

In a card file, a cross-reference card may be identical with all others in size and color, or it may be distinctively different in color to make it stand out clearly from the other cards.

For Review and Discussion

1. What are the first, second, and succeeding indexing units in each of the following names?

   a. Cleston Burgess
   b. Mathew Campbell-Brown
   c. Mary J. L'Assanza
   d. Wm. Lawson, Sr.
   e. Thos. Raymond Le Bar
   f. Rev. Jno. Harry George
   g. Mrs. Laura Smith Downs
   h. Father Whiting
   i. Harry Brooks, II
   j. Sister Mary Alice Simmons
   k. Ruth Barlow Beauty Shop

   l. Anne-Marie Haynes
   m. Dr. D'Italo Verrini
   n. R. Richard St. John
   o. Miss Maria Matthews
   p. Mrs. H. A. (Elaine) Kane
   q. Rabbi Joel Post
   r. Ven Tru Zidek
   s. Mlle. Louise Marie
   t. Betty O. A'Bris
   u. Brother John Adams
   v. Roy A. Pross, Ph.D.

2. The three names in each of the following groups of names are in correct alphabetic order. A fourth name is given in parentheses below each group. Should this fourth name, when added to the group, be placed first, second, third, or fourth in the group?

   a. Robert Bandi-Crane
      J. H. Davidson
      James Davidson

      (Robt. H. Crane)

   b. D. Louis Cox
      Louis H. Cox
      Louis Henry Cox

      (Louis Cox, Jr.)

   c. Ms. Alice Leonard
      Mrs. Enda Lester
      Dr. Bernard Lewin

      (Madame Lenora)

   d. Bro. John Ragan
      Dr. John A. Ragan
      Mr. John Andrew Ragan

      (Charles John-Ragan)

3. Are the two names in each of the following pairs in correct alphabetic order?

   a. Robert L. Smythe
      Robert Lawrence Smythe

   b. Thomas St. Germain
      Thomas Saint Germaine

   c. Mrs. Russell (Eva) Smith
      Rose A. Smith

   d. Rev. Ralph D. Beeker
      Father Adamson

e. Mrs. Arthur (Ann)
    Hanson
    Mrs. Anne Hanson

f. Don Schmidt Bakery
    Hubert Crawford Downey

g. David Thomas-Earl
    David Timothy Earl

h. Edward O'Donnel
    Nancy O. Donnell

i. Raymond Cleary, Agent
    Albert S. Agin

j. L. C. Hargrove, Sioux City, Iowa
    L. C. Hargrove, Springfield, Illinois

k. Perry Elliott, Florist
    Perry A. Elliott

l. Mrs. Roy (Anne) Fox, Durham,
    North Carolina
    Mrs. Anne Fox, Elgin, Illinois

m. Clifford Hardesty, M.D.
    Mrs. Clifford L. Hardesty

n. Connie Marie Attermeyer
    Clement Adams, Attorney

Laboratory Assignment 1

You should now complete Laboratory Assignment 1 (Card Filing —Names of Individuals) in *Records Management—Laboratory Materials*. The instructions for the assignment and the supplies needed in completing it are provided in the set.

SECTION 2: ALPHABETIC RULES FOR BUSINESS NAMES

11: *Order of Indexing Units*

a. The general rule is that names of businesses, except those containing the full name of an individual, are indexed as they are written.

b. If the full name of an individual appears in a business name, the units in the individual's name are transposed in the same way the units would be transposed if the individual's name stood by itself.

c. A business name consisting of a title followed by a single given name, a surname, or a coined name (such as "Mademoiselle Marie Dress Shoppe," "Mrs. Ryan Candy Shop," or "Mister Softee Ice Cream") is indexed as it is written. If the title is abbreviated, it is indexed as if it were spelled in full. However, the titles "Mr." and "Mrs." are filed alphabetically as they are written. If the full name of an individual is contained in a firm name, it is transposed in the usual manner and the title is disregarded.

Names	| Alphabetic Index Order			
	Units: 1	2	3	4
E. E. Benson Limited	Benson	E.	E.	Limited
Bond Typewriter Sales	Bond	Typewriter	Sales	
Bonfield Answer Service	Bonfield	Answer	Service	

(*Illustrative examples continued on page 49.*)

Names	Alphabetic Index Order			
Units:	1	2	3	4
Canadian Aluminum Products	Canadian	Aluminum	Products	
Dr. Brown Clinic	Doctor	Brown	Clinic	
Forest Dale Terrace Apartments	Forest	Dale	Terrace	Apartments
Gordon Book Mart	Gordon	Book	Mart	
W. C. Gordon Associates	Gordon	W.	C.	Associates
Alice Graham, Cosmetics	Graham	Alice	Cosmetics	
Graham Cosmetics Company	Graham	Cosmetics	Company	
Gruver Furniture Store	Gruver	Furniture	Store	
Mary Gruver Bakery	Gruver	Mary	Bakery	
Gruver, Paige, Rush, Attorneys	Gruver	Paige	Rush	Attorneys
T. Gruver Tile Setters	Gruver	T.	Tile	Setters
Gunthers Furs Limited	Gunthers	Furs	Limited	
Greta Hudson Candies	Hudson	Greta	Candies	
Hudson Linen Company	Hudson	Linen	Company	
Donald Lee Drygoods Store	Lee	Donald	Drygoods	Store
Marsh Business Supplies Limited	Marsh	Business	Supplies	Limited
Miss Jane Tutoring School	Miss	Jane	Tutoring	School
Mountain Duplicators	Mountain	Duplicators		
Mr. Repair Television Service	Mr.	Repair	Television	Service
Mrs. Hartley Catering Company	Mrs.	Hartley	Catering	Company
Mrs. Tendercare Baby Sitters	Mrs.	Tendercare	Baby	Sitters
Marshall G. Page Repairs	Page	Marshall	G.	Repairs
Seaway Paper Bag Company	Seaway	Paper	Bag	Company
Señor Morales Western Store	Señor	Morales	Western	Store
Sir Albert Toggery	Sir	Albert	Toggery	
Valley Farm Ice Cream	Valley	Farm	Ice	Cream
Paul Walters Drug Corner	Walters	Paul	Drug	Corner

12: *Identical Business Names*

If all the units in two or more business names are identical, filing order is determined by addresses, which are used as auxiliary means of indexing rather than as indexing units.

The auxiliary means (or identifying elements) are considered in order as follows: (1) city names, (2) state names if the city names are identical, (3) street names, including the designations "Avenue," "Street,", and "Drive," and the directions, such as "East" and "West," transposed, and (4) building numbers, with the lowest number filed first. (The name of the building is used as an identifying element only when the street name is not known.)

Names	Alphabetic Index Order			Identifying Elements
Units:	1	2	3	
Graham Paint Shop Ware, Massachusetts	Graham	Paint	Shop	(Ware)
Graham Paint Shop Warren, Michigan	Graham	Paint	Shop	(Warren, Mich.)

(Illustrative examples continued on page 50.)

Names	Alphabetic Index Order			Identifying Elements
	Units: 1	2	3	
Graham Paint Shop Warren, Minnesota	Graham	Paint	Shop	(Warren, Minn.)
Graham Paint Shop Warwick, Rhode Island	Graham	Paint	Shop	(Warwick)
Graham Variety Store 2296 First Avenue, Waterbury, Connecticut 06710				
Graham Variety Store 905 Second Avenue, Waterbury, Connecticut 06710				
Graham Variety Store 2867 Second Avenue, Waterbury, Connecticut 06710				
Graham Variety Store Terminal Building, Waterbury, Connecticut 06711				
Graham Variety Store 1918 Vine Street, Waterbury, Vermont 05676				

13: *Articles, Prepositions, and Conjunctions*

English articles, prepositions, and conjunctions in a business name are generally not considered to be indexing units. These disregarded words are enclosed in parentheses to set them off from the indexing units. "The," when appearing as the first word in a business name, is placed at the end of the name and is enclosed in parentheses. (If two or more individuals' names are connected by "and" or "&" to form a business name, a cross-reference should be prepared in the manner explained on page 57.)

Exception: When a preposition is the first word in a business name, the preposition is considered to be the first indexing unit. In addition, when a word that is normally classified as a preposition is used as a modifying word or as part of a compound name, that word is considered to be an indexing unit.

Names	Alphabetic Index Order		
	Units: 1	2	3
The Farr Manufacturing Company	Farr	Manufacturing	Company (The)
Fourth & Elm Grocery	Fourth (&)	Elm	Grocery
Fruit of the Loom, Incorporated	Fruit (of the)	Loom	Incorporated
The In Between	In	Between (The)	
In and Out Service	In (and)	Out	Service
The Jones & Peterson Company	Jones (&)	Peterson	Company (The)
The Off Beat	Off	Beat (The)	
Over the Rhine Restaurant	Over (the)	Rhine	Restaurant
Persons and Persons, Incorporated	Persons (and)	Persons	Incorporated
Save A Minute Laundry	Save (A)	Minute	Laundry
Side by Side Loans	Side (by)	Side	Loans

(Illustrative examples continued on page 51.)

Names	Alphabetic Index Order		
Units:	1	2	3
Signs of Business	Signs (of)	Business	
Travel with Lucille	Travel (with)	Lucille	
West or East Truckers	West (or)	East	Truckers

Note: Contrast the foregoing treatment of business names containing articles, prepositions, and conjunctions with the treatment of business names containing hyphens, Rule 16, page 52.

14: *Abbreviations*

Abbreviations in a business name are indexed as though they were spelled in full. The files operator should be absolutely sure of spelling and meaning, however; he should not guess.

Names	Alphabetic Index Order		
Units:	1	2	3
Arctic Eq. Co.	Arctic	Equipment	Company
AP Internat'l	Associated	Press	International
B & O RR	Baltimore (&)	Ohio	Railroad
Belanger Asphalts Ltee.	Belanger	Asphalts	Ltee.
Calif. Vinyl Prods.	California	Vinyl	Products
Cartier Brands Reg'd	Cartier	Brands	Registered
Citywide Mtge. Loans	Citywide	Mortgage	Loans
Custer & Co. Ltd.	Custer (&)	Company	Limited
Darwin Constr. Co.	Darwin	Construction	Company
Farnsley Dept. Store	Farnsley	Department	Store
GE Co.	General	Electric	Company
Gen'l Eng. Corp.	General	Engineering	Corporation
Gen'l Mfg. Co.	General	Manufacturing	Company
General Mdse. Assn.	General	Merchandise	Association
Hopkins Bros.	Hopkins	Brothers	
Hopkins Hdwe. Co.	Hopkins	Hardware	Company
Hopkins Ins. Co.	Hopkins	Insurance	Company
I. Magnin & Co.	Magnin	I. (&)	Company

Note: Unless all the files operators in the office know the meaning of "Ltee.," the abbreviation should be filed exactly as it appears in the name. Files operators are expected to know English abbreviations, but they may not know abbreviations in foreign languages.

15: *Single Letters*

a. A single letter (with or without a period) in a business name is considered to be a separate unit.

b. In a business name composed of two or more single letters, each letter is considered to be a separate indexing unit, no matter whether the letters are written separately or are written together. Punctuation of the letters also is immaterial.

Names	Units: 1	Alphabetic Index Order 2	3	4
A B C Waxers	A	B	C	Waxers
A to B Lines, Inc.	A (to)	B	Lines	Incorporated
BBD Bottlers	B	B	D	Bottlers
Bar X Ranch	Bar	X	Ranch	
D and G Motors	D (and)	G	Motors	
Dale & Roy Cleaning Service	Dale (&)	Roy	Cleaning	Service
The D'Amico	D'Amico (The)			
F Sharp Music Store	F	Sharp	Music	Store
G.B.L. Caterers	G.	B.	L.	Caterers
G. C. H. Corporation	G.	C.	H.	Corporation
Gladys and Helen Dress Shop	Gladys (and)	Helen	Dress	Shop
H A & R Laboratories	H	A (&)	R	Laboratories
H and W Market	H (and)	W	Market	
C. Chas. Howard Gallery	Howard	C.	Charles	Gallery
B. Shell and J. West	Shell	B. (and)	West	J.
The T V Man	Television	Man (The)		
TV Repair Service	Television	Repair	Service	

Note: An alternate plan for filing the familiar abbreviation "TV" is to consider it as two single letters and not as the complete word "television." If this plan is used, "T" is the first unit and "V" is the second unit.

16: *Hyphenated Business Names*

a. When two or more initials, words, names, word substitutes, or coined words in a business name are joined by a hyphen, the hyphen is disregarded and each part of the name is considered to be a separate indexing unit. (If a surname and a coined name are used to form a business name, a cross-reference should be prepared in the manner explained on page 58.)

b. Articles, prepositions, and conjunctions that are joined to other words by hyphens also follow this rule: Each is a separate indexing unit.

c. When a hyphen joins two parts of a single word, both parts are considered together as one indexing unit. Words of this type often begin with *anti-, bi-, co-, inter-, intra-, mid-, non-, pan-, pre-, re-, self-, trans-, tri-, un-,* and the like.

Names	Units: 1	Alphabetic Index Order 2	3	4
A-A Laundry	A-	A	Laundry	
A-One Cleaners	A-	One	Cleaners	
A-Z Variety Store	A-	Z	Variety	Store
Anti-Defamation League	Anti-Defamation	League		
C-Clear Window Shop	C-	Clear	Window	Shop

(Illustrative examples continued on page 53.)

Names	Alphabetic Index Order			
Units:	1	2	3	4
Carson-Wells Drug Laboratories	Carson-	Wells	Drug	Laboratories
Chat-N-Chew	Chat-	N-	Chew	
Co-operative Scale Co.	Co-operative	Scale	Company	
Eat-More Foods, Inc.	Eat-	More	Foods	Incorporated
Geneva Drive-In Theater	Geneva	Drive-	In	Theater
Go-to-Europe Fund	Go-	to-	Europe	Fund
In-and-Out Service	In-	and-	Out	Service
Inter-Ocean Ins. Co.	Inter-Ocean	Insurance	Company	
On-Time Answering Service	On-	Time	Answering	Service
Sav-Ur-Self Markets	Sav-	Ur-	Self	Markets
Self-Service Variety Store	Self-Service	Variety	Store	
Sno-Blo Ski Shop	Sno-	Blo	Ski	Shop
Trans-Canada Chapeau Ltee.	Trans-Canada	Chapeau	Ltee.	
Tri-City Credit Bureau	Tri-City	Credit	Bureau	
Wash-a-Car, Inc.	Wash-	a-	Car	Incorporated

Note: Unless this rule is followed consistently, misfiling will result and much time will be consumed in looking in two or more places in the files for such names.

17: *Words That Can Be Written Singly or Together*

In a business name when a word that appears as one word, as two words, or as a hyphenated word may be correctly written as one word, it is considered to be one indexing unit, no matter which way the word is written. This rule applies to words such as *airport, co-operative, everybody, goodwill, lakeside, pre-eminent, railroad, worthwhile,* and points of the compass words such as *northeast, northwest, southeast, southwest,* and their variations.

Names	Alphabetic Index Order		
Units:	1	2	3
Down Town Operators Assn.	DownTown	Operators	Association
Downtown Printers	Downtown	Printers	
Down-Town Rental Agency	Down-Town	Rental	Agency
Lakeland Resort	Lakeland	Resort	
Lemon Lake Side Rentals	Lemon	LakeSide	Rentals
Lemon-Ade Parlor	Lemon-Ade	Parlor	
Lemonade, Unlimited	Lemonade	Unlimited	
Main WavaCurl Shoppe	Main	WavaCurl	Shoppe
The Main-Stay Corner	Main-Stay	Corner (The)	
Robert North & Son	North	Robert (&)	Son
North East Health Center	NorthEast	Health	Center
Northeastern Airlines	Northeastern	Airlines	
Northern Calif. Bureau	Northern	California	Bureau
North Western Business Service	NorthWestern	Business	Service
Sea Board Floral Co.	SeaBoard	Floral	Company
Capt. William B. Worth	Worth	William	B. (Capt.)
Worth While Tailors	WorthWhile	Tailors	
Worthwhile Thrift Shop	Worthwhile	Thrift	Shop

18: *Numbers and Symbols in Business Names*

Numbers and symbols within a business name are considered as though they were spelled out. The complete number is considered to be one word. If the number is accompanied by a symbol, the symbol is considered separately as a word. Four-place numbers are expressed in hundreds, not in thousands (resulting in a smaller number of letters to indicate the number).

Names	Units: 1	Alphabetic Index Order 2	3	4
5th Street Florists	Fifth	Street	Florists	
53 Lucy Street Barbers	Fiftythree	Lucy	Street	Barbers
$5 Daily Rentals	Five	Dollar	Daily	Rentals
5 Mile House	Five	Mile	House	
4-Square Caterers	Four-	Square	Caterers	
490 Post Street Bakery	Fourhundredninety	Post	Street	Bakery
4th Avenue Garage	Fourth	Avenue	Garage	
The House of 9	House (of)	Nine (The)		
9¢ Novelty Nook	Nine	Cent	Novelty	Nook
905 Sutter Repair Serv.	Ninehundredfive	Sutter	Repair	Service
1900 Pacific Apts.	Nineteenhundred	Pacific	Apartments	
19th & Q Corporation	Nineteenth (&)	Q	Corporation	
#1 Delivery Co.	Number	One	Delivery	Company
The 3 Cooks	Three	Cooks (The)		

Note 1: Some files operators consider numbers in the hundreds without the word "hundred." For example, "490" would be "fourninety"; "1010" would be "tenten." This method of indexing is also correct. One plan, however, must be followed consistently in one office.

Note 2: Even though a number is considered to be spelled out in indexing, it is written in figures if that is the way it is normally used.

19: *Possessives*

When a word contains an apostrophe showing possession, all of the word up to the apostrophe is considered. If an "s" follows the apostrophe, the "s" is disregarded.

Names	Units: 1	Alphabetic Index Order 2	3
Irene's Alteration Shop	Irene'(s)	Alteration	Shop
Irene & Bob's Hobbies	Irene (&)	Bob'(s)	Hobbies
James's Coffee Shop	James'(s)	Coffee	Shop
James' Hardware Store	James'	Hardware	Store
The Jameses' College Bowl	Jameses'	College	Bowl (The)
Janson's Brick Corp.	Janson'(s)	Brick	Corporation
Harold W. Janson	Janson	Harold	W.
Jansons' Ambulance Co.	Jansons'	Ambulance	Company
Jones's Barber Shop	Jones'(s)	Barber	Shop
Jones' Beauty Loft	Jones'	Beauty	Loft
King's Furniture Store	King'(s)	Furniture	Store
Kings' Boat Repair	Kings'	Boat	Repair
Klem's Auto Shop	Klem'(s)	Auto	Shop
Klem-Emos' Nursery	Klem-	Emos'	Nursery
Klems' Bicycle Repair	Klems'	Bicycle	Repair

20: *Compound Geographic Business Names*

Each English word in a compound geographic business name is considered to be a separate indexing unit. A similar rule applies to the Spanish words "San" and "Santa," which are commonly known to mean "Saint."

Names	Units:	1	2	3	4
			Alphabetic Index Order		
Lake Wells Gun Club		Lake	Wells	Gun	Club
Lakeport Grocery		Lakeport	Grocery		
Lakeview Industries		Lakeview	Industries		
Mt. Hope Pen Shop		Mount	Hope	Pen	Shop
Mountain Home Candles		Mountain	Home	Candles	
Mountainview Apothecary Shop		Mountainview	Apothecary	Shop	
New Castle Riders Group		New	Castle	Riders	Group
New York Lightoliers, Inc.		New	York	Lightoliers	Incorporated
St. George Pharmacy		Saint	George	Pharmacy	
Saintsburg Workshop		Saintsburg	Workshop		
San Gabriel Mission		San	Gabriel	Mission	
Santa Rosa Iron Works		Santa	Rosa	Iron	Works
The Meadows Stationery Store		The	Meadows	Stationery	Store

Note 1: "The," when it is part of the actual name of a city (as "The Meadows"), is considered in filing to be the first unit. The letterhead in a real situation would indicate the occurrence of "The" in a city name.

Note 2: Another commonly accepted plan of filing treats each geographic name as one word regardless of the number of words in the name. Thus, "New York" would always be considered as one unit; "St. George" would be considered as one unit. The plan to be used must be decided upon in the office and followed without exception. In the examples given above and in the practice material accompanying this chapter, Rule 20 is used as stated.

Note 3: Because many geographic names may be (and are) spelled as one or two English words, the files operator must be alert so that papers pertaining to the same firm will not be filed in two places because of two spellings of the name.

21: *Foreign Business Names*

a. Each separate word (but not a particle or prefix) in a foreign business name is considered to be a separate unit.

Names	Units:	1	2	3	4
			Alphabetic Index Order		
Monte Rio Grande Mar		Monte	Rio	Grande	Mar
Nueva Rosita Tomales		Nueva	Rosita	Tomales	
Palo Alto Veterans Club		Palo	Alto	Veterans	Club
Ste. Agathe Importing Co.		Sainte	Agathe	Importing	Company
San Francisco Spice Co.		San	Francisco	Spice	Company
Sault Sainte Marie Electronics		Sault	Sainte	Marie	Electronics
Terre Haute Appliance Serv.		Terre	Haute	Appliance	Service
Trois Rivieres Steamship Lines		Trois	Rivieres	Steamship	Lines

b. A foreign particle or prefix (the translated form of which often includes articles, prepositions, and conjunctions) is combined with the word following it, and the combination of the two is considered to be one unit. Examples of prefixes are *d', de, des, do, dos, du, el, il, l', la, las, le, les, los.*

Names	Units:	1	2	3	4
			Alphabetic Index Order		
Bayou La Batre Packing & Supply		Bayou	LaBatre	Packing (&)	Supply
Compagnee D'Auvents de Quebec		Compagnee	D'Auvents	deQuebec	
Decker Variety Store		Decker	Variety	Store	
De Kalb Excavating Co.		DeKalb	Excavating	Company	
Delman Jewelers		Delman	Jewelers		
Del Norte Abstract Co.		DelNorte	Abstract	Company	
D'Lo Engraving Co.		D'Lo	Engraving	Company	
Elbert Shoe Company		Elbert	Shoe	Company	
El Dorado Ranch Properties		ElDorado	Ranch	Properties	
L'Epiphanie des Etoiles		L'Epiphanie	desEtoiles		
Losacker Grocery		Losacker	Grocery		
Los Angeles Lock Co.		LosAngeles	Lock	Company	
Notre Dame du Lac Resort		Notre	Dame	duLac	Resort

c. Unusual foreign business names are indexed exactly as they are written.

Names	Units:	1	2	3	4
			Alphabetic Index Order		
Alta Loma Gift Shop		Alta	Loma	Gift	Shop
Aquiles Serdan Tourist Bureau		Aquiles	Serdan	Tourist	Bureau
Arroya Grande Racing Assn.		Arroya	Grande	Racing	Association
Bella Vista Shell Station		Bella	Vista	Shell	Station
Bon Secour Tourisme		Bon	Secour	Tourisme	
Bonbons Julienne Enr.		Bonbons	Julienne	Enr.	
Contra Costa Constr. Co.		Contra	Costa	Construction	Company
Cuidad Acuna TV Service		Cuidad	Acuna	Television	Service
Dorion-Vaudreuil Press		Dorion-	Vaudreuil	Press	
Gu Achi Cuisine		Gu	Achi	Cuisine	

CROSS-REFERENCING OF BUSINESS NAMES

Frequently, business names are so composed that information pertaining to a business may be called for under two or more forms of the name. For this reason cross-references are prepared to enable the files operator to find the requested material regardless of the name used in the request for the material.

Types of business names for which cross-references should be prepared are as follows:

1. Business names composed of two or more surnames
2. Names of companies doing business under more than one name
3. Names of companies that are affiliates or branches of other companies
4. Unusual company names that do not clearly indicate whether they are composed of one individual's complete name, two or more surnames, or an individual's name combined with a coined name
5. Company names that are commonly referred to by initials or abbreviations
6. Company names that have been changed

Business names composed of two or more surnames. When a business name is composed of two or more surnames or names that appear to be surnames, the card or correspondence pertaining to the business is filed according to the name as it is written. A cross-reference, however, is prepared for each surname after the first one so that if a request is sent to the filing department with the surnames in incorrect order, the files operator will have no difficulty in finding the material. For example, cross-references would be prepared for the firm of Walters, Whelan & Young (original card at right) as follows:

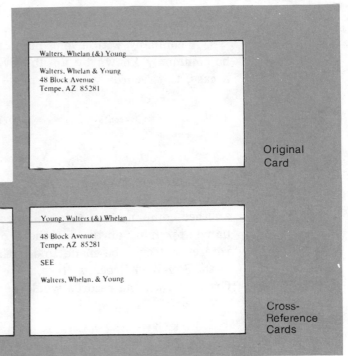

Walters, Whelan (&) Young

Walters, Whelan & Young
48 Block Avenue
Tempe, AZ 85281

Original Card

Whelan, Young (&) Walters

48 Block Avenue
Tempe, AZ 85281

SEE

Walters, Whelan & Young

Young, Walters (&) Whelan

48 Block Avenue
Tempe, AZ 85281

SEE

Walters, Whelan, & Young

Cross-Reference Cards

Similarly, if an original card is made out for Gorin-Francis-Kahn, Importers, two cross-references would be made: one under the name Francis-Gorin-Kahn, Importers, and one under the name Kahn-Francis-Gorin, Importers.

The important point to remember is to use each of the surnames once as the first unit in a cross-reference. The order of the other names in a cross-reference is not of importance so long as each form of the name contains all the surnames.

Names of companies doing business under more than one name. If a company is organized under one name but conducts its business under another name, its correspondence would be kept under the name under which it does business. A cross-reference would be prepared under its organization name, however, in case material was called for by that name at some future time. For example, the

Galesburg Manufacturing Company does business under the name "Gamco, Inc." Its records would be filed as follows:

Original Card	Cross-Reference Card
Gamco, Inc.	Galesburg Manufacturing Company
	SEE
	Gamco, Inc.

A company with a long name may, for the sake of convenience, be commonly known by an abbreviated form of the name. In such a case, the records would be made as follows:

Original Card	Cross-Reference Card
Dawson's	Dawson Furniture Designing & Manufacturing Co.
	SEE
	Dawson's

Names of companies that are affiliates or branches of other companies. When one company is affiliated with or is a branch of another company, the original record would be prepared under the name appearing on the letterhead of the branch or affiliate. A cross-reference would be made under the name of the parent company. If the Sav-Well Grocery Store, for example, is affiliated with National Grocers, Inc., the records would be prepared as follows:

Original Card	Cross-Reference Card
Sav-Well Grocery Store	National Grocers, Inc.
	SEE
	Sav-Well Grocery Store

Unusual or difficult company name combinations. The names of some companies are composed of words that could be an individual's name, a combination of surnames, or a combination of an individual's name and a coined name. Because it is difficult to determine by which rules such names should be indexed, the files operator codes the names as written and prepares cross-references to the other possibilities.

Original Cards	Cross-Reference Cards
Bronson-Sprinkles Candies	Sprinkles-Bronson Candies
	SEE
	Bronson-Sprinkles Candies
Graham Brougham Sportswear	Brougham Graham Sportswear
	SEE
	Graham Brougham Sportswear

Original Card	Cross-Reference Card
Katazalov Makai Company	Makai Katazalov Company
	SEE
	Katazalov Makai Company

A well-known example of a company name containing an individual's unusual name is "Marshall Field & Company." Although most people know that "Marshall Field" is the name of an individual, some may not. Therefore, the files operator would handle the name as follows:

Original Card	Cross-Reference Card
Marshall Field & Company	Field, Marshall, & Company
	SEE
	Marshall Field & Company

The similarity between this kind of cross-reference and that used for a business name composed of two or more surnames should be apparent.

Initials and abbreviations. Many businesses and associations are commonly referred to by initials rather than by names or abbreviations of the names. The files operator should prepare cross-references for all names of this type. Four examples of cross-reference cards are as follows:

ABC	GE
SEE	SEE
American Broadcasting Company	General Electric Company
AT&T	P & G
SEE	SEE
American Telephone and Telegraph Company	Procter and Gamble Company

Change in company name. At times a company may deem it desirable to change its name. The files operator must then change the records to indicate the name change and to insure that the new name will be used for filing purposes. The cards or correspondence already in the files are refiled under the new name, and the former name is put in the records as a cross-reference. For example, if the Brown Hat Manufacturing Company changes its name to American Chapeau Designers, the names will appear in the files as follows:

Original Card	Cross-Reference Card
American Chapeau Designers	Brown Hat Manufacturing Company
	SEE
	American Chapeau Designers

The name on the first line of the cross-reference card or sheet is always the one that is used to determine placement in the file and is the one to be indexed and coded. The first units in the examples given in the cross-references on pages 57, 58, and 59 are "Whelan," "Young," "Francis," "Kahn," "Galesburg," "Dawson," "National," "Sprinkles," "Brougham," "Makai," "Field," "A," "A," "G," "P," and "Brown."

For Review and Discussion

1. What are the first, second, and succeeding indexing units in each of the following names?

   a. New World Mdse. Mart Ltd.
   b. Nancy Wilson Bakery
   c. Madame Helga Cosmetics
   d. The Ball Meat Market
   e. Sir George Restaurant
   f. Gen'l Mdse. Co.
   g. A to Z Office Supply Co.
   h. Buy-On-Time Appliance Shop
   i. Taste-Good Sandwich Stand
   j. Tri-State Bus Corp.
   k. Bart-Jacks Hdwe. Store

   l. South-Eastern Air Port Gifts
   m. 122 Items, Inc.
   n. Ed's Excavating
   o. Mrs. Clara Jones's Pastries
   p. New York Supply Company
   q. Bay View Motor Mart
   r. Guabi & Fransci-Porenti
   s. Major Jones Military Suppliers
   t. Kailua Kona Rest Home
   u. CCC Blacktop Corp.
   v. La Salle Toy Mfrs.

2. The names in each of the following groups of names are in correct alphabetic order. A fourth name is given in parentheses below each group. Should this fourth name, when added to the group, be placed first, second, third, or fourth in the group?

   a. New Haven Printers, Inc.
      Newark News Market
      Newport Donut Shop

      (New Rochelle Dept. Store)

   b. Miss Margie Babycare Agency
      Miss & Mrs. Dress Shop
      Miss Nora Stafford Home
      Candies

      (Seldom-Miss Dart Co.)

   c. DDD Advertising Co.
      D & D Used Car Lot
      D. Wallingford & Sons Co.

      (Wallingford-Cane Co.)

   d. Good & Will Foundry
      Good Will Engravers
      Goodwill Hdwe. Store

      (Good Will Rental Agency)

   e. 7th City Importers
      70 Townley Avenue Apt.
      77th Street Terminal

      (770 Products for Milady)

   f. Adam's Delicacies, Akron, Ohio
      Adams' Delicatessen, Canton, Ohio
      Adams' Delicatessen, Dayton, Ohio

      (Adams' Delicacy Foods, Inc.)

g. In-Drive Theatre
Inter-City Loan Co.
Interstate Bus Lines

(Interborough Movers, Inc.)

h. Serv-All Food Products
Servall Motors, Inc.
Service Center for Bikes

(Serv-Self Fruit Market)

i. Henry Mark's Jewelry Store
The Marks's Meat Market
Markstroms-Ross Co.

(Markstrom's Ins. Agency)

j. La Porte Sign Co.
La Salle Grocery
Las Cruces Shoe Store

(Laredo Coach Lines)

3. Indicate the indexing order of the units in each of the following names (a) on the original card in a card file and (b) on the cross-reference card or cards in a card file.

  a. Ulu Mau Village

  b. Lane Ladies' Wear Mfg. Co.
  (commonly called Lane's)

  c. NBC

  d. Johnson-Crockett Company
  (formerly known as Johnson & Son)

  e. Clifton Hdwe. Store
  (branch of Hanes Hdwe. Stores, Inc.)

Learning Projects

1. Write the following names according to the indexing order of the units in the names. Then list the names in correct alphabetic order.

  a. Charles F. St. John, M.D., Anchorage, Alaska

  b. W. Roy Sainte Nurseries, Bangor, Maine

  c. Leo Saint John, Key West, Florida

  d. Mrs. Frank (Maria) Santa, Erie, Pennsylvania

  e. George L. Saint, Tulsa, Oklahoma

  f. Maria Santa, M.A., Miami, Florida

  g. Maria Santa-Anna, Detroit, Michigan

  h. Mary Clyde-Santa, Canton, Ohio

2. On a 5" by 3" index card or on a slip of paper of that size, carefully type or write each of the following names in indexing order. Then, a triple space below the name, type or write the name and address as they would appear on an envelope. Prepare the usual cross-references as you type or write the cards. Arrange all the cards in alphabetic order.

  a. Carl A. Norman, Jr., 622 Idaho Blvd., Boise, ID 83701
  b. Norvell-Craven Corp., Columbia at Main, Saint Paul, MN 55107
  c. N-and-Out Diner, 2295 Adams Lane, St. Louis, MO 63111
  d. MacDuff & North, Florists, 4160 Light Drive, Las Vegas, NV 89102
  e. Father Normand, 10 Sea Breeze Blvd., Juneau, AK 99801
  f. Madame Nora Dressmaking, Lua Lua Bldg., Honolulu, HI 96803
  g. 962 North Side Apt., 962 East Blvd., Helena, MT 59601

   h. Normand, Jones & Charles, 2265 Smith Avenue, Chicago, IL 60605
   i. Carl Norvell Pharmacy, 169 Second Avenue, Terre Haute, IN 47801
   j. North Miami Gift Shop, 22 Ocean Way, North Miami, FL 33121
   k. Mrs. George (Bertha) Norvell, 1606 Cherry Grove, Eugene, OR 97401
   l. NFC Repair Shop, 62 Chaney Avenue, Norwood, OH 45212
  m. Chas. Normand-Jones, 365 Cottage Lane, Denver, CO 80210
   n. No-Waste-Meat Market, 33 Elm Avenue, Houston, TX 77006
   o. Ed M. Nakai, d/b/a Edward Enterprises, Inc., 641 Waiakamilo Road, Honolulu, Hawaii 96817
   p. North East Auto Parts Co., 3d and Plum, Portland, ME 04102
   q. Carl A. Norman, Sr., 290 Tenth Avenue, Boise, ID 83701
   r. Non-Skid Carpet Mfrs., Warren, OH 44481
   s. Mrs. Carl A. Norman Knitting School, 22 Joyce Blvd., Canton, OH 44702
   t. Northside #3 Variety Store, 222 Long Street, Evanston, IL 60201
   u. Normand, Jones & Charles, 1600 Michigan Blvd., Chicago, IL 60603

Laboratory Assignment 2

    You should now complete Laboratory Assignment 2 (Card Filing—Names of Businesses) in *Records Management—Laboratory Materials*.

SECTION 3. ALPHABETIC RULES FOR OTHER NAMES

22: Names of Schools

a. *Elementary and Secondary Schools.* Elementary and secondary school names are indexed first by the names of the cities in which the schools are located and then by the names of the schools. An individual's name within a school name is transposed in the usual manner. If a school name begins with a city name, the city name is considered only once. State names are considered only if the city names in two or more states are identical, in which case state names are considered second as identifying elements.

| Names | Alphabetic Index Order | | | |
	Units: 1	2	3	4
Alameda High School Alameda, California	Alameda	High	School	
Elementary School Albany, California	Albany (California)	Elementary	School	
Albany Elementary School Albany, Indiana	Albany (Indiana)	Elementary	School	
St. James Boys' School Camden, Arkansas	Camden (Arkansas)	Saint	James	Boys'
Notre Dame Academy Camden, New Jersey	Camden (New Jersey)	Notre	Dame	Academy

(Illustrative examples continued on page 63.)

| Names | Alphabetic Index Order | | | |
	Units: 1	2	3	4
Rundlett Junior High School Concord, New Hampshire	Concord	Rundlett	Junior	High
Holmes High School Covington, Kentucky	Covington	Holmes	High	School
Euclid Elementary School Daytona Beach, Florida	Daytona	Beach	Euclid	Elementary
St. Paul's School Daytona Beach, Florida	Daytona	Beach	Saint	Paul'(s)
Du Vall Elementary School Dearborn, Michigan	Dearborn	DuVall	Elementary	School
Edsel Ford High School Dearborn, Michigan	Dearborn	Ford	Edsel	High
Grant Preparatory School Dearborn, Michigan	Dearborn	Grant	Preparatory	School
John Adams High School Des Moines, Iowa	DesMoines	Adams	John	High
St. Joseph Academy Des Moines, Iowa	DesMoines	Saint	Joseph	Academy
Stanley Consolidated School Des Moines, Iowa	DesMoines	Stanley	Consolidated	School

b. Colleges, Universities, and Special Schools.

A college, university, or special school name is indexed first by its most distinctive word. The words "College" and "University" are never considered to be first indexing units. In the case of identically named schools, addresses are used for indexing, as explained in Rule 12, page 49. An individual's name within the name of a college, university, or special school is transposed in the usual manner; and often, a cross-reference is made to the first name. If a city name appears in the name, the city name is considered to be an indexing unit or units.

| Names | Alphabetic Index Order | | | |
	Units: 1	2	3	4
Albert School of Decorating	Albert	School (of)	Decorating	
Grace Ball Secretarial College	Ball	Grace	Secretarial	College
Berlitz School of Languages	Berlitz	School (of)	Languages	
Capital College	Capital	College		
John Carroll University	Carroll	John	University	
Cleary School of Electronics	Cleary	School (of)	Electronics	
Concord Hearing-Speech Center	Concord	Hearing-	Speech	Center
Cornell University	Cornell	University		
East Carolina University	East	Carolina	University	
Emerson Junior College	Emerson	Junior	College	
Iowa State University	Iowa	State	University	
University of Missouri	Missouri	University (of)		
Arthur Murray Dance School	Murray	Arthur	Dance	School
New York Professional School	New	York	Professional	School
College of the Pacific	Pacific	College (of the)		
St. Olaf College	Saint	Olaf	College	
San Francisco State University	San	Francisco	State	University
Agnes Scott College	Scott	Agnes	College	
Trinity College (Burlington, Vermont)	Trinity	College (Burlington)		
Trinity College (Hartford, Connecticut)	Trinity	College (Hartford)		

23: Churches, Clubs, and Other Organizations

a. Churches. The names of churches, temples, cathedrals, synagogues, and the like, are indexed under the most distinctive word within the name. The denomination, if known, is indexed first. The word "Church" is never considered to be the first unit. If a city name is the first word in the name of a nondenominational church, the city name is used as the first indexing unit or units.

Names	Units: 1	2	3	4
	Alphabetic Index Order			
Calvary Baptist Church	Baptist	Church	Calvary	
Bethel Full Gospel Church	Bethel	Full	Gospel	Church
Jeng Sen Buddhism & Taoism Assn.	Buddhism (&)	Taoism	Association	Jeng
Calvary Cross Church	Calvary	Cross	Church	
Memorial Christian Church	Christian	Church	Memorial	
First Christian Reformed Church	Christian	Reformed	Church	First
All Saints Episcopal Church	Episcopal	Church	All	Saints
I Am Temple	I	Am	Temple	
Idaho Falls Community Church	Idaho	Falls	Community	Church
Congregation Ner Tamid	Ner	Tamid	Congregation	
Our Lady of Mercy of Troy	Our	Lady (of)	Mercy (of)	Troy
Broadmoor Presbyterian Church	Presbyterian	Church	Broadmoor	
St. Ignatius Church	Saint	Ignatius	Church	
Cathedral of St. Paul	Saint	Paul	Cathedral (of)	
Temple Sherith Israel	Temple	Sherith	Israel	
First Unitarian Church	Unitarian	Church	First	

b. Clubs, Lodges, and Other Organizations. The names of clubs, lodges, and similar organizations are indexed according to the most clearly identifying word in the name.

In names like American Brotherhood of Railroad Trainmen and American Institute of Accountants, *Railroad, Trainmen,* and *Accountants* are the most clearly identifying words and should be considered first. Stated another way, everything up to and including the word "of" should be transposed as of secondary importance when the most clearly identifying words appear in the name after the word "of." NOTE: Some filing authorities recommend cross-referencing names of this kind according to the first word of the complete name.

A city name appearing in the name of an organization is considered as an indexing unit or units wherever it appears.

When the names of organizations in two or more cities are identical, city names are considered last as identifying elements.

Names	Units: 1	2	3	4
	Alphabetic Index Order			
Beta Sigma Phi, Enid, Okla.	Beta	Sigma	Phi (Enid)	
Beta Sigma Phi, Omaha, Nebr.	Beta	Sigma	Phi (Omaha)	
Canton Better Business Bureau	Canton	Better	Business	Bureau

(*Illustrative examples continued on page 65.*)

Names	Units: 1	Alphabetic Index Order 2	3	4
Commonwealth Club of San Diego	Commonwealth	Club (of)	San	Diego
Corporate Officers of America	Corporate	Officers (of)	America	
Fraternal Order of Eagles	Eagles	Fraternal	Order (of)	
Independent Order of Foresters	Foresters	Independent	Order (of)	
Indiana University Alumni Assn.	Indiana	University	Alumni	Assn.
Loyal Order of Moose	Moose	Loyal	Order (of)	
American Federation of Musicians	Musicians	American	Federation (of)	
Pattern Makers Assn. of Chicago	Pattern	Makers	Assn. (of)	Chicago
Rotary Club, Albany, N. Y.	Rotary	Club (Albany)		
Rotary Club, Miami, Florida	Rotary	Club (Miami)		
Sew-&-Save Club	Sew-	and-	Save	Club
University Club	University	Club		

24: *Banks, Trust Companies, and Building and Loan Associations*

a. If correspondence with banks, trust companies, and the like, is with local firms only, the names are indexed as written.

b. If correspondence is with both local and out-of-town banks, trust companies, and the like, the name of the city is considered first and the name of the institution is indexed next, in the order in which it is written. (If the city name appears in the name of the firm, the city name is used only once.) If city names are identical, the names of the states are considered next as identifying elements. This method of indexing is similar to that followed in indexing the names of elementary and secondary schools.

Names	Units: 1	Alphabetic Index Order 2	3	4
Ohio Security Savings Bedford, Ohio	Bedford (Ohio)	Ohio	Security	Savings
Bedford Union Trust Bank Bedford, Virginia	Bedford (Virginia)	Union	Trust	Bank
Boston Federal Savings Assn. Boston, Massachusetts	Boston	Federal	Savings	Association
First National Bank Camden, New Jersey	Camden	First	National	Bank
Central Trust Company Cincinnati, Ohio	Cincinnati	Central	Trust	Company

25: *Newspapers and Magazines*

a. **Newspapers.** The name of the city in which the newspaper is published is the first indexing unit or units. The name of the newspaper as it is written is indexed next; however, the city name is used only once. (A cross-reference may be made to the name of the publisher in the manner described on page 72.)

b. **Magazines.** The name of a magazine is indexed as it is written. (A cross-reference may be made to the name of the publisher in the manner described on page 72.)

Names	Alphabetic Index Order		
Units:	1	2	3
The Beacon Journal, Akron, Ohio	Akron	Beacon	Journal (The)
American Home	American	Home	
The Atlanta Journal	Atlanta	Journal (The)	
The News-Post, Baltimore, Maryland	Baltimore	News-	Post (The)
Better Homes and Gardens	Better	Homes (and)	Gardens
Business Week	Business	Week	
Changing Times	Changing	Times	
The Commonweal	Commonweal (The)		

26: *Hotels and Motels*

The distinctive word in the name of the hotel or motel is indexed first. The word "Hotel" or "Motel" is never considered to be the first indexing unit; it is transposed to follow the distinctive word. The names of hotel or motel services that include the name of the hotel or motel in their titles are indexed in the same manner.

Names	Alphabetic Index Order			
Units:	1	2	3	4
Hotel Lerner Coffee Shop	Lerner	Hotel	Coffee	Shop
Mali Hai Inn	Mali	Hai	Inn	
Hotel Milton Florists	Milton	Hotel	Florists	
Motel Napoli	Napoli	Motel		
Nob Hill Motel	Nob	Hill	Motel	
O'Presto Motel	O'Presto	Motel		
John Pressman Motel	Pressman	John	Motel	
Prince George Hotel	Prince	George	Hotel	
Raleigh Hotel	Raleigh	Hotel		
Larry Simmons Motel	Simmons	Larry	Motel	

27: *Historical Names and Nursery Rhyme Names*

a. Historical Names. Historical names are indexed according to the rules for individuals' names and business names previously given.

b. Nursery Rhyme Names. A name containing a nursery rhyme character name is indexed in the order in which it is written.

Names	Alphabetic Index Order			
Units:	1	2	3	4
French Revolution Antique Shop	French	Revolution	Antique	Shop
Humpty Dumpty Toyland	Humpty	Dumpty	Toyland	
Jack & Jill Toy Shop	Jack (&)	Jill	Toy	Shop
General Robert E. Lee's Candies	Lee'(s)	Robert	E.	Candies (General)
Little Miss Muffet Frocks	Little	Miss	Muffet	Frocks
Magna Carta Printing Co.	Magna	Carta	Printing	Company
Mother Hubbard's Bakers	Mother	Hubbard'(s)	Bakers	
Old King Cole's Grill	Old	King	Cole'(s)	Grill
Queen Anne Textile Imports	Queen	Anne	Textile	Imports
Sir John, the Tailor	Sir	John (the)	Tailor	

28: Radio and Television Stations

The names of radio and television stations may be indexed in one of two ways: (1) by call letters, each letter being considered as a separate unit; or (2) by the words "Radio Station" or "Television Station," considered as the first two units and followed by the call letters, each letter being considered as one unit. Since the call letters may be unknown, partly known, or incorrectly remembered, the second way is used in this text and is considered better when correspondence with radio and television stations is filed alphabetically with other papers.

Names	Alphabetic Index Order					
Units:	1	2	3	4	5	6
Race Car Repair Shop	Race	Car	Repair	Shop		
KFRC	Radio	Station	K	F	R	C
KSCJ	Radio	Station	K	S	C	J
WLBC	Radio	Station	W	L	B	C
WOW	Radio	Station	W	O	W	
Radium Supply Company	Radium	Supply	Company			
Select Bait Shop	Select	Bait	Shop			
Travis C. Tamson	Tamson	Travis	C.			
KQED--TV	Television	Station	K	Q	E	D (TV)
WLBC--TV	Television	Station	W	L	B	C (TV)
Television Stores, Inc.	Television	Stores	Inc.			
Ward's Radio Service	Ward'(s)	Radio	Service			

Note: "TV" is not considered a second time since "Television" is already the first unit.

29: Government Agencies and Offices

Of primary importance in the filing of governmental correspondence is a method that will effectively separate the many types of American names at the various governmental levels—local, regional, state, and national—as well as names of foreign governments. Proper identification of the name is a necessity. Every files operator must be meticulous in filing this type of material because of the similarity of names at all levels of government.

If a great deal of correspondence is carried on with one branch of the government, a special section of the file may be set aside for this material, with the names of the agencies and offices being filed alphabetically within the special section.

If governmental correspondence is filed with other correspondence, the following rules apply:

a. United States Government Names. The first three indexing units for any federal government office are "United States Government." They should be written on any correspondence to which they apply if they do not already appear there. The fourth and succeeding units are the principal words in the name of the department and the name of the bureau, division, board, or commission. The words "Department of," "Bureau of," "Division of," and the like are transposed; the word "of" is disregarded.

An authentic list of United States Government agencies and offices is necessary and can be secured from the U. S. Superintendent of Documents. The *U. S. Government Organization Manual* and the *Congressional Directory*, published annually, contain such lists.

Names	Units: 4*	5	6	7	8	9
		Alphabetic Index Order				
Meat Inspection Lab. Agric. Research Serv.	Agriculture	Department (of)	Agricultural	Research	Service	Meat
Weather Bureau	Commerce	Department (of)	Weather	Bureau		
2d Armored Marine Corps Reserve	Defense	Department (of)	Navy	Dept. (of)	Marine	Corps
General Services Administration	General	Services	Administration			
Social Security Administration	Health	Education (and)	Welfare	Dept. (of)	Social	Security
National Park Service	Interior	Department (of)	National	Park	Service	
Federal Bureau of Investigation**	Justice	Department (of)	Federal	Bureau (of)	Investigation	
Immigration and Naturalization Service	Justice	Department (of)	Immigration (&)	Naturalization	Service	
U. S. Employment Service	Labor	Department (of)	Employment	Service		
Main Post Office	Post	Office	Department	Main	Post	Office
Internal Revenue Service	Treasury	Department	Internal	Revenue	Service	

b. State Government Names. The first indexing unit is the name of the state; it must be written on any correspondence where it does not already appear. The next indexing unit is the word "State." The succeeding units are the principal words in the name of the bureau, department, board, or office. The words "Department of," "Bureau of," and the like, are transposed.

Names	Units: 1	2	3	4	5
		Alphabetic Index Order			
Alabama National Guard	Alabama	State (of)	National	Guard	
Florida State Board of Education	Florida	State (of)	Education	Board (of)	
Florida State Fair Board	Florida	State (of)	Fair	Board	
Iowa State Highway Patrol	Iowa	State (of)	Highway	Patrol	
Nebraska State Beverage Control Board	Nebraska	State (of)	Beverage	Control	Board
New York State Athletic Commission	New	York	State (of)	Athletic	Commission
Texas Dept. of Public Health	Texas	State (of)	Public	Health	Department (of)
West Virginia Div. of Highways	West	Virginia	State (of)	Highways	Division (of)

* The first three units in each name are *United States Government*.
** The Federal Bureau of Investigation is so well known by its full name and by its initials, FBI, that this name is often filed in the order in which it is written, rather than in the order given in these examples.

c. *County and City Government Names.* The first indexing unit is the name of the county or city; it must be written on any correspondence where it does not already appear. The next indexing unit is the word "County" or "City." The succeeding units are the principal words in the name of the department, bureau, board, or office. Such words as "Department of" and "Bureau of," are transposed; the word "of" is disregarded. If two or more city or county names are identical, state names are considered second as identifying elements.

Names	Alphabetic Index Order			
Units:	1	2	3	4
Waste Dept., Adams, Mass.	Adams	City (of)	Waste	Department
Probate Court, Adams County, Colo.	Adams (Colorado)	County (of)	Probate	Court
Welfare Dept., Adams County, Ill.	Adams (Illinois)	County (of)	Welfare	Department
Water Dept., Akron, Alabama	Akron (Alabama)	City (of)	Water	Department
Fire Dept., Akron, Colorado	Akron (Colorado)	City (of)	Fire	Department
Police Dept., Akron, Iowa	Akron (Iowa)	City (of)	Police	Department
Health Dept., Akron, Ohio	Akron (Ohio)	City (of)	Health	Department
Traffic Court, Alameda, Calif.	Alameda	City (of)	Traffic	Court
Highway Patrol, Alameda County, Calif.	Alameda	County (of)	Highway	Patrol
Police Dept., Albany, New York	Albany	City (of)	Police	Department
County Court House, Albany, Wyo.	Albany	County (of)	Court	House
Assessor, Clarksburg, W. Va.	Clarksburg	City (of)	Assessor	
County Auditor, Clermont County, Ohio	Clermont	County (of)	Auditor	
Dept. of Welfare, Davis County, Utah	Davis	County (of)	Welfare	Department (of)
Park Dept., Dayton, Kentucky	Dayton (Kentucky)	City (of)	Park	Department
School Board, Dayton, Ohio	Dayton (Ohio)	City (of)	School	Board

30: *Foreign Governments*

The distinctive English name of the foreign country is considered first. Divisions, by whatever title, are considered in the same manner as are departments of the United States Government.

If foreign-language names are to be filed with English names, the foreign-language names are properly translated into English and indexed accordingly. A cross-reference may be made to the foreign-language spelling, as explained on page 73.

Names	Units:	Alphabetic Index Order			
		1	2	3	4
República Argentina		Argentina	National	Bank	
Banco de la Nación					
Chung-Hua Jen-Min Kung-Ho Kuo		China			
Československá Socialistická		Czechoslovakia	National	Committee	
Republika					
Národni vybór					
Kongeriget Danmark		Denmark	State	Council	
Statsraadet					
Republiken Finland		Finland	Supreme	Court	
Korkein oikeus					
République Française		France	Defense	High	Council (of)
Conseil Supérieur de la					
Défense Nationale					
Armeé de l'Air		France	Air	Force	
Bundesrepublik Deutschland		Germany			
Bundesrat		Germany	Federal	Council	
Bundeswehr		Germany	Federal	Defense	Force
Bundestag		Germany	Federal	Diet	
Kongeriket Norge		Norway			
Storting		Norway	Parliament		
Høyesterett		Norway	Supreme	Court (of) Justice	

Note 1: The names of foreign countries may be in English or in the native spelling. To keep uniformity, the files supervisor keeps a complete list of countries with their foreign spellings and the English translations used in the office.

Note 2: If only a very few foreign-language names are to be filed, some files operators prefer to leave them in their original spelling and file according to that spelling alone.

Note 3: A variation of this rule consists of using the formal English name of each foreign country in transposed order. For the names given above, the order of indexing units would be:

Argentine	Republic (The)	National	Bank	
China	People's	Republic (of)		
Czechoslovakia	Socialistic	Republic (of)	National	Committee
Denmark	State	Council		
Finland	Republic (of)	Supreme	Court	
France	Republic (of)	Defense	High	Council (of)
France	Republic (of)	Air	Force	
Germany	Federal	Republic (of)		
Germany	Federal	Republic (of)	Federal	Council
Germany	Federal	Republic (of)	Federal	Defense
Germany	Federal	Republic (of)	Federal	Diet
Norway	Kingdom (of)			
Norway	Kingdom (of)	Parliament		
Norway	Kingdom (of)	Supreme	Court (of)	Justice

Note 4: A good source for determining translations is the **Statesman's Yearbook**, to which the files operator may go for reference.

31: Subjects

Within an alphabetic arrangement, correspondence may sometimes be filed and found more conveniently by a subject title than by a specific name. Beware, however, of using so many subjects that the file becomes predominantly a subject file with alphabetic names as subdivisions! A few typical examples of this method are:

1. Applications correspondence—the job for which applications are being made is far more important than the names of the applicants.

2. Bids or projects correspondence—similar pieces of correspondence are kept together regardless of the names of the writers, as all of the papers pertain to the same bid or the same project.

3. Special promotions or celebrations—all correspondence relating to the event is grouped together by subject instead of being dispersed throughout the files by the names of the writers.

4. Branch office memos and duplicated Information sent to many different offices—material of this nature is kept together to keep the files from becoming filled with duplicate papers in many different folders.

The filing procedure for subject filing is explained in greater detail in Chapter 8. Its application at this time consists of writing the subject title on the piece of correspondence if it does not already appear there. The main subject is the first consideration in indexing. Subdivisions of the main subject may be considered as successive units. The name of the correspondent is considered last.

For correspondence pertaining to applications, the word "Applications" is the name of the main subject; the specific job applied for is a subdivision of the main subject; the applicant's name is last in consideration in indexing. Examples are:

Applications	Accountant	
Applications	Clerk	Factory
Applications	Clerk	Office
Applications	Maintenance	Factory
Applications	Maintenance	Office
Applications	Secretary	
Applications	Stenographer	
Applications	Vari-Typist	

CROSS-REFERENCING OF OTHER NAMES

Certain names, referred to as "Other Names," may be called for in a form in which they were not indexed. Names for which cross-references can be very helpful include:

1. Newspapers
2. Magazines
3. Guardians, trustees, receivers
4. Foreign-language names of businesses and governmental agencies
5. Stores

Newspapers. If the city of publication of a newspaper is not the first unit or units in the newspaper name, a cross-reference should be prepared under the newspaper name.

At times the name of a newspaper may be forgotten, but the name of the publisher may be remembered. If a cross-reference has been made to the publisher, the files operator will be able to locate the name of the newspaper after referring to the cross-reference.

Original Cards	Cross-Reference Cards
Cleveland: Plain Dealer (The)	Plain Dealer (The) SEE Cleveland: Plain Dealer (The) Forest City Publishing Co. SEE Cleveland: Plain Dealer (The)
Columbus Daily Journal	(No cross-reference necessary because (1) the city name is the first unit in the newspaper name and (2) the name of the newspaper and the name of the publisher are alike.)

Magazines. Similar to the difficulty encountered with respect to newspapers is that relating to magazines: Sometimes the name of the magazine is temporarily forgotten; reference to a cross-reference card that has been made for the publisher's name will remind the files operator of the correct name of the magazine.

Original Cards	Cross-Reference Cards
Business Week	McGraw-Hill, Inc. SEE Business Week
Sunset Magazine	Lane Magazine & Book Company SEE Sunset Magazine

Guardians, trustees, receivers. Records pertaining to anyone considered to be an agent for an individual or an organization are indexed under the name of the individual or organization for whom the agent is acting. Guardians, receivers, trustees, and the like, may also be financial institutions or companies. A cross-reference is made under the name of the guardian, receiver, or trustee to refer the files operator to the name of the individual or organization for whom the agent is acting. For example, if the Security National Bank is the trustee for Connie D. Peterson, a minor, the original record is filed under the name of Connie D. Peterson. A cross-reference is prepared for the bank.

Original Card	Cross-Reference Card
Peterson, Connie D. (Miss)	Security National Bank, Trustee SEE Peterson, Connie D. (Miss)

Foreign-language spellings of foreign governmental agencies. The spelling of the name of a foreign government and its agencies is often a native spelling that is usually translated into English for indexing purposes. If the translation has not been made on the document to be filed or on the requisition for materials, the files operator will find a cross-reference bearing the original spelling an aid to finding the records. Special care should be taken to type correct spellings and markings since these may differ markedly from the English form.

Original Cards	Cross-Reference Cards
Burma	Pyee-Daung-Su Myanma-Nianggan-Daw SEE Burma
Sweden	Sverige SEE Sweden

"SEE ALSO" REFERENCES

Another kind of reference, useful primarily in card filing and sometimes called a cross-reference, is a SEE ALSO reference. An application of its use in a card file is as follows: Many grocery stores may be affiliated with the National Grocers, Inc., chain. The name and address of each grocery would be typed on a separate original card. The SEE ALSO reference card, bearing the name and address of the National Grocers, Inc., would read as follows:

```
National Grocers, Inc.
432 Life Building
Des Moines, Iowa    50310

SEE ALSO

Night & Day Foods, Cayuga, Indiana
Owl Grocery, Priest River, Idaho
Sav-Well Grocery, Lawrence, Kentucky
Spink Grocery, Fargo, North Dakota

(and all other groceries affiliated with
National Grocers, Inc.)
```

Another form of SEE ALSO reference is found in card files that have a great number of names. Difficulty may arise in locating surnames that are pronounced the same but spelled differently. A SEE ALSO reference may be prepared to be inserted at each place where a difference in spelling could cause trouble, to direct the files operator to other suggested spellings. The following are examples:

```
Brown--SEE ALSO Braun, Broun, Browne
Kimbal--SEE ALSO Kimball, Kimbel, Kimbell, Kimble
Waal--SEE ALSO Wahl, Wahle, Wall, Whall, Wohl, Woll
```

Still another cross-reference found useful in card files reflects a change in the spelling of a name when it has been translated from a foreign spelling to English spelling. For example:

```
Müller--SEE Mueller
```

SEE ALSO references can be made also for a newspaper publisher and for a magazine publisher. Examples are:

SEE ALSO Reference for a Newspaper Publisher	SEE ALSO Reference for a Magazine Publisher
Thorpe Publications, Publisher 307 East Walnut Street Des Moines, Iowa 50309	Curtis Publishing Company (The) Independence Square Philadelphia, Pennsylvania 19105
SEE ALSO	SEE ALSO
Ankeny Times Beaverdale News Carlisle Citizen	Holiday Jack and Jill Ladies' Home Journal

Syndicates or chain stores may also be located through a SEE ALSO card.

Learning Projects

1. On a 5″ by 3″ index card or on a slip of paper of that size, carefully type or write each of the following names in indexing order. After you have typed all the cards, arrange them in alphabetic order. (Keep the cards for use in Problem 6.)

1. St. Paul Church
2. Nat'l Assn. of Osteopaths
3. Loyal Order of Foresters
4. Central Trust Company
5. City Bank and Trust Company
6. Springfield Savings & Loan Co.
7. Hotel Chamber Coffee Shop
8. John Bardon Motel
9. Little Jack Horner Drums
10. WKRC-TV
11. Radio Station WLW
12. Calvary Baptist Church
13. Carousel Motel
14. Sir Henry Motel
15. Fairmont Temple
16. Florists Club of Akron
17. Central Savings Assn.
18. Matthew United Church
19. Canton Chamber of Commerce
20. Cathedral of St. Richard
21. Civil War Antique Shoppe
22. Hope Presbyterian Church
23. Motel Springfield Restaurant
24. Trinity Episcopal Church

2. On a 5″ by 3″ index card or on a slip of paper of that size, carefully type or write each of the following names in indexing order. After you have typed all the cards, arrange them in alphabetic order. (Keep the cards for use in Problem 6.)

25. Mary Immaculate Seminary, Northhampton, Pennsylvania
26. Ruth Simpson Business School, Baltimore, Maryland
27. The *New York Times,* New York, New York
28. Trinity College, Washington, D. C.
29. *Kent's Home Magazine,* Kent Publishers, Kingsport, Tennessee
30. Harrison School of the Arts, Los Angeles, California
31. Senior High School, Tavares, Florida
32. Miami University, Oxford, Ohio
33. *Home Gardener Magazine,* Home Publications, Philadelphia, Pennsylvania
34. St. Paul's Academy, Rockford, Illinois
35. Young Dramatic School, Providence, Rhode Island
36. *Good Housekeeping,* The Hearst Corporation, New York, New York York
37. College of Idaho, Caldwell, Idaho
38. Hart Institute of Electronics, Chicago, Illinois
39. *Long Island Press,* New York, New York
40. Howard Miller University, Denver, Colorado
41. Elementary School, San Luis Obispo, California
42. *The Daily Journal,* Montgomery Publishing Co., Greensboro, North Carolina
43. Lawes School of Commerce, Detroit, Michigan
44. John F. Kennedy High School, Springfield, Massachusetts
45. College of the Northwest, Spokane, Washington
46. *Fair Mount Youth Magazine,* Bardwell Printers, Chicago, Illinois
47. Elementary School, Harrison, Pennsylvania
48. *Wall Street Journal,* New York, New York

3. Prepare the necessary cross-reference cards for Nos. 29, 33, 36, 39, 40, 42 (two), 46, and 48 in Problem 2. (Keep the cards for use in Problem 6.)

4. Prepare the original index cards and the necessary cross-reference cards for the following names. (Keep the cards for use in Problem 6.)

49. Mrs. George (Mae) Harrison
50. Avery Dennis
51. Whitfield, Wayne & Co.
52. John-Bardon Corp.
53. *Home Designer Magazine* West Publishers, Topeka, Kansas
54. Sinclair's (name commonly used to refer to Sinclair Town and Country Mart)
55. Montgomery, Hart & Company
56. YMCA
57. *The Daily News,* Tulsa, Oklahoma
58. Laulu Mua Importers
59. Wells, Bard, & Spring, Inc.
60. Marie L. Jones (Miss) Union Trust Co., Trustee
61. Bardon & Son (name recently changed from John Bardon, Agent)

5. Prepare an index card for each of the following names. If a name is incomplete, add the necessary words. (Keep the cards for use in Problem 6.)

62. Internal Revenue Service
    Treasury Department
    Dover, Delaware
63. State Highway Patrol
    Woodward, Oklahoma
64. Board of Health
    Woodbury County
    Sioux City, Iowa
65. City Purchasing Department
    New York, New York
66. Veterans Employment
    Service
    U. S. Department of Labor
    Tampa, Florida
67. County Public Library
    Montgomery County
    Montgomery, Alabama
68. FBI
    Department of Justice
    Washington, D. C.

69. State Environmental Control
    and Consumer Protection
    Board
    New York, New York
70. Bureau of International
    Commerce
    U. S. Department of Commerce
    New York, New York
71. State Dept. of Industrial
    Relations
    Frankfort, Kentucky
72. U. S. Army Recruiting Service
    Department of the Army
    San Francisco, California
73. Office of the Director
    Bureau of the Mint
    Treasury Dept.
    Washington, D. C.

6. Combine all the original and cross-reference index cards prepared in Problems 1 through 5. Arrange them in alphabetic order.

Laboratory Assignments 3 and 4

You should now complete Laboratory Assignments 3 (Card Filing —Other Names) and 4 (Card Filing—Review) in *Records Management—Laboratory Materials*.

Chapter 4

Alphabetic method
of records storage

An alphabetic method for filing records is used in almost every office. This method—a dictionary method using letters of the alphabet as determiners of order—underlies the geographic, numeric, and subject methods; and it is used also in filing by sound. It can even be combined with chronologic filing, although chronologic storing is the one method least likely to use alphabetic arrangement.

Because of its importance to the other methods of filing, alphabetic filing is explained fully in this chapter before the other methods are presented. The advantages and disadvantages of this much-used method of records storage are as follows:

ADVANTAGES	DISADVANTAGES
1. Direct reference to filed materials is possible because there is no need to have an index.	1. Misfiling may result when rules are not followed consistently or when there are no established rules.
2. The dictionary order of arrangement is simple in operation.	2. Similar names may cause confusion.
3. Cross-referencing is not difficult.	
4. Misfiling is easily checked by alphabetic sequence.	

Although the practice of consistently following the rules for alphabetic indexing is of primary importance to the files supervisor, certain other types of knowledge are also important if he or she is to understand the alphabetic and other methods of filing, to be able to supervise others in their use, and to be able to analyze, protect, and find records entrusted to his or her care.

The records manager needs to be informed about the "tools" that are necessary to alphabetic filing. His or her suggestions are followed in purchasing supplies, in setting procedures, in revising and updating the systems. His or her knowledge or lack thereof may mean the difference between a smoothly functioning office and one in disarray.

SECTION 1. BASIC SUPPLIES FOR ALPHABETIC FILING

A large alphabetic file is comprised of many small sections, each of which represents one alphabetic division of the file and contains a primary guide, individual folders, a miscellaneous folder, and, in some cases, auxiliary guides and special folders. These items appear in the illustration of part of a typical alphabetic file drawer shown in Figure 4-3, page 82; hereafter, reference will frequently be made to this illustration.

TYPES OF GUIDES

Guides are rigid drawer dividers that, as the name implies, point the way or guide the eye to the sections of the file being sought. They also protect folders from extensive wear as the hand passes quickly from guide to guide, not touching the folder tops.

Guides are available in sets that divide the alphabet into *divisions*. The simplest set is a 23- or 25-division index, the latter having a tab for each letter from *A* to *W*, a tab labeled *Mc*, and a last tab with the combination *XYZ*. Suppose, however, there are 60 to 70 folders for names beginning with the letter "A." Obviously, a number of guides will be needed in the "A" section of the file drawer; that is, guides showing subdivisions of the "A" section will be needed in order to have signposts at more frequent intervals. Thus, a sequence of guides might be used that, instead of running *A-B-C-D*, would run *A, Ah, Am, An, Ar,* and *At*. Subdivisions for the alphabet are available in sets numbering from 20 to 225,000. A comparison of guides in 40-, 80-, 120-, and 160-division sets of the A-Z index is shown in Figure 4-1.

Several filing authorities recommend determining the correct number of subdivisions to be used by counting the number of drawers and using about 20 guides for each drawer. Guides furnished by different manufacturers vary even though each one may divide the

40 Div. A-Z		80 div. A-Z				120 div. A-Z						160 div. A-Z (Larger divisions available up to 10,000 div. A-Z)							
A	1	A	1	L	41	A	1	Gr	41	Pe	81	A	1	E	41	L	81	Ron	121
B	2	An	2	Le	42	Al	2	H	42	Pi	82	Ah	2	Eg	42	Lar	82	Rot	122
Bi	3	B	3	Li	43	An	3	Han	43	Pl	83	Am	3	El	43	Le	83	Ru	123
Br	4	Be	4	Lo	44	As	4	Has	44	Pr	84	An	4	Er	44	Len	84	S	124
C	5	Bi	5	M	45	B	5	He	45	Pu	85	Ar	5	F	45	Li	85	Sam	125
Ch	6	Bo	6	Map	46	Bar	6	Hen	46	Q	86	At	6	Fi	46	Lo	86	Sch	126
Co	7	Br	7	McA	47	Bas	7	Hi	47	R	87	B	7	Fl	47	Lu	87	Scho	127
D	8	Bro	8	McH	48	Bc	8	Ho	48	Re	88	Bal	8	Fo	48	M	88	Sci	128
Do	9	Bu	9	McN	49	Ber	9	Hon	49	Ri	89	Bar	9	Fr	49	Mad	89	Se	129
E	10	C	10	Me	50	Bl	10	Hu	50	Ro	90	Bas	10	Fu	50	Mar	90	Sh	130
F	11	Ce	11	Mi	51	Bo	11	I	51	Rog	91	Be	11	G	51	Mas	91	Shi	131
Fl	12	Co	12	Mo	52	Br	12	J	52	Ru	92	Ber	12	Ge	52	McA	92	Si	132
G	13	Coo	13	N	53	Bre	13	Jo	53	S	93	Bi	13	Gi	53	McD	93	Sm	133
Gi	14	Cr	14	O	54	Bro	14	K	54	Sch	94	Bl	14	Go	54	McG	94	Smi	134
H	15	D	15	P	55	Bu	15	Ke	55	Scho	95	Bo	15	Gr	55	McN	95	Sn	135
He	16	De	16	Pl	56	C	16	Ki	56	Se	96	Bop	16	Gri	56	Me	96	Sp	136
Ho	17	Do	17	Q	57	Car	17	Kl	57	Sh	97	Br	17	Gu	57	Mes	97	St	137
I-J	18	Dr	18	R	58	Ce	18	Kr	58	Shi	98	Bre	18	H	58	Mi	98	Ste	138
K	19	E	19	Re	59	Ci	19	L	59	Si	99	Bro	19	Ham	59	Mim	99	Sti	139
Ki	20	En	20	Ro	60	Co	20	Lar	60	Sm	100	Brow	20	Har	60	Mo	100	Su	140
L	21	F	21	S	61	Com	21	Le	61	Sn	101	Bu	21	Has	61	Mu	101	T	141
Li	22	Fi	22	Sch	62	Cop	22	Len	62	Sp	102	C	22	He	62	N	102	Th	142
M	23	Fo	23	Se	63	Cr	23	Li	63	St	103	Can	23	Hen	63	Ne	103	Ti	143
Mc	24	G	24	Sh	64	Cu	24	Lo	64	Sti	104	Cas	24	Hi	64	Ni	104	To	144
Me	25	Ge	25	Si	65	D	25	M	65	Su	105	Ce	25	Ho	65	Nu	105	Tr	145
Mo	26	Gi	26	Sm	66	De	26	Map	66	T	106	Ci	26	Hom	66	O	106	U	146
N-O	27	Gr	27	St	67	Di	27	McA	67	Th	107	Cl	27	Hor	67	On	107	V	147
P	28	H	28	Sti	68	Do	28	McD	68	Tr	108	Co	28	Hu	68	P	108	W	148
Pi-Q	29	Har	29	Su	69	Du	29	McH	69	U	109	Col	29	Hy	69	Pe	109	Wam	149
R	30	Has	30	T	70	E	30	McN	70	V	110	Con	30	I	70	Pf	110	We	150
Ro	31	He	31	To	71	El	31	Me	71	W	111	Cop	31	J	71	Pi	111	Wel	151
S	32	Her	32	U	72	Er	32	Mi	72	Wam	112	Cr	32	Jo	72	Pl	112	Wh	152
Se	33	Hi	33	V	73	F	33	Mo	73	We	113	Cu	33	Jon	73	Po	113	Wi	153
Sm	34	Ho	34	W	74	Fi	34	Mu	74	Wh	114	D	34	K	74	Pr	114	Wil	154
St	35	Hu	35	We	75	Fo	35	N	75	Wi	115	Dav	35	Ke	75	Pu	115	Wim	155
T	36	I	36	Wh	76	Fr	36	Ne	76	Wil	116	De	36	Kem	76	Q	116	Wo	156
U-V	37	J	37	Wi	77	G	37	No	77	Wim	117	Di	37	Ki	77	R	117	Woo	157
W	38	K	38	Wo	78	Ge	38	O	78	Wo	118	Do	38	Kl	78	Re	118	Wr	158
Wh	39	Ki	39	X-Y	79	Gi	39	On	79	X-Y	119	Dos	39	Ko	79	Ri	119	X-Y	159
X-Y-Z	40	Kr	40	Z	80	Go	40	P	80	Z	120	Du	40	Kr	80	Ro	120	Z	160

NOTE: Number on alphabetic heading appears only on file guides, not card guides

Figure 4-1   Comparison of Guides in A-Z Indexes

Oxford Pendaflex Corporation

alphabet into 50 divisions. Before a records administrator purchases a set of guides, he should get a list of the divisions of the alphabet from the manufacturer to see if they fit the office requirements. The type of correspondence to be filed determines which kinds of guides should be used.

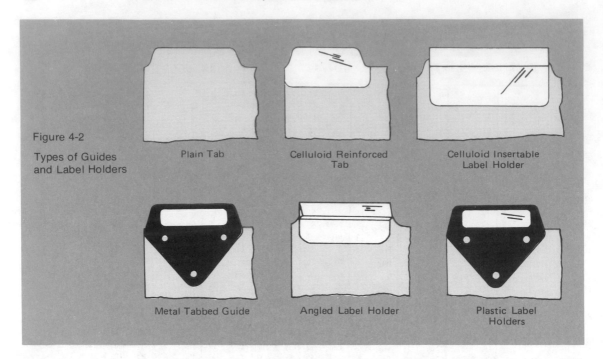

Figure 4-2

Types of Guides
and Label Holders

Plain Tab

Celluloid Reinforced
Tab

Celluloid Insertable
Label Holder

Metal Tabbed Guide

Angled Label Holder

Plastic Label
Holders

Some guides have letters printed on their tabs at the time of manufacture. Other guides have tabs with slotted holders into which can be inserted labels showing whatever sections of the alphabet are needed. Guides are usually very sturdily made since they are expected to last many years. Pressboard and bristol are usually the stock of which they are manufactured. Aluminum and plastic guides also are available. The same set of guides may be used year after year with no change, or they may be added to or changed as the file expands. Because of their thickness and rigidity, guides serve also to keep the contents of a drawer upright. Figure 4-2 illustrates several types of guides.

Guides that have projections with eyelets on the bottom, through which a rod is fastened, are more serviceable than straight-bottom guides. Since eyeleted guides are held in the file drawer by the rod that has been inserted through them from front to back of the drawer, the guides will not be lifted out by mistake when folders are removed. Loose guides have a tendency to "ride up" when the drawer is filled; a careless shutting of the drawer ruins the tabs. Guides with projections for a rod cannot be used in equipment that does not have the rod, unless the projection is cut off, as the projection must fit into a depression in the drawer.

Guides should be grasped by their sides or well down from the top edge, never by the tab. Continual pulling forward or upward on the tab will weaken it and ultimately cause it to break from the body of the guide.

Inadequate use of guides, uneven distribution of guides throughout the files, or a system of guides that is too complicated can be a source of trouble in filing.

Primary guides. A *primary* or *main guide* is used to indicate one principal division of the alphabet. A primary guide always precedes all other materials in a section. In Figure 4-3, page 82, the A-1 and B-2 guides are primary guides. They are in first position. If the volume of correspondence with many individuals or firms is comparatively small, only primary guides need be used to divide the file into alphabetic sections.

Auxiliary guides. An *auxiliary* or *secondary guide,* which falls into the alphabetic range of the preceding primary guide, may have one of several uses:

(1) It may indicate the location of the folder of an individual or a company with which there is a large amount of correspondence. In Figure 4-3 the guide labeled *Atlas Baking Co.* is a special (auxiliary) name guide. Conceivably, a complete drawer may be needed for one correspondent; in this instance, a special (auxiliary) guide for that name may be followed by other auxiliary guides with monthly, weekly, or other designations to subdivide the materials housed in this section of the file.

(2) It may introduce a special section, such as one pertaining to *Applications, Bids, Conferences, Exhibits,* or *Speeches,* that may be found in an alphabetic file. The special subject section is necessary to bring together in one place all the correspondence relating to one subject rather than have it dispersed throughout the file by the names of the different correspondents. In Figure 4-3 the *Applications* guide is a special section guide (placed in alphabetic order in the *A* section) behind which is filed in properly captioned folders all correspondence concerning applications for employment as clerk, copywriter, and stenographer.

(3) It may introduce a section reserved for names that have the same first indexing unit. In Figure 4-3 the *Adams, Ayers,* and *Brown* auxiliary guides lead the eye to the sections in which are filed the numerous folders bearing names with *Adams, Ayers,* or *Brown* as

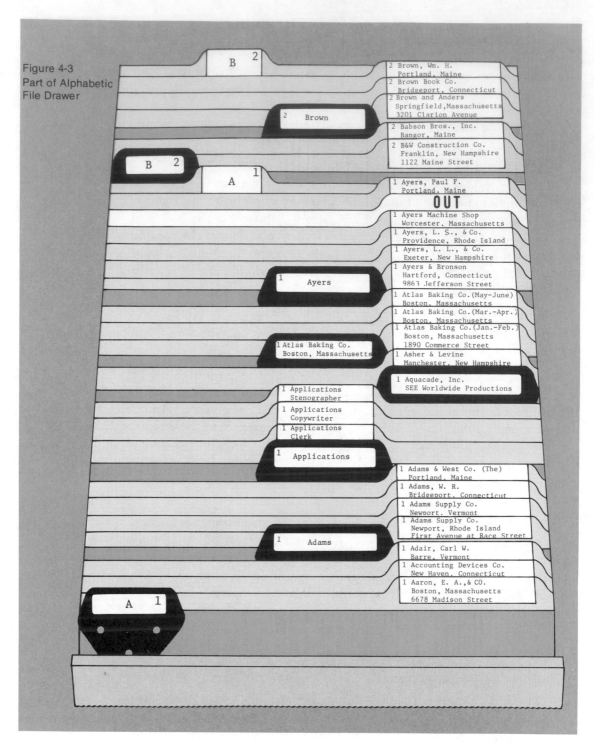

Figure 4-3
Part of Alphabetic
File Drawer

Figure 4-3.
Part of Alphabetic File Drawer

the first indexing unit. Again, there may be correspondence with a great many firms whose names begin with the word "General." An auxiliary guide for names beginning with "General" could be followed by additional auxiliary guides from *A* to *Z*, subdividing the "General" names according to their second units (General *Appliance,* General *Aquamarine,* and General *Asbestos* being behind the "General-A" auxiliary guide; General *Electronics,* General *Elevators,* and General *Engravers* being behind the "General-E" auxiliary guide; and so on).

OUT guides. An *OUT guide* is a piece of heavy paper stock—similar to cardboard—with "OUT" printed on its tab at a position and in a color so that it can be readily seen in the file. An OUT guide is used to replace a folder that has been removed from the files; the OUT guide remains in the files until the borrowed folder is returned and is replaced in the files.

TYPES OF FOLDERS

An ordinary *folder* is a piece of heavy paper (usually manila or kraft although pressboard may be used for heavy, bulky materials) folded in half so that the back is higher than the front. A folder may be reinforced across the top of the back edge, as that is the place receiving the greatest wear. Like guides, folders are available with a straight edge or with tabs of various widths (cuts) and in various positions. Plastic folders in attractive colors are also available.

Miscellaneous folders. For every primary guide there is a corresponding folder, called a *miscellaneous folder,* bearing the same caption as that on the guide. In Figure 4-3 the A-1 folder is a miscellaneous folder; it closes the "A" section of the file because it is the last item in that section. In a miscellaneous folder are filed the papers pertaining to all correspondents whose correspondence is limited in volume and whose names fall in the section of the alphabet indicated by the primary guide preceding the folder. Within the miscellaneous folder, papers are arranged first alphabetically by the correspondents' names and then by date in each group with the most recent date on top (Figure 4-4, page 84).

Individual folders. When papers pertaining to one correspondent accumulate to a predetermined number in the miscellaneous folder, they are removed from the miscellaneous folder and are placed in

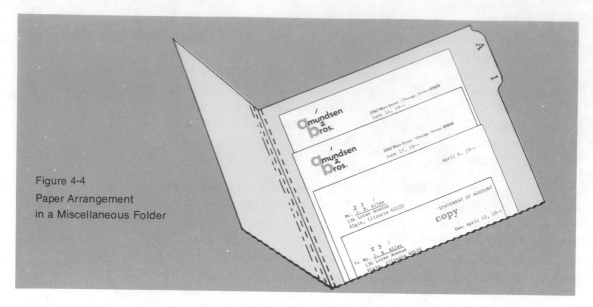

Figure 4-4
Paper Arrangement
in a Miscellaneous Folder

a new folder, called an *individual folder*, prepared especially for and bearing the name of that correspondent. Office policy determines whether the accumulation shall be five pieces, eight pieces, or some other number. In special cases, when correspondence is received from a customer who is destined to be an important client, an individual folder may be prepared when the first piece of correspondence is received from him. This is a situation that arises with more or less frequency in certain businesses. Within an individual folder, papers are arranged chronologically, with the most recently dated piece on top. When correspondence with one firm is very heavy and so important that all of it must be kept in the active files, the correspondence may be placed in several folders with the months indicated on the folder tabs so that reference to the correspondence will be facilitated. The three folders for the Atlas Baking Co. in Figure 4-3 are examples of this kind of individual folder.

In most filing systems, individual folders are placed in alphabetic order between the primary guide and the miscellaneous folder, which is the last item in the alphabetic section. In Figure 4-3 individual folders occupy fourth and fifth positions at the right side of the drawer.

Special folders. *Special folders* follow special (auxiliary) guides in an alphabetic arrangement. In Figure 4-3 the special folders contain correspondence pertaining to subdivisions of a special subject —Applications—and within which all papers on those subjects are arranged first by names of correspondents and then by date in each group of papers.

Folders of special construction. *Suspension folders* are folders that hang on metal rods at the sides of a drawer. Such folders have a "hem" at the top of the front and the back sides; and through each hem goes a rod with small end hooks that fit on the metal rods of the drawer. Suspension folders will not sag; and they can be creased at their bottom edges for expansion purposes. The Oblique hanging folder, a type of suspension folder, is described and illustrated in Chapter 10.

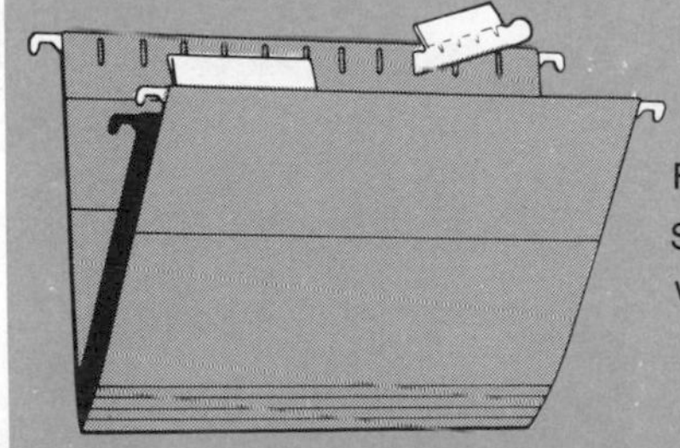

Heavy *binder folders* may have fasteners with which to bind papers within them. Since fasteners slow the filing operation because of the necessity of punching holes in the paper to be filed, opening the fastener, inserting the paper neatly, and closing the fastener, such folders are not often used in the usual business office. Legal offices frequently use folders with fasteners because of the necessity of keeping bound together the papers relating to one case for court purposes.

Figure 4-5
Suspension Folder
with Insertable Tab

Oxford Pendaflex Corporation

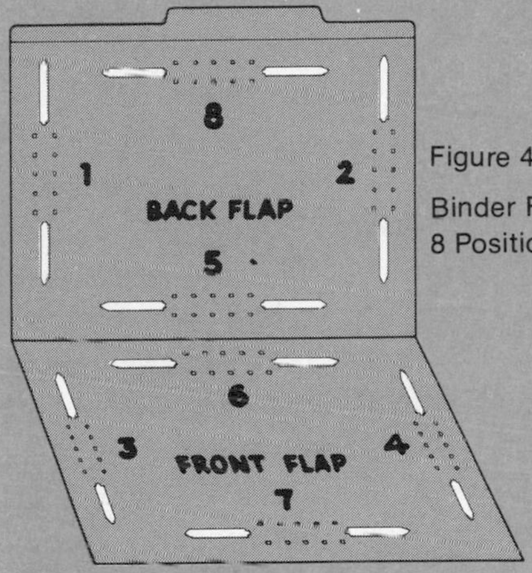

Figure 4-6
Binder Folder Showing
8 Positions for Fastener

Sperry Remington, Office Systems and
Machines, Sperry Rand Corporation

Binder folders (also referred to as *clasp fastener folders, tang fastener folders,* or *compressor folders*) may be purchased with the fastener in *one* of several positions (Figure 4-6).

When unusual protection from loss is desired, the fastening of papers securely becomes an important feature. On construction jobs, as an example, where papers may be exposed to the elements and subjected to loss by wind, the folder with fasteners is often used for security.

Overloading of folders. The number of pieces of correspondence that will fit in one folder obviously depends on the thickness of the papers. Papers should never protrude from the folder edges, and they should always be inserted with their tops to the left. Near the bottom edge of most folders are one or more score marks, which should be used as the contents of the folders expand. If folders are refolded at these marks (Figure 4-7), the danger of their bending and sliding under other folders is reduced, a neater-looking file results, and papers do not curl readily. Pressboard folders are often made with cloth-expanding hinges at the bottom edge.

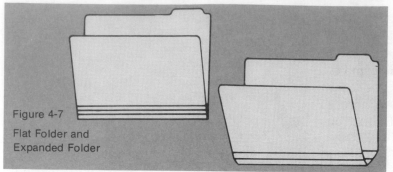

Figure 4-7

Flat Folder and
Expanded Folder

When papers start to "ride up" in any folder, the folder is overloaded. A folder lasts longer and is easier to use if it is not stuffed beyond its capacity. If too many papers are contained in the individual folder of a correspondent, it is time to open a second folder for him. The two folders may then be labeled to show that the papers are chronologically arranged in them; or the papers may be redistributed between the two folders by subjects.

If overloading occurs in a miscellaneous folder, the papers should be reviewed to determine the advisability of opening individual folders for some of the correspondents because of the accumulation of papers to, from, or about them. It might be that a finer alphabetic breakdown in primary guides would handle the problem by narrowing the alphabetic range of the materials filed in all the miscellaneous folders. For example, if the divisions of the alphabet used were *A-B-C-D,* etc., it might be wise to use *A-An-B-Be-Bi,* and so on. Another possible way to alleviate congestion in the miscellaneous folders is the setting up of special subject guides and corresponding folders to take care of papers that have accumulated in miscellaneous folders but could better be housed under subjects rather than correspondents' names. At times, older papers in any folder may be transferred to inactive files to relieve overloading. Further explanation of transfer is explained in Chapter 12.

Care of folders. Folders are kept upright by the proper use of guides and *follower blocks* at the back of the drawer. Follower blocks (or compressors) slide back and forth to allow for contraction or expansion of the contents within the drawer. A variation of this procedure is shown in Figure 4-8, wherein slim steel dividers are placed permanently throughout the file drawer to hold the contents upright.

Figure 4-8
Follower Blocks
and Uprights

Amberg File and Index Co.

Two sources of filing difficulty relate directly to folders: (1) folders that are made so cheaply that their tabs break easily and (2) overloading of folders. A records manager can study the needs of the office and prepare a workable system of alphabetic filing by purchasing blank guides and folders and making his own system. However, many businesses have found it more economical in the long run to ask for help from records management experts employed by filing equipment manufacturers. These experts study the needs of the office, consult with the records manager there, and recommend a satisfactory commercial system. With many kinds of systems available, designed for a wide range of business requirements, the records manager must be able to evaluate the special features of all and determine wisely which one will be a help and not a hindrance in his situation.

TABS

A *tab* is a projection on the top edge of a guide or a folder. It can be of the same material as that of the guide or folder of which it is a part; it can have a transparent covering to protect the printing and give additional strength; it can be of metal or of plastic with a "window" into which information can be inserted; or it can be of the insertion type to fit into slots on the tops of hanging folders. (See page 80.) If file expansion is anticipated, window tabs are preferable because they allow for change with a minimum of disruption. They are more costly at the outset, but they do not become obsolete or unusable unless they deteriorate with age or mishandling.

Tabs are available slanted (angled) or straight, printed or blank. Tabs should be constructed so that there are no rough edges to catch hands or papers in any way. Since a tab receives heavy wear, thought should be given to its choice. The writing space should be large enough for whatever caption is needed in the office. When all captions are short, smaller tabs should be used.

Varying heights and widths of tabs are available. The widths, referred to as *cuts* (illustrated on page 17), vary from straight-cut to one-twelfth-cut. Because cuts are in various *positions* across the top edge of folders and guides and are referred to by number from left to right, the cut and the position of tabs should be accurately described when supplies are ordered.

If folders are placed with their tabs in *staggered* positions, that is, alternating from left to right, additions to the file often throw the arrangement out of order. Advocates of the staggered arrangement say, however, that the eye can read the tabs on two folders side by side more quickly than it can read tabs one behind the other. (See the staggered folder arrangement on page 28, Figure 2-12, and on page 30, Figure 2-14.) Advocates of the *one-line* or *straight-line* arrangement (tabs one behind the other) argue that the eye travels faster down one line than in the zigzag manner necessitated by staggered arrangement. (See page 26, Figure 2-10, and page 31, Figure 2-16.)

Most individuals perform operations from left to right; therefore, the use of guide tabs positioned at the left and folder tabs positioned at the right speeds operations and should be used when possible. As the left hand finds the guide, the right hand locates the folder. Guides should be arranged so that their tabs will not obscure the tabs of the folders behind them.

CAPTIONS AND LABELS

The terms *caption* and *label* are often used interchangeably. These terms refer to the identification on the tab of a guide or of a folder or the identifying information on the front of a file container (drawer, box, shelf, and the like).

Guide labels. Captions on primary guides in an alphabetic system consist of letters of the alphabet or a combination of letters and numbers. The caption on a miscellaneous folder always agrees with the caption on the primary guide it follows. If the primary guides have numbers as well as letters on their captions, the auxiliary guides also should have numbers to correspond with the numbers on the primary guides they follow. The combination of letters and numbers, and sometimes the color of the label on which the caption is printed, help to avoid filing mistakes. For example, the files operator should almost unconsciously note the appearance of a green-tabbed folder within an otherwise tan section; he should note, too, a folder with the number "10" in a section with folders numbered "40."

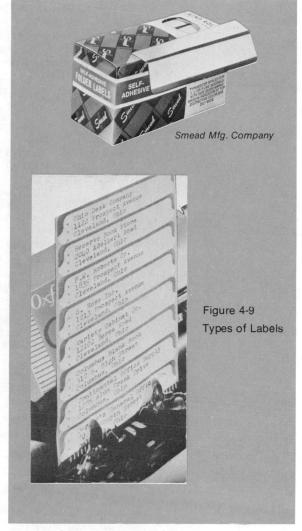

Smead Mfg. Company

Folder labels. Folders are often labeled with gummed strips. Gummed labels in various styles may be purchased either completely blank or with various markings printed on them. Rolls of labels in boxes, continuous folded strips, separate strips of eight or more labels together, or protected adhesive labels are only four of the various ways in which labels are packaged (Figure 4-9). Pastel colors are preferable so that the typing can be easily read. If a number code is used on a primary guide tab, that same number should appear on the label of every folder in the section behind that guide.

Figure 4-9

Types of Labels

A folder may be labeled by inserting the folder into the typewriter and typing directly on its tab; this is not the usual practice, however.

Typing format on the label is a matter of office preference combined with the style required by the type of label used. Handwritten labels are a source of trouble and should be avoided. Uniformity is the key word. Several practices are listed below:

1. All typing should begin the same distance from the left edge of the label (usually 2 or 3 typewriter spaces) and the same distance from the top of the label (usually 1 line space).
2. If the label is a double one with a score mark, the caption must be typed on the lower space. The score mark becomes the top edge of

the label after the upper space is folded down and attached to the back of the folder.

3. The captions may appear either in indexing order or in straight order. Compare the two lists of identical names that follow and note how much easier it is to check the alphabetic arrangement of the first list:

Indexing Order	*Straight Order*
Nichols, H. A.	H. A. Nichols
Nicholson Steel Company	Nicholson Steel Company
Nickerson, Charles P.	Charles P. Nickerson
Nisbett, A. R., Co. (The)	The A. R. Nisbett Co.
Noles, Jane L. (Miss)	Miss Jane L. Noles
Nyberg, John, & Son	John Nyberg & Son

4. The caption may consist of the name only; of the name on the first line and the city and the state on the second line; or the name on the first line, the city and the state on the second line, and the street address on the third line. The office manager should determine the style to be used in his company.

5. Punctuation may be used or omitted. The same is true of the use of the parentheses. Whichever way is adopted must be followed consistently.

6. The name may be typed with all capital letters, with capitalization of only the first letter of each important word, or with all capitals for the first unit and capitals and lower case for the other units.

7. Block style is preferred to conserve space. If a title is too long for the width of the label, however, the carry-over of the title is indented on the second line.

8. Labels should be affixed to the tabs of all folders at the same place. Uniform placement can be accomplished as follows: When a new box of folders is opened, remove all the folders and keep them tightly together standing upright on a flat surface. A ruler or stiff card is placed over the tab edges at the spot where all the labels are to be attached. A mark is made with a pencil across the top edge of all tabs; a very small pencil mark will show on each of the tabs at the same place and will serve as a guide for attaching the labels.

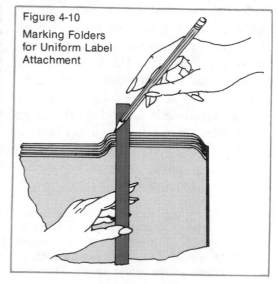

Figure 4-10

Marking Folders for Uniform Label Attachment

In preparing new folders, the files operator must use care to make sure the labels agree in placement and typing format with those on other folders. New folders may be necessitated because:

1. a new group of names is to be added to the file;

2. older folders have become full, and additional ones must be added to take care of the overload;

3. enough papers have accumulated for certain correspondents so that the papers can be removed from the miscellaneous folders and put into individual folders;

4. folders have worn out and must be replaced;

5. the regular time of the year has arrived for replacing folders and transferring older folders to inactive files.

Examples of various methods of typing labels are given below:

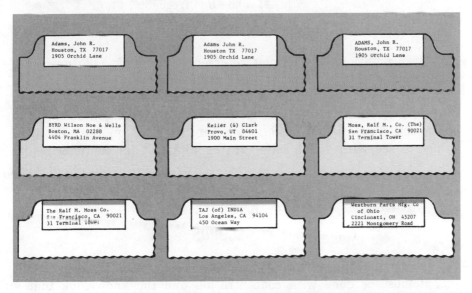

Satisfactory labels are made of good quality paper (1) that will not break when folded over the top of a tab; (2) that permits erasing easily and invisibly; (3) that has perforations that tear easily but are of sufficient strength to hold together for typing purposes; and (4) that is made of a color sufficiently muted that typing on it can be easily read. Color strips or bands are sometimes used on white or buff labels in lieu of solidly colored labels because typing is more legible on the buff or white backgrounds than on other colored surfaces.

File cabinet labels. Labels on file cabinets or containers should be as brief and clear as possible. The notations indicating the alphabetic range of the contents of the container may be one of three types:

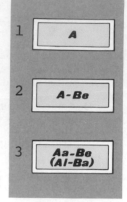

1. *Open notation,* showing only the beginning letter of the alphabetic section within the container.
2. *Closed notation,* showing both the beginning and the end of the alphabetic section within the container.
3. *Multiple-closed notation,* showing not only the alphabetic range of the material in the container but also the frequent combinations within that range (example, the range *Aa* to *Be,* with *Al* and *Ba* frequent combinations in the *Aa* to *Be* range).

Open notations (sometimes referred to as *single notations*) are easily read, and they allow for quick expansion by subdivision. Closed notations (sometimes referred to as *double notations*) indicate at once to the reader the entire alphabetic span of the contents of the container. There is no need to look at the label on the next container to see with which letter in the alphabet its contents begin.

SECTION 2. FILING PROCEDURES FOR ALPHABETIZED RECORDS

The actual filing (storing) operation is an exacting responsibility; it must be done with concentration and the knowledge that a mistake may be costly. In any enterprise, key personnel should see that there is centralized control of all files even if centralized physical placement is not possible.

Centralization of physical storage will probably be advantageous if the following can be accomplished:

1. less duplication of effort
2. greater efficiency in finding
3. saving of office space
4. improved cooperation from involved personnel

Decentralized location with *centralized control* (everyone files in his own department according to the same rules and procedures) is very workable. And, if the following conditions exist, decentralization of records storage is probably warranted:

1. Highly technical records are maintained
2. Ready accessibility is of prime importance
3. Maintenance of confidentiality is required

Whether records are filed in individual offices (decentralized) or are sent to a common filing site (centralized), the filing procedures remain the same—papers must be (1) inspected, (2) indexed, (3) coded, (4) cross-referenced if necessary, (5) sorted, and (6) filed. Therefore, the filing operator must be dexterous, have a good memory, be a quick and adept reader, and enjoy detail work.

INSPECTION

Correspondence must not be filed until its contents have been noted by someone with authority; filing must not take place before whatever needs to be done with the correspondence has been done. Anyone who stores papers should be absolutely certain that the matters referred to in the papers have been (1) taken care of or (2) noted on a reminder calendar in some way so that the papers will be brought to the attention of the proper person at a future date. A cardinal rule of filing is: *Be sure the material to be filed has been released for filing (okayed by a person responsible!).* Filing papers before their contents have been noted and before appropriate action has been taken can sometimes cause irreparable damage to a business.

The assumption may be made that the carbon copy of an outgoing letter or other communication is ready to be filed when it is received by the filing department. But in most offices every original (or incoming) paper that is to be filed must bear a *release mark* showing that the paper is ready to be filed and, therefore, giving permission to the files operator to file it (see "R.K." on Figure 4-12, page 97). This mark, which is usually put on the paper by the secretary who has typed the reply or otherwise handled the matter, may be in the form of initials, a code or a check mark, a punched symbol, a stamp, a lightly drawn pencil line through the contents, or some other agreed-upon designation. If the mark is missing, the files operator knows he must ask about its omission. The secretary or other responsible person may have forgotten to place the release mark on the paper, or the paper may have gotten into the filing basket by mistake. A time stamp (Figure 4-11) is not a release mark. The one who opens the mail often stamps the correspondence with a

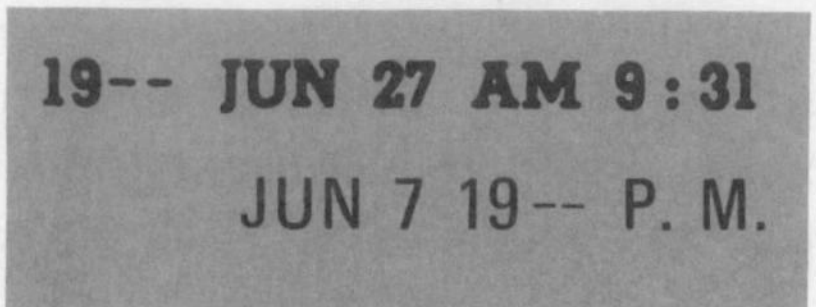

19-- JUN 27 AM 9:31

JUN 7 19-- P. M.

Figure 4-11 Time Stamps

time stamp showing date and time received, for reference purposes only.

Once a paper is put into the file, it is often left there for some time; if the contents of the paper are urgent and are not attended to before the paper is filed, a great deal of time and money could be lost as a result. This checking for "readiness to be filed" is known as *inspection*.

INDEXING

Before the files operator stores any item in a file container (usually a drawer or a shelf or a box), he should read or scan the item to determine where the item should be filed. The *mental process* required to determine this place is called *indexing*, some authorities may call this process *classifying*. In alphabetic filing, indexing means determining the name that is to be used as the basis for filing; in subject filing, it means ascertaining the subject or subjects referred to by the material and under which the material will be filed; in geographic filing, it means determining the location under which the material is to be filed; in numeric filing, it means finding the name and number to be used as the basis of filing; in chronologic filing, it involves a determination of the correct date of the material being scanned.

The indexing step is more difficult when correspondence is being filed than it is when cards are being put in order. On a card, the name, number, or subject is instantly recognizable; on correspondence, the name, subject, or location may appear in various places on the page. In order to select the correct indexing element (sometimes referred to as the *key title*), the files operator must keep in mind the following rules:

1. The name most likely to be used in calling for the paper is usually most important and is therefore the name under which the paper should be filed.
2. On original correspondence, the most likely name for filing purposes is usually the one in the letterhead.

3. Original correspondence that is on plain paper (paper without a letterhead) is most likely to be called for by the name in the signature line; this name is used as the basis for filing.

4. If a letterhead has no bearing on the content of the letter, the location of the writer, or the business connection of the writer, the letterhead name is disregarded for filing purposes. An example of this is a letter written on hotel stationery by a businessman who is out of town on a business trip.

5. When both the company name and the name of the writer seem to be of equal importance, the company name is used.

6. On the carbon copy of an outgoing letter, the most important name is usually that contained in the inside address.

7. When both the company name and the name of an individual are contained in the inside address of the carbon copy of an outgoing letter, the company name is used in filing unless the letter is personal in nature.

8. On the carbon copy of a letter that is personal in nature, the name of the writer may be most important and should be used as the basis for filing.

9. If a special subject section is used within an alphabetic file (such as an Applications section), the subject is given precedence over both company and individual names appearing in correspondence. Often, the files operator must write the name of the subject on the correspondence at the top right.

10. If a subject or a name that is given in the body of the letter is obviously the most important, it should be used for filing purposes.

11. In case of real doubt as to the most important name, the files supervisor should be consulted or the department from which the letter came should be questioned. If a filing manual is in use in the office, it should also be consulted.

12. Sometimes two names seem equal in importance. One is selected as the name under which the paper is to be filed, and the other name is cross-referenced at the time the paper is coded.

CODING

Coding is a physical act; it is the actual marking of the record to indicate its placement in the file. When a record has been released for filing, it may already have been marked or coded by the name under which it is to be filed. If this has been done, the files operator's job is simply that of scanning and indexing the contents of the paper to confirm that the coding has been done correctly. This quick scanning may also indicate a necessary cross-reference (further explained in the next section).

Often the one who files the paper is responsible for coding it. In coding, the name under which the paper is to be filed may be underlined; the name may be circled or checked or starred; an arrow may be directed to the name; a combination of underlining and numbering the indexing units may be used; and so on. Figure 4-12, page 97, shows a straight underline and numbering as the method of coding.

The importance of the coding step must not be minimized. Coding saves time when refiling is necessary. If a paper that does not show coding is removed from the file and is brought back at a later date to be refiled, the files operator must index the paper a second time. If the coding had been marked on the paper originally, the files operator would not have to index and code that paper again. In some offices a colored pencil is used for coding to make the code stand out; in other offices coding is done as unobtrusively as possible, with a pencil, to keep distracting marks at a minimum. The choice is an individual one.

Coding must be done carefully. In looking for the name to be marked, the reader may have to choose from many possible places: the letterhead, the inside address, the subject line, a name in the body of the message, the signature line. (See the list on pages 94 and 95 under Indexing.) Coding that is done too quickly may result in choosing the wrong name and, therefore, filing the paper in the wrong place. Extreme care must be taken to code the correct name.

CROSS-REFERENCING

The files operator may decide, while indexing a paper, that it is very likely that the paper may be called for by a name other than the one that has been selected as the most important for coding and filing. As in a card file, cross-referencing of individual, business, and other names is necessary because reference to a name can be made in more than one way, so, too, in a correspondence filing system a cross-reference is sometimes necessary.

After the correspondence is coded in the usual way, a mark is made on the piece to indicate that a cross-reference is to be made. This mark may consist of a wavy line under the name to be cross-referenced, an "X" beside it, or some other identifying code different from the marking used for the coding of the piece. Figure 4-12 shows a letter coded for filing by the use of a straight line and numbered units and distinctively marked with a wavy line, an "X" in the margin, and numbered units for cross-referencing.

Figure 4-12
Letter Properly
Released and Coded

weekly investments magazine
financial facts for all

1106 Michigan Boulevard   Chicago, IL 60610

June 20, 19--

JUN 22 19-- P.M.

Mr. Robert Peppard
11961 Terminal Tower
Public Square
Cleveland, Ohio   44102

Dear Mr. Peppard

In order to improve our magazine and serve our subscribers to an even greater extent, we have hired the Hyde Consulting Services firm to conduct a survey of the investment objectives of the subscribers to our magazine.

In the near future Hyde Consulting Services will send to each of our subscribers a questionnaire that will provide spaces for the listing of total yearly income, approximate yearly expenses, amount available for savings and investment, financial objectives, and other pertinent information. The questionnaire need not be signed and therefore you can give accurate information without sacrificing the confidential nature of the survey. Hyde Consulting Services will analyze the data received from all those who return the questionnaire and will then make recommendations for types of special articles and departments that will be of the greatest interest and benefit to our readers.

We ask that you fill out the questionnaire completely as well as accurately and return it to the Hyde firm shortly after you receive it.

We shall greatly appreciate your cooperation in this matter.

Sincerely yours

David Simpson
David Simpson, Editor

li

CROSS REFERENCE RECORD

FIRM NAME or SUBJECT Hyde Consulting Services   FILE NO.

DATE 6/20/-   REMARKS Survey conducted for
Weekly Investments Magazine

SEE Weekly Investments Magazine   FILE NO.
Chicago, Illinois
1106 Michigan Blvd.

DATE 6/22/-
L. S. Crandall   SIGNED

FILE CROSS REFERENCE RECORD UNDER NAME OR SUBJECT LISTED AT TOP OF THIS SHEET, AND IN PROPER DATE ORDER.
THE PAPERS REFERRED TO SHOULD BE FILED UNDER NAME OR SUBJECT LISTED UNDER "SEE".

FORM NO. 099CR

Figure 4-13
Cross-Reference
for Letter

Figure 4-14
Carbon Copy of
Outgoing Letter

CROSS REFERENCE RECORD

FIRM NAME or SUBJECT Crane Music House   FILE NO.

DATE 5/19/--   REMARKS Referral of customer for purchase
of hi-fi speaker cabinet. Recommend
Imperial model.

FILE NO.

SEE Jackson, M. L.
Painesville, Ohio
2215 Jefferson Street

DATE 5/19/--   SIGNED R. D. Sellers

FILE CROSS REFERENCE RECORD UNDER NAME OR SUBJECT LISTED AT TOP OF THIS SHEET, AND IN PROPER DATE ORDER.
THE PAPERS REFERRED TO SHOULD BE FILED UNDER NAME OR SUBJECT LISTED UNDER "SEE"

FORM NO. 099CR

Figure 4-15
Cross-Reference for
Carbon Copy of Letter

May 19, 19--

Mr. M. L. Jackson
2215 Jefferson Street
Painesville, Ohio 44077

Dear Mr. Jackson

The hi-fi speaker cabinet, about which you inquired in your
May 16 letter, is certainly available in your city.

For the convenience of our customers living outside the Cleveland area, we supply their needs through home-furnishings
dealers in their home cities. In Painesville the dealer who
takes care of our customers is the Crane Music House. They
have a copy of our latest catalog in which we illustrate our
complete line of hi-fi speaker cabinets. We have written them
to call on you so that you can look over the catalog to determine the model you prefer. You can then place your order with
them.

From the information in your inquiry, we believe that you would
especially like the new, graceful lines of the Imperial model,
illustrated in color on pages 12 and 13 of the catalog.

We shall be pleased to fill your order through the Crane Music
House.

Sincerely yours

Claudine Prentiss

Claudine Prentiss
Sales Manager

my

Cross-referencing must be done with discretion; each cross-reference requires valuable operator time, creates at least one additional sheet that must be filed, and requires additional space for filing in the equipment.

A *separate cross-reference sheet* may be prepared for the alternative name or an *extra copy* of the original piece of correspondence (a photocopy or other facsimile) may be made for cross-reference purposes. Figures 4-15 and 4-16 show two examples of cross-references. The cross-reference sheet shown in Fig-

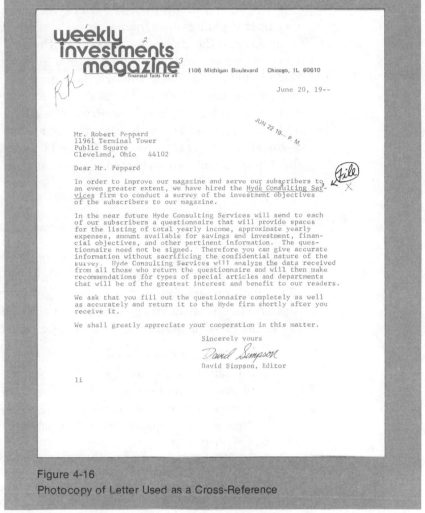

Figure 4-16
Photocopy of Letter Used as a Cross-Reference

ure 4-15 is a type that may be purchased in quantity and filled in with the required information as needed. The cross-reference in Figure 4-16 is an extra copy of a letter that was prepared for the purpose and properly marked as a cross-reference. The name at the top of the separate cross-reference sheet is coded for filing in exactly the same way as is any piece of correspondence—the name is straight underlined and the units numbered.

At times a *permanent cross-reference* in the file takes the place of an individual folder. The permanent cross-reference is a guide with a tab in the same position as the tabs on the individual folders. The caption on the tab of the permanent cross-reference consists of the name under which the cross-reference is filed, the word "SEE," and the name under which the correspondence may be found. When a company changes its name, for instance, the folder is removed from the file, the name is changed on the folder, and the correspondence is refiled under the new name. A permanent cross-reference guide is prepared under the original name and is placed in the position of the old folder in the file. For example, *Maynard & Phelps* changes its name to *Bayshore Products, Inc.* The *Maynard & Phelps* folder is removed from the file, the name on the folder is changed to *Bayshore Products, Inc.*, the folder is refiled under the new name, and a permanent cross-reference guide is made as follows:

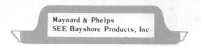

In Figure 4-3 in this chapter, a permanent cross-reference guide for Aquacade, Inc., appears in proper alphabetic sequence at the right of the file drawer.

Cross-references are prepared for the following types of names (as is the case in preparing cross-references for a card file):

1. Unusual and foreign names
2. Names of married women
3. Business names composed of two or more surnames
4. Names of companies doing business under more than one name
5. Names of companies that are affiliates or branches of other companies
6. Unusual company names that do not clearly indicate whether they are composed of one individual's complete name, two or more surnames, or an individual's name combined with a coined name
7. Company names that are commonly referred to by initials or abbreviations
8. Company names that have been changed
9. Names of newspapers
10. Names of magazines
11. Guardians, Trustees, Receivers
12. Foreign-language names of business and governmental agencies
13. Stores that may be affiliated with chains or other identifying-group names

The method of cross-referencing each of these names is explained in detail in Chapter 3, pages 45, 46, 57, 58, 59, 71, 72, and 73.

In most instances, a *sorting* step precedes filing. Especially if filing must be delayed, it is very important that sorting be done as soon as possible after coding and cross-referencing. Papers can be found with less delay if they have been roughly sorted instead of being in a stack on someone's desk or in a "to-be-filed" basket.

Sometimes coding and sorting are done in sequence. As the coding is finished, the paper is immediately put into a pile of like pieces —all of the A-B-C's together, all of the D-E-F's together, and so on. Coordination of inspection, indexing, coding, and sorting means handling each piece of paper only once. Delaying sorting until all pieces have been coded means handling each piece twice and therefore consuming more time and energy.

If sorting is delayed until all coding is finished, the material to be stored may then be grouped into a rough arrangement: all the A's together in no special order; all the B's together at random; all the C's together in mixed-up order; and so forth. This sorting may be done on top of the desk, with the papers placed in separate piles. It might be facilitated with desk-top sorters that have holders or pockets for various sections of the alphabet (Figure 4-17).

If many pieces are to be filed, finer sorting may be advantageous. Two of the more elaborate sorters available are shown in Figure 4-18.

First, papers are roughly sorted according to the alphabetic sections; then they are removed section by section, alphabetized properly within

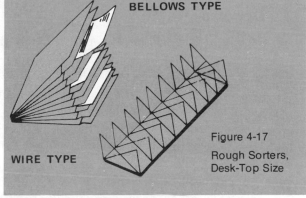

BELLOWS TYPE

WIRE TYPE

Figure 4-17
Rough Sorters,
Desk-Top Size

each section, and finally replaced in order in the sorter for temporary storage. After the papers in all sections have been alphabetized and the files operator is ready to file the papers, he removes them in sequence from all divisions of the sorter. Because of the sorting, time at the files is saved; there is no running from one section to another—first to the *B* section, then to the *I* section, back to the *D* section, then to the *S* section, and so on. Waste motion is reduced to a minimum because all papers are in strict alphabetic order. The greater the volume of papers to be stored, the finer the sorting should be to make the work easier, quicker, and less tiring.

Materials that are to be kept for extremely short periods of time may kept in a sorter until they are destroyed.

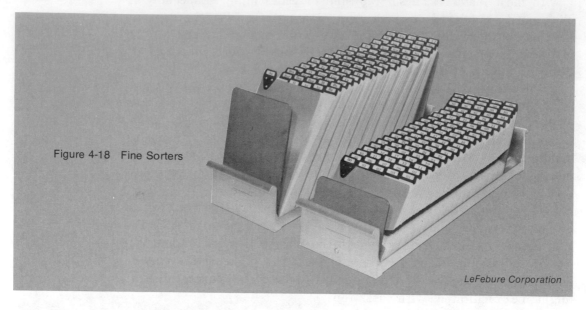

Figure 4-18   Fine Sorters

LeFebure Corporation

FILING (STORING)

Filing is a physical job of great importance. A misfiled piece is often a lost piece; and a lost piece means loss of time, money, and peace of mind while the files operator is looking for the paper.

The time at which papers are actually put into the storage containers depends upon the work load during the day. In some offices, filing is the job performed first in the morning; in others, all filing is done in the early afternoon; in others, filing is the last job performed each day; in still others, filing is taken care of whenever there is anything to be filed and when there is a lull in other work. In a centralized filing department, there is no lull in filing. It takes place all day every day—filing, finding, tracing, and refiling.

Paper clips and pins should be removed from materials to be filed. If papers should be kept together, it is satisfactory to staple them together in the upper right corner so that other papers kept in the folder will not be inserted between them by mistake. Torn papers should be mended before they are filed.

A quick glance at the label on the container (drawer, shelf, box) will show in which place the files operator should begin filing. Upon opening a drawer, the files operator scans the guides until the proper alphabetic section is reached. The section is checked visually to see if there is an individual or a special folder already prepared in which the piece of correspondence should be filed. If there is none, the miscellaneous folder is located. Usually the left hand pulls the guides forward, while the right hand searches quickly for the correct folder.

Before a paper is put into the folder, the folder should be raised slightly. Many folders are reinforced at the top with a double or triple thickness of material that helps to increase the life of the folders, as they are grasped repeatedly by their top edge. The files operator should avoid pulling by the tab, however, as continual pulling will weaken it.

If the folder is raised, its front and back will be clearly seen; and the paper to be inserted will therefore be put *into* the folder and not in front of or behind it. Much inaccurate filing results from the files operator's failure to pull up the folder when intending to put a piece of correspondence into it. A quick glance at the label and the top piece in the folder will further verify the fact that the piece to be filed is correctly placed, as all will bear the same coded name. This is another precaution against misfiling.

Each paper goes into the folder with its top to the left. When the folder is removed from the file and placed on a desk to be used, it is opened like a book with the open edge at the right; and all the papers therein are in proper reading position (Figure 4-19). Left-handed people may find it somewhat awkward to file in this manner and will want to

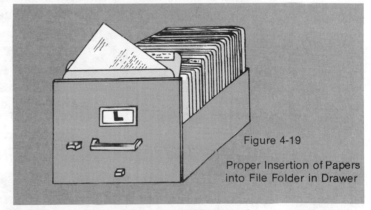

Figure 4-19

Proper Insertion of Papers into File Folder in Drawer

put papers top right into folders; this practice is not correct and must be avoided. All papers in a folder should be even; jogging of the folder may be necessary to even up the papers.

The most recent paper placed in an individual folder is always placed in the front and therefore is on top when the folder is opened. The oldest piece of correspondence is the one at the back of the folder. Pieces that are removed from the folder and later refiled must be placed in their correct chronological sequence, not on top of the contents of the folder.

Since a miscellaneous folder contains papers pertaining to a number of correspondents, papers in a miscellaneous folder are filed first alphabetically by correspondents' names and second by date, with the most recently dated piece on top of each group.

Papers filed in a subject folder (such as an Applications folder) are filed first alphabetically by correspondents' names and second by date, in a manner similar to that used with a miscellaneous folder.

Two file drawers in one cabinet should not be opened at the same time because a person could be injured by a filing cabinet that falls forward when it becomes overbalanced by having two or three loaded drawers opened at the same time.

Many offices have banks of files, perhaps four or five drawers in height, and five or more of these cabinets side by side. The top-most drawer and the very bottom one are the hardest for most people to reach. Therefore, the active, current, and most frequently used folders are often placed in the drawers in the middle section. Inactive and seldom-used files are placed in the top and bottom drawers. (See Figure 4-20.) If the file setup is a large one and frequent reference is made daily to the contents, this arrangement can save many an aching muscle and many a fatigued back.

Figure 4-20
Laborsaving
Arrangement
of
File Drawers

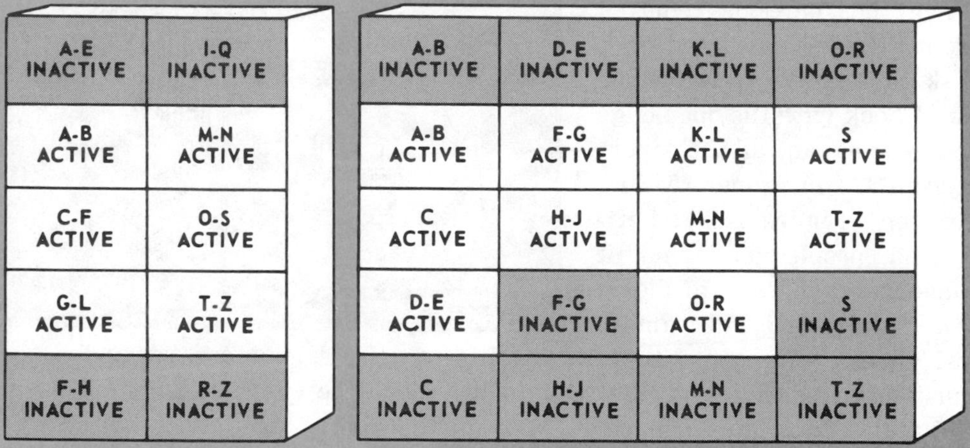

A-E INACTIVE	I-Q INACTIVE
A-B ACTIVE	M-N ACTIVE
C-F ACTIVE	O-S ACTIVE
G-L ACTIVE	T-Z ACTIVE
F-H INACTIVE	R-Z INACTIVE

A-B INACTIVE	D-E INACTIVE	K-L INACTIVE	O-R INACTIVE
A-B ACTIVE	F-G ACTIVE	K-L ACTIVE	S ACTIVE
C ACTIVE	H-J ACTIVE	M-N ACTIVE	T-Z ACTIVE
D-E ACTIVE	F-G INACTIVE	O-R ACTIVE	S INACTIVE
C INACTIVE	H-J INACTIVE	M-N INACTIVE	T-Z INACTIVE

Sperry Remington, Office Systems and Machines, Sperry Rand Corporation

The files operator who (1) recognizes the value of the release mark, (2) knows and applies the rules for alphabetic indexing well, (3) codes papers properly, (4) prepares cross-references skillfully,

(5) invariably sorts papers preparatory to filing, and (5) knows about and uses advantageously the basic equipment for filing, is well on the way to success in alphabetic arrangement. The real test of competency, however, comes in being able to *find* papers once they have been filed.

For Review and Discussion

1. In order to file properly, what must a files operator know?

2. Although a files operator may know the rules for indexing very well, he or she may not be able to do an acceptable job of filing papers alphabetically. Why?

3. If a files operator tells you that he uses "the dictionary method," is this information sufficient for you to be able to file in that office? Why or why not?

4. If correspondence is heavy in volume and if 50 file drawers are needed to contain it, why would a 30-division set of alphabetic guides be inadequate?

5. What is the difference between an individual folder and a miscellaneous folder? How are they similar?

6. What is a *score* on a file folder? What is its use?

7. Of what value would a set of guide and folder tabs printed by the manufacturer be? When would blank ones be of greater use?

8. A file drawer has a label bearing the following information:

Ta-Ti
(Te-Th)

What does the label mean?
What is this type of caption called?

9. Why would a bright red label or a deep violet label be inadvisable to use? Would a buff-colored label with a bright red band across the top be advisable? Why or why not?

10. Turn to the four alphabetic systems shown on the colored inserts. Without referring to the text copy, locate the following:

    (1) Primary guides
    (2) Auxiliary guides
    (3) Individual folders
    (4) Miscellaneous folders
    (5) Staggered arrangement
    (6) Straight-line arrangement
    (7) The cut and position of the tabs on guides and folders; identify each

Learning Projects

1. From a filing supply catalogue or from a local filing supplies representative, find a description of an alphabetic subdivision different from those shown on page 79. Prepare a typed copy of it, captioned for bulletin-board display.

2. Bring to class a blank guide or an unused folder secured from a business office. Be prepared to comment on its features; prepare a typed statement about it that would be suitable for bulletin-board use.

3. Be prepared to demonstrate to the class a method of marking folder tabs so that all labels will be attached at the same place on the tabs.

4. Observe files used in 3 or 4 offices. What evidences do you find of improper use of filing supplies and of a need for better storage procedures? Be prepared to comment to the class with illustrations, if possible.

5. What method of releasing papers for filing can you locate in addition to those specifically mentioned on page 93?

6. Type the names and addresses given on pages 107 and 108 in correct form as though they were being typed on labels. If actual labels are available, use them. If not, rule typing paper for the width of a label according to this sample:

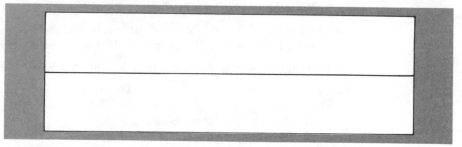

Triple-space between the label items if you use plain paper.

(1) Start typing on the third space from the left edge.

(2) Space down 1 line from the top edge before beginning to type. (Remember to type *below* the score mark.)

(3) Use block style (all lines begin at the left margin) and single spacing.

(4) Type the names in indexing order, using punctuation, abbreviations, and wording exactly as in the name. Transpose words as necessary. Use upper and lower case as in regular typing.

(5) Type "(*Miss*)" or "(*Mrs.*)" at the end of a woman's name. Use "(Ms.)" if you do not know the correct courtesy title.

(6) Enclose in parentheses everything that is not considered in indexing. Examples:

> Garner, Shirley R. (Miss)
> Harris, R. Shirley (Mr.)
> Hoover, Howes (&) Lane, Contractors
> Johnson, Paul J., (and) Sons
> Williams, Walter L., (&) Co. (The)

Note the commas and the spacing in the preceding examples. They are important for consistency.

(7) Type the state and city on the next line; the street address on the last line.

(8) If a line of typing is too long for the label, carry it to the line below and indent it two spaces. Example:

> Farber, Newton, Morrison, Bowles
>   (&) Lesikow
> Palo Alto, CA

(9) Avoid using abbreviations except for states in the address lines. Type the words completely unless space is too limited.
The names and addresses are as follows:

1. L. Richard McMillan & Son, 692 Crane Blvd., Mobile, AL   36612

2. Tsuki's Hair Styling, 1906 Main Street, Waterbury, CT   06704

3. The Scholastic Magazine, Wilson Building, Flat River, MO   63601

4. Senator Oliver Lewis, 219 Federal Building, Newport, RI   02840

5. 15th Street Garage, 1196 15th Street, Dayton, OH   45402

6. Vermont Daily News, News Bldg., Bennington, VT   05201

7. Dr. John Lewis-Jones, 694 South Hart St., Custer, SD   57730

8. Tampa Unitarian Church, 4th & Palm Streets, Tampa, FL   33609

9. Out Door Tennis Players Association, 2222 Longacre St., Eugene, OR   97401

10. Brotherhood of Shipping Clerks, 1110 Arthur Avenue, Port Arthur, TX   77640

11. U. S. Shippers, Inc., 16 Haleiwa Blvd., Haleiwa, HI   96712

12. Mrs. Joe (Amy) St. Charles, 210 Faith Ave., Anchorage, AK   99501

13. One Hundred Diners Club, 191 Lincoln Bldg., Lincoln, NB 68508

14. AOK Repair Service, 3406 Clay Avenue, Helena, MT   59601

15. Mrs. Towner's Beauty Shop, 1904 Main Avenue, Paoli, IN 47454

16. McMillian's Hdwe. Store, 215 Yorkshire Street, Sparks, NV 89431

17. Sister Mary Claire Histed, 1906 Academy Drive, Memphis, TN 38128

18. Serv-U-Well Caterers, 2190 Sixth Avenue, Phoenix, AZ   85004

19. Tri-State Movers, Inc., 886 Elm Street, Fort Knox, KY   40121

20. Lewis High School, 1121 Darwin Boulevard, Pittsburg, KS 66762

Laboratory Assignments 5 and 6   You should now complete Laboratory Assignments 5 (Alphabetic Correspondence Filing—Names of Individuals) and 6 (Alphabetic Correspondence Filing—Names of Individuals and Businesses) in *Records Management—Laboratory Materials.*

Chapter **5**

Correspondence
retrieval
procedures

When a record is created, unnecessary papers concerning it should be destroyed, excessive duplicate copies avoided, and papers of temporary value prominently marked so that the files do not become jammed with records of little or no value. This is a process of control which is continued as papers are dated and time stamped upon receipt, started through the flow pattern from office to office, and stored for retrieval when needed. Efficient records control includes the first-try location of the needed files to avoid duplication of effort, the standardizing of the purchase of equipment and supplies to allow interchange among departments, the adequate training of personnel, and the following of standard procedures of requisition, charge-out, and follow-up.

If filed records cannot be found when they are needed, the most willing files operator, the most modern filing equipment, and the most neatly kept files will be to no avail. Material is placed in the files because it may be useful in the future—to help in making decisions, to provide a record of the past, to furnish information too complicated to be trusted to memory, to assist departments in communicating with each other, to substantiate claims, to divulge information useful for legal purposes. The files operator, therefore, must be able to find instantly any information contained in the filed records.

Because the files operator is responsible for the material that he has filed, orderly methods of keeping track of the material must be established. In a small department file, memory rather than a written record may be relied upon; but memory is never adequate. In those offices that do not follow a formal procedure, much time is wasted trying to find missing papers; tempers become frayed; accusations, real or implied, are made; and control over stored papers is almost nonexistent.

A well-organized filing department has a plan for keeping a record of the papers that are taken from the files. Minutes, or even hours, can be spent searching for a lost paper, while less than one minute is needed to make a note at the time of the lending of that paper. Frantic searching is avoided and the borrower is much more conscientious about returning the material when he knows papers have been charged out in his name than he is apt to be if no record has been kept.

Effective records management, in general, enables the files operator to answer these five questions:

1. *What* material is out of the file?
2. *Who* took the material?
3. *When* was the material taken?
4. *How long* will the material be gone?
5. *Where* will the material be refiled when it is returned?

Ideally, one person should be responsible for removing papers from the files. In practice, the files may be consulted by many persons. Regardless of who removes material from the files, the same procedure should be followed in every instance.

A request for filed papers may come orally from the next desk, over the telephone or intercom, or by messenger. The request may be in written form in a memo or in a letter or on a requisition form, delivered in person or sent by pneumatic tube or conveyor system. The gist of the request is, for example, "Please send me the recent letter from Firth-Jones, Inc., that has a list of supplies and current prices in it." Because a name of this type has been cross-referenced, the files operator will be able to find the letter even if the person requesting it has mistakenly transposed the surnames in the company name (which correctly is Jones-Firth, Inc.).

The letter must be found quickly in the files and given to the one requesting it. At the same time, some method must be used to keep track of the paper and to make sure that it is returned to the files. In filing terminology, this practice is referred to as "using a requisition, charge-out, and follow-up system." "Requisition" and "charge-out" are so interwoven that discussion of one inevitably leads to consideration of the other.

SECTION 1. REQUISITIONS AND CHARGE-OUTS

A *requisition* is somewhat like an IOU; it is an acknowledgment that the borrower has taken a record and that he intends to return it. The requisition may become a stand-in for the borrowed record and thus is an indicator of the location of the record. The arrangement of the information on a requisition may take one of several forms, but the information must provide answers to the five questions stated on the previous page.

The requisition asking for records may be (1) prepared by the requester or (2) made out by the files operator from information given orally or in writing by the requester. The form of the requisition is subject to these variables:

1. The filing supplies available
2. The confidential nature of the papers
3. The method of passing borrowed papers from one person to another
4. The possibility that the material has already been loaned to someone else

FILING SUPPLIES AVAILABLE

Requisition card or slip. The records supervisor or purchasing agent has selected cards, slips, guides, or folders for use in controlling records that are removed from the files. One of the most frequently used is the *requisition card* or *requisition slip* (usually 5" by 3" or 6" by 4"), printed with blanks to be filled in to give an accurate description of the material borrowed, the name and location of the

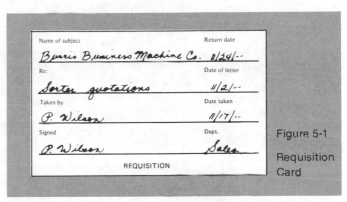

Figure 5-1

Requisition Card

borrower, the date the material is borrowed, the date appearing on the borrowed material, and the date on which the material is to be returned to the file. Figure 5-1 is an example of a requisition card.

A requisition slip differs from a requisition card only in that the slip is printed on paper stock instead of on card stock. The information on the requisition slip is the same as that found on a requisition card. The requisition card or slip may be prepared in duplicate. The use of the second copy is explained in detail on page 119 with the discussion of the tickler file and follow-up procedures.

OUT (substitution) cards and sheets. When a requisition card or slip requesting one paper or a few related papers is presented to the files operator, he uses the card to search for the papers wanted. When he finds them, he removes them from the folder and inserts an *OUT* or *substitution* form in the folder in place of the papers he has just removed. Three types of OUT forms are in general use.

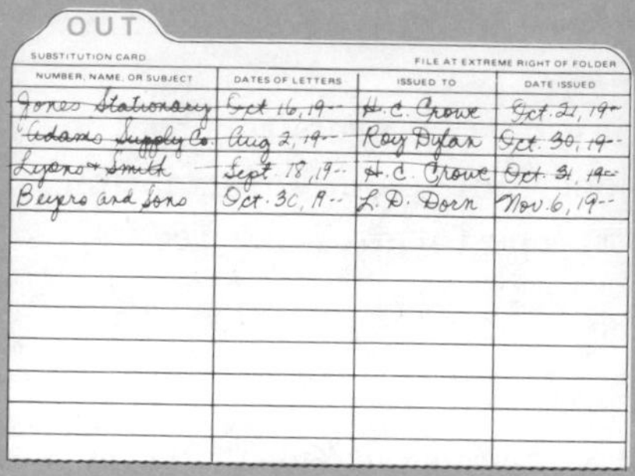

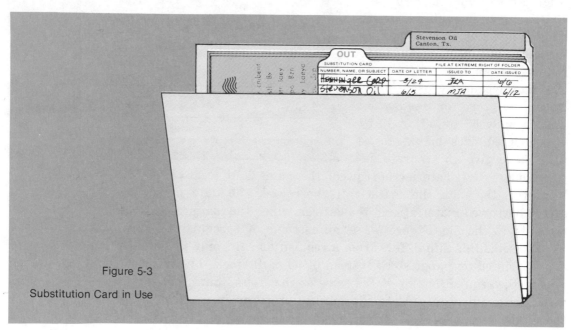

Figure 5-2

OUT Card with Printed Lines

(1) An *OUT card* has lines on which the necessary information may be written when material is requested. Figure 5-2 shows such a card, which may be used over and over again since each line contains space for the information necessary to identify the paper that has been removed from the file. Some substitution cards are one half to one third the width of a guide, equally as high, and have the words "File at extreme right of folder" printed on them so that all these cards are uniformly placed in the file. Figure 5-3 shows such a substitution card in use. OUT or substitution cards are usually made of lightweight card

Figure 5-3

Substitution Card in Use

stock in a distinctive color. When the borrowed paper is returned, the information on the OUT or substitution card is crossed out, and the card is again ready for use.

(2) An *OUT (substitution) card*, made of a stock lighter than pressboard, may contain slots into which the requisition card or slip is placed. Figure 5-4 shows this type of OUT card with its tab in a position and of a color that can be readily seen in the file. The OUT card is inserted in the file at the place where borrowed material is removed, and it remains in the file until the borrowed material is re-

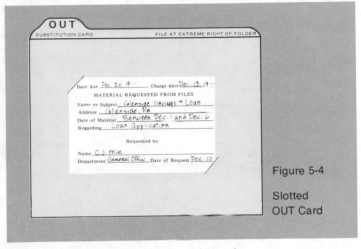

Figure 5-4

Slotted OUT Card

turned and refiled. At that time, the requisition card or slip is removed, and the OUT card is ready for use again.

(3) An *OUT sheet* (or *OUT slip*) is approximately one half to one third the width of a guide but as high as a guide. The information recorded on the OUT sheet is the same as that recorded on the requisition card formerly discussed. The requester may have completed the OUT sheet, using it instead of a requisition card, or the files operator may have filled it out from the information on the requisition given to him by the requester. The OUT sheet has a tab with the word "OUT" on it; when the sheet is inserted into the folder at the place where papers are removed, the tab shows above the top edge of the folder. OUT sheets are usually bound in pads of brightly colored paper. (See Figure 5-5.)

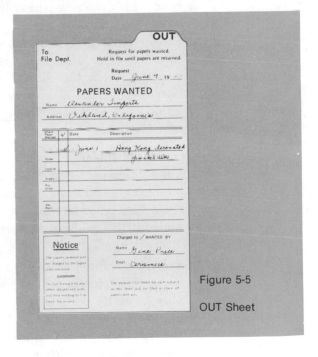

Figure 5-5

OUT Sheet

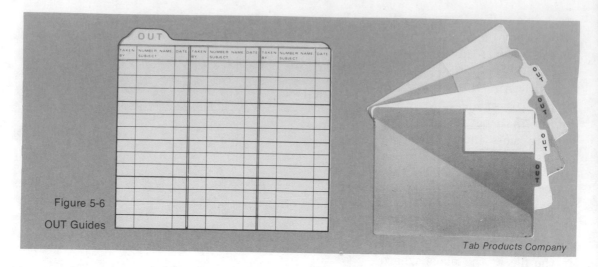

Figure 5-6

OUT Guides

Tab Products Company

OUT guides. The *OUT guide* is a heavy (usually pressboard or plastic) guide with the word "OUT" printed on its tab at a position and in a color so that it can be readily seen in the file. Two types of OUT guides are illustrated in Figure 5-6—one with a holder, designed to contain the original requisition for material, and one with lines on it on which the requisition information is handwritten. The holder on a guide is usually placed so that the top edge of the requisition slip or card that is inserted into it can be seen with a minimum of effort. The OUT guide is used to replace a folder that has been removed from the files. The guide remains in the files until the borrowed folder is returned and refiled. At that time, if the OUT guide holds a requisition card or slip, the card is removed. Both types of OUT guides may be used many times.

OUT folders. When an entire folder is removed from the file, filing of papers for that correspondent must be held up unless a temporary folder is inserted in its place. For continuity in filing, some files operators prefer to substitute an *OUT folder* to take the place of the one that is borrowed.

(1) An OUT folder with the word "OUT" printed on its tab and lines printed on the front of the folder may be used. It is usually a manila or kraft folder, light in color so that writing on the lines may be easily read (Figure 5-7). A plastic back with a clear plastic half-front folder may also be used as an *OUT* folder.

Information contained on the original requisition card is transferred by handwriting to one line on the folder front. While the original folder is out of the files, papers for the correspondent are filed in the OUT folder. When the borrowed folder is returned to the file, the papers are removed from the OUT folder and are refiled

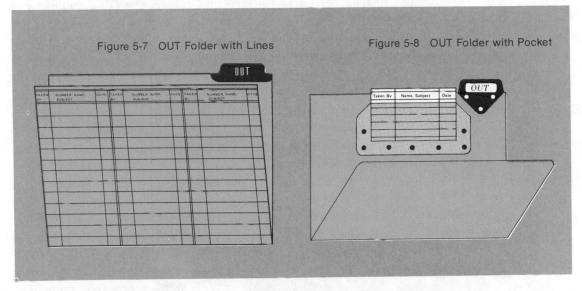

Figure 5-7 OUT Folder with Lines   Figure 5-8 OUT Folder with Pocket

in their proper place in the original folder. This type of folder can be used again and again as each succeeding line can be used for new information (other lines having been marked out).

(2) An OUT folder may have a pocket on the inside into which the requisition card or slip is inserted (Figure 5-8). The folder is used in the same manner as is the OUT folder described above. When the original folder is returned to the file, the contents of the OUT folder are transferred to the original folder, the requisition card or slip is removed, and the OUT folder is again ready to be used.

A translucent folder is also available with features the same as those of a pressboard *OUT* folder.

Carrier folders. It is valuable in the preservation of folders to leave the original folder in the file but transfer its entire contents to a temporary, brightly colored *carrier folder*. This folder is then sent to the person requesting the original folder. An OUT indicator is placed in the original folder with information on it indicating the whereabouts of the folder contents. The color of the carrier folder serves as a reminder to the borrower that he has papers that must be returned to the files. Often the carrier folder has "Return to Files" printed prominently on its front cover as a further reminder to the borrower. The unusual wear and tear to which the original folder would be subjected were it to leave the file is avoided when the carrier folder is used. When the carrier folder is returned to the file, its contents are transferred to the original folder, the OUT indicator is removed, and the carrier folder is ready to be used again.

One disadvantage of lending a complete folder is the possibility that some of the papers will be missing from it when the folder is returned. Unless the papers are fastened together in some way, the loss of some papers is a risk that must be taken.

Multiple-copy requisition form. At times, materials that are borrowed from the files are passed from the original borrower to several other persons before the papers are returned to the files. When it is known that several people may wish to see the materials, a *multiple-copy requisition form* is prepared (Figure 5-9). Each carbon copy after the first is longer than the one preceding it, to allow space for an additional line of information. The requester or the files operator completes the multiple form with information similar to that on all well-designed requisition forms.

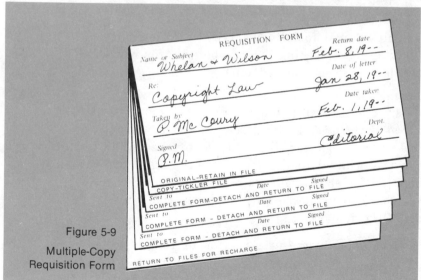

Figure 5-9

Multiple-Copy Requisition Form

If a folder is removed from the file, the original copy of the multiple form may be put in a pocket of an OUT guide or folder and the OUT guide or folder inserted in the file drawer at the place where the folder has been removed. If individual papers have been removed, the original copy of the multiple form may be inserted in the slots of an OUT card that is placed in the file where the papers have been removed; or the information may be written on a separate OUT indicator that is placed in the file where the papers have been removed. The second copy of the multiple form may be used for follow-up purposes. The remaining copies are attached to the borrowed material.

As each individual finishes with the material, he notes on the top copy of the multiple form the name of the person to whom the material is being sent, dates it, initials or signs it, detaches it, and sends the form to the files operator. The files operator then places this slip (sometimes referred to as a *transfer slip*) in the OUT folder, guide, or card pocket or writes the information on the OUT indicator. The original information on the OUT indicator is then obsolete and must be either crossed out or removed and disposed of. An up-to-date control is thereby kept of the whereabouts of the borrowed material without the necessity of securing the material again for recharging. When the last copy of the multiple form has been used, the material must be sent back to the files.

The success of this method depends on the cooperation of each person who transfers the records to someone else. If one person or several persons fail to fill out a transfer slip and return it to the files operator, the whole system breaks down. The files operator must do the tracing to find the papers if they are needed or if they are due, beginning with the one to whom the papers were originally loaned.

On-call (wanted) card. Material that has already been borrowed by someone else will occasionally be requested from the files. When this occurs, the files operator must immediately notify the requester that the material has been loaned. If the request is urgent, the files operator notifies the original borrower of the request and asks him to return the material so that it can be loaned to someone else. The notification may be made orally or on a *wanted card* or *on-call card* (Figure 5-10). The card is similar to one of the forms of an OUT (substitution) card.

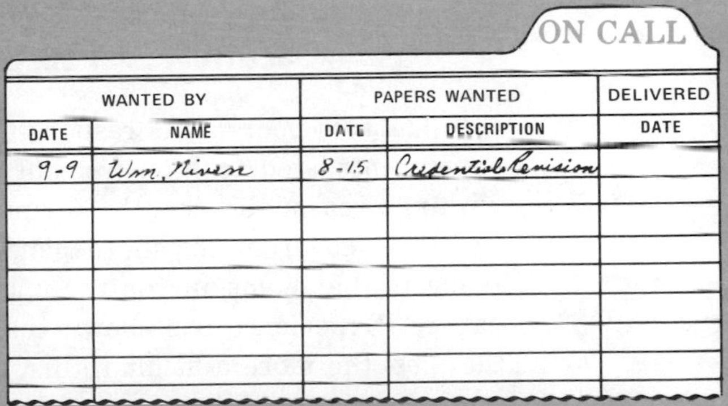

WANTED BY		PAPERS WANTED		DELIVERED
DATE	NAME	DATE	DESCRIPTION	DATE
9-9	Wm. Rivers	8-15	Credentials Revision	

Figure 5-10   Wanted Card or On-Call Card

The wanted card is usually made in duplicate, the first copy going to the original borrower and the second copy being placed in the file behind the original OUT indicator. As soon as the original material is returned to the file by the first borrower, it is charged out to the second borrower by the usual method of charge-out or by noting on the wanted card the date on which the material was delivered to the second borrower. Although the practice of keeping on-call or wanted cards in a tickler file is followed in some offices, the advantages lie with the use of on-call or wanted cards in the file. When the material is returned to the file by the original borrower, it is immediately seen that the material is wanted by someone else. If the request has been placed in a tickler file, it might be several days before reference to the tickler file reveals that the material is wanted by a second person.

CONFIDENTIAL PAPERS

All filed papers are considered valuable or they would not be in the file. Some, however, are so valuable as to be marked "Confidential," "Secret," "Vital," "Personal," and the like. The files operator must be very careful in releasing these papers from the files without proper authority. In some offices, a written request bearing the signature of a designated officer of the company is required for the release of such papers.

Some records are so valuable or confidential that they are not to be taken from the file under any circumstances. The records must be inspected at the files. This inspection is not accompanied by any requisition form or charge-out procedure other than the required signature of someone in authority as the requisite to inspection.

SECTION 2. FOLLOW-UP PROCEDURES

The files operator is responsible not only for knowing where the papers entrusted to him are, but also for checking on their return within a reasonable length of time. The length of time papers may be borrowed from the file depends on the business, the number of requests that come in for the specific papers, and the value of the papers. Experience has shown that the longer papers remain out of the files, the more difficult return of them becomes. Many businesses stipulate a week to ten days with two weeks being the absolute maximum time papers may be borrowed.

CONFIDENTIAL MATERIAL

The rule concerning confidential material is usually that the material (if it may be borrowed at all) must be returned to the file each night. A special memory device should be used by the files operator to remind himself of the absence of these papers. Notation of their whereabouts is made in the same way as that used for any other borrowed paper—by using a requisition and an OUT indicator. An additional reminder must be made for the files operator to secure the return of the paper before leaving for the day. This reminder may be a card note to himself prominently displayed on his desk, a copy of the requisition impaled on a spindle reserved for urgent matters requiring attention before the day's end, a special flag or signal in plain view on his desk as a memory jogger. Whatever the device used, it should be adopted because of its unusualness and its unfailing ability to remind the records manager or the files operator of confidential material that must be recovered.

TICKLER FILES

Many files operators request that every requisition be made in duplicate so that the carbon copy can be used for follow-up purposes. The follow-up or reminder method most frequently used is that of a *tickler file*, mentioned briefly in Chapter 2. Two forms of a tickler file, used in connection with a correspondence file, are shown in Figures 5-11 and 5-12. They are:

1. A card file
2. A folder file

The basic form of a tickler file is always the same: a chronological arrangement. This arrangement usually takes the form of a series of 12 guides or folders with the names of the months of the year printed on their tabs and 31 guides or folders whose tabs are printed with 1 through 31 for the days of the month. Guides or folders for the years following the present one may also be provided.

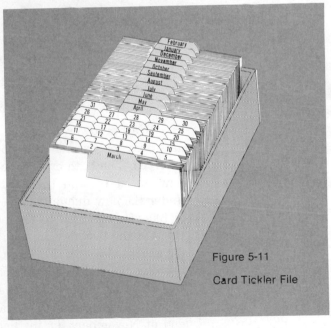

Figure 5-11

Card Tickler File

Behind the appropriate month or day guide are put reminders of items that need attention. The tickler file must be checked the first thing each day. According to the notes there, papers that are to be brought to the attention of someone are found in the regular files. OUT indicators are inserted in their places and the original papers are sent to the persons who are responsible for whatever is to be done with them. Borrowed materials that are indicated as due that day are requested from the borrowers.

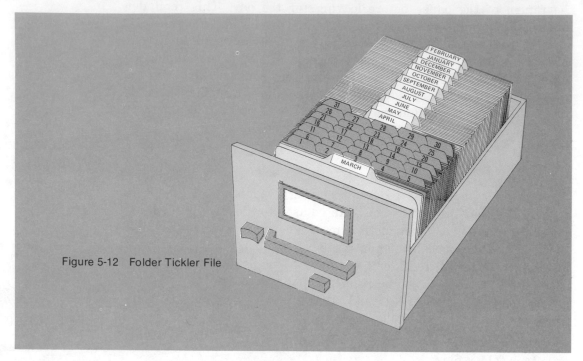

Figure 5-12   Folder Tickler File

If a borrower wants to keep materials beyond the due date, the date may be extended if no other request for the papers has been received. The date on the tickler file reminder is then changed to the new due date, and the card or sheet is returned to the tickler file under the new due date. The date on the OUT form that is in the files is likewise changed to the new date.

On the last day in each month, the one in charge of the tickler file checks through the date cards or folders to be certain nothing has been inadvertently overlooked during the month. Then he removes all the cards or papers from behind the next month's guide and redistributes them behind the daily numbered guides. If it were at the end of November, for instance, he would check behind the November daily guides, move the November guide to the back of the file, and put the December guide in the front. All the cards, slips or papers pertaining to December would be redistributed behind the guides labeled 1 through 31, according to the dates on the cards or on the papers.

Many executives use a card tickler system as a reminder for events that happen yearly, for payments that occur periodically throughout the year, for recurring meeting reminders, for annual meeting arrangements, and for anything else of a recurring nature.

No matter which type of tickler file is used, it is a means of controlling records. When records are returned and refiled, the tickler notation is destroyed (that is, the card, requisition, or sheet is torn and disposed of); the extra copy is shredded and thrown away. This destruction must be done carefully, as it is possible to tear the wrong card, requisition, or copy. In a few offices, charge-outs are kept for comparison purposes, to see how often the files are being consulted, to attempt to determine the work load of the files operators, to see what types of materials are being used frequently and which ones are not. Totals are often kept by day, week, month, or year.

If the file is a small one, no tickler system may be necessary for the follow-up of borrowed material since the files operator can open the file drawers daily and quickly scan the folders for OUT signals. Each OUT record can be checked individually to see if the material should be returned that day. If so, a request for it can be made immediately. The use of a tickler file to remind the files operator of some future action, however, is important. And the use of OUT indicators is likewise important, no matter how small the file.

Card tickler file. To use for follow-up of borrowed materials, card-size requisitions or index cards may be filed in card tickler files. In an office where duplicate copies of requisitions are made for all materials requested from the files, the carbon copy of the requisition becomes the card placed in the tickler file. The date by which it is filed is the date on which the material is to be returned to the files. The card in Figure 5-13, therefore, would be filed behind the 21 guide since the material is to be returned on April 21.

If an oral request or a request written on other than a requisition slip or card is received and a paper or folder is to be removed from the file, the files operator completes a requisition card or makes a separate index card containing complete information. An example of a separate index card made for a

Name or Subject	Return date
Ball Furniture Store	4/21/--
Re:	Date of letter
Order for Sales Dept.	4/5/--
Taken by	Date taken
J. E. Morrow	4/14/--
Signed	Dept.
J. E. Morrow	Sales
REQUISITION	

Figure 5-13

Completed Requisition Card

paper loaned on November 6 and to be returned on November 20 is shown here:

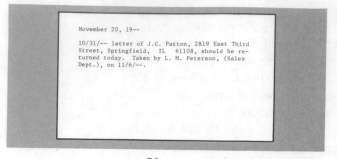

November 20, 19--

10/31/-- letter of J.C. Patton, 2819 East Third Street, Springfield, IL 61108, should be returned today. Taken by L. M. Peterson, (Sales Dept.), on 11/6/--.

The card would be placed behind the 20 guide because its date is within the current month. If the letter were to be returned on December 7, the card would read "December 7, 19--" on its top line, and it would be filed behind the December guide in the card tickler file.

If a paper that is ready to be filed is to be brought to someone's attention on a future date, the files operator notices that fact while inspecting the correspondence. A special notation may appear on the paper, usually made by the one who released it, to the effect that the paper is to be brought up again on a future date. The notation may take one of many forms—a penciled date, a stamp reading "Wanted," "Bring up," "Pending," "Follow-Up," "Future use," and the like. The files operator may attach a follow-up sticker to the original piece of correspondence as a further aid in locating the right piece of correspondence on the date it is wanted. Follow-up stickers are usually brightly colored and have adhesive backs that stick to the paper and may be easily removed without marring the surface of the paper. If a letter from Plymale Products Co., 106 Basin Street, New Orleans, Louisiana, dated November 1, is filed on November 6 and

December 6, 19--

Take letter of 11/1/-- from Plymale Products Co., 106 Basin St., New Orleans, LA 70112, to Mr. Niven.

is to be brought to Mr. Niven's attention on December 6, the files operator makes a tickler card like that at the left. The files operator then places the card behind the December guide in the card tickler file. The card may be handwritten or typed. Handwritten records, however, must be very readable; and any tickler record must contain complete information. Unintelligible scrawls and incomplete information are two inexcusable errors that can lead to lost time and frayed dispositions.

Sometimes a request may be received in advance of the date on which a record is wanted. For instance, on October 15 a note is received requesting the entire folder of the Midwest Brick Corporation on October 20. The information on the note is transferred to a requisition (made in duplicate) that is then placed behind the 20 guide in the tickler file. When the tickler is checked on the morning of the 20th, the Midwest Brick Corporation folder is pulled from the file, an OUT indicator is put in its place with the original requisition card or slip attached to it, and the borrowed material is delivered to the one who requested it. The date on the duplicate requisition card or slip is corrected to reflect the due date of the borrowed material, and the requisition card is filed in the tickler file behind the due date.

Folder tickler file. Refer again to Figure 5-12 on page 120. The *duplicates* of OUT sheets and substitution cards are filed in tickler folders according to the dates on which the OUT slips need attention. Using a duplicate requisition system eliminates the need for writing the information twice and, therefore, eliminates errors and saves time.

If an extra copy (typed or reproduced by mechanical means) has been made of a paper that will be needed at a future date, the extra copy is placed in a folder tickler file in the folder bearing the date on which the original paper is to be brought up. If the paper is to be attended to on a date within the current month, the copy would go into the correct date folder. If the date is in a succeeding month, the copy would go into the folder bearing that month's name. The files operator may make this extra copy himself, since original correspondence belongs in the regular file. Original papers should NEVER be filed in a tickler file, since finding them involves looking first in the regular files (and not locating the papers) and then having to go through all the folders in the tickler file to locate them. Only extra copies belong in the tickler file.

Special follow-up folders. To house specialized materials that will need attention at a series of dates in the future, special follow-up folders may be used. They may be placed either in the regular file or in the tickler file. Their tabs are the complete width of the folder and have printed on them the months of the year and the days of the month (Figure 5-14, page 124). Two movable, colored signals are used to indicate the month and day on which the folder is to be followed up. If the folder is placed in the regular file, the files operator must check the regular files daily to be sure no follow-up folders are overlooked. In a large filing installation, this practice may be very impractical; in a small file setup, daily inspection may be relatively easy.

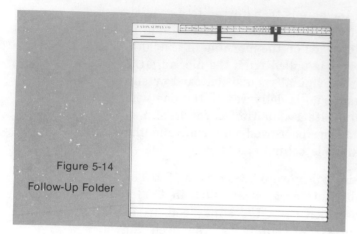

Figure 5-14

Follow-Up Folder

If the follow-up folder is kept in the tickler file, a permanent OUT guide should be placed in the regular file at the position originally occupied by the removed folder, indicating the presence of the folder permanently in the tickler file. OUT folders should never be used for this purpose since the papers of one correspondent will then be filed in two places—in the regular file in the OUT folder and in the tickler file in the follow-up folders. Special follow-up folders are often used in a deskside file for equipment maintenance purposes, insurance policy information, production control, special projects deadlines, purchase order follow-up, and sales prospects.

DISPOSITION OF CHARGE-OUTS

When borrowed materials are returned to the files, all OUT indicators inserted while the materials were gone must be immediately removed. If the charge-out information has been written on the OUT indicator itself, this information is crossed out and the indicator is stored for reuse. Requisition cards are removed from holders and are destroyed, and the holders are stored for reuse. If any duplicates of OUT slips or OUT cards have been made (for the tickler file, for instance), they should be located and immediately destroyed also.

LOST PAPERS

The records manager knows from experience that sometimes papers get lost. Searching for them involves:

1. Looking in the folder in front of and behind the correct folder
2. Looking between the folders
3. Looking on the bottom of the file, under all the folders, where the paper may have slipped
4. Looking completely through the correct folder because alphabetic or other order may have been neglected due to carelessness
5. Checking transposition of names
6. Looking for the second or third or succeeding units of a name instead of for the first unit

7. Checking for misfiling because of misreading of letters—*e* for *i*, *n* for *m*, *t* for *l*, *k* for *h*, *C* for *G*, and the like

8. Checking alternate spellings

9. Looking under other vowels (for a name beginning with *Ha*, look also under *He, Hi, Ho,* and *Hu*)

10. Looking for a double letter instead of a single one (or the reverse)

11. Looking for anglicized forms of a name (*Mueller* for *Müller*)

12. Checking transposition of numbers

13. Looking in the year preceding or following the one in question

14. Looking in a related subject if the file is a subject file

15. Being aware that the papers may be en route to the files by mechanical conveyance or messenger

16. Looking in the sorter

17. Getting the person in whose desk or briefcase the material may be to search for it!

If every search fails to produce the missing paper, some records managers try to reconstruct the paper from memory, typing up as much as is known. This information is placed in a folder labeled "LOST," and the folder is filed in its correct place in the file as a constant reminder to the files operator to be on the alert for the missing paper.

The loss of papers can be prevented by permanently binding them in book form. Binding in this manner assures neatness and precludes the borrowing of individual papers. Binding, therefore, is not recommended for individual papers to which frequent reference is made. Bound volumes can be placed on shelving, releasing drawer space and utilizing space that might not otherwise be used. But binding creates bulk; the transporting of borrowed papers is difficult; bound volumes are usually stored in hard-to-reach places. Papers that are active should not be bound because so many unnecessary papers must be loaned along with the one that is requested; correspondence files, therefore, do not lend themselves to binding.

Efficient records control is also dependent upon the equipment and layout of the files as they affect the flow of work. These topics are discussed in Chapter 13.

For Review and Discussion

1. Why is memory inadequate for keeping track of records in a department that has only two file drawers of material?

2. What psychological element enters into the use of written requisitions for material that is borrowed from the files?

3. In keeping a record of papers removed from the files, efficient records personnel should be able to answer what five questions?

4. Why is it difficult to explain "requisition" without talking about "charge-out" also?

5. Three dates are usually found on a requisition form. What are they? Why are all three necessary?

6. Why is it important that the eye see an "OUT" indicator quickly when the file drawer is opened?

7. Which of the various OUT forms do you believe to be the quickest to use? Why?

8. Why is an OUT slip or substitution card not a good OUT signal to use to replace a folder that has been removed from the files?

9. Turn to the colored inserts following page 12. Locate any OUT tabs in the four filing systems. Can you determine which ones are guides, folders, or slips? What type of material do you believe was borrowed from the file where an OUT indicator appears?

10. The entire contents of a folder may be transferred to a carrier folder. What advantages are there for using this method of borrowing papers from the files? Are there any disadvantages to this method?

11. What types of material that are highly valuable (confidential, secret, personal, and the like) might be kept in the files? What precautions should be taken in filing them? in charging them out? in following up on the charge-outs? in refiling them?

12. A tickler file may be used as a follow-up method for requisitions made from the files. Why do you suppose that such a reminder file is called a tickler file?

13. A handwritten requisition comes to your desk. The requisition is rather difficult to read, but you believe it is a request for a letter dated November 17 and addressed to Lytle, Brown & Casgill. You spend several minutes searching for that name but cannot locate it in its correct alphabetic position. Where would you then look?

Learning Projects

1. From filing supply catalogs and brochures or from other printed sources in the library, secure pictures of (a) requisition forms and (b) OUT forms. (Do not cut pictures from library sources, of course! Duplicate them!) Post the pictures on a bulletin board and compare your samples with those brought by other students. Be prepared to comment on similarities and differences.

2. Visit an office and ask to see a tickler file or other follow-up file that is in use. Make notes of its form, its size, and why it is used. Be prepared to comment before the class on your findings.

Laboratory Assignments 7 and 8

You should now complete Laboratory Assignments 7 (Alphabetic Correspondence Filing and Tickler File Usage) and 8 (Requisition and Charge-out Procedures) in *Records Management—Laboratory Materials.*

PART TWO

OTHER METHODS OF RECORDS STORAGE

Chapter **6**

Numeric method
of records storage

As its name implies, numeric filing is a method of filing by *numbers* instead of names, and two of the most common arrangements are illustrated on page 131. Numbers as a means of classification are encountered daily by individuals; for example, numbers identify checks, Social Security records, drivers' licenses, ZIP codes, insurance policies, and hospitalization plans, as well as credit cards for department store purchases, gasoline purchases, restaurant dining, and telephone calls.

The numeric method of filing is particularly advantageous for the following types of business situations:

1. Insurance companies, law firms, and social welfare agencies which maintain papers according to policy or case numbers.
2. Firms in the building trades which use contract or job numbers and stock numbers.
3. Architects who assign contract numbers to their clients to insure clear-cut identification of all pieces of correspondence or other materials pertaining to contracts.
4. State automobile license files and Social Security files which use numbers because of their large-scale operations.

SECTION 1. NUMERIC SYSTEMS BASED ON SERIAL NUMBERING

The simplest example of numeric filing is a sequence arrangement of numbered office forms in consecutive order, with no duplicates occurring. Invoices, purchase orders, and sales tickets are

examples of this numbering system. Even though these invoices, purchase orders, and sales tickets may be prepared at various locations,
they are stored in numerical sequence, all together. They may be
bound permanently, put in sturdy loose-leaf binders, or placed in
folders, all of which contain certain serially numbered sections and
are so labeled.

The simplest kind of numeric correspondence filing is that
described as *serial* or *consecutive numbering*. The numbers begin
with *1* and progress upward; or they may begin with *100, 1,000,* or
some other number and go upward. The numbers have no meaning
other than relative sequence.

BASIC FEATURES OF A NUMERIC FILE

All serial numbering filing systems consist of four parts:

1. Numbered guides and folders
2. An alphabetic miscellaneous file
3. A card file
4. An accession book

Numbered guides and folders. A numeric file (Figure 6-1) contains guides and folders with captions made up of numbers. A series
of numbered guides (100, 110, 640, 650) divide the file into easy-to-
find numeric segments. The guides may be purchased with numbers
printed on the tabs, or they may be made from blank guides of any
kind. Numbers may be inserted into slots on the tabs, stamped on
the tabs with a numbering machine, typed on, or hand lettered.
Guides may be in a straight-line arrangement or staggered across
the drawer. The numbers guide the eye to certain segments of the
numeric sequence. Usually one guide is provided for every five to ten
folders.

The folders are consecutively numbered (in the two illustrations
in Figure 6-1, 100 through 109 and 640 through 650) and are placed
behind the guides indicating the corresponding numbered sections.
Some folders bear also the names of the correspondents if secrecy
is not a factor or if office practice requires the names in addition to
the numbers. Since the sequence of numbered folders will never vary
(1, 2, 3, 4, 5, etc.; or 100, 101, 102, 103, 104, 105, etc.), the folder
tabs may be in one position or staggered. In Figure 6-1, the illustration at the left shows staggered arrangement; the illustration at
the right, straight-line arrangement.

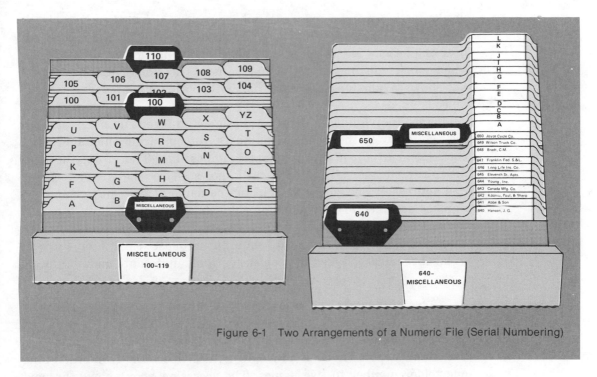

Figure 6-1   Two Arrangements of a Numeric File (Serial Numbering)

Alphabetic miscellaneous file. The miscellaneous file contains a primary guide labeled "Miscellaneous." This guide may be followed by other guides to indicate the alphabetic breakdown. In Figure 6-1, the Miscellaneous guide is in center position to avoid interfering with any other information. Behind the Miscellaneous guide is an arrangement of alphabetically captioned folders into which are filed the papers of correspondents who have not yet been assigned numbers because the volume of correspondence with them is so small that individual folders are not yet considered advisable. The entire miscellaneous section of guides and folders may be placed at the beginning of the numeric sequence (as in the illustration at the left of Figure 6-1) or at the very end of it (as in the illustration at the right of Figure 6-1). Because expansion occurs at the end of a numeric file, placement of the miscellaneous section at the front of the file is recommended.

Card file. The card file is an alphabetic file of the names of the correspondents and of any subjects in the file. Although the cards show the folder numbers assigned to the correspondents and to the subjects, the cards are arranged alphabetically. Cards may or may not be made for correspondents whose papers are filed in the miscellaneous file. If cards are made for these correspondents, the cards bear the letter "M" to show that the correspondence with those individuals or companies is in the miscellaneous section of the file. Figure 6-2 shows a portion of a card file with both numbered and miscellaneous cards.

Since individuals or firms are assigned different numbers and the file may grow to thousands of numbers, remembering the names that correspond to all of the numbers is impossible. Therefore, the card file is the "memory," for each card shows either the complete name and address of one correspondent or the name of one subject and the number assigned to that name or subject. Mistakes made in the card file are very serious because the card file is the first item to which reference is made in order to locate any requested name or subject; great care must be taken to keep the card file up to date and absolutely correct.

Accession book. The accession book, which is sometimes called an *accession record*, an *acquisition book*, or a *number book*, is a record of the numbers already assigned to correspondents and subjects. The use of an accession book prevents a files operator from assigning one folder number to two names. The accession book shows the next number available for assignment. If a numbered folder is lost or misplaced, reference to this book would indicate the name that had been assigned that number, and the full information could be obtained from the card file to help in locating the folder. Only complete

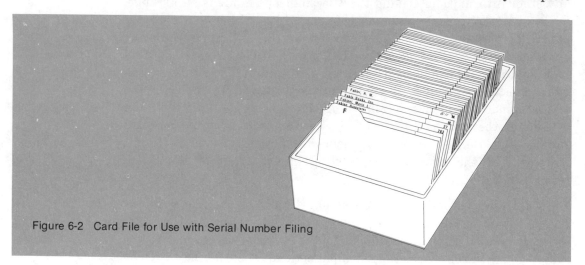

Figure 6-2   Card File for Use with Serial Number Filing

names need be written in the accession book since the card file shows all the information about each correspondent.

An accession book in bound form with prenumbered lines is usually purchased at an office supply store. Unnumbered, lined pages may be used if extreme care is exercised to number the lines in sequence. Figure 6-3 shows part of a page of an accession book; this

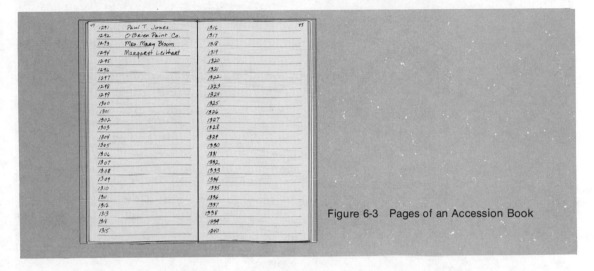

Figure 6-3   Pages of an Accession Book

page indicates that No. 1294 was the last number used and that No. 1295 is the next number to be assigned.

ILLUSTRATIVE SYSTEMS

Direct Number Filing System (Yawman & Erbe Corporation of California). This system (Figure 6-4, page 134) is used when the contents are referred to first by number. The primary divisions, which are indicated by guides with red tabs, are hundreds; the subdivisions, which are indicated by second-position guides with blue tabs and third-position guides with yellow tabs, are tens. All guide labels are of the insertable type that provide flexibility for any office situation. Individual folders have one-third cut tabs which show both numbers and names because this combination reduces errors in filing and makes finding quicker and earier.

Numeric-Name System (Shaw-Walker, Muskegon, Michigan). In this system (Figure 6-5, page 135) numbered guides are provided in center position for every ten folders. Folder tabs are one-half cut,

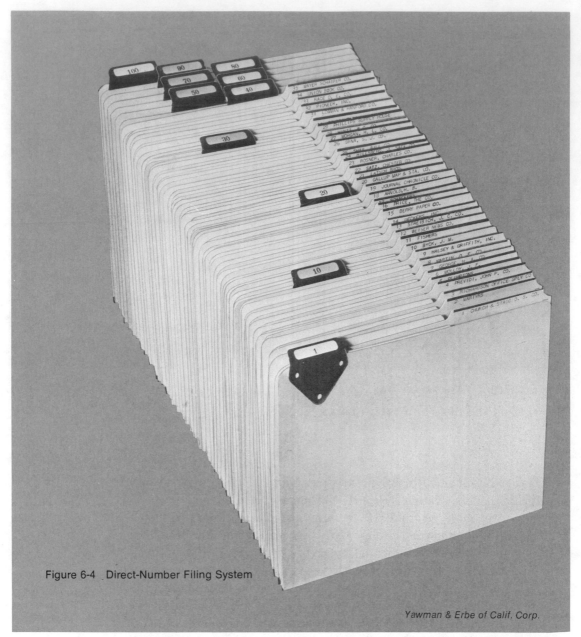

Figure 6-4   Direct-Number Filing System

Yawman & Erbe of Calif. Corp.

alternating from left to right. All folders with tabs at the left have even numbers; all folders with tabs at the right have odd numbers. In addition to numbers, the names of the correspondents are typed on the folder labels for aid in identification.

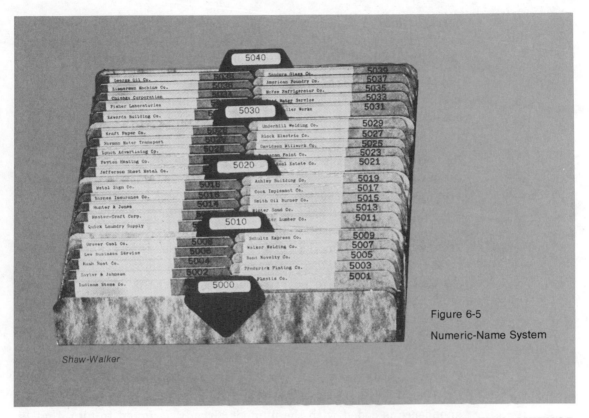

Figure 6-5

Numeric-Name System

Shaw-Walker

FILING PROCEDURES FOR NUMERIC METHOD

The basic steps of filing (inspection, indexing, coding, cross-referencing, sorting, and filing), charge-out, and follow-up are as important with the numeric method as with the alphabetic method.

A numeric file that is already in operation contains numbered guides and folders, a miscellaneous section with its alphabetic guides and folders, a card file with cards in alphabetic name order, and an accession book with numerous entries already made. The procedure to be followed in filing correspondence is as follows:

Inspection. Correspondence is inspected for release marks and is mentally indexed to ascertain the name or subject under which each piece is to be filed.

Name coding and cross-referencing. If the alphabetic coding of the name or subject has been previously done, the files operator checks it for accuracy. If the coding has not been done, the files operator marks the correspondence in the usual manner (according to the practice of the office). If cross-references should be prepared, the coding should include a notation to that effect.

Alphabetic sorting. If the volume of correspondence is large, a preliminary rough sorting by alphabet will speed the filing process because reference to the alphabetic card file is the next step.

Numeric coding. Before the files operator assigns a number or the letter "M" to a piece of correspondence, he should first consult the card file. This step will tell him whether or not a card has already been prepared for that particular correspondent and, if so, whether a number or the letter "M" has been assigned to that correspondent.

In some offices, a number is automatically assigned to a correspondent the first time he writes. For example, an order letter might be the signal to the files operator to assign a number, regardless of the fact that there are no other pieces of correspondence from this individual or firm. At times, an officer of the company may indicate that a new correspondent is of such importance that he is to be considered an active client and that a number should be assigned to him immediately.

Correspondents with numbers already assigned to them. If the card file contains a card for the correspondent, the piece of correspondence is coded with the number already assigned to him, that is, the number typed in the upper right corner of the card. The number is written in the upper right corner of the letter. The coded piece is then placed in a numeric sorter for later filing in the proper numbered folder in the file.

Correspondents with the letter "M" already assigned to them. If the card in the card file shows an "M," the previous correspondence for that correspondent has been filed in the miscellaneous alphabetic file. The piece of correspondence is therefore coded with a letter "M" in the upper right corner. The piece is then placed in an alphabetic sorter for later filing in the miscellaneous section of the file.

New correspondents to be assigned numbers. If a correspondent is important enough to warrant the immediate opening of an individual folder, the files operator takes the steps listed here and on the next page.

1. The files operator consults the accession book. On the first unused numbered line, he makes a notation of the correspondent's name.

2. He then marks the assigned number on the correspondence in the upper right corner.

3. He types an index card for the correspondent. He includes the complete information—name, address, and assigned number.

4. If any cross-reference cards are necessary, he prepares them immediately after he prepares the original card and puts the assigned number on each of them. Figure 6-6 illustrates an original index card and its accompanying cross-reference card. In order to emphasize the fact that a card is a cross-reference, it is advisable to use a distinctive color for it. If the cross-reference card is the same color as all other cards in the file, however, a number followed by an "x" should be used to indicate clearly that the card is a cross-reference. Typing format, capitalization, and punctuation should be the same as on the original card and consistent on all cards.

5. He opens a new folder for the correspondent and places on its tab the assigned number (and, in some cases, the correspondent's name). (See page 136.)

6. He places the correspondence in the folder in the usual manner according to date with the most recent piece on top.

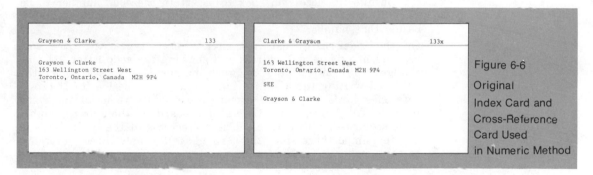

Figure 6-6

Original Index Card and Cross-Reference Card Used in Numeric Method

After these steps have been taken, the folder may be placed in the numeric sorter according to its number for later filing in numeric sequence in the file drawer, or the folder may be laid aside in a separate pile to be taken to the file drawer at the time the filing of other papers is done.

New correspondents to be assigned the letter "M." If the files operator does not find a card for the correspondent in the card file, he may prepare a card for him and place the letter "M" in the upper right corner. At this time he makes out the necessary cross-reference cards also, placing the letter "M" on each cross-reference. He codes the correspondence with the letter "M" and places the correspondence in the alphabetic sorter for storage until the letter is filed. He files the newly typed cards in their correct alphabetic sequence in the card file.

Filing. Coded papers are removed from the sorters, are kept in numeric and alphabetic sequences, and are taken to the files. All correspondence coded with numbers is filed in the correspondingly numbered folders in the usual manner; all correspondence coded with the letter "M" is filed in miscellaneous alphabetic folders first according to the indexing units in the correspondents' names and then by date within each name group.

Opening a numeric folder for accumulated correspondence. Office policy governs the number of accumulated pieces that call for the assignment of a permanent number to a correspondent. When three, five, seven, or some other predetermined number of papers to, from, or about a correspondent accumulate in a miscellaneous alphabetic folder, the files operator removes the correspondence from the folder and then takes the following steps:

1. He consults the accession book to ascertain the code number to be used. He writes the name of the correspondent in the accession book beside that number.

2. On the index card that has already been typed with the correspondent's name and address and showing the code letter "M," he changes the "M" to the assigned number by crossing out the "M" and writing the assigned number above or beside it. If cross-reference cards have been prepared, he treats them in the same manner. The files operator then files the cards in their proper alphabetic sequence in the card file. The correctness of the index cards is of great importance since the card file is the only direct reference to the numbered folders in the file drawers. Figure 6-7 shows two index cards properly typed.

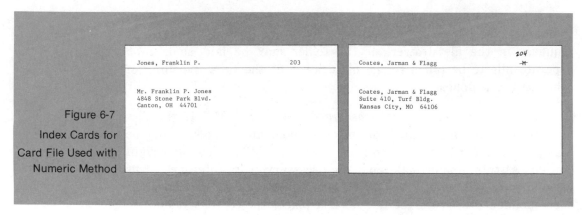

Figure 6-7

Index Cards for Card File Used with Numeric Method

Jones, Franklin P.   203

Mr. Franklin P. Jones
4848 Stone Park Blvd.
Canton, OH 44701

Coates, Jarman & Flagg   204

Coates, Jarman & Flagg
Suite 410, Turf Bldg.
Kansas City, MO 64106

3. The files operator then recodes all pieces of correspondence with the newly assigned number.

4. He opens a new folder with the assigned number on its tab (and, possibly, the correspondent's name). He places all papers concerning the correspondent by date into the folder, with the most recently dated paper on top.

5. He places the numbered folder in its correct numerical sequence in the file drawer.

Charge-out and follow-up. Whenever material is removed from a numeric file, requisitions, charge-out cards or slips, and OUT indicators must be used in the same way as they are for alphabetic filing. The purpose of these controls, of course, is to help the files operator know at all times what materials are missing from the files, where the materials have gone, and how soon they may be expected to be returned.

Follow-up procedures to locate missing materials, including the use of a tickler file or other reminder system, are also identical to those used in the alphabetic method and described in Chapter 5.

CONVERSION OF AN ALPHABETIC FILE TO A NUMERIC FILE

At the time an alphabetic correspondence file is being converted to a serially numbered file, the alphabetic card file index may follow an exact alphabetic and numeric sequence arrangement for a time because folders are customarily removed from the alphabetic file drawers in A-to-Z sequence. New numbered labels may be affixed to the old folder tabs, or the assigned numbers may be added to the folder tabs already in existence.

After all the existing individual folders have been converted to a numbered sequence and as new correspondents are added to the file, parallel alphabetic-numeric sequence in the card file will not be found. Ordinarily, several weeks are required to change from one filing method to another. During that time, new correspondents for whom folders were never present in the alphabetic file will have been added to the numeric file.

The procedure to be followed in converting an alphabetic file to a numeric file is as follows:

1. As the individual folders are removed from the file drawer in A-to-Z order, the correspondents are assigned consecutive numbers. New labels are made, or the numbers are added to the old ones.

2. Notation of the name of each correspondent is made in the accession book beside the number assigned to each correspondent.

3. An index card is typed for the name of each correspondent, and all cross-reference cards necessary are typed immediately. The assigned number is typed on each card for reference purposes.

4. Cross-reference sheets are removed from the individual folders, since the cross-reference cards take the place of cross-reference sheets. Cross-reference cards are also made for any permanent cross-references that may be encountered within the group of folders being converted to numeric method. The index cards are filed in the card file alphabetically by correspondents' names.

5. Each piece of correspondence in every folder is coded with its newly assigned number in the upper right corner of the piece. If any piece is removed from any folder, refiling of the piece will be easy because of the number appearing on it.

6. The numbered folder is returned to the file in its correct numeric sequence.

After all individual folders have been removed from the alphabetic file, assigned numbers, and placed in the new numeric file, the folders remaining in the alphabetic file will be the miscellaneous A-to-Z folders. These become the miscellaneous section of the numeric file. All the correspondence in each miscellaneous folder should be coded with the letter "M," and each correspondent should have an index card prepared with the letter "M" typed on it. Since this task takes a considerable amount of time, some files operators prefer not to include miscellaneous cards in their card indexes.

As is the case with other methods of filing, a subject may be considered of more importance for coding purposes than are the names of the correspondents. In numeric filing, therefore, a subject may be assigned a number. The index card for the subject "Annual Meeting" would be typed in the same manner as is a card for an individual correspondent. The accession book entry would be made, a numbered folder would be prepared, pertinent papers would be coded with the assigned number, the folder would be filed in the numeric file, and the card would be filed in alphabetic sequence in the card file.

In a numeric file having names and numbers on folders, special guides may be used in a file drawer to guide the eye to the active correspondents. In a numbers-only file, however, special guides are usually not in use since they destroy the anonymity inherent in a series of numbered folders.

The illustrations in Figure 6-8 show two pieces of correspondence correctly coded for numeric filing. At the left is a letter

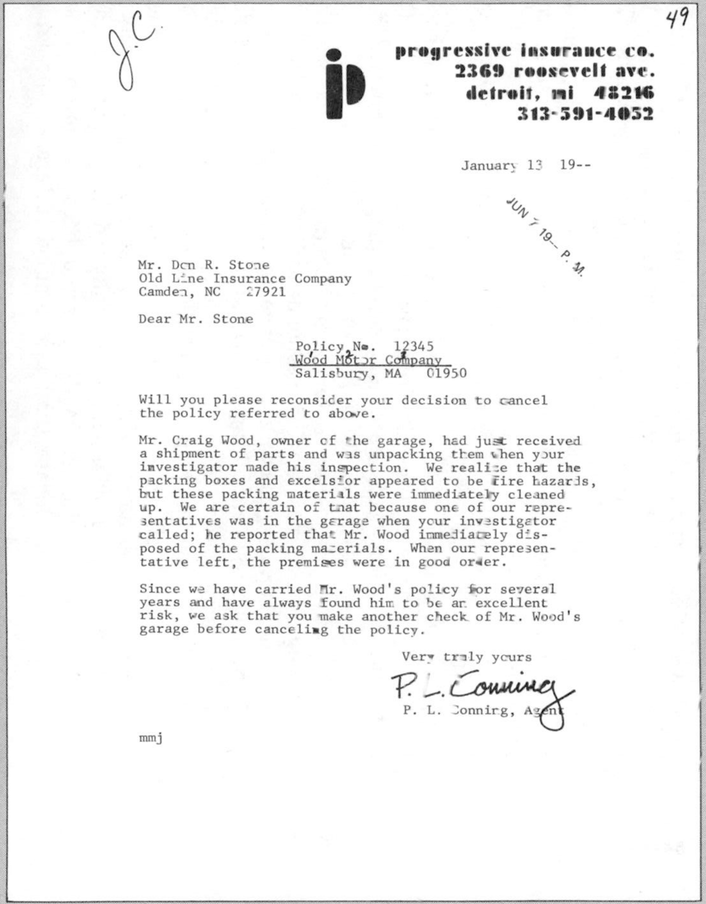

C P S

INSTITUTE for CERTIFYING SECRETARIES

A Department of THE NATIONAL SECRETARIES ASSOCIATION (International)
SUITE 410 • 1103 GRAND AVENUE • KANSAS CITY, MISSOURI 64106 • GRAND 1-0514

September 1, 19--

JUN 7 19-- P. M.

Mr. A. L. Lee, Personnel Manager
Big Three Insurance Company
492 Brock Building
Phoenix, AZ 85002

Dear Mr. Lee

The Dean of our Institute has asked me to write to you **3** because your company recently participated in an <u>accelerated reading program</u> for executives.

Several of our members speak, from time to time to civic groups, secretarial meetings, and management conferences. We are very eager to know the reactions of those who have taken specific courses in the speeding of reading. Will you please take a few moments to answer the following questions?

1. What is the average number of hours a day your executives spend in business reading?

2. What have you found to be the best method for developing greater efficiency in reading?

3. What were the results your executives achieved from their formal reading instruction?

I shall be most grateful if you can give me your answers to these questions within the next two weeks so that I can report to the Dean in time for the annual meeting.

Sincerely yours

Lillian M. Foreman

Lillian A. Forman
Secretary to the Dean

---

progressive insurance co.
2369 roosevelt ave.
detroit, mi 48216
313-591-4052

January 13 19--

JUN 7 19-- P. M.

Mr. Don R. Stone
Old Line Insurance Company
Camden, NC 27921

Dear Mr. Stone

Policy No. 12345
Wood Motor Company
Salisbury, MA 01950

Will you please reconsider your decision to cancel the policy referred to above.

Mr. Craig Wood, owner of the garage, had just received a shipment of parts and was unpacking them when your investigator made his inspection. We realize that the packing boxes and excelsior appeared to be fire hazards, but these packing materials were immediately cleaned up. We are certain of that because one of our representatives was in the garage when your investigator called; he reported that Mr. Wood immediately disposed of the packing materials. When our representative left, the premises were in good order.

Since we have carried Mr. Wood's policy for several years and have always found him to be an excellent risk, we ask that you make another check of Mr. Wood's garage before cancelling the policy.

Very truly yours

P. L. Conning

P. L. Conning, Agent

mmj

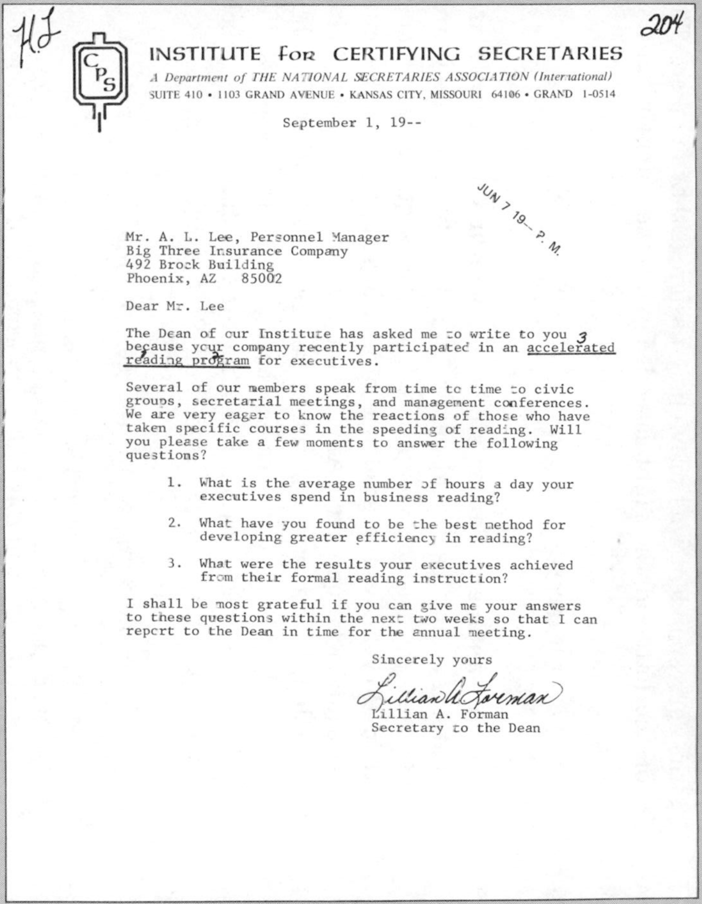

Figure 5-8 Coding of Correspondence for Numeric Method

assigned the number "49"; reference to the card file had shown that the correspondent was previously assigned that number. The subject of the letter at the right is coded with the number "204."

ADVANTAGES AND DISADVANTAGES OF THE SERIAL NUMBERING METHOD

Advantages. Earlier study has shown that records are filed so that they may be found easily and quickly when they are needed. Because the majority of people know the sequence of numbers better than they know the sequence of the alphabet, filing by number can be said to be quicker. An instant response (173) is elicited to the question, "What number comes before *174?*" But when the question is asked, "What letter comes before 'x'?" the response "w" is not nearly so quickly given. The filing of *72* behind *71* is much quicker than is the filing of *Swift* behind *Sutter*, for example.

Other advantages of the serial numbering method are:

1. Refiling of coded materials is rapid.
2. Expansion is easy and unlimited. New numbers may be assigned without disturbing the arrangement of the existing folders.
3. Transfer of inactive records is facilitated, especially in the offices where case numbers or contract numbers are used. The oldest cases or contracts have the lowest numbers and are together in the files rather than scattered throughout the filing equipment. The folders for the completed cases or contracts may be removed to storage quickly and put into numeric sequence easily. Entire drawers or cabinets may be released for numbers that are being assigned to new cases and contracts.
4. All cross-references appear in the card file and do not congest the file folders or drawers.
5. A file drawer filled with guides and folders with tabs containing *only* numbers is secure from curious eyes or intentional seekers of information. This need for secrecy may be important for patents, research projects, formulae, or clients' names.
6. In an office using a serial numbering method, orders, invoices, ledger accounts, and correspondence of one customer all bear the same number, making reference to them very easy. Fewer errors may occur in matching invoice and payment, for example.
7. A complete list of the names and addresses of correspondents is instantly available in the alphabetic card index.
8. Time and effort in labeling are saved because numbers can be affixed much more quickly than can correspondents' names or names of subjects. Folders may be numbered in advance of their use.
9. Misfiled folders are easily detected because numbers out of place are easier to locate than are misfiled letters of the alphabet.

Disadvantages. Disadvantages, too, are evident in the serial numbering method:

1. Transposition of numbers, inaccuracy in copying, and the omission of a digit are frequent errors that may not be easily detected. Carelessness results in misfiling—carelessness on the part of the person who wrote the original number as well as carelessness on the part of the files operator who filed the paper.
2. Numeric filing is an indirect method. Reference to an alphabetic index is necessary to ascertain whether or not a number has been previously assigned to the case, contract, or correspondent whose papers are being handled. Whenever filing routine is expanded and more time is required to get papers into the file, more mistakes can be made.
3. More equipment is necessary for the numeric method than for the alphabetic method; the cost is therefore somewhat higher.
4. Because of the necessity of consulting an alphabetic index in order to file papers by the numeric method, congestion around the card file can arise if there is frequent reference to its contents by more than one person.
5. Two methods of filing are involved—alphabetic and numeric. All of the disadvantages inherent in the alphabetic method are therefore found in numeric filing, in addition to the disadvantages of the numeric method.
6. Because of the necessity of checking each piece of correspondence with an alphabetic card file, sorting alphabetically may be done first. Then resorting is done numerically prior to filing. This double sorting requires extra time.
7. If the card file and the accession book are not kept meticulously, one correspondent's papers might be in several folders in the file; a number could be assigned twice; part of the papers of one correspondent could be in a miscellaneous folder and part of his papers in a numbered folder.

The serial numbering method is seldom used for ordinary correspondence filing because the alphabetic systems have been found less costly to operate. However, in offices such as those mentioned on page 129, numeric filing can fill a definite need.

SECTION 2. NUMERIC SYSTEMS BASED ON NONCONSECUTIVE NUMBERING

Two examples of nonconsecutive filing arrangements are known as terminal digit and middle digit filing. They are so named because filing order is first determined by the end or 'terminal" digits or by digits in the "middle" of a number.

TERMINAL DIGIT FILING

In a serially numbered file, growth occurs always at the end of the file, as numbered folders are added in consecutive order. As a result, a high percentage of work at the files usually takes place at the end of the files and therefore leads to congestion. Possibly the folders with the highest numbers are the most active, and reference to them by several people simultaneously is physically difficult because the files operators get in each other's way. As the file grows and the numbers become larger (as in the case of serially numbered items such as checks, mortgages, savings accounts, hospital cases, and insurance policies, with large numbers of six, seven, eight, or more digits), the large numbers often cause misfiling and confusion.

To surmount these difficulties, *terminal digit filing* was developed. It is used for material that is numeric in character, such as motor vehicle serial numbers, box car numbers, insurance policy numbers.

The numbers are read in groups from *right to left* instead of from left to right. The digits in the number are usually separated into groups of twos or threes. For example, the number 293746 could be divided 293 746 or 29 37 46 (sometimes written with hyphens: 29-37-46). The groups of digits are identified as primary, secondary,

and final numbers: $\underline{29}$ $\underline{37}$ $\underline{46}$
                              Final   Secondary   Primary

The primary digits usually indicate a drawer number. If the volume of papers filed is great, more than one drawer may be needed to house all items with numbers ending in the same primary digits. Figure 6-10 shows the arrangement of folders or numbered cards in drawer No. 46. All papers within that drawer bear numbers ending in *46*. The guide numbers in a drawer are determined by the numbers of the secondary digits, beginning with *00* and ending with *99* in each primary-numbered section of the file. The order of arrangement behind a certain guide is determined by the final digits. The numbered material filed in Figure 6-10 is correctly arranged. If the next item added to the file were numbered 8-37-47, the item would not go in this drawer but would be placed in the No. 47 drawer. Thus, as numbered material is added to the file, all the new material would be distributed among different drawers according to the last two digits of the new numbers. (In a serially numbered drawer, all new items would go at the end of the file, with the numbers increasing consecutively.)

Guides for final digits may be used as the file expands. Final digit guides would be in a position at the left of the file drawer, separating every ten or twenty folders. When expansion occurs in the file indicated in Figure 6-9, the first section in the drawer would look like the illustration in Figure 6-10.

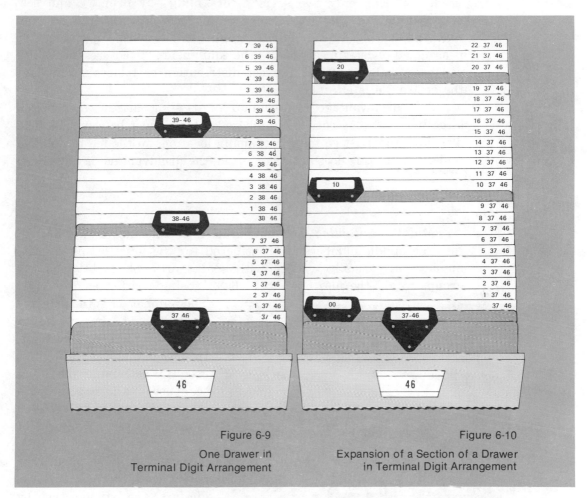

Figure 6-9

One Drawer in
Terminal Digit Arrangement

Figure 6-10

Expansion of a Section of a Drawer
in Terminal Digit Arrangement

ADVANTAGES AND DISADVANTAGES OF TERMINAL DIGIT FILING

Once a files operator has been trained to use terminal digit filing, fewer errors may occur with this system than with consecutive or serial numbering. Because the folder numbers are divided into groups of two or three digits, the files operator is concerned with only two or three numbers at one time. Transpositions and misreading of numbers are less likely to occur. Several operators can be looking for consecutively numbered folders at the same time because they need not wait until someone else moves; they will be working in separate drawers. Material can be sorted faster than it can be with serially numbered items; a 100-division sorter can be used, requiring only two sorts before filing—by primary and secondary numbers. The use of color coding on folders is frequent and reduces misfiling. In especially large file installations, a files operator is assigned to certain sections of the equipment; "fixed" responsibility can be effectively placed. Perfect distribution of folders throughout the entire file is effected.

One disadvantage of terminal digit filing arises whenever a large block of consecutively numbered folders must be removed. The files operator must go to each of many locations in the file to pull the folders. Since this does not occur often, the disadvantage is not great.

MIDDLE DIGIT FILING

Middle digit filing is a modification of terminal digit filing in that the middle numbers are considered for the first sorting. Again, numbers are usually written with spaces or hyphens between the groups to aid the files operator: 764321 being written as 76 43 21.

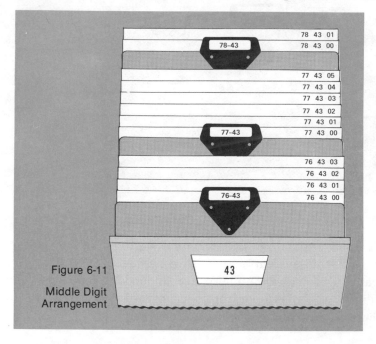

78 43 01
78 43 00
78-43

77 43 05
77 43 04
77 43 03
77 43 02
77 43 01
77 43 00
77-43

76 43 03
76 43 02
76 43 01
76 43 00
76-43

43

Figure 6-11

Middle Digit Arrangement

The number *43* is the primary digit, *76* is the secondary digit, and *21* is the final digit. In this example, *43* is first used to determine the filing sequence. All papers with the middle digits *43* are filed in one drawer or section of the file. (See Figure 6-11.) Sequence within the *43* drawer is determined first by the digits at the left and then by the digits at the right. Guide numbers are determined by the secondary digits.

In middle digit filing a block of 100 sequential papers will be kept together. Middle digit arrangement is often used in large insurance companies where it has been found desirable to keep together blocks of outstanding policies issued by one agent. Figure 6-11 shows that agent "76" has on file four policies (Nos. 4300, 4301, 4302, and 4303) and that there is space in his section of the file for ninety-six additional policies. Agent "77" has six policies on file (4300 through 4305) ; agent "78" has only two policies on file.

It is simpler to convert from a straight numerical filing arrangement to a middle digit filing arrangement than from a straight numerical file to a terminal digit file. Blocks of 100 consecutively numbered folders can be transferred at one time. The sorting operation for middle digit filing is reduced to two sorts—by primary and then by secondary numbers. Middle digit filing works most effectively with numbers not exceeding six digits; if more than six digits are used, the secondary digits would expand from two digits to three. Because of the necessity of "reading" a number beginning with the *middle* digits of it, moving to the left and then to the right, a period of re-training of files operators is needed. This reading is contrary to normal reading and is difficult to learn.

If terminal or middle digit filing is contemplated with the use of hanging or suspension file equipment, a revision of the guiding system described above is necessary. In hanging files, folders serve as guides. In any office where conversion of existing files to a terminal or middle digit system is considered, the help of a trained files analyst should be sought.

SKIP NUMBERING

Omission of numbers in a sequence may be used when assigning numbers to names, so that alphabetic as well as numeric sequence may be maintained. This method is known as *skip numbering, alpha numbers,* or *alpha-numeric.*

Names originally arranged in alphabetic sequence may be assigned numbers. The assignment is made with intervals or skips of 100 between the names. As new names appear to be filed between the original names, they are assigned numbers between those originally assigned; alphabetic arrangement may still be maintained. Obviously, a large expansion of names in some section of the file would soon cause difficulty in maintaining the absolute alphabetic sequence. In this event, alternatives are (1) to accept less than strict alphabetic sequence by assigning a number out of order; (2) to renumber all names; or (3) to add another digit at the end of each already assigned number so that nine new numbers are provided between names.

For example, a sequence was started as 100, 200, 300, 400, and so on. (Figure 6-12.) All numbers between 100 and 200 have been used (100, 101, 102, 103, 104, 105, 106, etc.). It is necessary to add a new name between that assigned 100 and the one assigned 101. By adding a zero at the end of all assigned numbers, the sequence then becomes 1000, 1010, 1020, 1030, 1040, 1050, 1060, and so on. Nine new numbers are available between all of the original ones. (Between 100 and 101, which are now numbered 1000 and 1010, are 1001, 1002, 1003, 1004, 1005, 1006, 1007, 1008, and 1009.) Colleges are frequent users of alpha numbers for assignment to student names.

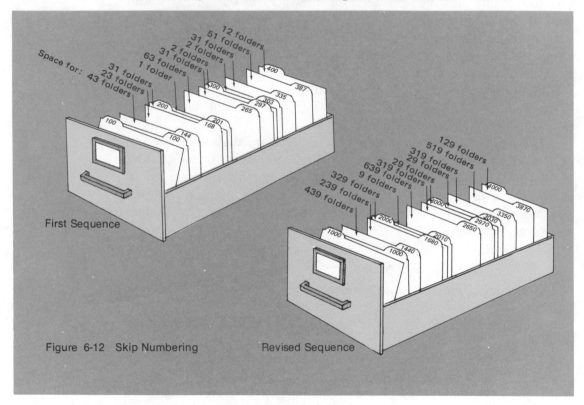

Figure 6-12   Skip Numbering

PHONETIC OR SOUND METHOD

An adaptation of the numeric method is one that combines sound and spelling into a numbered code. In the straight alphabetic method, as described in Chapter 4, names are filed as they are spelled. An estimate has been made, however, that over 100,000 surnames can be spelled in two or more ways. This presents difficulty to the files operator, especially when he is called upon to find a name for which the exact spelling is not known. For example, the surname *Beal* can be spelled *Beel, Behl, Bael, Beale, Biehl, Beall, Beil, Bealle,* and *Beyl,* among others. In a large file based on the alphabetic method, correspondence records for these correspondents might be far apart, and the time consumed in locating the names would be extremely great unless the files operator knew the correct spelling in each instance. He might not know the exact spelling because of poor handwriting, typing errors, or a telephoned request for the name by someone who was uncertain of the spelling of the name.

Large files containing many folders for common surnames (such as *Anderson, Brown, Johnson,* and *Smith*) have an extreme congestion of similar names with a resulting problem of correct filing. For any filing operation in which multiplicity of names and spellings offer almost endless possibilities for error, a group-name method employing *sound* may be more efficient.

Soundex. A system using the phonetic method of filing is manufactured by Sperry Remington, Office Systems and Machines, Sperry Rand Corporation. Named *Soundex,* this system, by means of a special coding process, eliminates the necessity for knowing the exact spelling of names. The Soundex system groups together names that are spelled or pronounced in a similar manner but that would be widely separated if they were arranged in alphabetic order. This method of filing is especially useful where files containing many surnames are found; for example, in hospitals, credit bureaus, insurance companies, banks, public utilities, and government offices. The Social Security Administration of the federal government uses this system, as do some auto license bureaus in various states.

In the Soundex system, the first indexing unit of a name (the surname of an individual or the first coded unit of a company name) is given a code consisting of one letter and three digits. The letter in the code is the first letter of the surname or the first company unit (such as "A" in Adams); the three digits are numbers that are assigned to, and therefore represent, certain consonants in the surname or first unit. The digits are assigned according to the table on page 150, which shows (1) the digits 1 to 6, which are used in making up the numeric part of the code, and (2) the consonants after the first letter of the name that are represented by each of the six digits.

Code Numbers	Letters Represented by the Code Numbers
1	b, f, p, v
2	c, g, j, k, q, s, x, z
3	d, t
4	l
5	m, n
6	r

The vowels (a, e, i, o, u) and the consonants w, h, and y are not represented by code numbers; therefore they are disregarded.

If a name does not contain enough consonants represented by code numbers to make up a three-digit code, enough zeros are used at the right to make a complete three-digit code.

Examples of Soundex coding are as follows:

Smith: S 530 S (initial letter); m is "5"; i is disregarded; t is "3"; h is disregarded; since there are only two digits, "0" is added as the third number in the code.

Jolson: J 425 J (initial letter); o is disregarded; l is "4"; s is "2"; o is disregarded; n is "5."

Masterson: M 236 M (initial letter); a is disregarded; s is "2"; t is "3"; e is disregarded; r is "6." Three digits have been assigned; no more than three digits are ever used even though the name is long and has many more letters.

Shea: S 000 S (initial letter); h is disregarded; e and a are disregarded. Since there must be three digits, three zeros are used.

Loso: L 200 L (initial letter); o is disregarded; s is "2"; o is disregarded. Since there must be three digits, two zeros are added to make a total of three.

Some additional rules needed for applying Soundex coding are:

1. Never assign a digit code to the initial letter.

2. Double, triple, or quadruple letter equivalents are considered as one letter. This rule refers to identical letters (tt, nn, rr) and to letters that fall into the same category (dt, sq, cs, mn, pf). Examples are:

Schmidt: S 530 *S* (initial letter); *c* is in the same category as (is "equivalent" to) the *S* and is therefore disregarded; *h* is disregarded; *m* is "5"; *i* is disregarded; *d* is "3"; *t* is equivalent to *d* and is therefore disregarded. Since there are only two digits, a zero must be added for the third digit in the code.

Jackson: J 250 *J* (initial letter); *a* is disregarded; *c, k,* and *s* are all equivalents and are considered as one letter, that is, "2"; *o* is disregarded; *n* is "5." Since there are only two digits, a zero must be added to complete the code.

Wosczinsky: W 252 *W* (initial letter); *o* is disregarded; *s, c,* and *z* are all equivalents and are considered as one letter, that is, "2"; *i* is disregarded; *n* is "5"; *s* and *k* are equivalents and are considered as one letter, that is, "2." The three digits in the code have been determined.

Kjolsen: K 425 *K* (initial letter); *j* is in the same category as *K* and is therefore disregarded; *o* is disregarded; *l* is "4"; *s* is "2"; *e* is disregarded; *n* is "5."

3. When the same letter equivalents are separated by a vowel or *y,* the letters are coded separately.

4. When the same letter equivalents are separated by *h* or *w,* only one of the letter equivalents is coded. Examples of (3) and (4) are:

Brennan: B 655 *B* (initial letter); *r* is "6"; *e* is disregarded; *n* and *n* are the same, that is, "5"; *a* is disregarded but is **considered to be a "divider"**; *n* is "5."

Colgyser: C 422 *C* (initial letter); *o* is disregarded; *l* is "4"; *g* is "2"; *y* is disregarded but is considered to be a "divider"; *s* is "2." The letters *e* and *r* are not considered because the code already has three digits.

Brochson: B 625 *B* (initial letter); *r* is "6"; *o* is disregarded; *c* is "2"; *h* is disregarded; *s* would ordinarily be coded "2" but it is considered to be right next to the *c* which was coded "2"—the *h* is not a "divider"— therefore, *s* is not coded; *o* is disregarded; *n* is "5."

Erkwxsol: E 624 *E* (initial letter); *r* is "6"; *k* is "2"; *w* is disregarded and is not considered to be a "divider"; *x* and *s* are equivalents to *k* and are therefore not coded; *o* is disregarded; *l* is "4."

Brocoson: B 622 *B* (initial letter); *r* is "6"; *o* is disregarded; *c* is "2"; *o* is disregarded but it is a "divider"; *s* is "2." No other letters need be considered because there are now three digits in the code.

Sysnnal: S 254 *S* (initial letter); *y* is disregarded but it is a "divider"; *s* is "2"; *n* occurs twice and is coded only once, that is, "5"; *a* is disregarded; *l* is "4."

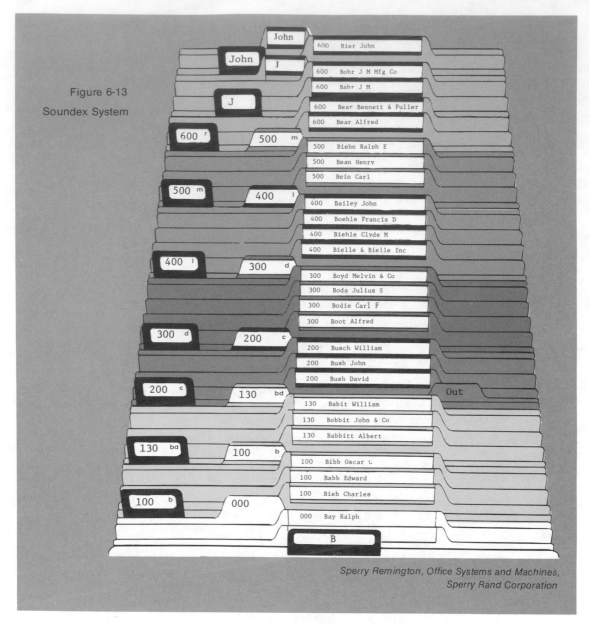

Figure 6-13

Soundex System

John	
John	J
	600 Bier John
	600 Bohr J M Mfg Co
	600 Bahr J M
J	600 Bear Bennett & Fuller
	600 Bear Alfred
600 r	500 m
	500 Biehn Ralph E
	500 Bean Henry
	500 Bein Carl
500 m	400 l
	400 Bailey John
	400 Boehle Francis D
	400 Biehle Clyde M
	400 Bielle & Bielle Inc
400 l	300 d
	300 Boyd Melvin & Co
	300 Boda Julius S
	300 Bodie Carl F
	300 Boot Alfred
300 d	200 c
	200 Busch William
	200 Bush John
	200 Bush David
200 c	130 bd	Out
	130 Babit William
	130 Bobbit John & Co
	130 Babbitt Albert
130 bd	100 b
	100 Bibb Oscar L
	100 Babb Edward
	100 Bieb Charles
100 b	000
	000 Bay Ralph
	B

Sperry Remington, Office Systems and Machines,
Sperry Rand Corporation

Figure 6-13 shows the arrangement of guides and folders in a drawer organized according to the Soundex system. Primary alphabetic guides corresponding to the first letter of the surname or the first company unit are white and are in fourth position. Guides in first position bear code numbers and code letters. This same arrangement of numbered guides is found behind every alphabetic guide (for example, Guide B in Figure 6-13) in a file based on the Soundex system. All the "100" guides are red; all the "200" guides are orange; all the "300" guides are yellow; all the "400" guides are green; all the "500" guides are blue; and all the "600" guides are violet. All guides and folders within any group of 100 numbers are color coded to match the color of the first-position guide in that series.

Because of the heavy use of the second indexing unit in an individual's name or a company name to determine alphabetic sequence within each number group, second-position alphabetic guides (see "J" and "John" in Figure 6-13) may be used to separate the second-unit names for ease of location.

Individual folders bearing code numbers and names have double-width tabs in fourth and fifth combined positions. Special indicators occupy the sixth position.

A miscellaneous folder with its tab in third position and bearing the same caption and color as the guide it follows is the last item within each numbered section.

The selection of the first-position guides depends on the volume of names in a particular alphabetic section of the file. The *"B"* section pictured in Figure 6-13 shows the guides for numbers 100, 130, 200, 300, 400, 500, and 600. The "S" section might have guides numbered 500, 510, 513, 516, 520, 525, 530, and 545. The individual folders with code numbers S510, S511, and S512 would be the only ones behind the 510 guide in the "S" section; but there might be hundreds of them. The "R" section might have guides numbered 500, 510, 520, etc. Only folders with numbers R510, R511, R512, R513, R514, R515, and R516 would be behind the 510 guide in the "R" section, as no number higher than 6 is ever used in the Soundex System.

In all sections, names on the folders behind the guides are in numeric order and not in alphabetic order according to the first units because the first unit has been preempted by the Soundex Code. Folders bearing the same number are arranged alphabetically according to the second units of the names. In the 100 section in Figure 6-13, *Charles* comes before *Edward,* which is in front of *Oscar;* in the 400 section, *Bielle* precedes *Clyde,* which comes before *Francis,* which is in front of *John.* This point is so important that it bears repeating: Filing arrangement is first by alphabet according to the letter preceding the code number; all numbers after that letter are arranged in numeric sequence according to the three numbers in the code; and if there are several identically numbered individual folders, arrangement of those folders is alphabetically determined by the *second and succeeding* units of the names. Papers of correspondents who do not have individual folders are filed in the miscellaneous folders in third position. Papers coded with the same code are filed in the same miscellaneous folder, and they are arranged first according to the alphabetic order of the second and succeeding indexing units, and second according to date in each group.

Rules for the arrangement of names alphabetically (such as those given in Chapter 3) are very important in determining the order of the folders. Only the first unit is almost completely removed from alphabetic consideration because it has been used for determining the numeric code. Its only connection with alphabetic arrangement is that its initial letter indicates the alphabetic section in the file drawer in which the folder is placed. At this time a knowledge of and strict adherence to the rules of alphabetic filing are absolutely necessary.

Some of the advantages claimed for the Soundex system are:

1. Every name has a positive, unchanging number.
2. 98 percent of all family names are automatically grouped regardless of spelling.
3. Unlimited expansion is possible.
4. Only 6 numbers are used instead of the 26 letters of the alphabet.
5. Numeric sorting, filing, and finding—the speediest of all methods—are used.
6. Checking of the files is rapid.
7. File folders used in other types of files can be converted into folders suitable for a Soundex file.

SECTION 3. OTHER NUMERIC FILING METHODS

One of the simplest of the numeric methods is chronologic filing—filing by date—which is explained on pages 22 and 23. The numeric method may also be combined with geographic filing, to be explained in the next chapter, and with subject filing, discussion of which will be found in Chapter 9.

With the use of computers and other mechanical means of storing data growing each year, the use of numbers is very important in identifying data, in storing it, and in retrieving it. The special coding systems needed in this age of mechanization are discussed in Chapter 11.

For Review and Discussion

1. Examples of various numbers that may be used by individuals in their everyday life are given in the first paragraph on page 127. What additional ones can you think of?

2. Why is a serial numbering method seldom used for filing ordinary correspondence?

3. Is a numeric method of filing considered a speedy method of filing? Why or why not?

4. The comment has been made that numeric filing is a secret method of filing. What does this mean?

5. Is the numeric method a direct or an indirect method of filing? Explain the difference between the two methods.

6. Are cross-references made only in the alphabetic card index in a numeric file? If so, why? If not, why not?

7. Why are misplaced folders bearing numbers on their tabs easier to locate than are misplaced folders that have complete names typed on their tabs?

8. In a numeric file is an alphabetic arrangement used? If not, why not? If so, in what places?

9. In what order are papers placed in the numbered folders in numeric filing?

10. Why are mistakes in the card file serious?

11. How could it happen that some of a correspondent's papers would be filed in a numbered folder while other papers of this same correspondent would be filed in a miscellaneous folder?

12. Can a number that has been assigned to one correspondent be used for another correspondent at a later time, say, ten years later? Why or why not?

13. In a system in which each correspondent is assigned a number, why is cross-referencing necessary?

14. Will fewer errors probably occur in terminal digit filing or in consecutive (serial) numbering filing? Why?

15. How does the addition of folders to the file in terminal digit or middle digit filing differ from the addition of folders in a serially numbered file?

16. Why or why not are an accession book and a card file necessary in:

    (a) Skip number filing?
    (b) Soundex filing?
    (c) Terminal digit filing?
    (d) Middle digit filing?

17. Compare the kinds of equipment needed for numeric filing with that needed for alphabetic filing. Which requires the most equipment? Why?

18. In Soundex filing, how are the rules for alphabetic filing used?

19. If you were searching in the Soundex files for a name that sounded like "Cavanaugh," you would probably look under the code *C 152.* If you could not find it there, where might you look next?

Learning Projects

1. Write a short memo report describing the use of numeric filing in one business office in your community. Explain in sufficient detail so that the reader will understand what types of records are filed numerically and what type of numeric method is used.

2. Code each of the following names with the correct Soundex code:
   - (1) Byron E. Bergdall, Tama, Iowa
   - (2) W. Bergdolt & Sons, Salt Lake City, Utah
   - (3) The Bird Enterprises, Inc., Hilo, Hawaii
   - (4) Burraror Building & Loan Assn., Burckdall, Massachusetts
   - (5) Dr. Robert I. Byrd, Binghamton, Maryland
   - (6) Claussen Implement Co., Boise, Idaho
   - (7) Anita Clawson, Albany, New York
   - (8) Robert Closson-Hewitt, Hershey, Pennsylvania
   - (9) Eldredge-Frame-Blodgett, San Rafael, California
   - (10) Mary Thomasina Hicks, Reno, Nevada
   - (11) Hubert A. Janssen, Hartford, Connecticut
   - (12) Elmer Jensen & Associates, Tucson, Arizona
   - (13) Kjaer Imports, Chicago, Illinois
   - (14) Victor A. Klaussen, Victoria, B. C., Canada
   - (15) Michael J. Kobricz, Gary, Indiana
   - (16) Kobritz Advertising Agency, Tulsa, Oklahoma
   - (17) Harry E. Lee, Tampa, Florida
   - (18) Maynard C. Linnekens, Louisville, Kentucky
   - (19) Lloyd V. Lloyd, Providence, Rhode Island
   - (20) Lloyd A. Nelson, Augusta, Maine
   - (21) Harold J. Niehlsson, Minneapolis, Minnesota
   - (22) Peter M. Nilssen & Son, Kansas City, Missouri
   - (23) Nimau Grocery, Brunswick, New Jersey
   - (24) The Nomeau Upholsterers, Washington, D. C.
   - (25) Hazel I. Peifer, Berne, North Carolina
   - (26) Pfeffer, Mayne & Jolson, Seattle, Washington
   - (27) Mark I. Pfeifer, Juneau, Alaska
   - (28) Jerry A. R. Phiffer, Memphis, Tennessee
   - (29) Schadlich Bros., Huntington, West Virginia
   - (30) Jos. Schaefer Company, Dallas, Texas
   - (31) Joseph A. Shaefer, Omaha, Nebraska
   - (32) The Shafer Specialty House, Detroit, Michigan
   - (33) Helen O. Sheaffer, Eau Claire, Wisconsin

(34) Professor Richard M. Stephens, Columbus, Ohio
(35) Stevens Optical Co., Springfield, New Hampshire
(36) Whighom & Whighom, Bozeman, Montana
(37) Thos. P. Whitcher, Minot, North Dakota
(38) Wan Kyung Wong, Portland, Oregon

3. In what order would you file the names having the same code number in Learning Project No. 2?

4. An office has converted its files from the alphabetic method to skip numbering. The names of the customers are listed below with the assigned numbers opposite their names:

Ace Engineering Company—100
American Ink Products Co.—150
Bartels, William E.—200
Brower, George L.—250
Buffalo Insurance Co.—275
Buy & Save Meat Co.—290
By-Line, The—295
Byers & Butterfield—298
Byrd, James L.—299
Byron's Shoes—300
C & A Consumers—301
C F C Forms—305

How would you maintain strict alphabetic sequence if the next correspondents' names were:

(1) Cafferty Bros.
(2) Biltmore Hotel
(3) Aaronson & Sons Builders
(4) Burry Bakeries
(5) Byzantine Mosaics
(6) Harold P. Byrne & Sons

5. You work for the regional sales manager of a company whose product is automatic coffee-making machines. His region includes the states of California, Nevada, Arizona, and Hawaii. He wants you to set up a numeric coding system that will show three pieces of information in code: the state, the size of the city, and the number of salesmen he supervises in each city. His reason for using code numbers is so that folder labels in the files will not reveal information to the casual observer, yet your employer and you can see at a glance the population range within which the city falls, and you can easily pull all folders where, for instance, three salesmen are indicated.

It is suggested that your coding system be something like this: NV.1a (the *NV* meaning Nevada, the *1* meaning city such as Carson City with a population of under 15,000, and the *a* meaning 1 salesman in that city). Set up the coding table that could be given to anyone who was assigned the task of giving code numbers to cities, their population, and the number of salesmen within the various cities.

Laboratory Assignments 9 and 10   You should now complete Laboratory Assignments 9 (Numeric Correspondence Filing) and 10 (Numeric Correspondence Filing—Review) in *Records Management—Laboratory Materials.*

Chapter **7**

Geographic method
of records storage

Where the primary interest of a business lies in *place* information, geographic filing is advantageous as it is a method of alphabetic arrangement based first upon the location of the correspondents and second upon their names. This method of filing, therefore, is particularly useful for those businesses having sales organizations in charge of many branches; those licensed to operate in certain states but not in others (such as insurance companies); public utilities, where street arrangement is of primary importance (a specialized kind of geographic arrangement); and real estate firms that have listings according to plats of land areas. Mail-order houses and publishers whose primary business is conducted through the United States mail must arrange their addressing plates or stencils by geographic areas so that the second-class mail will be accepted by the Post Office. Frequently, the correspondence files of such companies are similarly arranged. Governmental agencies often file by state or by county. Jobbers, wholesalers, manufacturers, and subscription departments find the geographic method extremely adaptable to their use. In addition, businesses with overseas branches and customers may find the geographic method to be of value.

Type of business being operated, the geographical areas in which the correspondents are located, and the way in which the files are to be used are factors which determine the divisions of a geographic file. Generally, a geographic arrangement is one of two types: (1) the location name guide plan and (2) the lettered guide plan.

SECTION 1. LOCATION NAME GUIDE PLAN FOR
GEOGRAPHIC METHOD

BASIS OF PLAN

A geographic filing system based on the location name guide plan has location names (names of countries, provinces, states, counties, cities) as the main sections into which the file is divided and according to which correspondents' names are filed alphabetically.

ILLUSTRATIVE SYSTEM ANALYSIS

Figure 7-1 shows part of a drawer in a filing system based on the location name guide plan. The setup of the system is as follows:

1. The first item in the drawer is the guide for the state name *Illinois*. Since the state is the largest geographic division into which the file is divided, the tab of the guide is double width and centered to give the guide prominence.

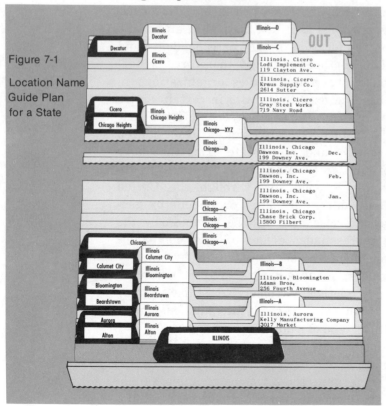

Figure 7-1

Location Name
Guide Plan
for a State

2. The second item in the drawer is a city guide for *Alton*, the first location name guide after the state guide.

3. The third item is a miscellaneous city folder for *Alton*. In this folder are filed the materials from all correspondents located in Alton.

4. The fourth item is a city guide for *Aurora*.

5. The fifth item is an individual folder for *Kelly Manufacturing Company*, located in Aurora, Illinois. This folder was opened when the correspondence with the company (originally filed in the miscellaneous Aurora city folder) increased to the number of pieces requiring the opening of an individual folder. It is placed after the *Aurora* city guide but before the miscellaneous city folder.

6. The sixth item is the miscellaneous city folder for *Aurora.*

7. The last item in the "A" section of this file drawer is a miscellaneous state folder with the caption *Illinois—A.* In this folder are filed materials from correspondents located in cities beginning with the letter A for which there is not yet a city folder.

8. The next six items in the drawer are those that fall under "B."

9. Since Chicago is the location of so many correspondents, one miscellaneous city folder (in addition to the individual folders for correspondents in that city) is not large enough. Therefore the names of those correspondents will have to be filed in alphabetic groups, each group in a separate folder. To make these folders stand out from the other city folders in the drawer, the *Chicago* section is introduced by a double-width tab in positions 1 and 2, and the *Chicago* alphabetic folders are placed in position 3. Individual folders for correspondents located in Chicago are placed in alphabetic order among the Chicago alphabetic folders, with each individual folder preceding the Chicago folder bearing the letter that corresponds to the first letter of the first unit of the correspondent's name.

10. If the correspondence with one individual or firm is very heavy, monthly individual folders are provided (see *Dawson, Inc.*). These are placed in the file according to state, city, name, and finally, date.

11. An OUT guide is placed so that the word "OUT" is in fifth position.

ADAPTATIONS OF THE LOCATION NAME GUIDE PLAN

Foreign countries. The location name guide plan can be readily adapted to the needs of various companies. For example, if a business has correspondence with a large number of individuals and firms in Canada, it might have a filing arrangement similar to that in Figure 7-2 on page 162. The name "Canada" appears on the label of the file drawer. In the illustration, the following arrangement is used: (a) the double-width tabs in combined third and fourth positions indicate the names of the Canadian provinces—the largest geographic sections of Canada; (b) position 1 is used for city guides arranged alphabetically after the provinces in which they are located; (c) position 2 is used for guides to indicate alphabetic breakdown of correspondents' names in cities; (d) position 3 is used for miscellaneous city folders; (e) position 4 is used for miscellaneous province folders; (f) the last two combined positions are used for individual folders; and (g) OUT guides occupy fifth position.

This same type of arrangement can be set up for other countries. A filing system for Mexico, for example, would show states and cities; a filing system for Italy would show regions and cities.

Figure 7-2

Location Name Guide Plan
for a Country

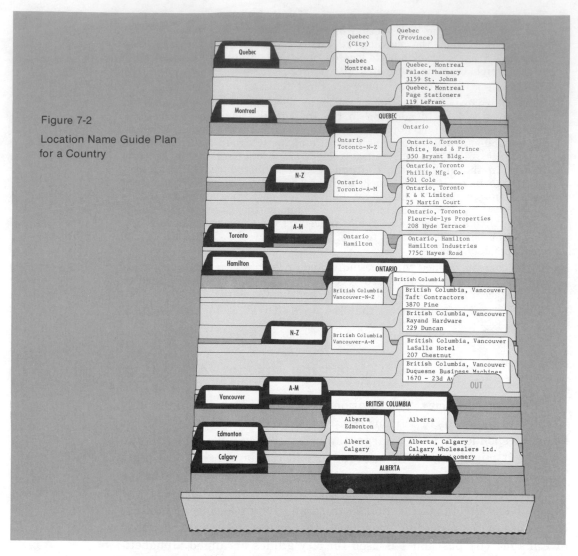

States. If a business needs to break its geographic arrangement of states into both counties and cities, it could have a location name guide plan similar to that in Figure 7-3 on page 163.

Districts within states. If the nature of the business demands a breakdown of the states into regions or districts, the filing system can reflect this aspect of the business by the arrangement of the captions on the guides. Figure 7-4 on page 163 shows how the filing system of a business operating on the West Coast divides the state of California into regions.

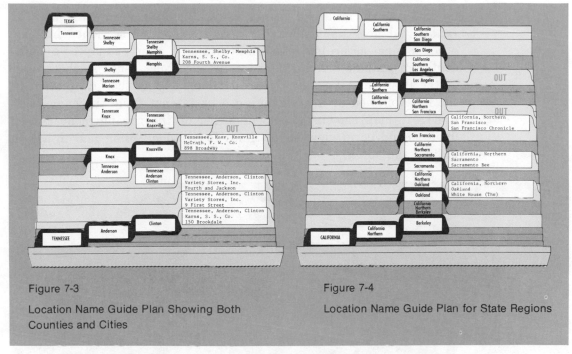

Figure 7-3

Location Name Guide Plan Showing Both
Counties and Cities

Figure 7-4

Location Name Guide Plan for State Regions

Local correspondence. Some businesses (public utility companies, for example) that have customers in a restricted area, such as a city or a county, must have the filing system geared to the actual locations of the customers. Therefore, the filing system must indicate names of suburbs, names of streets, and names of customers with their house or building numbers. Such a system is illustrated in Figure 7-5. Note that in this filing system there are no miscellaneous folders; each folder is an individual folder for one person, one business, or one organization. The guides indicate suburbs and streets in the suburbs.

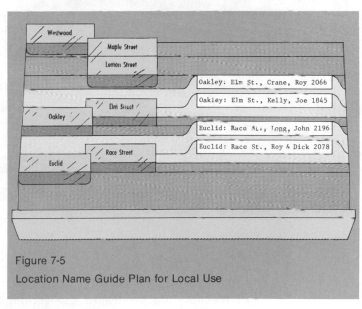

Figure 7-5

Location Name Guide Plan for Local Use

Other arrangements. The primary guide arrangement may be for regions without regard to the alphabet. A region arrangement may be small (such as areas within a city, as in Figure 7-5), may be fanned out geographically from a central spot or sectioned in some other manner according to areas drawn on a map, or may be a continental geographic arrangement by distance zones, such as those used by the Post Office (the area nearest "home" being the first section in the file, followed by areas ranging ever farther from the home location). A map showing the boundaries of the arrangement agreed upon should be in view at all times to avoid misfiling and to aid in coding and filing.

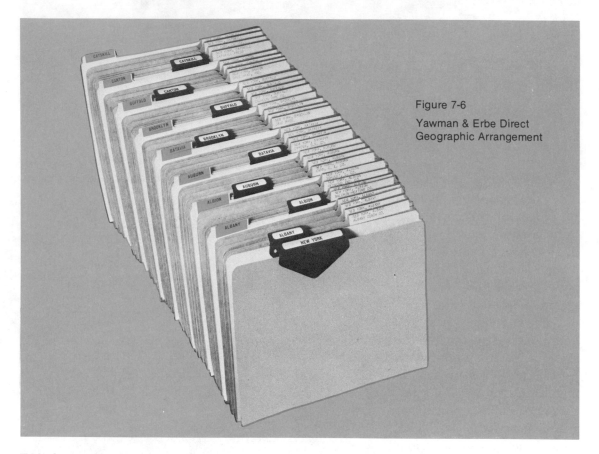

Figure 7-6

Yawman & Erbe Direct Geographic Arrangement

TAILOR-MADE SYSTEM

The *Direct Geographic System* (Yawman & Erbe of California Corporation) is a location name guide arrangement, containing two-fifths-cut state guides in the second and third combined positions, with fifth-cut city guides arranged alphabetically in alternating second and third positions. (See Figure 7-6). Miscellaneous folders are filed in first position and have tabs that correspond to the names on the city guides. Individual folders are in fourth and fifth combined positions.

SECTION 2. LETTERED GUIDE PLAN

BASIS OF PLAN

The lettered guide plan, like the alphabetic filing plan, divides the filing system into alphabetic sections, each section introduced by a lettered and numbered guide (A-1, for example) and closed with a miscellaneous folder with a corresponding caption (A-1 to match the A-1 guide). Individual folders and city folders are opened as the volume of correspondence with individual correspondents or in certain cities increases.

ILLUSTRATIVE SYSTEM ANALYSIS

Figure 7-7 shows part of a drawer in a filing system based on the lettered guide plan. The setup of the system is as follows:

1. The first item in the drawer is the guide for the name of the state, *Michigan* — the largest geographic division into which the file is divided. The tab of the guide is double width and centered to give it prominence.

2. The primary guides are alphabetic guides that divide the state into alphabetic sections. The guides are staggered in positions 1, 2, and 3. Each guide indicates the section of the alphabet within which are filed city names in that section. The guide tabs are numbered consecutively so that they will be kept in correct order.

3. Each primary guide is accompanied by a corresponding miscellaneous alphabetic folder, which is placed at the end of

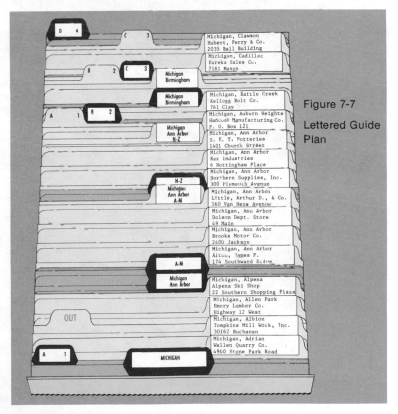

Figure 7-7

Lettered Guide Plan

that particular alphabetic section. The folder has the same caption as that of the primary guide, and it is placed in the same position as the primary guide. Each miscellaneous alphabetic folder houses materials from correspondents located in cities with names beginning with the letter of the alphabet on the folder.

4. In fourth position appear several types of equipment: (a) special city guides to indicate cities for which there is a considerable volume of material (*Michigan, Ann Arbor*); (b) special alphabetic guides that provide an alphabetic breakdown of correspondents' names in the cities identified by the special city guides (*A-M* and *N-Z*); (c) special city folders to accompany the special city guides (*Michigan, Ann Arbor, A-M* and *Michigan, Birmingham*); and (d) OUT guides that are used as substitutes for folders or papers that have been removed from the files.

5. Individual folders with double-width tabs appear in fifth and sixth positions. Note that the caption for an individual folder contains the name of the state and that of the city in which the correspondent is located as the first line on the label. The second line bears the correspondent's name; the third line, the street address.

TAILOR-MADE SYSTEM

Another system based on the lettered guide plan is the Sperry Remington Geographic System, shown below in Figure 7-8. Insertable

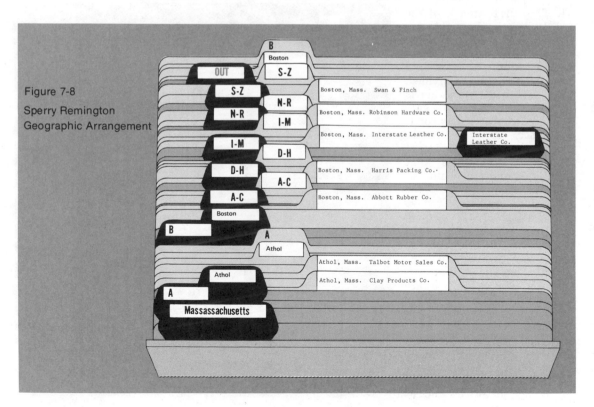

Figure 7-8

Sperry Remington

Geographic Arrangement

tabs are used to allow for variation and individuality in this lettered guide arrangement. A guide with a two-sevenths-cut tab is located in first position for each state. Also in first position are sixth-cut alphabetic guides that divide the file into alphabetic city sections. Guides with printed tabs in second position bear the names of cities and towns and are arranged alphabetically in each group. Also in second position are alphabetic guides for subdividing names in large cities. Miscellaneous folders occupy third position; the *Athol* and *A* folders are examples of miscellaneous folders in Figure 7-8. Individual folders occupy fourth, fifth, and sixth combined positions. In the last position are special guides for extremely active correspondents and OUT indicators.

SECTION 3. SUPPLIES FOR GEOGRAPHIC METHOD

GUIDES AND FOLDERS

Guides. Guides printed with state, county, and important city names are available for purchase from some manufacturers of filing equipment. Since the needs of offices are so varied, the usual practice is to use guides with insertable tabs and to prepare folder labels as needed. The file can then be set up with whatever captions are necessary to the business. Additions are made as they are needed, and subdivisions are made when the file becomes crowded at certain places.

Whatever the arrangement decided upon, the primary guides ordinarily bear the names of the largest divisions. An exception is the placement of the name of the largest division, such as the name of a country or of a state, on the drawer label. If this is done, the primary guides can bear the names of the largest divisions, such as states or provinces. Secondary guides are used to subdivide the divisions indicated by the primary guides.

If the file drawers are equipped with rods that go through openings in bottom tabs of the guides, the guides cannot be removed from the file drawers without pulling out the rods. In this case, the guides cannot be taken out of a drawer by mistake or changed in position; therefore, the captions need not contain the name of the state as well as that of the city.

If the file drawers are not equipped with rods, the guides can be taken out of the drawer or changed in position by mistake; therefore, it is best for the guide captions to include the name of the state as well as the name of the city.

Folders. With certain rare exceptions, for every guide there is a similarly labeled miscellaneous folder into which all miscellaneous correspondence pertaining to that locality is filed.

Folder labels may be typed in several ways, but all the folder labels in one filing system should be consistent in style. In each case, however, the top line shows the location of the correspondent; the

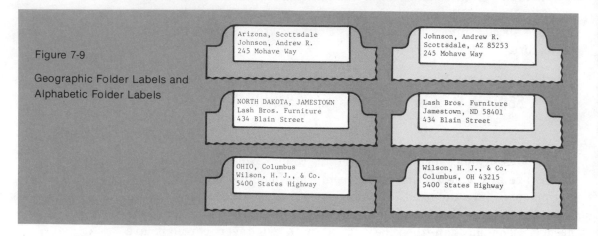

Figure 7-9

Geographic Folder Labels and Alphabetic Folder Labels

Arizona, Scottsdale
Johnson, Andrew R.
245 Mohave Way

Johnson, Andrew R.
Scottsdale, AZ 85253
245 Mohave Way

NORTH DAKOTA, JAMESTOWN
Lash Bros. Furniture
434 Blain Street

Lash Bros. Furniture
Jamestown, ND 58401
434 Blain Street

OHIO, Columbus
Wilson, H. J., & Co.
5400 States Highway

Wilson, H. J., & Co.
Columbus, OH 43215
5400 States Highway

second line shows the name of the correspondent. Figure 7-9 illustrates three different ways of typing the information on folder labels. Reference should be made also to the illustrations of file drawers in this chapter.

In every instance, both the state name and the city name must appear on the tabs of folders to insure their replacement in the file at the proper places. It is wise but not always required to have the state as well as the city name on a guide tab. Because of duplication of city names in several states, confusion would result if the state names were omitted from the folder labels. The same principle holds true for miscellaneous folders showing alphabetic state or city breakdowns; if such folders were labeled only with letters of the alphabet, it would not be possible to determine in which state or city they belonged, once they were removed from their places in the files, without opening the folders to inspect the contents.

Positions of guides and folders. The positions of the tabs on the guides and the folders vary according to the preference of the records manager and the kind of supplies purchased. A basic rule to follow, however, in setting up a geographic file is that the file should be kept uncluttered in appearance. Guide and folder tabs should be arranged for ease in filing and finding. Straight-line arrangement of similar guides and of similar folders (rather than a staggered arrangement) provides for easier expansion. Because the left hand usually does the preliminary searching for the correct position and the right hand moves along the folders, many geographic files are set up with the primary and secondary guides at the left positions and the folders at the right. Often OUT indicators are found at the extreme right where they may be quickly seen.

SUPPLEMENTARY ALPHABETIC CARD INDEX

An alphabetic card index is considered important to geographic filing. Correspondence may be called for by the name of a correspondent rather than by his address if his address has been temporarily forgotten. A card file, consisting of index cards on which are typed the names of the correspondents in alphabetic filing order, followed by their complete addresses, gives all necessary information when the files operator must locate correspondence without knowing the location. The usual typing arrangement is that described on page 168.

If material pertaining to a correspondent is to be filed in a miscellaneous folder, the files operator types the letter "M" for miscellaneous in the upper corner of the index card to identify the type of folder in which the correspondence will be placed.

When the pieces of correspondence with one correspondent reach the number that calls for the opening of an individual folder, the files operator changes the "M" on the index card to an "I" to indicate an individual folder, removes the correspondence from the miscellaneous folder, opens an individual folder, and files the correspondence.

If no card file arranged alphabetically by name is available, finding is seriously delayed. Since it is important to keep the card file current, a quick check should be made before any paper is filed in a geographic file to ascertain whether there is a card for the correspondent and whether the information is correct in the card file. Variations of card filing are explained in greater detail in Chapter 9.

SECTION 4. FILING PROCEDURE FOR GEOGRAPHIC METHOD

The steps in filing (inspecting, indexing, coding, cross-referencing, sorting, filing, charging-out, and following-up) are just as important in the geographic method as they are in the alphabetic and numeric methods.

INSPECTING AND INDEXING

Inspecting and indexing take place at the time a piece of correspondence is picked up by the files operator. Checking to see that the piece has been released for filing and scanning it for content to determine its proper place in the file are always important.

CODING

Coding in geographic filing consists of marking the correspondent's location first. This can be done by circling the pertinent words. The order in which the words are to be considered is sometimes indicated by numbers written above or below the units. The name of the correspondent is then coded in the usual manner (by underlining, checking, starring, and the like). Figure 7-10 shows (1) a letter properly coded for the geographic method of filing and for the preparation of a cross-reference and (2) the cross-reference sheet prepared.

CROSS-REFERENCES

In the geographic filing method, cross-references are made in two places: (1) the alphabetic card file and (2) the files where the correspondence is housed.

In the alphabetic card file, it is necessary to have a card for every name by which a correspondent may be known or by which his materials may be called for. Names of married women, unusual names of individuals, company names composed of several surnames, names of companies that have more than one address, and companies located at one address and doing business under other names in other locations are examples of names that must be cross-referenced. The cards made up for the letter in Figure 7-10 are illustrated in Figure 7-11.

In the file drawers, three kinds of cross-references are used: (1) cross-reference sheets that are filed in folders to refer to specific pieces of correspondence, (2) visible cross-reference guides that are placed in the drawers as permanent cross-references, and (3) SEE ALSO cross-reference notations on folder tabs.

CROSS REFERENCE SHEET

Name or Subject _Pennsylvania , Pittsburgh_
Porter- Hall & Co.
2964 Broadway

Date of Item _August 4, 19--_

Regarding _Programmed learning_

SEE

Name or Subject _Indiana , Muncie_
Porter- Hall & Co.
49 Kimberly Lane

Authorized by _J. Bradley_ Date _8/6/--_

PORTER · HALL

Educational Consultants

49 Kimberly Lane, Muncie, IN 47304

August 4, 19—

AUG 5 19- 9:31 AM

RC

Miss Ester L. Dawes
School of Business
Yorkshire University
Terre Haute, IN 47805

Dear Miss Dawes

We have referred to our Pittsburgh, Pennsylvania, office your request
for fifty brochures explaining in detail the programmed learning
materials we have available for use in summer workshop programs.

We are out of stock of these brochures because of the extraordinary
number of requests which we have filed. Interest in this exciting
and novel material has been extremely high, and we have been pleased
that professors are finding it so worthwhile. You will find the
information in the brochures helpful as well as interesting. Within
the next two weeks you should receive the number you requested.

Very truly yours

H. A. Hall
H. A. Hall
Educational Consultants

sl

2964 Broadway (Pittsburgh) PA 15216

Figure 7-10

Letter Properly Coded and
Cross-Referenced for Geographic Method

Figure 7-11

Card File Cards

A *cross-reference sheet* is used to call attention to a specific piece of correspondence filed in another folder but relating to the material in the folder in which the cross-reference is filed. The cross-reference sheet pictured in Figure 7-10 would be filed alphabetically by the letter "P" in the *Pittsburgh, Pennsylvania,* folder to guide the files operator to the *Muncie, Indiana,* folder, in which the piece of correspondence with Porter-Hall & Co. is filed. Some files operators prefer to eliminate this type of cross-reference by making a facsimile copy of the correspondence to which reference may be made and by placing the facsimile copy in the folder in lieu of a cross-reference sheet. When this procedure is followed, reference to another part of the files is not necessary.

A *visible cross-reference guide* (Figure 7-12) is placed in the file to indicate to the files operator that all correspondence of a company that has several branches, for instance, is filed under the home office address. If the home office of Mortenson, Incorporated, is in San Francisco, and if a branch office is in Monterey, California, all the correspondence would be filed at the home office location; and a visible cross-reference guide would be placed in the file at the proper place for Monterey, California. The cross-reference would be a tabbed sheet of the size and weight of a guide. The caption on the tab would be typed as shown in Figure 7-12. This cross-reference would indicate that all correspondence is filed under the San Francisco ad-

Figure 7-12

Visible Cross-Reference Guide for Geographic Method

dress even though it bears a Monterey address on the letterhead. The words "San Francisco" should be written on each piece of correspondence when it is coded. The cross-reference guide is filed according to the location on the top line of the caption, in geographic sequence with other geographically labeled guides and folders.

SEE ALSO cross-references are used to direct the files operator to sources of related information. If a company has two addresses (for instance, Nardley Supply Company, Inc., in Chicago, Illinois, and also in Peoria, Illinois) with correspondence filed under both addresses, two cross-references would be used. They would be SEE ALSO references, indicating that information is to be found in both places in the files. If these cross-references are sheets of paper, they would always be kept as the first items in their respective folders so that they would not be overlooked (see Figure 7-14).

This cross-reference information may be given on the tabs of the two folders for the Nardley Supply Company instead of on separate cross-reference sheets. (Figure 7-13.)

Illinois, Chicago
Nardley Supply Company, Inc.
SEE ALSO Illinois, Peoria

Illinois, Peoria
Nardley Supply Company, Inc.
SEE ALSO Illinois, Chicago

Figure 7-13

SEE ALSO Reference on Folder Tabs

SORTING

Correspondence is sorted by location, the distinctive feature of the geographic method. The papers are sorted first by the largest geographic unit (such as a state), next by the first subdivision (such as a city), and last by the names of the correspondents in a strict alphabetic arrangement.

FILING

Before any paper is placed in the file, the name of the correspondent must be quickly checked in the card file (if one is used). If a card for that correspondent is found, the files operator will know whether the correspondence is to be filed in a miscellaneous or an individual folder. He may then proceed with the filing in the usual manner. If a card for the correspondent is not found, the files operator must prepare a card at that time. Because of the complexity of a geographic arrangement—individual correspondents' folders, special city folders, alphabetic subdivisions of cities with their corresponding miscellaneous folders, miscellaneous folders for alphabetic

CROSS REFERENCE SHEET

Name or Subject _Illinois, Chicago_

Nordley Supply Company, Inc.

1313 North Sixth Street

Date of Item

Reguarding

SEE ALSO

Name or Subject _Illinois, Peoria_

Nordley Supply Company, Inc.

2264 Evanston Avenue

Authorized by _G. Collins_ Date _2/4/--_

CROSS REFERENCE SHEET

Name or Subject _Illinois, Peoria_

Nordley Supply Company, Inc.

2264 Evanston Avenue

Date of Item

Reguarding

SEE ALSO

Name or Subject _Illinois, Chicago_

Nordley Supply Company, Inc.

1313 North Sixth Street

Authorized by _G. Collins_ Date _2/4/--_

Figure 7-14

SEE ALSO Cross-Reference Sheets

groupings of cities, and miscellaneous state folders—the files operator must be extremely careful in filing papers within a geographic arrangement of guides and folders.

The proper drawer is located by reference to the label showing the geographic range within it. In that drawer the files operator finds the guide that shows the correct geographic section, the state, for instance. Because of the variance of guides and folders behind state names, caution must be used here to locate the proper folder into which to insert the paper.

Arrangement within every miscellaneous folder is alphabetic first by location and then by correspondents' name. In an individual folder, correspondence is arranged in the usual manner with the most recent date on top.

Location name guide arrangement. After the files operator finds the state, he looks for the correct city name. If he finds a city guide, he then looks for an individual folder for the correspondent; and if he finds one, he files the paper in it according to date. If there is no individual folder, he files the paper in the correct city miscellaneous folder according to the name of the correspondent, in alphabetic order, with the other papers within the folder. If more than one paper is filed for a correspondent, he arranges the papers chronologically with the most recent date on top. If there is no city miscellaneous folder, he places the paper in the miscellaneous state folder first according to the alphabetic order of city names and then by correspondents' names and addresses (if necessary), according to the rules for alphabetic filing. The papers for each correspondent are always arranged with the most recent date in front.

Lettered guide arrangement. After the files operator finds the state, he uses the lettered guides to locate the alphabetic state section within which the city name falls. After finding that section, he looks for an individual folder for the correspondent; and if he finds one, he files the paper in that folder in chronologic order. If there is no individual folder, he looks for a miscellaneous city folder; and if he finds one, he files that paper in it according to correspondent's name in the same manner as in an alphabetic arrangement. If there is no miscellaneous city folder, the files operator files the paper in the miscellaneous alphabetic folder within which the city name falls. Again, arrangement is according to the rules for alphabetic filing. The names of cities are arranged alphabetically, the names of correspondents are arranged alphabetically by names within a city, and the papers of one correspondent are grouped together with the most recent date on top. If there are identically named correspondents in one city, the rules for identical names are followed.

The folder into which a paper is to be filed should be pulled up slightly while the paper is being inserted to avoid misfiling.

CHARGING OUT MATERIALS

The process of charging out materials in a geographic file is the same as charging out papers from any other kind of file. An OUT indicator is inserted at the place where a folder or papers are removed. The OUT indicator shows what material has been taken, who has taken it, when it was taken, and when it is expected to be returned. The order of the information on the OUT indicator is arranged geographically, that is, with the location information first; but the total information on the indicator is the same as that found on an OUT indicator in alphabetic filing.

FOLLOW-UP PROCEDURES

The follow-up procedures in a geographic file, used to secure the return of borrowed materials, are the same as those used in any other method of filing. A tickler file or other reminder system is employed to make sure that papers are returned to the files at designated times and to remind the files operator of items needing attention in the future.

SECTION 5. ADVANTAGES AND DISADVANTAGES OF GEOGRAPHIC METHOD

ADVANTAGES

Speed of reference to specific geographic areas is the main advantage of a geographic file. All the advantages of alphabetic filing are inherent in this method also since this is basically an alphabetic arrangement. Many geographic systems use color as a safeguard to give the files operator another check against misfiling. All the records for one geographic section would be of one color; a different section would mean a different color.

The volume of correspondence within any given geographic area can be seen by glancing at the files. An analysis of the information contained in a geographic file section could be used in sales work to note areas with the most complaints, to note aggressive selling effort or the lack thereof, to note areas where additional work seems needed, or to show where territories need to be combined, separated, or subdivided. If territories are combined, enlarged, or subdivided, geographic files may be readily rearranged. Each location is a unit, a group; and the shifting of groups is relatively easy because it is mechanical.

Geographic reference is often used for trouble-shooting purposes. For instance, if trouble develops with the gas, electric, or water meter at a certain address, reference is made to the address rather than to the name of the person or business at that location. Geographic reference is often helpful because of the nature of the business. Real-estate firms may arrange their listings by areas within a city for ease in location of properties. Companies may base business-promotion efforts on geographic locations.

Although the advantages of geographic filing are many, several disadvantages must be kept in mind when the appropriate filing method is being selected.

DISADVANTAGES

One disadvantage of the geographic method may be the complexity of the guides and folders. Because the nature of geographic method calls for variety and much subdivision, a geographic file requires more time to set up than does an alphabetic file. Getting records into and out of geographic files is time consuming because reference must be made first to area, then to a certain point within that area, and finally to a name (state, city, individual customer—for instance).

If the location of a correspondent is not remembered and no alphabetic card file is kept, much time is lost by the files operator in searching through several sections of the file before he remembers the address or locates the correspondence by chance. Even with the use of a card file of alphabetized names, delay is occasioned because two operations are necessary in order to file material—a quick check of the card file to be sure the correspondent is included correctly in it plus the actual filing in the correct geographic section of the file. Two operations may also be necessary in order to find material—a check of the card file, if only the individual's name is given, to find the address to which reference must first be made, and then the actual searching of the file for the records of the individual.

Often a geographic file arrangement is set up and is then kept unchanged for years as a result of habit. The ledgers of the company could give information needed by territory. An alphabetic file might prove more efficient, but custom lingers on.

Misfiling can result because of the similarity of state names (*Ohio* and *Iowa, North Carolina* and *South Carolina, North Dakota* and *South Dakota, Vermont* and *Virginia*) and the frequency of identical city names within various states. ("Springfield" is found in Arkansas, Colorado, Florida, Georgia, Idaho, Illinois, Kentucky, Louisiana, Maine, Massachusetts, Michigan, Minnesota, Missouri, Nebraska, New Hampshire, New Jersey, Ohio, Oregon, Pennsylvania, South Carolina, South Dakota, Tennessee, Vermont, Virginia, and West Virginia!) Carelessness in filing will result in misplacement of folders in geographic filing just as it will in any other method.

SECTION 6. EXPANSION IN GEOGRAPHIC METHOD

When enough correspondence has accumulated to warrant opening a separate folder for a certain city, for a certain geographical section, or for an individual correspondent, the files operator removes the papers from the miscellaneous folder; if necessary, makes the required changes in the index card file (for example, changing the "M" to an "I" in the upper right corner of the card when an individual folder is opened for a correspondent); opens a new folder with the geographic location on the first line of its tab above the name of the correspondent; prepares a corresponding guide if one is required; and then places the guide and the folder in the correct place in the file.

While the practice varies on the requirements for setting up a separate folder for a specific geographic location, such as a city, a good rule of thumb is this: When correspondence is carried on with five or more correspondents located in one geographic location, a separate folder should be opened for correspondents in that location. For example, in the location name guide file in Figure 7-1 on page 160, materials pertaining to correspondents located in Alton, Illinois, were filed originally in the *Illinois-A* miscellaneous folder. When papers accumulated from five or more correspondents in Alton, a new guide labeled *Illinois-Alton* and a new miscellaneous city folder labeled in the same manner were prepared. The papers were removed from the *Illinois-A* folder and were transferred to the *Illinois-Alton* folder; and the new guide and the new folder were inserted in the drawer in alphabetic order after the *Illinois* state guide. When the correspondence with the Kelly Manufacturing Company accumulated to the predetermined number of pieces, these papers were removed from the *Illinois-Aurora* folder and were placed in an individual folder to be inserted in front of the *Illinois-Aurora* city folder.

Similarly, in the lettered guide plan in Figure 7-7 (page 165), materials pertaining to correspondents located in Birmingham, Michigan, were filed originally in the *B-2* miscellaneous folder. When papers accumulated from five or more correspondents in Birmingham, a new guide labeled *Michigan-Birmingham* and a new miscellaneous city folder labeled in the same manner were prepared. The papers were removed from the *B-2* folder and were transferred to the *Michigan-Birmingham* folder; and the new guide and the new folder were inserted in the drawer in correct alphabetic order after the individual folder for the Kellogg Bolt Co., which is filed according to the city, Battle Creek.

The principles applying to the opening of an individual folder in an alphabetic filing system apply to opening such a folder in a geographic system. The only differences are that in the geographic system the top line of the caption on the folder consists of the geographic location and the identifying letter "M" is changed to an "I" in the upper right corner of the card in the card file.

SECTION 7. COMBINATIONS OF THE GEOGRAPHIC METHOD

GEOGRAPHIC AND ALPHABETIC METHODS

Geographic arrangements are sometimes found in an alphabetic file. For instance, correspondence with one company can become so voluminous that it is necessary or expedient to file the company correspondence geographically for ease in locating material. Such an arrangement might be found within the "I" section of an alphabetic file, as shown in the illustration at the left of Figure 7-15 (page 180). The "I-L-M Products" folders are arranged geographically by states.

Another geographic arrangement in an alphabetic file might occur if correspondence were carried on with several officers of one organization having, for instance, five vice-presidents who are from different districts and whose term of office is only for one year. An example would be the group of *National Office Workers* folders, filed behind the *N* guide of an alphabetic file. The folders for the vice-presidents might be filed as shown in the illustration at the right of Figure 7-15.

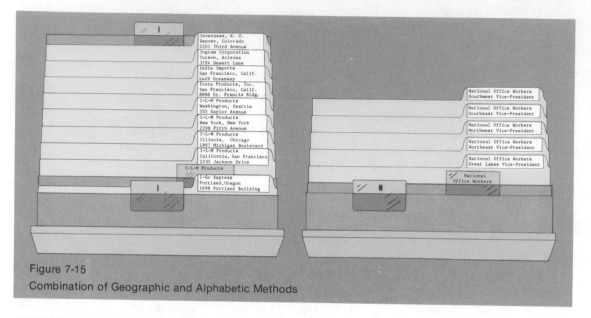

Figure 7-15
Combination of Geographic and Alphabetic Methods

GEOGRAPHIC AND NUMERIC METHODS

A combination of geographic and numeric methods may be used. All correspondents within a certain area, for example, may be given identical numbers. If the United States were divided into seven sections, for instance, each section could be numbered as shown below.

Midwest—100	South—500
Northeast—200	Southeast—600
Northwest—300	Southwest—700
Off-Continent—400	

A map must be marked to show the boundaries of each of these sections. If Washington, Oregon, Idaho, Montana, and Wyoming were considered the Northwest, a correspondent located in Portland, Oregon, would have the number "300" placed on his correspondence for coding purposes. The same would be true of a correspondent located in Boise, Idaho; or Great Falls, Montana; or Laramie, Wyoming; or

Seattle, Washington. In sorting the correspondence before it is filed, all pieces would be sorted (1) according to the number "300" to indicate that they are to be filed in the Northwest section of the file, (2) according to the state, and (3) according to the city. The first sorting by number would be quicker than sorting by name. Eventually, however, unless the states and the cities within them were given numbers, filing would become an alphabetic determination.

The use of long numbers separated by hyphens or dashes or spaces is becoming more frequent. A records manager could designate 300-2-172 to mean Northwest section of the United States —(State of) Washington—(City of) Seattle. A numbered index of states and cities within those states would have to be set up and consulted constantly to be sure the correct numbers were used. The ZIP code numbering instituted by the United States Post Office may have implications for the combining of geographic and numeric filing methods. The state indicator might be changed to a two-letter abbreviation, as advocated by the Post Office.

Transposition of numbers and all other disadvantages of a numeric method are ever-present hazards whenever numbers are used.

GEOGRAPHIC AND SUBJECT METHODS

Within a geographic file, arrangement might be by topic or subject, as further subdivisions of the correspondence. For instance, within "Texas" there might be subdivisions labeled *Retailers, Schools, Wholesalers,* and *U. S. Government.* The subdivisions within each of these topics could be by cities; within each city, by individuals' names. All of these subdivisions, however, are alphabetical within the geographic framework.

A further combination of subject and geographic methods might occur if a special subject folder were needed because correspondence is more likely to be called for by subject than by location. Examples might be *Applications* or *Advertising* or *Form Letters.* To attempt to give a geographic location to these subjects might entail considerable difficulty because the material involves a number of different locations. The best solution seems to be that of grouping all special subject files together alphabetically in one part of the files separate from the geographic arrangement. Usually this group of folders will appear in the front of the first file drawer or at the end of the last file drawer.

A more comprehensive discussion of subject filing is contained in Chapter 8.

For Review and Discussion

1. How can geographic filing be combined with alphabetic filing? with numeric filing?

2. How could guides and folders used in alphabetic filing be used with the geographic method?

3. How do cross-references used in geographic filing vary from those used in alphabetic filing? How are they similar?

4. Is the geographic method of filing a slow or a fast method? Explain.

5. Is geographic filing a direct or an indirect method? Explain.

6. In preparing the arrangement of guides and folders for a geographic file, what principles should the operator keep in mind?

7. If a geographic file were arranged by regions of the North American continent, what visual aid would be needed to assure correct filing and finding of papers?

8. Refer to the geographic arrangements on pages 160 and 163. Give as many examples as you can of the types of businesses that might find each arrangement useful to them. Explain your choices.

Learning Projects

1. Draw a picture of the type of geographic file that might be used in each of the following companies:

   a. A large oil company
   b. A domestic automobile manufacturer
   c. A company publishing a popular magazine
   d. An executive office of a professional organization

2. What type of geographic file does the utility company in your city use?

3. Are the names in each of the following pairs in correct order if this is a geographic filing arrangement according to state first, city second, street designation third, and individual or company name fourth?

   a. L. Richard McDuff and Son
      692 Crane Blvd.
      Mobile, AL 36612

      L. Richard MacDuff
      392 Crane Road
      Mobile, AL 36611

   b. Vermont Daily News
      News Building
      Bennington, VT 05201

      Foremost Dairies
      1872 River Road
      Bennington, VT 05201

c. The National Navigation Magazine
Wilson Building
Flat River, MO   63601

Four Seasons Restaurant
W. O. W. Building
Flat River, MO   63601

d. Thomas' School of Cosmetology
1906 Main Street
Waterbury, CT   06706

Thomas F. Colt
1900 Main Street
Waterbury, CT   06706

e. Senator Oliver Lewis
219 Federal Building
Newport, RI   02840

Sarah E. Wells
4318 Oak Drive
N. Kingstown, RI   02852

f. 15th Avenue Garage
1196 15th Avenue
Dayton, OH   45402

Foreman & Sons
86-B 15th Avenue
Dayton, OH   45402

g. All-Steel Equipment Inc.
Route 31 and Ashland Avenue
Aurora, Illinois   60507

Western Manufacturing Company
P. O. Box 1266
Aurora, Illinois   60507

h. Western Piedmont Day
School
Beseler Avenue
Skokie, Illinois   60076

Western Piedmont Dental
Society
Beseler Avenue
Skokie, Illinois   60076

i. Dr. John Lewis-Jones
694 South Hart Street
Custer, SD   57730

Lewis Jones
694 South Heart Street
Custer, SD   57730

j. Tampa Unitarian Church
7th and Palm Streets
Tampa, FL   33602

First Methodist Church
8th and Palm Streets
Tampa, FL   33605

k. Out Door Tennis Players
Assn.
2222 Longacre Street
Eugene, OR   97401

Oregon Players Club
University of Oregon
Box 870
Eugene, OR   97403

l. Brotherhood of Shipping
Clerks
1110 Kalakaua Avenue
Honolulu, HI   96814

U. S. Shippers, Inc.
16 Haleiwa Blvd.
Honolulu, HI   96813

m. Audio Visual Corporation
George Washington Way
Richland, Washington 99352

Audiovisual Products
Unlimited
2900 Washington Way
Richland, Washington 99352

n. The Hughes Company
Summit Avenue
Sandford, NC   27330

Thomas Hughes
Summit Avenue
Sandford, NC   27330

4. Ascertain the meaning of the ZIP code numbers being used by the Post Office. Work out a sample geographic arrangement combined with a

numeric method based on the ZIP numbering system for a national magazine subscription agency that wants to set up a geographic file of subscribers.

Laboratory Assignments 11, 12, and 13

You should now complete Laboratory Assignments 11 (Card Filing—Geographic Method), 12 (Geographic Correspondence Filing), and 13 (Geographic Correspondence Filing—Review) in *Records Management—Laboratory Materials*.

Chapter **8**

Subject method
of records storage

The subject method of records storage is that method of filing
in which records are labeled and stored according to the *subject
matter* of the record. Even though the majority of offices use a
records storage system based on the names of individuals or firms,
almost every business has at least one type of subject file. Such files
are frequently found in the offices and departments where interest
lies not in names but in topics relating to the various operations
of the company; they are also referred to as *data, executive, information,* or *topical* files. Subject files often contain such classifications as:

Annual Reports	Incorporation Papers
Associations	Insurance Papers
Blueprints	Leases
Clippings	Minutes of Annual Meetings
Dissolution Papers	Ordinances
Financial Statements	Price Lists
Government Publications	Speeches
House Organs	Surveys

A drawer of a typical executive subject file might look like that
in Figure 8-1 on page 186, with main subject divisions, several subdivisions of that subject, individual folders, and special classifications
clearly indicated.

When the volume of material to be filed by subject is small compared with the correspondence to be filed by name, both subject
material and name material may be filed in the same alphabetic files.
Examples might be Applications and Contracts as subjects appearing
within an otherwise alphabetic name file.

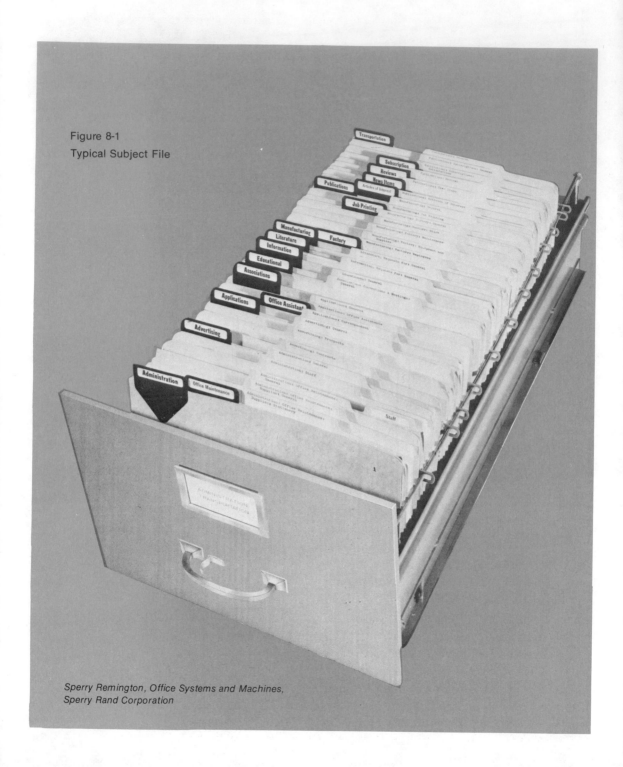

Figure 8-1
Typical Subject File

Sperry Remington, Office Systems and Machines,
Sperry Rand Corporation

Sometimes, too, subject folders are used as subdivisions in a geographic file. (See page 181.)

Subject filing is a very difficult and costly method of storage. The costs of operating a subject file are high since every paper must be carefully read to determine the single subject or the several subjects to which its contents refer. No two persons think exactly alike about any one topic. In an alphabetic system the name "Brown" is not confused with the name "Ackerman"; but in a subject file, two persons can easily think of one topic by similar or synonymous (though different) terms, such as "Far Eastern Trade" or "Oriental Trade"; "Company Newspapers" or "House Organs"; "Rugs" or "Carpets" or "Floor Coverings."

Businesses, departments, or offices in which subject files are often found include department stores that may keep all papers relating to window dispays or promotional activities by subject; trade organizations that deal with groups of businesses engaged in similar activities; school offices where correspondence is stored by such subjects as "accidents," "accrediting," "athletics," "budgets," "cafeteria," "certification," and the like. Engineering departments of manufacturing firms where specialized equipment is made often use subject arrangement of correspondence pertaining to each kind of equipment, stored according to the equipment name. Research department papers may be stored according to the various studies being made and the projects under way.

Personnel offices may use the subject arrangement in the storage of correspondence related to the various departments within the business. A purchasing agent for a firm will probably keep his files according to subject (types of items) rather than according to the names of suppliers. A file maintained by a vice-president in charge of production in a number of plants or factories may be arranged by subjects such as "equipment," "labor contracts," "safety," and the like; within each of the subject categories, folders would be maintained for each plant or factory.

Every subject file, no matter how small, must be accompanied by a written list of subjects used. The written list, either on cards or sheets of paper, is often referred to as an *index*. It is an alphabetically arranged control list of main headings, subdivisions under the main headings, and cross-references. The index gives a quick review of the contents of a subject file when new headings are chosen and aids in identifying material requested under unusual headings.

Good subject headings are exact, concise, specific, technically correct, clearly descriptive, and composed of terms in common usage that are capable of one interpretation only. Seldom do all persons in a business refer to the contents of a paper in the same way. For that reason, the selection of subject headings should be made by those thoroughly familiar with the material to be stored and with a good working knowledge of the firm's operations. Only the most skilled files supervisors and records managers are competent to select subject headings. If files operators use headings assigned at random by members of different departments, soon the same type of material may be stored under two or more synonymous terms and the files will be hopelessly confused. The files supervisor must be alert to unify subject headings. Once the subjects have been chosen, they must be adhered to and all future subjects added must not duplicate or overlap the subjects selected previously.

No two indexes are alike even in similar businesses because the functions of every business vary and the files must be adapted to the business. Suggested indexes can be of value only in giving ideas. The requirements of a good index are: (1) It should be standardized within a department if not throughout the company so that agreement is reached on the headings under which material shall be filed; (2) it must be flexible to allow for growth and the eventual inclusion of entirely new material; and (3) it must be understandable to all who use it.

A records supervisor or manager is fortunate to be able to find a printed list of subjects that can be adapted to his company's needs. Printed subject lists that might be used as guides are available from the following sources:

Agriculture

Agricultural Index. H. W. Wilson Co. (Publisher)
950 University Avenue, Bronx, New York   10452

Architecture

Architecture (Decimal)
University of Illinois Press, Urbana, Illinois   61803

Business

Advertising, Banking, Management, Selling
Hayden Book Companies, 116 West 14th Street, New York, New York   10011

Advertising, Marketing, and Communications Media
Elin B. Christianson and Edward G. Stroble (Editors)
Special Libraries Association, 31 East 10th Street, New York, New York 10003

American Institute of Certified Public Accountants
666 Fifth Avenue, New York, New York   10019

Banking and Financial Subject Headings
Special Libraries Association, 31 East 10th Street, New York, New York
10003

Business Periodicals Index. H. W. Wilson Co. (Publisher)
950 University Avenue, Bronx, New York   10452

Communication in Organizations: A Guide to Information Sources
Robert M. Carter (Author), Gale Research Company, Book Tower
Detroit, Michigan (Published as their Management Information Guide 25)

Economics and Public Affairs

Public Affairs Information Services Bulletin
11 West 40th Street, New York, New York   10018

Electricity

General Electric Catalog, General Electric Company, Schenectady, New York
12305

Engineering

Engineering Index. Engineering Index, Inc. (Publisher)
3452 47th Street, New York, New York   10017

General

American Library Association List of Subject Headings
American Library Association, 50 East Huron Street, Chicago, Illinois
60611

Industrial Arts Index. H. W. Wilson Co. (Publisher)
950 University Avenue, Bronx, New York   10452

Library of Congress List of Subject Headings
Library of Congress, Washington, D. C.   20025

Readers' Guide to Periodical Literature. H. W. Wilson Co. (Publisher)
950 University Avenue, Bronx, New York   10452

Medicine

Medical Subject Headings. U. S. National Library of Medicine
Superintendent of Documents, U. S. Government Printing Office
Washington, D. C.   20402

Social Sciences and Humanities

Social Sciences and Humanities Index. H. W. Wilson Co. (Publisher)
950 University Avenue, Bronx, New York   10452

SECTION 1. ARRANGEMENT OF SUBJECT FILES

The standard arrangements of subject files are (1) alphabetic,
(2) simple numeric, (3) duplex numeric, and (4) decimal.

ALPHABETIC SUBJECT ARRANGEMENT

The alphabetic subject file is the arrangement most frequently used. It may be expanded almost indefinitely, and employees other than the regular files operator can easily use this arrangement. The two methods of arranging subject material alphabetically are (1) straight dictionary arrangement and (2) encyclopedic arrangement.

Straight dictionary arrangement. Practically all small subject files are suited to the straight dictionary method of storing materials with no thought given to the grouping of like subjects. Subject names are written on folders with wide labels, and the folders are filed behind alphabetic guides. Every subject has its own folder, and subjects that are exceptionally active may be made conspicuous by the use of special subject guides similar to name guides.

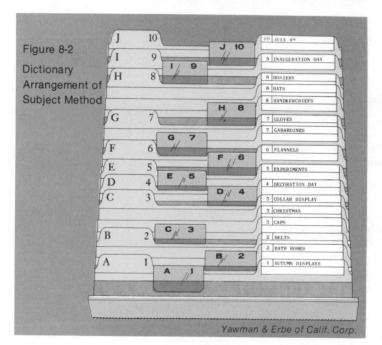

Figure 8-2

Dictionary Arrangement of Subject Method

Yawman & Erbe of Calif. Corp.

The illustration in **Figure 8-2** shows a typical subject file used by a large department store for filing window-display ads. It uses subject folders in straight-line arrangement behind alternating alphabetic guides. Miscellaneous alphabetic folders with first-position tabs are provided for filing material that, because of the limited quantity, does not warrant the use of subject folders. The possible subjects filed within any miscellaneous folder can be many, and papers filed in miscellaneous folders are often lost.

Encyclopedic arrangement. The encyclopedic arrangement is especially adapted to filing material by subject; it requires guides and folders similarly labeled with subject notations. The guides are of the insert type and are arranged in alphabetic order. The *Subject Index System* in Figure 8-3 on page 191 has as its basic foundation 172 main subject and subclassification headings printed on guide and folder labels. This system is intended for executive use; the

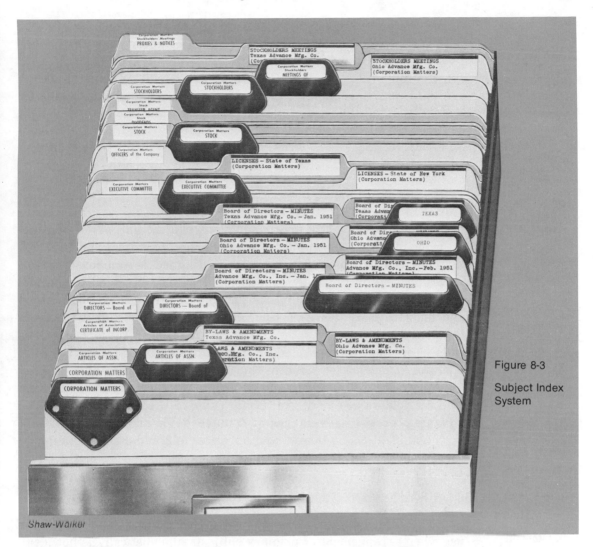

Figure 8-3

Subject Index System

executive selects the headings he needs from the list of those available. One-fifth-cut guides show primary subjects in first position. Subclassification guides in second position are also one-fifth-cut. Subject folders with one-fifth-cut tabs in first position are used to correspond to primary and subclassification guides. Additional subject folders may be inserted for which guides are not used.

Individual or company name folders may be added as sufficient papers justify using middle- and third-position one-third-cut folders. Their tabs should be labeled first with the subject or classification heading and next with the name. (See the two individual folders behind the guide labeled "Corporation Matters, Stockholders MEET-INGS OF.") To classify individual folders, labels have distinctive color stripes across their tops.

For unusual subjects or especially active subjects, metal-tabbed guides are provided at the right in two sizes. The longer tabs signify especially important subjects; the shorter tabs are for divisions within the subject indicated on the longer tab. (See "Board of Directors—MINUTES" and "OHIO" and "TEXAS" at the right of the drawer.)

SIMPLE NUMERIC ARRANGEMENT

The simple numeric arrangement of subject matter is identical in principle with the numeric arrangement of correspondence for individuals or firms. Each subject is assigned a number from an accession book in the order in which the subject is added to the file. An alphabetic index of subjects, usually a card file, is maintained and must be consulted each time a paper is filed or called for from the files. Every similar subject title by which each subject might be called for must be included in the card index to refer the files operator to the subject used in the file. The file number must appear on every card in the index and on every piece of paper in the files. The file folders are arranged *numerically* in the file equipment. The advantages and disadvantages of a numeric file arrangement of subjects are identical to those listed on pages 142 and 143 pertaining to the filing of individual and firm names by the numeric method.

DUPLEX NUMERIC ARRANGEMENT

The duplex numeric arrangement of subject filing is designed for use when arrangement of primary subjects alphabetically is not ideal. Usually the file develops with the growth of the business, or the file grows as a project progresses toward completion. Main subject headings receive numbers in the order in which they are added to the file; an alphabetic card index is used as in a straight numeric file. For example, if the first subject placed in the file is *Equipment,* the file number would be *1.* The card in the card file will read as follows:

Equipment	1

The guide in the file will read as follows:

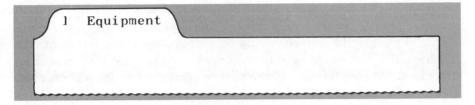

The subdivision of each main subject heading receives the file number assigned to the main heading and also a number that indicates its place in the classification. Examples are:

1-1 Equipment—Desks
1-2 Equipment—Chairs

Subsequent subdivisions may receive a letter, in addition to the numbers assigned to the main heading and to the first subdivision. Examples:

1-1a Equipment—Desks—Roll Top
1-1b Equipment—Desks—Flat Top
1-1c Equipment—Desks—Modular

If more than 26 subdivisions are anticipated, letters are not feasible; an additional number would be used, separated from the other numbers by a colon, a dash, a period, or some other distinguishing symbol.

Occasionally another subdivision is added by the use of another number or letter, but such notations as 1-2c4 or 1-2-3a or 1-4-7-6 are confusing and increase the possibility of error.

The advantage of the duplex numeric method of filing subject material is that it provides for an unlimited number of primary headings and an unlimited number of subdivisions. The disadvantages of this method are the dangers inherent in the transposition or misreading of numbers and the fact that any subdivisions using letters are limited to the 26 letters in the alphabet.

The American Institute of Architects Standard Filing System, (page 194, Figure 8-4), available from many manufacturers, is a variation of the duplex numeric method. The 41 main classifications and their file number designations conform in general to those headings usually included in mechanical and equipment specifications. The master heading classifications and numbers are supplemented by subdivision classifications and numbers referring particularly to individual types of materials, appliances, equipment, and the like. Every folder tab bears the number of its correspondingly numbered master heading. The files operator may use only the master heading classifications and add subdivisions in the future according to individual preferences and needs.

Figure 8-4
A.I.A. Standard Filing System

DECIMAL ARRANGEMENT

The first decimal classification method was worked out in 1873 by Dr. Melvil Dewey for classifying library materials. Its suitability for this type of material is proved by the fact that today it is in use in more than 90 percent of the public and private libraries in the United States and is widely used in other countries because it covers every subject upon which anything has been written. The system, developed in accordance with the expansion of the world's knowledge, has ten general classes or main divisions:

000 Generalities (encyclopedias, periodicals, and other books of a general character)
100 Philosophy and related disciplines (the science of living)
200 Religion (the principles of spiritual life)
300 The Social Sciences (including business topics)

400 Languages
500 Pure sciences (classified knowledge of the physical world)
600 Technology (applied sciences)
700 The Arts (creation of aesthetic pleasures)
800 Literature (record of the thoughts and ideas of men)
900 General geography and history and their auxiliaries

Each of these major groups is divided into ten parts, which in turn can be divided into ten additional groups, and so on indefinitely. For example, group *300 Sociology* is subdivided as follows:

300 Sociology
310 Statistics
320 Political Science
330 Economics
340 Law
350 Public Administration
360 Social Pathology, Social Services, Association
370 Education
380 Commerce, Communications, Transportation
390 Customs and Folklore

The *370 Education* group has these subdivisions:

370 Education
371 The school
372 Elementary education
373 Secondary education
374 Adult education
375 Curriculums
376 Education of women
377 Schools and religion
378 Higher education
379 Education and the state

The Dewey Decimal System is used only when classifying library material and is not adaptable to a correspondence file. However, many government offices and companies have devised systems based on the decimal classification principle because their material will fit into ten or fewer main headings.

One of the best-known examples is the Williams Decimal System, devised for the use of railroads. There are only eight main subjects and two blank categories (000—General, 100—Executive and Legal, 200—Finance and Accounts, 300—Roadway and Structures, 400—Equipment and Shops, 500—Transportation and Storage, 600—Traffic (Rates), 700—blank, 800—blank, 900—Local Facilities and Affairs. The two blank categories are provided for expansion.

The success of any decimal system depends primarily upon the original classifications selected. If the main divisions prove too specific or limiting, if they overlap, or if they fail to cover the entire subject, the system will not work. Mere knowledge of the subject matter is not sufficient; ability is needed to analyze and classify clearly and accurately. A trained files operator, however, should be able to operate a decimal system efficiently.

The advantages of a decimal system are unlimited expansion; papers can be called for more quickly and easily by number than by name; materials for each subject and all its allied topics are grouped in the same section of the file. The disadvantages of a decimal system are that the main divisions are limited to ten; the cost of operation is high because of the need for highly trained persons; and carelessness in the use of numbers can cause the loss of papers for indefinite periods of time.

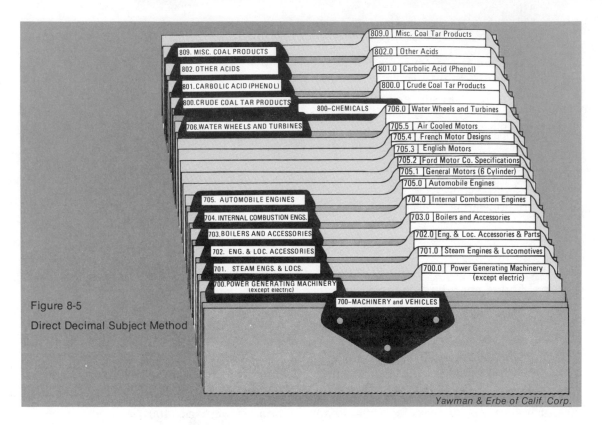

Figure 8-5

Direct Decimal Subject Method

Yawman & Erbe of Calif. Corp.

A direct decimal system, as shown in Figure 8-5, can be designed for a large volume of papers accumulating under any general subject. The example shown has the primary classification "700" for "Machinery and Vehicles." The number *705* is the sixth subclassification in this group and it bears the title "Automobile Engines." Further subdivision is secured under this group by expanding the decimal digits—"705.1 General Motors," "705.2 Ford Motor Co. Specifications," and so forth. For additional expansion, the file folder numbers may be extended to the next decimal place: 705.10, 705.11, 705.12; 705.20, 705.21, 705.22; etc.

ALPHANUMERIC ARRANGEMENT

Some operators set up the files by subject titles that are arranged according to a pattern that reflects in an organized way the activities of the various functions of the business. The subject titles are given numbers that indicate main divisions and subdivisions. The captions on the guide and folder tabs may show both the subject titles and the numbers assigned to those titles, or they may show only the numbers. In the first case, numbers *may* be used instead of subject titles to save time in coding and filing; in the second case, numbers *must* be used in coding and locating folders. If the captions on the tabs consist only of numbers, a supplementary card index file must be set up to arrange the subjects alphabetically. This index file is used in the same way that an index file is used in a numeric correspondence file.

A list of subject titles and their corresponding numbers for a simple alphanumeric file is as follows here and on page 198.

Subject Number	Main Subject	Division of Subject	Subdivision of Subject
100	Advertising		
110		Direct-mail	
120		Trade Journals	
200	Bookkeeping		
300	Credit		
310		Credit Managers' Association	
320		Retail Credit Bureau	
400	Equipment		
410		Office	
420		Shipping	
430		Store	
500	Filing		
600	Personnel		
610		Applications	
611			Office
612			Shipping
613			Store
620		Employee Data	
630		Policy Manual	
640		References	

Subject Number	Main Subject	Division of Subject	Subdivision of Subject
700	Purchasing		
800	Sales		
810		End-of-Month	
820		Holiday	
830		Special	
900	Shipping		
910		Air	
920		Railroad	
930		Truck	

SECTION 2. SUPPLIES FOR SUBJECT FILING

GUIDES

The guides used in any subject arrangement are determined by the kind of subject arrangement used. If the file consists of many small headings, these headings may be arranged according to the *dictionary method,* that is, with an alphabetic set of guides similar to those used in name filing. If, on the other hand, the file consists of but a few major subjects that have a number of divisions, the headings may be arranged according to the *encyclopedic method,* that is, with the major subjects and the divisions arranged alphabetically, or with the subject titles arranged according to the importance of the major headings.

Figure 8-6 shows an encyclopedic subject file that is used in an advertising agency. The primary guides in first position bear captions that correspond to the main headings in the file; the secondary guides in second position correspond to the divisions of the main headings. If the primary guides were numbered, the secondary guides and the folders would also be numbered according to the primary guides they follow.

The use of color (either one color for each main heading and its divisions or one color for the main headings and different colors for the divisions) will be a check against misfiling.

FOLDERS

Individual folders following each subject guide often have double-width tabs; one-half-cut tabs in right-hand position are shown in Figure 8-6. At times so much information may be required on the

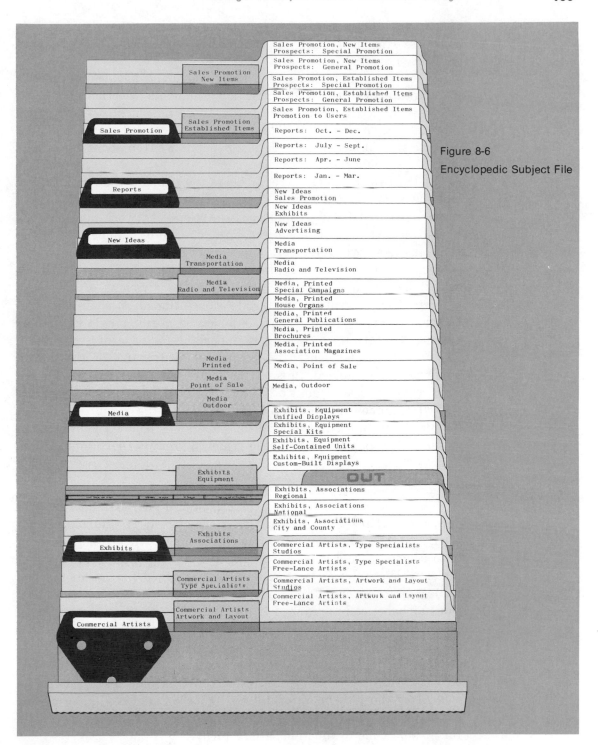

Figure 8-6

Encyclopedic Subject File

folder tab that larger tabs may be necessary. Where material is bulky, expansion folders of pressboard with metal tabs may be needed.

The use of miscellaneous folders should be avoided. A miscellaneous category usually indicates an incomplete selection of subject headings or divisions. If there seems to be no place to file a paper except under the heading of "miscellaneous," careful study should be given to the subjects in use. Every paper is written about something and there should be no miscellany.

A *label* for a folder correctly bears the name of the main subject and the name of a division, if any. The first individual folder in Figure 8-6 is labeled "Commercial Artists, Artwork and Layout Free-Lance Artists." If a subject is referred to by number and if the subjects are assigned numbers, the number may be substituted for the subject title on the label. Typing of main subjects may be done in all capital letters to distinguish them from the divisions of the main subjects. The quantity of material to be included on each label will determine typing style—block or indented form, single or double spacing. Uniformity of typing is important for ease of recognition. The size of the label used is determined by the size of the tab on which it is to be affixed. In turn, the folder tab will have been chosen with regard to the amount of material normally to be typed thereon.

OUT guides in Figure 8-6 are placed at the right for ease in finding. They mark the location of papers or folders removed from storage. Here one folder has been removed from the Exhibits section.

SUBJECT INDEXES

An alphabetic *index* for a correspondence file, arranged by subject, is necessary to all subject filing systems. It is valuable in that a quick review of all subjects used can be made when a new heading is to be chosen, and it is also valuable in finding the correct heading under which material is stored when it is asked for by an unusual subject title. A card file, or typed sheets, with the subject classifications alphabetically arranged is usually sufficient for a simple, small alphabetic subject index. A more complex arrangement requires a *relative index,* in which all main headings and division headings and all possible variations of subjects are listed. A relative index is used also as a cross-reference device since it contains unused subject entries that refer the files operator to the topics or subjects under which the material actually is filed. Without an index, it is almost impossible for a subject file to function satisfactorily.

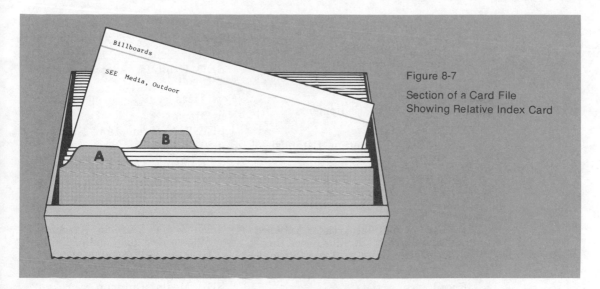

Figure 8-7

Section of a Card File
Showing Relative Index Card

Figure 8-7 shows the card file containing the index that is kept as a guide to the subject file illustrated in Figure 8-6. The complete list of captions on the cards in the card file is as follows:

Advertising
SEE New Ideas
SEE ALSO Media, Printed

Agency Fees
SEE Commercial Artists, Artwork and Layout, Studios; *and* Commercial Artists, Type Specialists, Studios

Artwork
SEE Commercial Artists, Artwork and Layout

Association Magazines
SEE Media, Printed, Association Magazines

Associations
SEE Exhibits, Associations; *and* Media, Printed, Association Magazines

Billboards
SEE Media, Outdoor

Brand Names
SEE Media, Printed, Brochures; *and* Media, Printed, House Organs

Brochures
SEE Media, Printed, Brochures

Campaigns
SEE Media, Printed, Special Campaigns

Car Cards
SEE Media, Transportation

City Association Exhibits
SEE Exhibits, Associations, City and County

Commercial Artists

Commercials
SEE Media, Radio and Television

County Association Exhibits
SEE Exhibits, Associations, City and County

Creative Advertising
SEE New Ideas

Custom-Built Displays
SEE Exhibits, Equipment, Custom-Built Displays

Displays
SEE Exhibits, Equipment, Custom-Built Displays; *and* Exhibits, Equipment, Unified Displays

Equipment
SEE Exhibits, Equipment

Established Items
SEE Sales Promotion, Established
Items

Exhibits
SEE ALSO New Ideas

Fees
SEE Commercial Artists, Artwork
and Layout, Studios; *and* Commercial Artists, Type Specialists, Studios

Free-Lance Artists
SEE Commercial Artists, Art-
work and Layout, Free-Lance
Artists; *and* Commercial Art-
ists, Type Specialists, Free-
Lance Artists

General Publications
SEE Media, Printed, General Publications

House Organs
SEE Media, Printed, House Organs

In-Company Advertisements
SEE Media, Printed, House Organs

Kits
SEE Exhibits, Equipment, Special
Kits

Labels
SEE Media, Printed, Brochures;
and Media, Printed, House Organs

Layout
SEE Commercial Artists, Artwork
and Layout

Magazines
SEE Media, Printed, Association
Magazines

Mass Advertising
SEE Media

Media

National Association Exhibits
SEE Exhibits, Associations, National

New Ideas

New Items
SEE Sales Promotion, New Items

Outdoor Media
SEE Media, Outdoor

Painted Bulletins
SEE Media, Outdoor

Periodical Advertising
SEE Media, Printed, Association
Magazines; *and* Media, Printed,
General Publications

Poster Advertising
SEE Media, Outdoor

Printed Media
SEE Media, Printed

Promotion Ideas
SEE Sales Promotion

Publications
SEE Media, Printed, General Publications

Radio Advertising
SEE Media, Radio and Television

Regional Association Exhibits
SEE Exhibits, Associations, Regional

Reports

Sales Promotion
SEE ALSO New Ideas

Self-Contained Units
SEE Exhibits, Equipment, Self-
Contained Units

Slogans
SEE Media, Printed, Brochures;
and Media, Printed, House Organs

Special Campaigns
SEE Media, Printed, Special Campaigns

Special Kits
SEE Exhibits, Equipment, Special
Kits

Spot Advertising
  SEE Media, Radio and Television

State Association Exhibits
  SEE Exhibits, Associations, State

Store Signs
  SEE Media, Point of Sale

Studios
  SEE Commercial Artists, Artwork
    and Layout, Studios; *and* Com-
    mercial Artists, Type Special-
    ists, Studios

Television Advertising
  SEE Media, Radio and Television

Trademarks
  SEE Media, Printed, Brochures;
    and Media, Printed, House Or-
    gans

Transportation Advertising
  SEE Media, Transportation

Type Specialists
  SEE Commercial Artists, Type
    Specialists

Unified Displays
  SEE Exhibits, Equipment, Unified
    Displays

Window Displays
  SEE Media, Point of Sale

A further example of a *relative index* is that found on the pages preceding the yellow classified section of many telephone directories. The index to the yellow pages contains all the subjects listed in the yellow pages as well as additional related subjects to which reference might be made. In a records storage department, the subject index is likely to be on cards rather than on sheets of paper or in bound book form since the use of cards permits expansion without retyping.

Color in a card index may be advantageous—one color of card might identify main headings, another color might identify cross-references, and a third color might identify subheadings of main subjects.

The listing immediately below the main subject of all cross-references made to it and of any subtopics related to the main subject quickly brings together related materials and may help to explain the nature of the subject. (See Figure 8-8.)

```
Commercial Artists
_____

SEE ALSO

Agency Fees
Artwork
Fees
Free-Lance Artists
Layout
Studios
Type Specialists
```

Figure 8-8
Cross-Reference Card Showing
Related Subjects in a Relative Index

Customarily, an index used with a subject file does not contain the names of individuals or companies. However, for many businesses a control card file may be established to contain a card for each correspondent. On the card are shown the name and address of the correspondent and the subject title under which the papers are stored. Because reference may be made to the name of the individual or the company, cards containing this information may save hours of time for the files operator.

Special subject indexes. A type of subject indexing that has saved valuable time is the index for corporate minutes, for annual proceedings of trade associations, and for regular meeting minutes of organizations. Finding what action has been taken on any topic (such as Convention Arrangements, Jewelry, Pensions, Salesmen's Meetings, or the Branch in Cleveland) over the past 25 or even 50 years is a time-consuming process if all minutes for those years must be read. The indexing is usually done on cards containing enough detail, including dates, to give necessary information without actual reference being needed to the minute books. The cards are arranged alphabetically by subject. The sample card below shows what action has been taken concerning "Convention Arrangements" through the years. The first entry indicates the arrangements for the first national convention, held in Erie, can be found by referring to the minutes of April 7, 1964, on page 7. The last entry on the card shows the report of the 1972 arrangement committee is on page 14 of the 10-9-72 minutes.

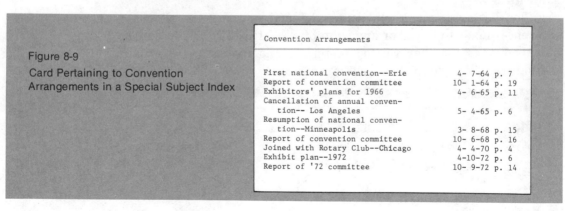

Figure 8-9

Card Pertaining to Convention Arrangements in a Special Subject Index

```
Convention Arrangements

First national convention--Erie        4- 7-64 p. 7
Report of convention committee        10- 1-64 p. 19
Exhibitors' plans for 1966             4- 6-65 p. 11
Cancellation of annual conven-
   tion-- Los Angeles                  5- 4-65 p. 6
Resumption of national conven-
   tion--Minneapolis                   3- 8-68 p. 15
Report of convention committee        10- 6-68 p. 16
Joined with Rotary Club--Chicago       4- 4-70 p. 4
Exhibit plan--1972                     4-10-72 p. 6
Report of '72 committee               10- 9-72 p. 14
```

Card files, typed sheets, or loose-leaf indexes are used with any numeric method of subject filing. If a card file is used, each main subject and each division thereof is typed on a separate card with its accompanying number beside it. The cards are filed alphabetically. If the topics are typed on sheets, the list is compiled alphabetically with the assigned number beside each topic in a continuous listing.

The operation of a decimal filing system requires an alphabetic index by subject, preferably on cards, with the assigned number appearing beside each subject. In addition, a listing of the decimal classifications is also necessary to indicate to those who code materials for storage the divisions and subdivisions being used.

SECTION 3. FILING PROCEDURE FOR SUBJECT METHOD

All the filing steps (inspection, indexing, coding, cross-referencing, sorting, filing, charge-out, and follow-up) are important in the subject method.

INSPECTION

The inspection of any paper is necessary to see that it has been released for storage.

INDEXING

Indexing, or classifying, is of great importance. This step consumes more time than in any other method of filing because of the necessity for the files operator to read the contents of each paper carefully to ascertain the subject or subjects under which it can be filed. If the correspondent has limited himself to only one subject, indexing is comparatively simple. The correct subject must be chosen from all the subjects available. If someone else has previously indicated the subject under which the paper is to be filed, the files operator must recheck the accuracy of the subject selection.

If the paper contains information about more than one subject, indexing will consist of the mental determination of the most important subject, the one under which the paper is to be filed, and the mental note that the other subjects must be cross-referenced.

CODING

Coding of the main subject heading and of any subdivisions of it consists of underlining or otherwise marking the selected words if they appear in the paper. If the subject title is not mentioned, it must be legibly written at the top of the sheet or in the upper right corner of it. A colored pencil is often used. If a numeric system is used, the code number must be determined from the index and written at the top or right corner of the material. Some files operators prefer to write both the subject heading and the code number on the material to be filed.

When more than one subject is indicated, only the most important one is underlined or written at the top of the paper; all other subjects are marked in some distinctive manner (marked with a wavy line, checked, x-ed, etc.) for cross-referencing.

CROSS-REFERENCING

The number of cross-references that may be made for one item may be many. If the record to be stored refers to several important subjects, sometimes copies (typed, photocopied, or the like) are made of the record and those copies are filed under the different subject headings to eliminate the need for cross-reference sheets for that record.

Figure 8-10

Tab of Permanent Cross-Reference

> Automobiles
> SEE
> Buses, Passenger Cars, Trucks

Figure 8-10 shows the tab of a permanent heavy sheet the size and weight of a guide bearing a label directing the searcher to the correct place in the file where papers may be found.

In Figure 8-11, the illustration at the left shows a card of a distinctive color to be inserted in the card index to show the searcher the correct subjects under which to look for information about automobiles. A cross-reference card of this type is a SEE reference used for synonymous or similar terms. In the files of which the illustrations in Figures 8-10 and 8-11 are a part, no paper would ever be filed under the heading "Automobiles." The SEE ALSO reference shown in Figure 8-11 is a reference to one or more places where helpful material connected with "Claims" may be found.

Figure 8-11

Three Cross-References Found in a Relative Index

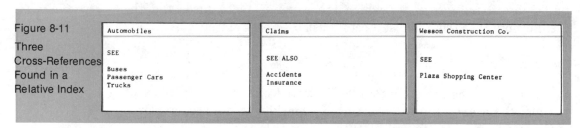

Automobiles	Claims	Wesson Construction Co.
SEE	SEE ALSO	SEE
Buses	Accidents	Plaza Shopping Center
Passenger Cars	Insurance	
Trucks		

The illustration at the right of Figure 8-11 shows an index card made for an individual correspondent whose name is often used in calling for records. Since the records relate to the Plaza Shopping Center, they have been filed under that subject title and the cross-reference card in the control file for correspondents indicates that.

SORTING

Sorting of records to be filed alphabetically by subject is usually done in an A-to-Z sorter. Records are sorted by main headings; any resorting by subdivisions is done at the time the records are inserted into the file folders. If the volume of records to be filed is great and many subdivisions are used, the sorter might be subdivided to save time at the files. A sorter with numeric divisions is required for material that has been coded by number. Sorting by number has been found to be faster than sorting by alphabetic character.

FILING

Careful filing of records into folders is always important. A careful look at the folder tab to see that the subject or number on it agrees with the subject or number coded on the record will help to avoid misfiling. A slight raising of the folder by the left hand before the record is inserted by the right hand will also avoid mistakes in filing. Material in a miscellaneous subject folder is arranged first by the alphabetic order of subjects. Material in a single subject folder is placed in alphabetic order according to the names of the correspondents. Each correspondent's papers are then arranged by date with the most recent date in front. If an individual correspondent's folder is used in a subject file, the records are arranged within it in the same manner as are papers in an individual folder in the alphabetic method.

CHARGE-OUT AND FOLLOW-UP

These procedures are the same as those used in any other method of filing. Knowing who has taken the papers, what the contents of the papers are, on what date the papers were borrowed, and on what date the papers are to be returned to the files are important in maintaining control over filed records. Follow-up is necessary to see that the papers are returned, to extend the charge-out time, or to call to the attention of someone in authority any matters needing consideration in the future. The only difference in procedure is that the order of the information on the OUT indicator will show the subject first and then the other information because the method of storage being used is the subject method.

SECTION 4. ADVANTAGES AND DISADVANTAGES OF THE SUBJECT METHOD

ADVANTAGES

Subject files save the time of executives since all written comments on a specific topic, a situation, a project, or a problem requiring managerial decision are grouped together rather than being separated into folders by the names of the correspondents.

Such grouped related information could include records of what transactions took place, what procedures were followed, what investigations have been undertaken or are contemplated, what developments are anticipated or have taken place, when they took place, and the results that were obtained.

Subject files can be expanded easily by adding subdivisions to main subjects. For example, if "Transportation" were a main heading and "Airplanes," "Automobiles," "Buses," and "Trains" were subheadings, "Rockets" could easily be added at some future time without rearranging the file in any way.

Statistical information may be obtained and relationships perceived that might not be apparent were other methods used, because in a subject system all related material has been brought together at a common point of reference.

DISADVANTAGES

The disadvantages of the subject method are many. Unless extreme caution is taken, subject lists and subdivisions grow until there are too many subjects chosen. The selection of subject classifications is difficult in that subject titles must be concise, definitive, and uniform. The classifications must not be terms used by specialists or subject to individual interpretation. A subject classification is not effective when the subject titles used establish no limitations. Many files (especially those in private offices and in department files) contain folders bearing subject titles that are meaningless. Only the secretary or the files operator knows what the folders contain. A folder bearing the title "Office Memoranda," "Miscellaneous," or "General" contains, in reality, unfiled papers.

The development and installation of subject files usually require the assistance of experienced records analysts. Furthermore, the staff that is to maintain the files must be thoroughly trained in the various phases of subject classification.

The subject method of filing is the most expensive method to maintain because it requires very experienced workers as files operators. Preparation of materials for the subject files always takes longer than in any other method of filing. The content of every paper must be thoroughly and carefully read; scanning will not suffice.

Duplex numeric and decimal methods have the disadvantages inherent in the use of numbers—transposition and misreading.

An inadequate subject index often prevents or seriously delays the finding of papers. Indexing and coding should be done with the thought that all individuals who are here today may be gone tomorrow. Memory should never be relied upon.

Although a folder may be properly labeled, the papers filed within it may not pertain to the subject except incidentally. The labels *Prices, Adjustments, Collections, Credits* may be correct when the folder contains administrative papers on these topics; but when a subject folder contains papers often called for by the name of the writer, and when no cross-reference card has been prepared for the relative index, delay is encountered when the paper is requested by name instead of by subject.

Within a subject file, the use of folders for officers' names leads to difficulty when the name of an officer is forgotten or unknown or when personnel changes. Too often papers are filed in folders made for the name of the officer (Paul Miller) in charge of the department instead of for the name of the department (Accounting Department); or under the name of the individual (Mary Alexander) who holds the position instead of under the position name (Corporation Secretary). Personnel may change in organizations, but the name of the department or position remains.

Records that are filed by subject in order that statistical information may be easily compiled or so that mailing lists can be quickly prepared require an extensive cross-referencing system that is impractical. It would be costly, for instance, to file customers' correspondence and orders under the headings of "Accounts—Out-of-Town" and "Accounts—City" just to find sales statistics for each salesman's territory or for each state or each city.

Most of the disadvantages mentioned here are based on inappropriate uses of the subject method. If reference to materials is to be made by name of individual, by firm name, or by location, subject filing is not the recommended method. However, after careful study of the needs of a company, a records manager may rightly decide that subject filing is the best method by which to store a portion of the company's records.

For Review and Discussion

1. Every subject file, no matter how small, must be accompanied by a written list of subjects used. Why is it so essential that this written list or index be prepared?

2. What is meant by the sentence, "Only the most skilled of files operators are competent to select subject headings"?

3. What factors make the cost of subject filing high?

4. What do the words "subdivision" or "subclassification" mean in the subject method?

5. Give several ways of identifying or separating one main heading and its subdivisions from other main headings and their subdivisions in a subject file drawer.

6. What is the difference between the straight dictionary arrangement and the encyclopedic arrangement of a simple alphabetic subject file?

7. Comment on the advantages or disadvantages of using straight-line arrangement and alternating arrangement of folders in a subject file.

8. How are special subject classification guides in subject arrangement similar to special name guides in an alphabetic subject arrangement?

9. What rules of label typing should be followed in the typing of captions for guides and folders for a subject file?

10. What is the basic difference between duplex numeric and decimal arrangements? How are they similar?

11. In the duplex numeric arrangement, for what levels of subject titles do the code numbers "1-7-5," "1-2a," and "7:1-5" stand?

12. Why is the Dewey Decimal System not adaptable to business office files?

13. How can subject filing be integrated with the alphabetic method of storing correspondence? with the numeric?

14. Can subject filing ever be used in a geographic method of filing correspondence? Explain.

15. How does a relative index differ from a simple index used in the subject method?

16. Explain at least four different forms in which indexes to subject files can be kept. Which form permits expansion with the least difficulty? Why?

17. If an executive's subject file has only ten subjects, why is it necessary to have a written subject index?

18. If a typed list of subjects is used in an office, and frequent reference to the files is made by a number of people, where might the typed list be kept for easy access by the files user?

19. If you were preparing a list of main headings and subdivisions for subject filing, why would the following be considered incorrect?

    Main heading   : Office equipment
    Subdivision   : Desks
    Sub-subdivisions: Mahogany
                      Executive

20. Comment on the following subjects contemplated for use as main headings:

    a. Data
    b. Instructions
    c. Letters
    d. Material
    e. Office Conditions
    f. Office Memos
    g. Office Supplies
    h. Purchasing
    i. Sales
    j. Trips

21. In Figure 8-5, page 196, subdivisions of each group are numbered with the main heading number and a decimal number. In the 705 group, what is the number of the miscellaneous folder?

22. Miscellaneous folders are provided in most filing systems. Why is it desirable to avoid the use of miscellaneous folders in the subject method of records storage?

23. Compare the following points as they pertain to the alphabetic method, the numeric method, the geographic method, and the subject method:

    a. The use of the rules for alphabetic arrangement (Chapter 3)
    b. The arrangement of guides and folders in the file drawers
    c. The coding step
    d. The cross-referencing step
    e. The charge-out procedure

24. Assume that you are the files supervisor responsible for the subject files of several departments. Letters that pertain to Department A are already coded with a subject; letters that pertain to Department B are sometimes coded and sometimes not; letters that pertain to Department C are not coded.

   a. What would be your procedure in relation to the filing of all the pieces of correspondence from the various departments?

   b. Often the letters are called for at some future time by subjects other than the ones that either you or the department have used in coding. What would you suggest to make your work easier?

Learning Projects

1. Visit the office of a company, a church, a bank or other financial institution, and a school. What kind of subject files are maintained in each? Write your findings in the form of a short report letter to your instructor.

2. Study the index preceding the yellow classified pages of a large telephone directory. How does the listing in the index pages differ from the subject listing in the yellow pages? Give specific examples.

3. Consult with a relative or a friend who is recording secretary of an organization. Ascertain whether any type of indexing of the minutes has been done. If so, see if the indexing corresponds to the type of indexing mentioned in this chapter. Be prepared to report orally.

4. If stores in your vicinity sell filing supplies, ask about and make a list of the kinds of guides and folders that are most often purchased for use with subject files.

5. From an office supply store in your area or from filing equipment manufacturers' catalogs, determine the kinds of guides and folders that are available for subject filing. Make a list to compare with others made by students in your class.

6. a. Use the relative index given on pp. 201-203 and Figure 8-6. Make an alphabetic list of the main subject captions and the subheads found in this subject file.

   b. Referring to Figure 8-6 and the relative index, in which folder would you file the following items:

      1. A printed advertising brochure
      2. A TV commercial script
      3. A picture of a prize-winning billboard
      4. A list of advertising slogans that have been used successfully during the past 10 years
      5. A rough draft of art work for a brochure soon to be printed
      6. A report on a special advertising campaign just concluded
      7. A report of advertising in TIME and COSMOPOLITAN magazines

8. A quarterly report prepared by your company to send to stockholders
9. A memo of promotion to increase sales of a certain item
10. A picture of the car card advertising to be used in public transportation vehicles (busses, trains, and cabs)

Laboratory Assignment 14

You should now complete Laboratory Assignment 14 (Subject Correspondence Filing) in *Records Management—Laboratory Materials.*

PART THREE

STORING AND
RETRIEVING
SPECIAL RECORDS

Chapter 9

Filing of card
and
visible records

Quite frequently, office records are maintained in a card or visible record file. These files are useful and necessary for keeping names and addresses alphabetically in geographic filing and in numeric filing and for keeping an alphabetic list of subjects and, perhaps, of authors' names and article titles in the subject files. Because of the frequent use of these types of records, it is essential that records personnel have a knowledge of the applications and mechanics of card and visible records filing, the type of equipment available for these records, the types of systems used, and the advantages and disadvantages of card and visible records.

SECTION 1. TYPES OF CARDS AND VISIBLE RECORDS

INDEX RECORDS

Card records usually fall into two classifications. The first classification consists of *index records*, which contain information used for reference only. Index records are used "to refer to"; they include the following data on cards: (The list is representative, not all-inclusive.)

Customers' names and addresses
Suppliers' names and addresses
Personnel records
Stock room or warehouse item information
Dealers' price lists, terms of sale, delivery terms, and discount terms
Telephone numbers and names and addresses of people with whom an
  employer frequently does business

POSTED RECORDS

The second type of card record consists of *posted records,* which contain information that is continually accumulated and recorded on the cards either by hand or by machine. Posted records are used "to record on" and are sometimes called *secondary records* since they contain information that has been copied from original or primary records. Examples include:

Stock control cards	Hospital records
Payroll cards	Student permanent record cards
Repair and maintenance cards	Dental and medical records
Sales records	Scientific research records
Inventory records	Ledger cards in bookkeeping and ac-
Purchase records	counting departments
Auto service records	Credit and collection records

The list given above is not meant to be inclusive; it is merely representative.

Figure 9-1 on page 217 shows a sample student permanent record card to which data may be added as the student progresses through his course of study. Figure 9-2 illustrates a credit card on which payments and charges are recorded as they are received in the office.

SECTION 2. EQUIPMENT FOR CARD AND VISIBLE RECORD FILING

Cards may be filed vertically in special drawers or boxes or be filed visibly in trays or other containers so that the edge or some portion of each card is exposed to view. The two methods of filing cards are directly related to the manner in which the cards are to be used.

VERTICAL CARD FILING

Guiding systems. Cards that are filed upright in drawers or boxes have only card guides to separate them into the desired sections: alphabetic, numeric, geographic, or other. No folders are used. Vertical card guiding plans are much the same in principle as are the guiding plans available for use with correspondence files. The notable exception is the use of an *end* or *terminal guide* at the end of a special name section to separate this section from the cards immediately behind it. The alphabetic method usually is a straight directory

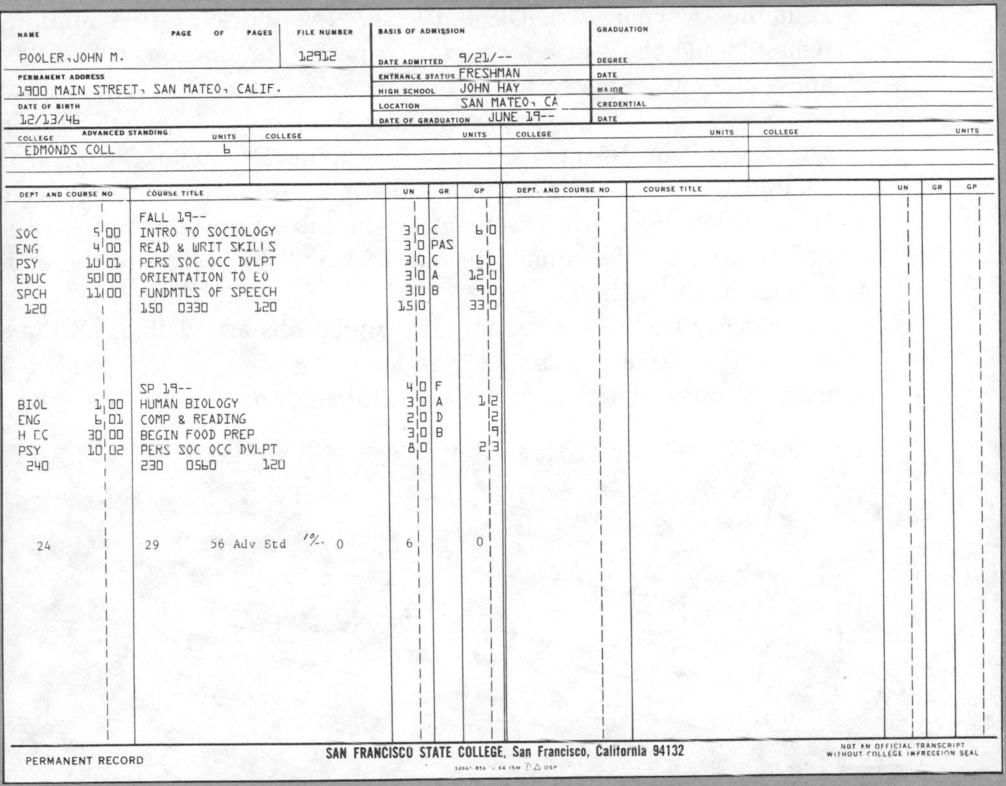

NAME: POOLER, JOHN M. | PAGE OF PAGES | FILE NUMBER: 12912

PERMANENT ADDRESS: 1900 MAIN STREET, SAN MATEO, CALIF.

DATE OF BIRTH: 12/13/46

BASIS OF ADMISSION
DATE ADMITTED: 9/21/--
ENTRANCE STATUS: FRESHMAN
HIGH SCHOOL: JOHN HAY
LOCATION: SAN MATEO, CA
DATE OF GRADUATION: JUNE 19--

GRADUATION
DEGREE
DATE
MAJOR
CREDENTIAL
DATE

ADVANCED STANDING

COLLEGE	UNITS	COLLEGE	UNITS	COLLEGE	UNITS	COLLEGE	UNITS
EDMONDS COLL	6						

DEPT AND COURSE NO		COURSE TITLE	UN	GR	GP
		FALL 19--			
SOC	5 00	INTRO TO SOCIOLOGY	3 0	C	6 0
ENG	4 00	READ & WRIT SKILLS	3 0	PAS	
PSY	10 01	PERS SOC OCC DVLPT	3 0	C	6 0
EDUC	50 00	ORIENTATION TO ED	3 0	A	12 0
SPCH	11 00	FUNDMTLS OF SPEECH	3 0	B	9 0
120		150 0330 120	15 0		33 0
		SP 19--	4 0	F	
BIOL	1 00	HUMAN BIOLOGY	3 0	A	1 2
ENG	6 01	COMP & READING	2 0	D	2
H EC	30 00	BEGIN FOOD PREP	3 0	B	9
PSY	10 02	PERS SOC OCC DVLPT	8 0		2 3
240		230 0560 120			
24		29 56 Adv Std 10/-- 0	6		0

PERMANENT RECORD | SAN FRANCISCO STATE COLLEGE, San Francisco, California 94132 | NOT AN OFFICIAL TRANSCRIPT WITHOUT COLLEGE IMPRESSION SEAL

San Francisco State University

Figure 9-1
Student Permanent Record Card

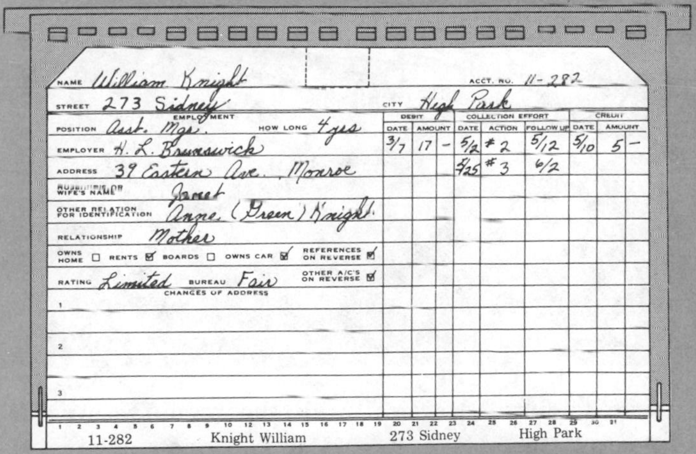

NAME: William Knight | ACCT. NO. 11-282
STREET: 273 Sidney | CITY: High Park
EMPLOYMENT
POSITION: Asst. Mgr. | HOW LONG: 4 yrs
EMPLOYER: H. L. Brunswick
ADDRESS: 39 Eastern Ave., Monroe
HUSBAND'S OR WIFE'S NAME: Janet
OTHER RELATION FOR IDENTIFICATION: Anne (Green) Knight
RELATIONSHIP: Mother
OWNS HOME ☐ RENTS ☑ BOARDS ☐ OWNS CAR ☑ REFERENCES ON REVERSE ☑
RATING: Limited | BUREAU: Fair | OTHER A/C'S ON REVERSE ☑
CHANGES OF ADDRESS
1
2
3

DEBIT DATE	DEBIT AMOUNT	COLLECTION EFFORT DATE	ACTION	FOLLOW UP	CREDIT DATE	CREDIT AMOUNT
3/7	17 –	5/2	#2	5/12	5/10	5 –
		5/25	#3	6/2		

11-282 Knight William 273 Sidney High Park

Figure 9-2 Credit Card

Sperry Remington, Office Systems and Machines, Sperry Rand Corporation method such as the Oxford *Flexindex System* (Figure 9-3, Oxford Pendaflex Corporation, Garden City, New York). Other similar systems include the *Variadex Index* (Sperry Remington, Office Systems and Machines, Sperry Rand Corporation, Blue Bell, Pennsylvania), the *Space Saver Expandex* (Shaw-Walker, Muskegon, Michigan), and the Alpha-Natural System (Datavue Products Corp., Wabash, Indiana). The variations among the manufacturers are minors ones: the positions and reinforcement of the tabs, the weight of card stock, and the use of "terminal" instead of "end" to designate the end of a special name section.

As Figure 9-3 shows, only the guide tabs are visible; all the cards are of the same size and lower than the tops of the guides. Each manufacturer determines the labeling on the card guides that will

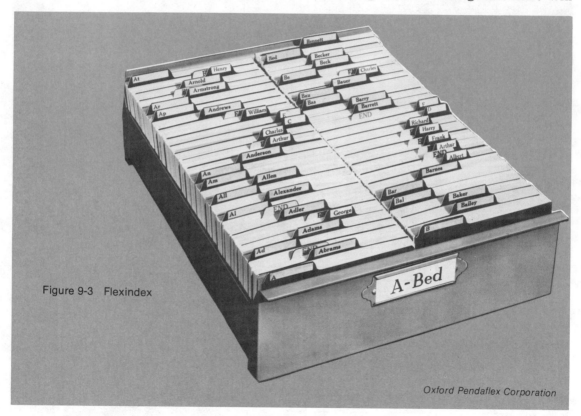

Figure 9-3   Flexindex

Oxford Pendaflex Corporation

be standard with its firm; practically all the manufacturers carry alphabetic, state, month, weekday, and daily guides. Some manufacturers also stock city, county, and recipe guides as standard items. Card record systems have been designed for special professions or businesses including attorneys, banks, educational institutions, insurance firms, and real estate houses. Blank guides may, of course, be used; on these guides are typed notations to fit the needs of the office.

In some cases, transparent card holders may be used as guides. The holders are one-half inch higher than the cards that are inserted into them. Because the holders are higher than the cards, the top of the plastic-covered card will be higher than the other cards in the file; the card is held in this higher position by a slot near the bottom of the plastic holder. Whatever is typed on the top line of the card becomes the guide to that section of the file.

Standard card sizes are 5 by 3, 6 by 4, and 8 by 5 inches. The first number indicates the width of the card; the second number indicates the depth. The 5-inch edge of a 5 by 3 inch card, therefore, is the edge resting on the bottom of the drawer. In requesting cards from a supplier, the records manager gives the width first although, traditionally, cards have been referred to as "3 by 5" and "4 by 6" cards.

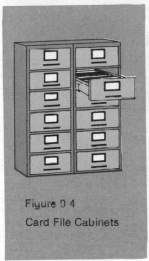

Figure 9-4
Card File Cabinets

Manual equipment. The variety of equipment available in which to house card files is great. Of the *hand-operated equipment*, perhaps the most widely used is the cabinet with drawers similar to correspondence file drawers but smaller (Figure 9-4). Tiers of cabinet files can be purchased in many heights. Card-file drawers combined with desks and with counters are frequently found in offices.

Card files used exclusively for punched cards may be housed in specially built cabinets with removable trays. These trays have high side walls, and the cards are tightly packed so that trays may be carried vertically. Some tab card trays have a hand hold at the back of the drawer for ease in carrying with two hands.

Specialized equipment, such as that for Acme's "Veri-Visible" (Figure 9-5), permits housing of cards in unit holders that can be moved separately. Several employees can work on different units of the records at the same time.

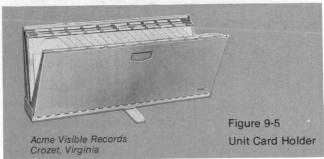

Acme Visible Records
Crozet, Virginia

Figure 9-5
Unit Card Holder

Rotary cabinets (Figure 9-6) permit more people to use records simultaneously; less floor space is required for more records than could be housed in file drawers; no walking is necessary to get to the files; tiers may be added for expansion; fewer misfilings occur because fatigue, discomfort, and poor visibility are reduced; records need not be duplicated since one set serves several departments. Many kinds of records can be filed in rotary equipment—cards, books, binders, folders, and papers. Sliding covers with locks can be procured for security purposes. Rotary equipment can be tailored to fit individual records requirements.

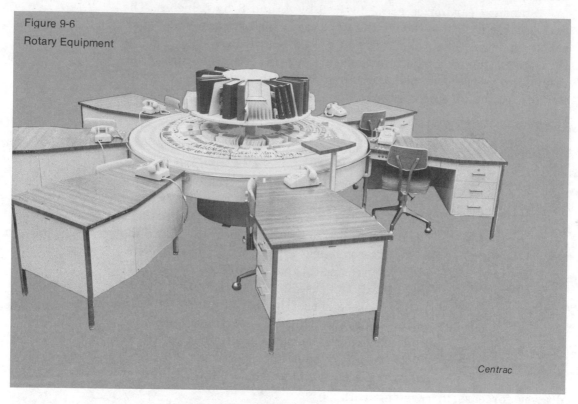

Figure 9-6
Rotary Equipment

Centrac

Bookkeeping and accounting records can be housed in trays that are quickly adjusted. Figure 9-7 shows closed locked position and open posting position. Once the tray is closed and the key removed, no sheet can be taken out or referred to. The compression squeezes out air to provide fire resistance.

Cabinets, racks, and easels for card books must be solid and sturdily constructed to hold heavy books. Single or double doors permit access from either side of a double work station; rollers in the cabinet bases permit books to glide in and out easily; index labels at the top or the bottom of the slots keep materials in order.

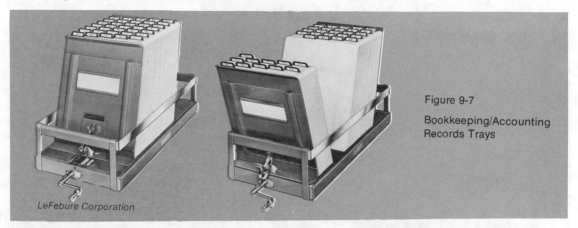

Figure 9-7

Bookkeeping/Accounting Records Trays

LeFebure Corporation

Trays of cards may be located in stationery cabinets, and the operator's chair situated on a sliding track in front of the files (Figure 9-8). A variation of this type of equipment is a stationery operator and cards housed in sliding trays.

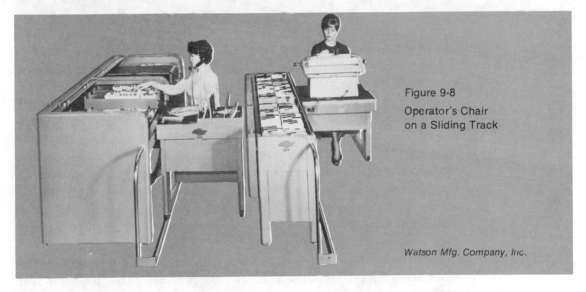

Figure 9-8

Operator's Chair on a Sliding Track

Watson Mfg. Company, Inc.

A wheel file or tubular-type file (left in Figure 9-9, page 222) contains cards that are snapped in place over a center rod and kept within bounds by the outer rims of a wheel. The size of the wheel may vary from a desk-top unit approximately 8 inches high to much larger motorized desk-size units. The *Instafile* (right in Figure

9-9) contains 200 to 500 cards instantly visible for right- or left-handed use. Each card is securely fastened with the card-lock rod and pivots to full readability.

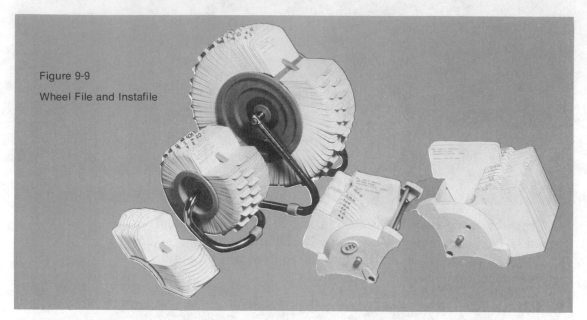

Figure 9-9

Wheel File and Instafile

Mechanized equipment. In addition to the wheel file described in the previous paragraph, mechanized equipment includes rotary equipment such as that shown in Figure 9-6 on page 220. Mechanization of card files is found in large records control installations.

Another type of motorized card file consists of card trays hung in cradles that do not tip or spill. The *Stratomatic* (Figure 9-10) places up to 700,000 card records before an operator within five seconds from the touch of a button. The file design allows units to be placed back to back or side by side. It can be used for cards, microforms, and specialty products and may be secured in a variety of widths. Remington Rand's Kard-Veyer System and Diebold's power files are similar types of equipment.

Cards may be filed in practically any order in the special equipment known as *Electrofile*. The equipment is designed to handle loan account records. The cards have metal teeth on the bottom that are cut according to a predetermined code (name, account number, due date, dealer, and the like). When a certain card is needed, the tray containing it is placed in a machine that has a special keyboard at the front of it. By typing the name or number of the wanted card

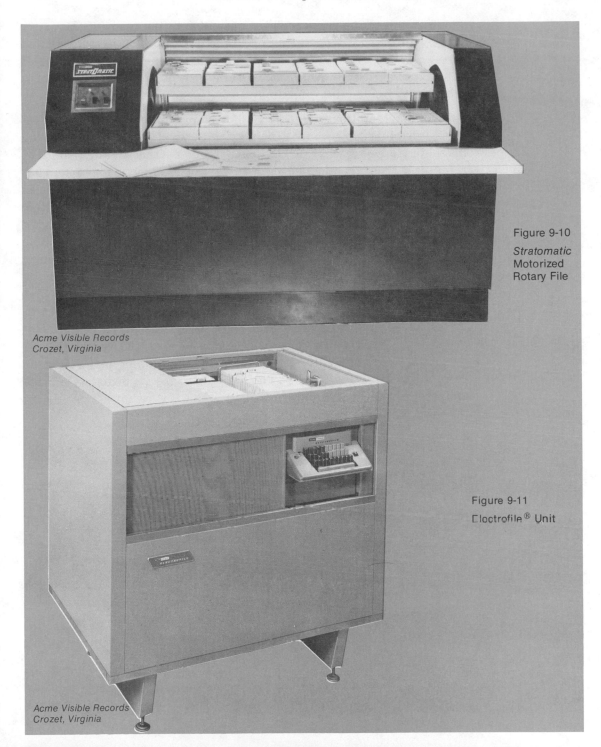

Figure 9-10

Stratomatic Motorized Rotary File

*Acme Visible Records
Crozet, Virginia*

Figure 9-11

Electrofile® Unit

*Acme Visible Records
Crozet, Virginia*

(conforming to the same code as was cut into the teeth of the card) and by pressing an operating bar, the operator raises the wanted card above the tray (Figure 9-11). With this equipment, cards need not be arranged according to any method; random insertion of cards into the tray cuts filing time immensely.

The Magne-Dex card tray shown in Figure 9-12, gives instant visibility to groups of vertically filed cards by utilizing magnetic force to separate one card from another at any point of reference. Each tray is equipped with two permanent magnets, running from front to rear on the sides of the tray. In each side near the top of every Magne-Dex card a small piece of steel is laminated. This steel (only .002 inches thick) has a mild temper so that it can be put into a typewriter or bookkeeping platen easily and yet is able to snap back to its original flat shape when not under pressure. Original records can be converted for use in Magne-Dex trays by attaching activator patches to the cards. The individual cards are magnetized to repel each other by the permanent magnets. Control plates, placed approximately every 150 cards, keep the cards compressed. A slight touch releases the pressure of the control plate; when any card is lightly pulled forward, a fanning-out action of from 15 to 20 cards results. The top edges are immediately visible and the required card can be found, read, or removed quickly as the need may be.

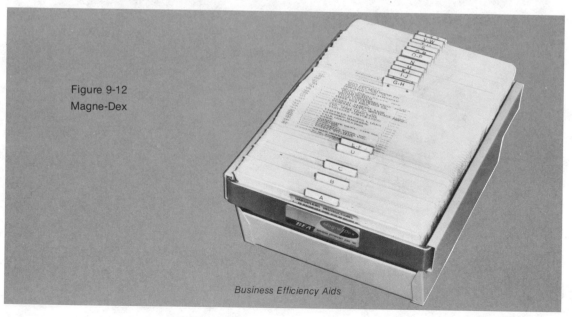

Figure 9-12
Magne-Dex

Business Efficiency Aids

Signals. The information on a card is not visible until the card has been located and exposed to view. So that some information may be instantly seen when the file drawer is opened or mass groups of cards are viewed at one time, permanent or temporary signals call attention to certain conditions of the records.

A distinctive color on the guide tabs may be significant. The cards themselves may be of several colors to show different types of information (the names of customers in a certain area may be indicated by green cards, for instance). The edges of all cards may be printed with codes to be cut in a special way. One of the best-known of these systems is *McBee Keysort*. In this

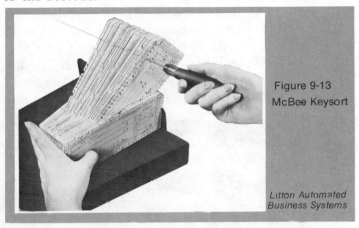

Figure 9-13
McBee Keysort

Litton Automated
Business Systems

system (Figure 9-13) all edges of the cards have holes through which a slender steel needle may be thrust. When the holes have been notched according to a code, all the cards with notched holes will remain in place while the uncut cards will be raised by the needle.

Movable transparent or opaque signal clips can be attached to the tops of the cards. Their position and/or color may signify special information. The difficulty with movable clips is that they are liable to be removed accidentally; a chance brushing across them may dislodge them.

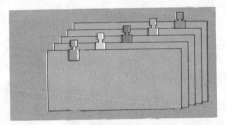

VISIBLE CARD OR STRIP FILING

Filing equipment for visible records is made so that a strip or at least one edge of a card is exposed on which information is instantly visible without any handling of the record. Of the various types of equipment manufactured, the kind used depends upon the requirements of the organization as to the number of cards or strips to be filed, the importance of their location to their use, their portability, their frequency of use, and whether they are to be used for reference or for posting purposes. The main kinds of visible files are (1) card visible files and (2) reference visible files.

Card visible files. A number of different forms of card visible files, also known as *posting visible files,* are available. The best-known holder of cards on which information is to be posted is probably the cabinet with shallow drawers or trays, each one containing a large number of overlapping cards held horizontally by hangers or hinges or in slots called *pocket holders.* Figure 9-14 shows a cabinet with drawers that can be pulled out and down but that remain attached to the cabinet by a hinge. Cards are held in pocket holders having a protective transparent edge. The holders are on wires that snap in and out of the drawer. Both sides of the card may be used since the card bends around the lower edge of the holder.

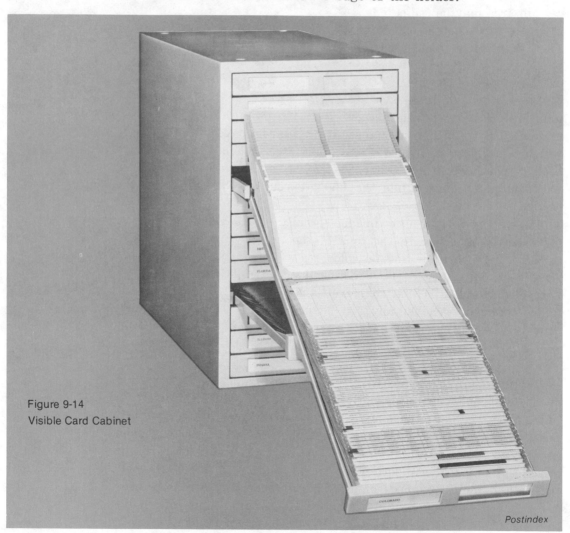

Figure 9-14
Visible Card Cabinet

Postindex

Other types of cabinets have more than one panel of horizontally held cards within the same drawer, to increase the capacity of the equipment. The capacity varies with the size of the equipment and the size and thickness of the cards used.

Each tray or drawer should be labeled with a closed notation showing the range of the contents. Cards are inserted so that one or two lines of each card are visible. The information on the visible edge of the cards is used to determine the alphabetic, subject, geographic, or numeric arrangement within the drawer or tray.

Information to be posted to a card is placed on the portion of the card that is exposed after the cards on top of it have been flipped back. Both sides of cards that are attached directly to hangers or hinges may be used since the hanger or hinge is flexible. Some cards are made so that they may be folded over the hanger rod, giving four surfaces on which to post information. Inserts may be used with some cards, giving additional posting surfaces.

Pocket holders (see Figure 9-14) are slotted to accommodate cards of various sizes. Some holders have transparent edge protectors, while some have the complete pocket made of transparent material. This see-through covering protects the edge of the cards from wear, tear, moisture, and dirt.

Where thousands of cards must be kept, frequent posting to them is required, and space is limited, equipment that is almost ceiling height may be necessary to utilize space well. To reach the highest card trays would be a physical impossibility without power-driven equipment.

Figure 9-15 shows the front of one mechanized cabinet. As many as 200,000 listings are available with a fingertip touch. To retrieve the proper frame housing the card that is needed, the operator first finds the appropriate code on the handy index panel. The appropriate code buttons are pushed in a numerical sequence, and the correct record frame appears within seconds. (See also page 276 of Chapter 11).

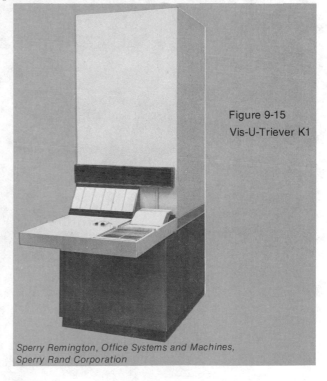

Figure 9-15
Vis-U-Triever K1

Sperry Remington, Office Systems and Machines, Sperry Rand Corporation

When portability is a factor, when the volume of cards to be filed is small, or when many operators need to post simultaneously, hinged pocket books may be used instead of cabinet trays. Card books may have fastenings at the top of the cards for ease in posting, or the cards may be snapped in and out at any point. Loose-leaf books with removable panels of cards provide portability and contain much data in a small space. Labeling of the contents of the book is done on the back binding.

Racks and cabinets are used to house card books. On the racks, books stand in upright closed position with the aid of bookends. Cabinets have compartments, and the books are stored in an upright position. The cabinet may be a revolving one so that several operators can refer to the information; opposite sides of the cabinet may be open so that operators may work from both sides; or the cabinet may be closed on three sides.

A file folder equipped with pockets for cards also gives portability, or the folder can be filed in a regular correspondence file or in a desk drawer. The folder is of heavy-duty construction to withstand the hard wear it receives from constant use.

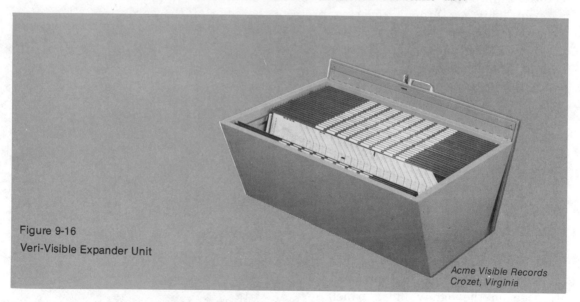

Figure 9-16
Veri-Visible Expander Unit

*Acme Visible Records
Crozet, Virginia*

Vertical-visible card files are especially useful to house cards on which data are posted by machine. One card file of this type has a tub of especially cut cards placed near the operator. Cards are filed in overlapping arrangement, their upper right corners being visible (Figure 9-16). The cards are notched at the bottom edge to straddle spacer rods located at the bottom of the tub in which they are kept. The solid line printed on the top of the following card becomes immediately visible when the card in front of any one card is removed.

Reference visible files. If but one line or a few lines of data are needed for reference purposes only, using an entire card on which to record a small bit of information is an unnecessary and wasteful method for keeping the information. Therefore, reference visible file information is placed on narrow strips, and the strips are inserted into visible files. Reference information that is often kept by businesses includes lists of employees, directories of various kinds (hospitals, hotels, motels, clubs), stock or tool location indexes, telephone listings, prospective customer lists, membership lists, publication subscription lists, and used-car listings.

Strips containing data are usually attached to panels or trays or frames. The illustration in Figure 9-17 shows one-line strips of information on panels attached to a revolving center post. This equipment is known as *single tier rotary equipment,* but double and triple tiers are also available. Although the illustration shows a desk model, floor equipment may also be purchased. Guide tabs at the sides of the panels are the primary dividers; they indicate the range of the names on each panel.

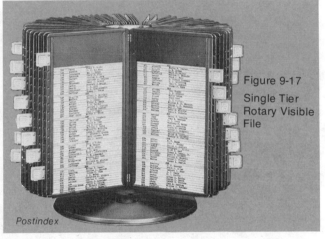

Figure 9-17

Single Tier Rotary Visible File

Postindex

Room for expansion is provided at the top of each panel; as names are added, the strips may be shifted upward since each strip is simply snapped into place. Removal of a strip allows the strips above it to shift downward.

Panels of these visible strips may be arranged on swinging brackets, in book form, in the form of flip-up indexes, or on stationary panels. Strips ordinarily are purchased in continuous sheet form with perforations between them. They may be typed upon, separated, and flexed into place; or they may be inserted into transparent tubes that are then snapped into position in the trays.

The shallow tray cabinet file referred to on page 226 in connection with card visible files may also be used with interlocking small card reference information. Figure 9-18 on the following page shows

Figure 9-18
Chaindex
Strips

B–620	Berc	Adam	S 127461
B–620	Berke	Albert E	S 56739
B–620	Berck	Alice	S 28061
B–620	Bourque	Armand	S 115038
B–620	Berke	Arthur	S 5873
B–620	Birke	Barbara	S 106927
B–620	Bork	Beatrice	S 74301

*Sperry Remington, Office Systems and Machines,
Sperry Rand Corporation*

Sperry Remington's *Chaindex* arrangement. Strips are supplied in sheets with a kraft backing or in sheets with perforations between the strips. Three widths, to accommodate one-, two-, or three-line information, can be obtained for insertion into equipment with special panels.

Signals. The signals that may be used for visible equipment include colored card stock, special printed edges that may be cut in various ways, and removable metal or plastic tabs of various colors

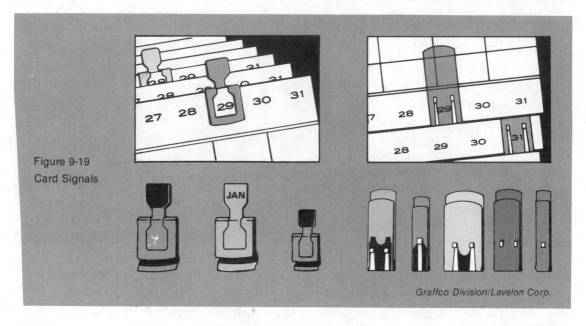

Figure 9-19
Card Signals

Graffco Division/Lavelon Corp.

and shapes. (Figure 9-19). Colored paper strips may be inserted in the clear plastic protectors; the plastic strips along the edge of the card may be tinted in at least ten different colors. Other methods of signaling include perforations in the card edge to allow different colors to show through according to color tabs inserted behind the holes. Card corners may be clipped to indicate special information. Some cards are so made that their tabs can be progressively cut (half-cut when the name is a prospect, for instance, and one-fifth-cut when the prospect becomes a customer).

Small L-shaped signals and V-shaped signals are used with certain pocket types of equipment. The V-shape signal fits around the visible edge so that the indicator may be seen on both sides of the card. Although space does not permit illustrating all the types of signals available, Figure 9-20 shows three different types: (a) Signals used with pocket type visible records that have protective strips along the margins may be secured in transparent or opaque

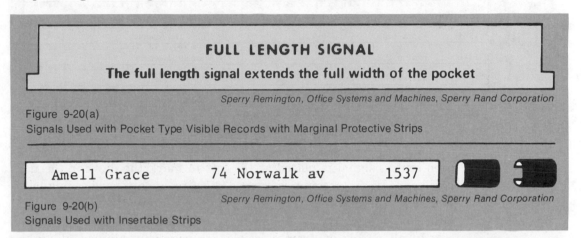

FULL LENGTH SIGNAL

The full length signal extends the full width of the pocket

Sperry Remington, Office Systems and Machines, Sperry Rand Corporation

Figure 9-20(a)
Signals Used with Pocket Type Visible Records with Marginal Protective Strips

Amell Grace   74 Norwalk av   1537

Sperry Remington, Office Systems and Machines, Sperry Rand Corporation

Figure 9-20(b)
Signals Used with Insertable Strips

materials. Some colors of the opaque signals have a matte finish for pen or pencil markings. (b) Signals used with insertable strips may be "C"-shaped transparent plastic or celluloid to be attached over the insert and moved freely along it. The sleeve or soda-straw type is opaque, to be slipped over the tip of the insert for temporary use. A brief notation can be written on the sleeve. (c) Clip-on signals, for use with exposed cards, are made to slip over the bottom edge of the card; the signals can be shifted or moved easily.

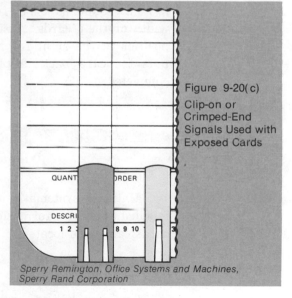

Figure 9-20(c)
Clip-on or Crimped-End Signals Used with Exposed Cards

Sperry Remington, Office Systems and Machines, Sperry Rand Corporation

An illustration of signals in use is shown in Figure 9-21 on page 232. Information about the status of many accounts may be seen at a glance. Since most customers pay on time, the signals at the right tend to form a straight line in the current month. Overdue accounts, indicated by out-by-line signals, are apparent. After the first collection letter has

1 3 5 7 9 11 13 15 17 19 21 23 25 27 29 31	2 4 6 8 10 12 14 16 18 20 22 24 26 28 30
1317 Badger, Ralph H.	257 Monroe Court
1 3 5 7 9 11 13 15 17 19 21 23 25 27 29 31	2 4 6 8 10 12 14 16 18 20 22 24 26 28 30
1320 Badgett, Paul R.	323 Courtland Drive
1 3 5 7 9 11 13 15 17 19 21 23 25 27 29 31	2 4 6 8 10 12 14 16 18 20 22 24 26 28 30
1323 Badgley, Frank	585 E. Hope
1 3 5 7 9 11 13 15 17 19 21 23 25 27 29 31	2 4 6 8 10 12 14 16 18 20 22 24 26 28 30
1330 Badina, Norma P.	Iroquois Building
1 3 5 7 9 11 13 15 17 19 21 23 25 27 29 31	2 4 6 8 10 12 14 16 18 20 22 24 26 28 30
1332 Badner, David	10 Avery Avenue
1 3 5 7 9 11 13 15 17 19 21 23 25 27 29 31	2 4 6 8 10 12 14 16 18 20 22 24 26 28 30
1336 Bannister, F. J.	2500 Delaware Avenue
1 3 5 7 9 11 13 15 17 19 21 23 25 27 29 31	2 4 6 8 10 12 14 16 18 20 22 24 26 28 30
1341 Banta, J.S.	283 Linwood Avenue
1 3 5 7 9 11 13 15 17 19 21 23 25 27 29 31	2 4 6 8 10 12 14 16 18 20 22 24 26 28 30
1346 Banton, P. L.	65 West 99 Street
1 3 5 7 9 11 13 15 17 19 21 23 25 27 29 31	2 4 6 8 10 12 14 16 18 20 22 24 26 28 30
1349 Banville, Francis	130 Post Avenue
1 3 5 7 9 11 13 15 17 19 21 23 25 27 29 31	2 4 6 8 10 12 14 16 18 20 22 24 26 28 30
1352 Banville, J. K.	654 Water Street
1 3 5 7 9 11 13 15 17 19 21 23 25 27 29 31	2 4 6 8 10 12 14 16 18 20 22 24 26 28 30

Figure 9-21

Status of Accounts Record Card with Signals   *Sperry Remington, Office Systems and Machines,*
Sperry Rand Corporation

been sent, a signal is placed at the left to mark the day for the next reminder. If the account is turned over to an attorney, a signal is placed at the extreme right margin. No signals at all indicate inactive accounts.

In all panels or frames, cards are regularly aligned along the left side. Some panels or frames are about a half-inch wider than the width of their cards. A slight nudge will move a card to an offset position at the right for immediate attention. Another little nudge puts the card back in place at the left edge when the work is completed.

SECTION 3. FILING PROCEDURE FOR CARD AND VISIBLE RECORDS

Unless a systematic method of filing is followed, cards will be misfiled and the information on them will be of no value because the cards cannot be located.

TYPING OF DATA

Typing a line of information on the edge of any card requires care because of the danger of card slippage. A special *bottom line card holder* (Figure 9-22) is recommended for use in typing the one line since the beginning word on each card should be in exact alignment with that on all other cards. Also, the typing must be visible in a specified area across the bottom (or top) edge of the card so it will not be obscured by the preceding or following card.

Care must be exercised when typing data on strips also. The beginning words on all strips must be in alignment, the typing format must be the same in regard to capitalization and punctuation, and proofreading is important.

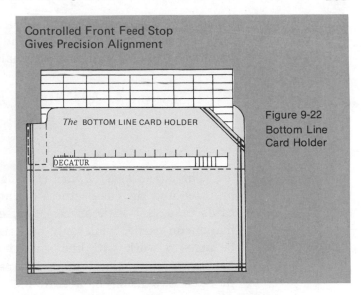

Controlled Front Feed Stop
Gives Precision Alignment

The BOTTOM LINE CARD HOLDER

DECATUR

Figure 9-22
Bottom Line
Card Holder

FILING ORDER

Alphabetic filing order, according to the principles of alphabetic filing of correspondence, is the method most frequently used. A geographic arrangement of the cards might be used, following any of the variations used for correspondence filing. Cards are sometimes arranged alphabetically according to subjects.

A file containing thousands of cards may be arranged alphabetically by grouping similar sounding names. All similar first indexing units, regardless of spelling, are filed together; the alphabetic arrangement is by the second and succeeding indexing units. At the beginning of a group of cards filed under similar surnames (similar in pronunciation but spelled differently), there is a master card that shows all possible spellings of the surname. Many cross-reference cards are necessary in this situation, one cross-reference at each place where a card would be placed were all cards filed in strict alphabetic sequence rather than in name groups. Because of the time necessary to make the cross-references and the difficulty in agreeing on what constitutes a similar name, this arrangement is seldom used.

Cards that are used for follow-up purposes are arranged chronologically instead of alphabetically.

CHARGE-OUT PROCEDURE

Cards used for reference purposes are usually not removed from the filing equipment. If a card is removed, however, a charge-out card should be inserted in its place. When groups of cards have been removed to be used elsewhere, a charge-out card should also be used. "Who," "what," "where," and "when" information is recorded on the charge-out card that is usually of a very brilliant color.

SECTION 4. ADVANTAGES AND DISADVANTAGES OF CARD AND VISIBLE RECORDS

CARD RECORDS

The advantages of card records are those relating to the saving of space and the compactness of information. Because of their size, cards take very little space. Many employees may work with information on cards, while only one employee or two employees would be able to work with the same information on a list. Cards are handled more easily than are papers because of their uniformity in size. Expansion in a card file is easy; just add another card. Obsolete records can be removed quickly and easily. Rearrangement in any preferred sequence is relatively simple because of the compactness of cards. Cards can be handled by machines for posting, sorting, and other processing. The use of cards for data processing is discussed in Chapter 11.

The disadvantages of card records include the fact that cards may be easily removed, mislaid, shuffled into incorrect order, or lost. Since information is usually transferred from another document to the cards, errors may arise. Time, also, is required to transfer information from one source to another.

VISIBLE RECORDS

The advantages of visible records are those related to the visibility of the information and the saving of space. The instant visibility of information reduces the time necessary to find it. Much information can be stored in little space. One employee can work with a great deal of information without changing position. Addition or deletion of information is sometimes easily handled by simply removing one strip of information and inserting another.

The disadvantages of visible records include the fact that visible equipment tends to be expensive, and some of it takes more space than would drawer files. Insertion and removal of items in many visible record systems are not easy or quick compared to the insertion of cards in or the removal of cards from a drawer. Because of the great number of items, misfiling or errors in recording information can cause great difficulties.

For Review and Discussion

1. Explain the differences between the terms listed in each of the following categories:

   a. Index record and posted record cards
   b. Vertically filed cards and cards filed visibly
   c. Posting visible files and reference visible files

2. In vertical card files, what terms are used to refer to the guides which separate a special name section from the cards immediately behind it?

3. Give as many examples as you can of instances when a wheel file of cards on a desk top might be more advantageous than a file drawer of cards.

4. How may the principle of vertical filing be used with visible records?

5. Contrast the "signaling" devices used with card records to those devices used with visible equipment.

6. Of what value is a solid line at the top of the vertical-visible card?

7. What types of records would be card files particularly suitable for storage in these card files:

   a. Electrofile
   b. Magne-Dex card tray
   c. Visible Card Cabinet
   d. Single Tier Rotary Equipment

8. Why does the typing of information on cards or visible strips require great care?

9. Why is it that cards used for reference purposes are usually *not* removed from the filing equipment?

10. Give as many examples as you can of instances when it is more advantageous to use visible records than it is to use card records.

11. Identify the disadvantages of using the following types of records:

    a. Card Records
    b. Visible Records

Learning Projects

1. Check with your instructor so that duplication does not occur and write to a manufacturer of filing supplies whose products are not illustrated in this chapter and ask for a catalog. Study it to determine the kinds of card guides and printed cards that are standard items of that manufacturer. Also note the types of equipment or systems that differ from those described in this chapter. Make complete notes for either a written or oral report to a small discussion group. Be prepared to report to the class the results of these discussion groups relative to the various types of equipment housing the records, the uses of the visible files, and the various kinds of signaling devices used.

2. Visit an office near you (checking with your instructor to avoid duplication) and

   (a) ask to see whatever card records are kept. Type a list of the various ways in which cards are used and the types of signals used. Bring the list to class to consolidate with the lists of others.

   (b) ask to see any reference visible files that may be used in that office. Type in tabular form (1) the types of equipment housing the records,
   (2) the use to which visible files are put, and
   (3) the various kinds of signaling devices used.

   Also be prepared to present your findings in a class discussion.

Chapter **10**

Noncorrespondence records: storage and control

Perhaps the greatest number of records stored in any office relate to correspondence within and outside the organization and they consist of paper and its byproduct—film. However, the kinds of non-correspondence, unusual, and nonpaper items that may be stored and retrieved are almost endless. Filing methods have been devised to keep account of small parts, of specimens and x-rays in the medical lab, of geological and archaeological discoveries, of marble samples used in construction, of receipted bills, of instruction tags, of recipe clippings, of swatches of fabric, and of costumes and props for dramatic productions—to mention only a few of the unusual items filed.

Items of unconventional size, shape, or weight more commonly encountered in business and professional offices can cause difficulty for the files operator who does not have a tested method of filing them so that they can be found quickly. Therefore, suggested filing methods for several types of noncorrespondence items are given in this chapter.

SECTION 1. TYPES OF NONCORRESPONDENCE RECORDS

BLUEPRINTS, DRAWINGS, MAPS, TRACINGS

Two methods often used for filing blueprints, drawings, maps, and tracings (transparent sheets on which a copy is made by super-imposing it on an original) are (1) hanging the items vertically from hooks or clips and (2) placing the items flat in shallow drawers in cabinets specially made for the purpose. If the latter method is used, the items are usually numbered, and an alphabetic list is kept in another place for reference. The labels on the drawers show the numbers of the items within them. One type of map file drawer has a bottom surface of material on which maps may be tacked, and both sides of the drawer bottom are used. The drawer is completely removed and turned over if the map on the lower side is to be used for reference.

If the items are hung vertically, a clip-on tab is usually affixed to the hanger to identify the article. The clips are attached to rods (Figure 10-1). One type is made of fabric pressure-adhesive tape with a cellulose acetate core to give it rigidity and at the same time flexibility for snapping on and off rods. The clip will pass through

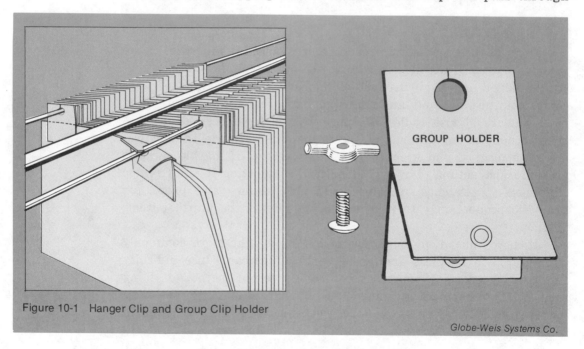

GROUP HOLDER

Figure 10-1 Hanger Clip and Group Clip Holder

Globe-Weis Systems Co.

blueprint machines and other types of reproducing equipment. Group holders to clip together complete sets of plans or papers related to one project are made of pressboard through which binding screws are fastened.

The practice of rolling large blueprints, maps, drawings, or tracings should be avoided because reference to rolled papers is extremely difficult.

BOOKS AND CATALOGS

Books are best filed in bookcases according to their titles alphabetically, according to the names of their authors alphabetically, or according to a numeric decimal method. Labeling is done on the back binding of each book.

Catalogs are best housed on shelves or in bookcases. Four methods of arrangement are found: (1) alphabetic order by names of firms issuing the catalogs, with a subject card file listing all catalogs on a given subject; (2) numeric order of catalogs according to the order of their receipt, with a card file containing (a) cards showing the names of the firms in alphabetic arrangement and (b) subject cards listing all catalogs on a given subject (a variation of the numeric arrangement is to assign numbers to vendors and to use those numbers on the catalogs coming from each vendor; a second catalog from the same vendor would be numbered with a decimal following the primary number); (3) by subject order if each catalog received pertains only to one subject, with a card file containing cards arranged alphabetically by names of firms; (4) in order by size, with the catalogs numbered in order of their receipt (large catalogs would stand alone on shelves while smaller ones would be filed in drawers), and a card file by name or subject would be kept alphabetically.

Flimsy supplements to catalogs are put into file folders to give them rigidity. Catalogs and their supplements should be kept together. When the items are filed by number, a record similar to an accession book is necessary to ascertain the last number used for each catalog or group of catalogs.

CASSETTES

Cassettes are best identified by typing labels and affixing them to the broad side of the housing. Then each cassette is numbered on its narrow side with an indelible pen (necessitating the use of an accession book); an alphabetic card file is made either by subject or by title and the cassettes themselves are filed by number. Special drawers or boxes hold the cartridges so that the numbers can be seen.

CHECKS AND VOUCHERS

Checks and vouchers are usually filed in check-file drawers made to accommodate checks. Filing is done by the number on the check or voucher and is, therefore, usually chronological also. Special check-file guides with insertable tabs are available. If checks or vouchers are filed by names of payees, alphabetic guides would be used.

CLIPPINGS

Temporary clippings should be separated from the permanent ones to avoid clogging the files with unnecessary pieces of paper. If clippings are filed with the regular correspondence, each clipping should be mounted on a letter-size sheet. The name and the date of the publication in which the clipping appeared should be typed or lettered on the sheet for reference (if it is not a part of the clipping). If unmounted clippings are to be filed as a group, the items should be placed in envelopes of folder size and labeled as to contents. Regular folders are sometimes used in place of envelopes, the folders being stapled shut on two sides to form a pocket.

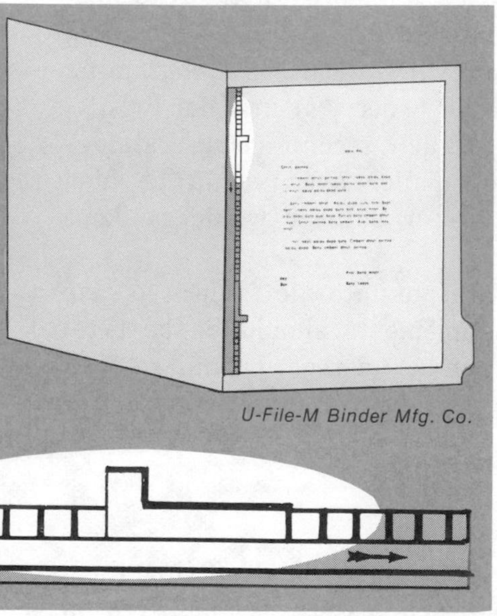

An aid to a clipping file is the "U-File-M" fastener. It is a gummed strip of paper with little tabs that project like teeth along one edge. The strip is glued to a folder at the inside crease. The tabs are glued to clippings, and the clippings can then be turned as are the pages in a book. This fastener is especially good for use when clippings are short. Several rows of the fasteners may be glued into each folder. Figure 10-2 shows a fastener being used with a letter.

Figure 10-2

"U-File-M" Fastener

U-File-M Binder Mfg. Co.

Newspaper clippings should not be folded since the quality of the paper is such that it breaks very easily along the fold. Newspaper items are sometimes clipped and pasted to cards if the items are very small and are to be used for contact purposes. Contractors, for instance, are interested in new buildings to be erected and notices of this type may be clipped, pasted on cards, and used for reference. Retailers follow social events and plan special promotions to coincide with the dates of the events; cards on which items are pasted often bear follow-up information across the top, to which movable signals may be attached. Frequently these cards become items placed in a tickler file. Clipping cards often have space for notations that are written on as contacts are made. Trade dailies carry lists of people who have moved to a community; prospect cards in the form of follow-up cards may be made from these lists so that solicitors can keep moving the indicators forward as solicitation progresses. A space for remarks is again usually provided on which to note the history of the calls made.

COMPUTER PRINT-OUTS

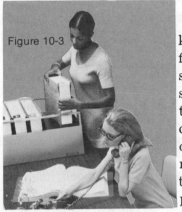

Figure 10-3

Wilson Jones Co.,
Division of Swingline, Inc.

Computer print-out sheets are often kept in binders with special prongs that fit into the holes on the sides of the sheets. These binders may be labeled with subjects, with dates, or with a combination of the two. Print-outs are heavy and can accumulate swiftly if careful control over their disposition is not someone's responsibility. Suspended V folders, pictured in Figure 10-7, can be used to hold print-outs of all sizes.

DICTATED BELTS, DISCS, AND RECORDS

After belts, discs, and records have been transcribed, some offices retain the dictated media for a certain period of time. The filing of these used belts, discs, and records is usually in a temporary container (box, drawer, file folder), chronologically placed according to the indication slip that is firmly attached to each item.

DOCUMENTS

DOCUMENT FILE BOX

Figure 10-4

Document File Box

Folded papers about 4 inches by 9½ inches are commonly found in law offices and city, county, and state governmental files. Abstracts, affidavits, certificates of incorporation, contracts, insurance policies, leases, mortgages, and vouchers are examples of documents sometimes filed in special document boxes (Figure 10-4). Extra heavy guides with insertable tabs are used or the boxes are filed on open-shelf equipment. The most common method of arrangement is by number with an alphabetic card file and accession book. Document files are still in use although the documents are unwieldy to read, the folded part often becomes worn and obliterated, and folded papers occupy more space than those that are filed flat.

ELECTROTYPES AND CUTS

An *electrotype* or *cut* is a thin printing surface of metal mounted on a wood or plastic block, making a bulky article for filing. Electrotypes or pictorial cuts are used by companies that advertise extensively or that issue periodically catalogs in which pictures of their products appear. Identification and coding should be done on the side of the block, not on the bottom because the bottom is often covered during the printing process with a layer of material which would obliterate whatever marks were made on the bottom.

The blocks should be filed in shallow drawers, face up to protect them from damage, in numbered order. The number on each block should be composed of at least two parts—the first number being the number of the drawer in which the block is filed and the second number being the identification of that particular cut. With a numeric file, of course, an alphabetic index and an accession book must be maintained. It is usually best to try to group like cuts together (all the cuts pertaining to one book, for instance, in one drawer). A proof file showing the actual printing of the cuts is usually kept vertically and numbered to correspond to the numbers on the cuts.

FILMSTRIPS

Filmstrips are ordinarily kept in small metal-covered cans that are placed in shallow drawers. The top of the can is labeled for identification with subject information, alphabetic title information, or a number.

MAGAZINES

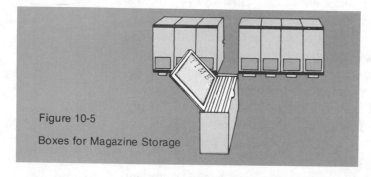

Figure 10-5

Boxes for Magazine Storage

Current issues of magazines are usually kept in stacks in chronological order, the most recent issue on top. If many magazines are received, the order of the stacks on the shelves is usually alphabetical by magazine name. Boxes with open backs, standing on edge

(Figure 10-5), may also be used to house current issues to keep them from becoming worn and dusty. As magazines accumulate, one year's issues (or several years' issues) are normally bound; the bound volumes arc labeled on the back binding and placed on end (as are books) in chronological arrangement.

MICRORECORDS

A thorough discussion of microrecords is contained in Chapter 11. Fiche microrecords may be filed in equipment arranged in tiers, as in Figure 10-6; each tier has several pockets in which fiche may be stored. These records may also be stored in file cabinets which have trays that hold 100 fiche and contain magnetic separators that allow fanning of each fiche as a separator is pulled forward. Aperture cards, illustrated in Figure 11-6, are usually filed in standard card file equipment; and, for various sizes of microfilm cartridges, standing shelves are available.

Figure 10-6
Rola-Scan

Retrieval Control Systems

MAGNETIC TAPE REELS AND MOTION-PICTURE FILMS

Chapter 11 contains information on the storage of magnetic tapes. Vertical filing by subject, alphabetically arranged, in open-wire racks is a common method of filing motion-picture films. Sometimes these reels are filed by a number system, necessitating an alphabetic card file for reference to titles or subjects and an accession book for help in assigning numbers.

OFFSET MATS AND PLATES

Offset mats and plates may be filed in the same type of equipment as are stencils (see page 246). Or they may be stored in suspended

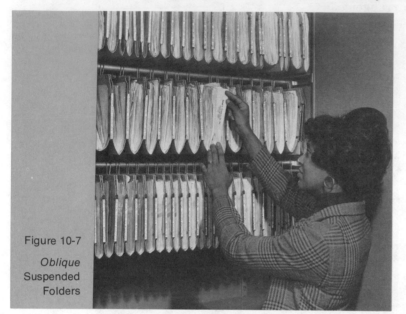

Figure 10-7

Oblique
Suspended
Folders

Robert P. Gillotte & Co., Inc.

V folders (Figure 10-7). These folders hang on two parallel rods that may be installed in existing storage cabinets, open shelving, or anywhere that there are two strong sides for support. The folders also snap together for compactness and are available in a variety of sizes from conventional letter sizes to 23½″ by 24½″. Plasticized label guides are 5½″ long, protected by curved shields that magnify the lettering therein.

PAMPHLETS

Because of the varying sizes, shapes, and thicknesses of pamphlets, they are usually filed in folders by subject. A card file is kept alphabetically by the subject titles, and cross-reference cards are made for those pamphlets that pertain to more than one subject. The use of the subject method for pamphlet filing parallels its use for the filing of correspondence by subject. A pamphlet file and its card index are best kept separately from correspondence files.

PHONOGRAPH RECORDS

Phonograph records are best filed on edge in protective jackets. A number is placed along the edge of the jacket or in the upper left corner on the front of the jacket for identification, again necessitating an alphabetic card file by title and an accession book with which to assign numbers.

PHOTOGRAPHS

Photographs may be inserted into envelopes for filing, the envelopes being labeled according to the filing method used—alphabetic, geographic, numeric, or subject. Photographs that are attached to correspondence may be protected by placing them in clear plastic envelopes or film bags of the kind known as sandwich bags. The photographs are then safe from scratches and mars.

PUNCHED PAPER TAPES AND CARDS

Figure 11-17 in Chapter 11 shows two methods of filing punched paper tapes. Punched cards are usually filed in drawer equipment built to the specific size of the card. Standard tabulating card drawers in a cabinet store the tab cards on their *long* dimension. A newer style cabinet has drawers holding cards on their *short* dimension edge, notched corner upward. The drawer fronts may take a small index card for identification or the holder may take a full-size tabulating card with the indexing information on it. (See Figure 10-8.)

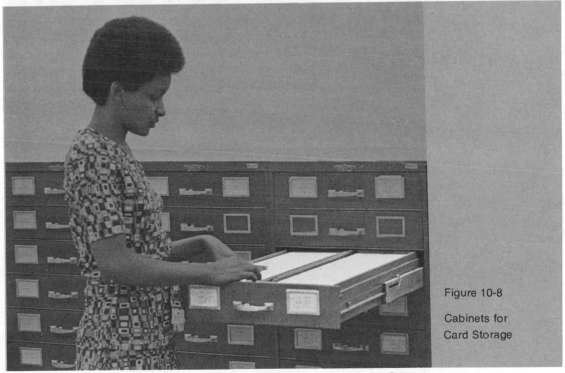

Figure 10-8

Cabinets for Card Storage

Ohio National Life Insurance Company

STENCILS

The word "stencil" may pertain to the long sheet on which typing or drawing is done for use on duplicating machines. This type of stencil is ordinarily blotted dry after use and hung from hangers in a cabinet known as a stencil file (Figure 10-9). Clip-on labels are used to indicate the contents of the stencil, the method of arrangement being suited to the needs of the office—by subject, by date, by salesman, by territory, by promotional scheme, and the like.

A stencil may also be an address plate (Figure 10-10). Stencil address plates are filed alphabetically by name, geographically by territory, numerically according to expiration date, or by some other plan, in specially made drawers or trays that can be inserted into the addressing equipment for processing.

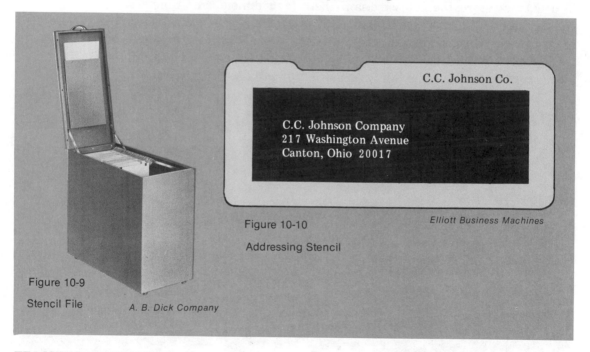

Figure 10-10

Addressing Stencil

Elliott Business Machines

Figure 10-9

Stencil File   *A. B. Dick Company*

TEACHING MATERIALS

Teachers who have accumulated worthwhile and usable pamphlets, clippings, reports, pictures, charts, booklets, articles, and other helpful materials are faced with the problem of filing them so that they can be located quickly when needed. Materials that can be used only in one course are easily filed by subject or type of course. But much material is usable in more than one teaching situation; one pamphlet, for instance, may be helpful in a correspondence course, in a secretarial course, in a general business course, in shorthand for dictation purposes, and in a records management course.

One magazine article may have interesting information that can be used in several courses at a later date; but the teacher does not want to cut the magazine and he has no equipment to reproduce the article. The magazine is therefore filed in its usual chronological order with other issues.

Finding the pamphlet once it has been filed in one of the course folders and locating the article in the magazine when it has been read long ago become problems. Cross-reference sheets are a solution but time consuming to make, and they soon clutter the course folders. A combination of subject and numeric methods has been found especially valuable for teachers' files.

Every item that is to be saved for future reference in some course (except for uncut magazine articles) is numbered in consecutive order beginning with *1*. An accession book is necessary to avoid giving any item the same number as that assigned to any other item. A card file by subject (course titles and course numbers may be changed and should be avoided) is started as the first item is numbered. Every subject to which item *1* might refer is listed on a separate subject card. The name of the item is indicated on the card with its number *1* beside it. The actual item is filed by number, preferably in a *box file* where the item cannot become lost as easily as it might be if it were in a folder in a file drawer. Also, bulky items, small items, and oddly shaped items do not fit well in a file drawer.

When the second piece of material is to be stored, it is marked with the number *2*. The subject cards already made are used to record the name or title of this item if it pertains to any of those subjects. If it does not, additional subject cards are made and the article is recorded on them with its number. When a subject card becomes filled with items, a second card is made with the same subject heading. As the name of the item is recorded on the card, abbreviate it to save space; but do not abbreviate so drastically that the meaning is lost to the reader.

Pieces are added to the file boxes as they accumulate; their titles and numbers are written on the subject cards already made, or new subject cards are made for them. Titles of magazine articles that may be very useful in future class sessions are also noted on the subject cards with the magazine titles and dates as the identification information.

The hypothetical subject cards in Figure 10-11 show the entry of 4 magazine references and 8 items that would be filed in boxes.

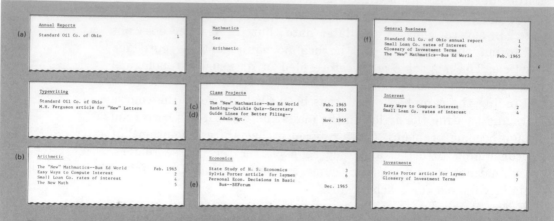

Figure 10-11   Subject Cards for a Teacher's File

(a) Item 1 might be listed also on a card headed "Typewriting" if information in the annual report could be used in a typewriting class; on a card headed "Calculators" if the content of the annual report would be useful as a checking problem in a calculating machine class; on a card headed "Office Machines" if the report contained pictures of up-to-date machines used in the Standard Oil Co. offices. **(b)** "Arithmetic" might be cross-referenced as "Mathematics." **(c)** The banking article on the Class Projects card would be listed also on a Banking card. **(d)** The filing card would be listed also on a Filing or Records Management card. **(e)** Abbreviations are sufficient for magazine information. **(f)** "General Business" might be cross-referenced as "Basic Business."

Boxes in which the numbered items are filed are labeled with the inclusive numbers of their contents; some boxes may hold only five or six items while other boxes hold twenty or thirty items. The size and bulk of the articles will determine how many can be housed in one box.

When a teacher wants the pamphlet on investment terms, for instance, he looks at his "Investments" card and notes the number is "7." He goes to the box containing that numbered item and finds it. It is marked "7" and can be quickly returned to its numerical sequence when the teacher has finished using it.

TEAR SHEETS

Tear sheets are items that have been torn from publications. In many instances, they may be large and require folding to fit into folders. Tear sheets are used as proof of advertising and are often filed alphabetically according to publication name or geographically according to the location of the publication. Frequently, they are pasted into loose-leaf notebooks according to a geographic or chrono-logic order.

SECTION 2. CHARGE-OUT AND FOLLOW-UP

Whenever any noncorrespondence material is removed from its file to be used by someone other than the files operator, an OUT guide or folder should be inserted in its place (as is done in the filing of correspondence). Knowing where every record has gone, who has it, when it was taken, and when it is due to be returned is important to the one in charge of the files.

For Review and Discussion

1. What problems are generated by the necessity for filing noncorre-spondence items?

2. Why is a knowledge of the rules for alphabetic indexing (Chapter 3) necessary for the filing of noncorrespondence items?

3. If you were following the practice of filing catalogs by vendors' numbers and if you had assigned the number *63* to Shaw-Walker, what number would you give to their second catalog that you had just received for filing? Why?

4. If checks are filed by their printed number, why are they said to be filed in chronological order also?

5. Why should clippings be mounted on full-sized sheets of paper before being filed in correspondence files?

6. A number on the edge of a phonograph record jacket or in the upper left corner is identification used for filing purposes. When could the number be better placed in the upper right corner?

Learning Projects

1. Visit an office that no one else has visited this year and ask what types of noncorrespondence items are filed. Ascertain the filing methods used. Be prepared to tell the class how the methods used parallel the sugges-tions in this text or differ from them. Be prepared to tell about and to illustrate the filing of any items not mentioned in this chapter.

2. Bring to class pictures (mounted on 8½ by 11-inch paper) of any of the equipment referred to but not illustrated in this chapter. Identify the mounting clearly and post it on the bulletin board as your instruc-tor indicates.

3. A list of the following items will be posted on the bulletin board. Indicate by your signature beside one of the items that you will be responsible for securing it. (If your class has fewer than 32 students, several of you may indicate you will bring more than one item listed.) Bring the item(s) to class on a designated day to participate in group discussion reviewing the methods of filing each of the items.

1. Blueprint
2. Large drawing
3. Large map
4. Large tracing
5. Catalog published by a vendor
6. Small newspaper clipping, prepared for filing
7. Clipping card used for follow-up
8. Voucher check
9. Computer print-out sheets
10. Dictated belt with indicator slip
11. Dictated disc with indicator slip
12. Folded bulky document
13. Electrotype or cut
14. Filmstrip in its can
15. Current business magazine
16. Microfilm reel
17. Microfilm strip holder
18. Aperture card
19. Microfiche card
20. Magnetic tape reel
21. Motion-picture film reel
22. Offset paper mat
23. Offset metal plate
24. Printed pamphlet
25. Phonograph record in its jacket
26. Photograph, ready to file
27. Punched paper tape
28. Deck of punched cards
29. Address stencil
30. Stencil (for page of typing)
31. Tear sheet
32. Cassette

4. Locate in the periodical indexes in your library an article that has been written within the last five years on the filing of noncorrespondence items. Read the article and type an abstract of it on a 6- by 4-inch card. Be sure to include title, author, and magazine information as well as your name on the card, as it will be used for bulletin board display.

After the cards have been posted on the board, read the abstracts for information. Type a list of the kinds of noncorrespondence items mentioned in the articles. Organize your list according to some system you believe is logical—alphabetic by name, like items together, according to industries or kinds of offices represented, etc. Submit the list to your instructor.

Information storage
and
retrieval systems

As modern business firms become more complex, procedures for filing and locating the vast storehouse of information required for their operation have also become more involved and sophisticated in nature. In fact, with the passage of time, information as an economic resource has become the key to management decisions.

To provide an accurate, orderly environment for maintaining organizational records, two specialized systems have been developed. These systems relate to the *storage* and *retrieval* of information by man and by machine and will be discussed in this chapter. Included also will be a review of the retrieval process and of the expanding role of microrecords in records management.

Since the late 1950's, more and more offices have adopted electronic computers and other related equipment that permit automated storage and retrieval of records. With the march of time, these machine-storage capabilities are "reaching" down into the smaller-scale businesses; therefore, workers in small as well as large offices should be familiar with both the manual and mechanical means of storing and retrieving information from the files.

RECORD CLASSIFICATIONS

Record systems analysts today classify records as being of two basic types: (1) transaction documents and (2) reference documents.

Transaction documents. These records, largely business forms, are familiar to all office workers. They include invoices, requisitions, purchase and sales orders, checks, and statements. Most of these records are simple to classify and to code, and they are filed according to commonly used numeric or alphabetic filing rules.

Reference documents. These papers include letters, memos, and reports. When they are indexed and coded according to their subjects by various file clerks, reference documents are subject to considerable variation in coding. Even though these records account for only 10 to 15 percent of the total paper work, they usually account for the greatest amount of difficulty in locating information in an office.

THE FILING (STORAGE) AND FINDING (RETRIEVAL) CYCLES

One of the foremost pioneers in records management, Robert A. Shiff, has described the key problem in controlling records in this way: [1]

> The key to retrieval usefulness is not the machine *but the design of the system.* For the average business firm, the problem is not one of machines at all, but how to identify and select information to be indexed, and then *how to file it so it can be found when needed.*

From the time a record is created and later filed and retrieved until such time as it is permanently stored or destroyed, many activities take place. Actually the same set of general steps are found for handling all types of records—those paper records found in the small office as well as the tape, card, and paper records created by computers found in the latest information systems. Only the specific operating procedures will differ.

The steps making up the filing and finding cycles are charted on page 253. In this chart one very basic point should be noted: that is, the close, interdependent relationship existing between filing and finding records—so much so in fact that if possible, the same clerks who file records should be responsible for finding those same records when requested.

For example, situations in which a department manager uses the files himself (for finding or later replacing correspondence folders in

---

[1] Robert A. Shiff and Alan G. Negus, *Administrative Management,* August, 1964, p. 24.

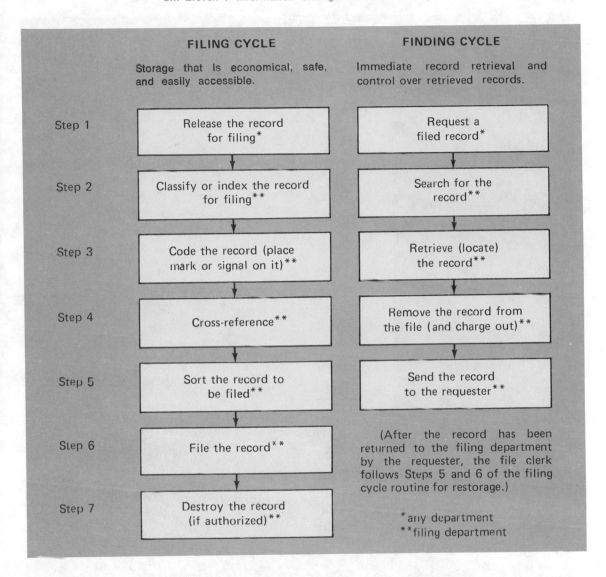

FILING CYCLE	FINDING CYCLE
Storage that is economical, safe, and easily accessible.	Immediate record retrieval and control over retrieved records.

	FILING CYCLE	FINDING CYCLE
Step 1	Release the record for filing*	Request a filed record*
Step 2	Classify or index the record for filing**	Search for the record**
Step 3	Code the record (place mark or signal on it)**	Retrieve (locate) the record**
Step 4	Cross-reference**	Remove the record from the file (and charge out)**
Step 5	Sort the record to be filed**	Send the record to the requester**
Step 6	File the record**	(After the record has been returned to the filing department by the requester, the file clerk follows Steps 5 and 6 of the filing cycle routine for restorage.)
Step 7	Destroy the record (if authorized)**	*any department **filing department

the files) rather than asking his secertary to do so eventually lead to lost records or difficulty in locating folders.

To illustrate the interdependence between the filing and finding phases, assume that the letter on page 254 is received by the Chairtown Lumber Company and is later released for filing. (See Figure 11-1.) For the Chairtown Lumber Company file clerk to file and later locate this record, he must follow all the steps necessary to file and find the record. The crucial steps, where the greatest opportunity for filing problems lies, are shown on page 254.

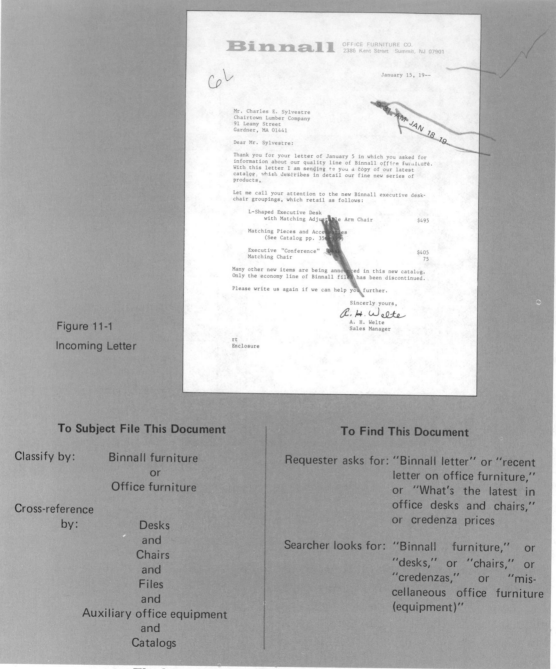

Figure 11-1

Incoming Letter

To Subject File This Document	To Find This Document
Classify by: Binnall furniture *or* Office furniture	Requester asks for: "Binnall letter" or "recent letter on office furniture," or "What's the latest in office desks and chairs," or credenza prices
Cross-reference by: Desks *and* Chairs *and* Files *and* Auxiliary office equipment *and* Catalogs	Searcher looks for: "Binnall furniture," or "desks," or "chairs," or "credenzas," or "miscellaneous office furniture (equipment)"

The key question is always whether the record is properly classified, coded, and cross-referenced in depth and then filed in such a way that the searcher will immediately recall these steps from the filing process and utilize them in searching for the requested document. Whenever various office personnel have access to the files, the indexer-coder and the searcher must, in a vernacular sense, "operate on the same frequency." *Step 2 of the filing cycle and Step 2 of the finding cycle,* therefore, are the most important (and most interdependent steps) in assuring an efficient filing system.

SECTION 1. SYSTEMS FOR CODING RECORDS

Leslie H. Matthies, one of the foremost administrative systems authorities, describes an ideal system for retrieving records. Briefly, it includes the following: [2]

1. Man needs to get back information.
2. He selects the right descriptors (words, numbers, or codes by which the record is filed).
3. He goes to the correct cabinet.
4. He finds the correct drawer.
5. His eyes follow the guides.
6. He pulls the correct folder.
7. He takes out the correct paper.
8. He reads the information he needs.

In the most efficient filing system, these steps can consume less than 10 seconds—just a little more time than it takes to dial a 7-digit telephone number.

In order that this finding process may be performed in an efficient manner, filed records are frequently given special code symbols for ease in identifying the records. Coding (which is an abbreviated form of data comprehensible only when interpreted with reference to a key) shortens and simplifies the processing of information as well as helps to maintain privacy over the information encoded. The majority of such coding systems involve numbers rather than alphabetic characters and should facilitate the easy classification of like items.

TYPES OF CODING SYSTEMS

While there are dozens of coding systems, several types are most commonly used and they are illustrated here. The student of records management should be aware of the various coding systems

---

[2] Leslie H. Matthies, *The Finding System* (Tulsa: Ross-Martin Company, 1963), p. 5.

by consulting appropriate references in data processing, accounting systems, library science, and information retrieval. And, a thorough review of the numeric method of records storage, which is discussed in Chapter 6 of this text, will provide a good foundation for understanding these various types of coding systems.

One of the simplest codes is the *sequence code*. It uses a consecutive numbering sequence starting with one and continuing in number until all items are coded. For example, a sequence code of the fifty United States would appear as follows:

  1. Alabama
  2. Alaska
   ·
   ·
  50. Wyoming

A more functional code is the *block code* which provides for blocks of numbers to represent data classifications. For example, forms to be numbered and used by various departments in a business might be block coded and numbered in this manner:

  100-149 accounting department
  150-199 purchasing department
  200-249 sales department

Group codes, on the other hand, are based upon major and minor classifications as represented by succeeding digits of the code. In an equipment inventory coding system, for example, office equipment might be coded in this way:

  1000 Equipment
  1100 Office Equipment
   1110 Furniture
    1111 Bookcases
    1112 Chairs
    1113 Coatracks
    1114 Desks
   1120 Machines

Many other versions of this group code are found. For example, the code "60*25*" could represent a code for 25-watt light bulbs; "60*40*," for 40-watt bulbs, and so on, with a natural memory jogger built in. Decimal coding is also common, as in the Dewey decimal coding system.

Other coding systems, incorporating alphabetic labels or alphanumerics can also be used. In a shoe company, shoe sizes are designated as 5AA, 4C, etc. In the Army, the classifications "1A" and

"4F" are commonly used. Shaw-Walker, a large office equipment firm, has identified its 4-drawer files as Nos. V1070F, V1071F, etc. All such numbers are artificial codes without any clue to the nature of the coded item.

Coding in the law office. Lawyers frequently assign consecutive numbers to cases in the order in which the cases are initiated. This system works well where these cases are complete within themselves, without involving other actions for the same client. In other instances, each client is assigned a number, which is further subcoded each time another action is undertaken for that client. Still another variation is the assignment of a separate series of numbers for each type of case. For example, partnership cases would take one series; probate cases, another series; divorce cases, a third series; and so on. No code number is usually assigned twice in the law office since the volume of cases is not so large as to require large-size numeric codes.

Growing use is being made of color in the coding process. In the law office, as an example, color-coding works well with either numeric or alphabetic codes. The color acts as a quick signal to the file user. Labels on divorce case folders may be edged in black; on probate case folders, in red; and on legal partnership folders, in blue.

Coding in the real estate office. Numeric coding may be useful in the filing systems of real estate offices, although for a somewhat different reason than in law offices. In law offices, numeric coding is frequently utilized to assure secrecy and to maintain the confidential nature of the files. In the real estate office where such secrecy is not so important, numeric coding may be employed to facilitate the filing and finding process.

Various filing methods may be used by the real estate firm to keep the listings of property in a logical order. Usually residential properties and industrial properties are kept separate. Sometimes, too, the property listings are maintained by section of the city. However, the most common arrangement seems to be listings by price in which case the price category becomes a natural code for filing the records relating to the listing. (If necessary, a cross-reference could be made to the owner's name.) Such a code might be:

code		*code*	
10-19	listings under $20,000	30-39	listings $30,000-$39,999
20-29	listings $20,000-$29,999	40-49	listings $40,000-$49,999

MACHINE CODING SYSTEMS

During the past two decades, a silent information explosion has occurred. Great advances have been made in the dissemination of information. For example, medical authorities relate that more research has been reported in their journals during this time than in all previous medical history. At the same time, improvements have been made in the means of collecting, manipulating or processing, and transmitting information by machine. Highly competitive, dynamic business people generate and demand more and more information to help in the decision-making process.

Machines from the punched-card, microfilm, and computer families are being used to store as well as to process information. When a complex machine is applied to a paper-processing operation, the total system must be carefully designed. A knowledge of machine functions and coding systems then becomes important for the records management personnel.

Coding in the Punched-Card System. The punched card (or tab card or unit record) has been employed for data processing work since about 1890. While some of the machines in which it is used are complex in operation, the principles by which the punched card functions are simple to understand. Today much large-volume data processing, such as payroll accounting and inventory control, still utilizes punched-card machines alone, although more and more punched-card machines now serve as peripheral equipment at the "introductory" (or input) and "exit" (or output) phases of a computer system.

For many years two types of punched cards were used in machine data processing systems: (1) the common 80-column card of IBM with the rectangular holes; and (2) the 90-column card of Remington Rand with the round holes. In 1966 Remington Rand announced they were discontinuing the round-hole card and adopting the standard 80-column card format used by IBM. Several years later IBM added a new data processing system for small-scale users called System/3. This new system uses a smaller size round-hole type of punched card with 96 columns arranged in three 32-column tiers for storing information. However, the punched-card "workhorse" continues to be the 80-column card shown in Figure 11-2. Punching positions are designated from the top of the card 12, 11 or X (usually *not* printed), 0, 1, 2, 3, 4, 5, 6, 7, 8, and 9 (usually printed). With 80 columns and 12 possible punching positions in each column, an IBM card has 960 possible punching positions.

As Figure 11-2 illustrates, *each card column* can accommodate a digit, a letter, or a special character, such as a "4," a "W," or a "%" sign. Accordingly with 80 columns, 80 pieces of information can be recorded in one card. Numbers or digits are recorded by holes punched in the digit punching area of the card (area 0 to 9). To record a "4" in column 19, one hole is punched in the "4 location" in that particular column (Figure 11-2). On the other hand, each of the 26 letters of the English alphabet is coded by 2 punches in a column— (1) a 12 punch for A through I *or* an 11 punch for J through R *or* a Zero punch for S through Z in the Zone Punching Area in the top section of the card and (2) a numeric punch in the Digit Punching

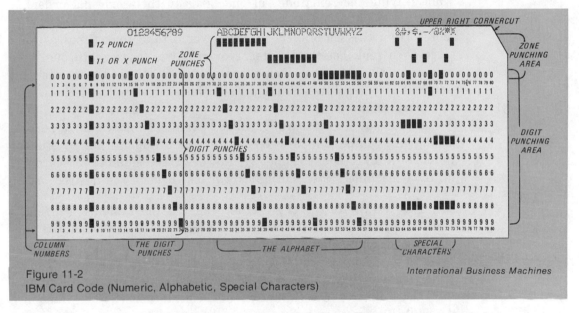

Figure 11-2
IBM Card Code (Numeric, Alphabetic, Special Characters)

International Business Machines

Area. In column 31 of Figure 11-2, the letter "A" has been encoded by a hole in the 12 punch in the Zone Punching Area and another in the 1 punch below "A." The letter "W" has been encoded by a hole in the Zero punch and another in the 6 punch (Column 53).

The special characters are recorded by one, two, or three punches. In column 71 (Figure 11-2), a threefold punch combination of 0, 4, and 8 encodes the "%" sign. Other symbols can be encoded in the machine also. With only one hole in the numeric code as compared with two holes for all alphabetic codes, it becomes simpler for punched card machines to process numeric data.

In the punched-card system, therefore, the manner in which the documents to be punched are coded plays an important role in how efficient the punched card is. For example, in classifying students in college as freshmen, sophomores, juniors, and seniors (or in classifying employees in business), it becomes more time-consuming for the machine to find and sort out students classified purely as "freshmen," "sophomores," etc., than it would if these classifications were coded. A typical, efficient coding system for these classifications would be:

Classification	Code	Classification	Code
freshman	1	junior	3
sophomore	2	senior	4

If such a coded number were then assigned to the punched-card document to which it referred, it would be possible to take a deck of 1,000 cards, "select out" or separate from such a deck all "2" cards while leaving the remainder of the cards in their original order. If this same machine had to separate on an alphabetic basis the sophomores from the seniors, the process would take *four* times as long since each alphabetic character requires two "passes" through the machine. Therefore, four such passes would be required before certain punched-card machines could differentiate between the letters "so" in *sophomore* and "se" in *senior*.

If the number of cards "pulled" from a punched-card deck is small, they can be manually refiled in their original order by student number or by student name. If, however, the number of cards is large, a machine sorter can quickly place them in the desired order.

The KWIC Retrieval System. Many of the systems utilized to store and retrieve information are available to both manual and machine systems. One of the newer concepts is the "KWIC" (Keyword in Context) method developed by IBM, which is discussed here. Other retrieval techniques are concept coordination or inverted indexing, and Selective Dissemination of Information (SDI) which are described in detail in information retrieval references.

In the KWIC indexing method a clerk reads or scans the document underlining key phrases or *descriptors,* subtitles or headings, assigning an arbitrary number to each record. The number or code assigned may be serial, block, or group coded, depending upon the coding system in use, and is used only as a cross-reference. Each descriptor and the record number is then keypunched into a card and used as input to a computer which later prints out a list of descriptor phrases. In the printout a center column in the list of phrases contains one key word of the phrase with the accompanying words to either side. This same phrase is then shifted to the right and to the left so that different key words appear in the center column. To help in locating key phrases, the computer program sorts each keyword phrase so that the center word is in alphabetic sequence. With several key phrases, each is cross-referenced with the appropriate record number. In Figure 11-3, a Keyword-in-Context Index is shown with each keyword in a document title arranged alphabetically in the center with document number listed on the right.

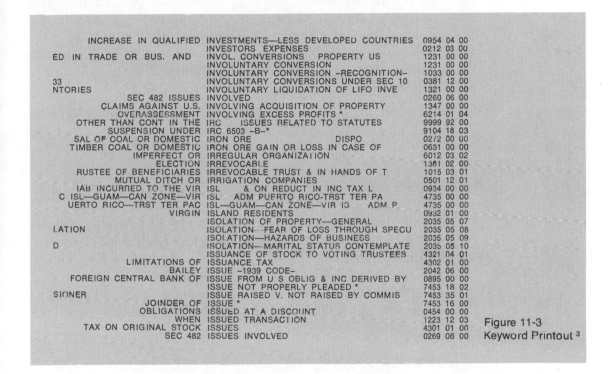

Figure 11-3
Keyword Printout [3]

To use the keyword printout, the user merely scans the list of center words (as shown in Figure 11-3) until he finds one of particular interest to him. He then reads the other words associated with the center word which give him a good idea of the nature of the reference. By noting the reference number and continuing his scanning of the list, he may find several other references to the same record number (and hence, the same subject).

---

[3] This illustration is taken from the *Records Management Handbook: Information Retrieval—Managing Information Retrieval*, General Services Administration, 1972, Federal Stock Number 7610-042-8762, p. 36.

The keyword concept lends itself to manual or machine retrieval. In effect, the person reading the document prior to coding attempts to anticipate every possible name or number by which the document will later be requested. All of these names or numbers, then, become the keywords by which this document is coded and cross-referenced. The actual document itself may be filed in a routine manner.

Coding in the Computer System. The use of numbers to code items to be classified has become very common in both manual- and machine-storage systems. Records that are stored on magnetic tape may be considered as a series of punched-cards filed side by side, reduced in size, and magnetized and "packed" into a small space on the tape. (See Figure 11-4.) In a similar manner, storage of information would be handled on magnetic disks.

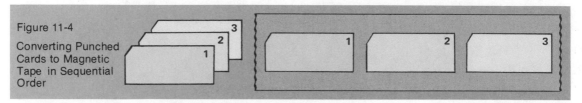

Figure 11-4

Converting Punched
Cards to Magnetic
Tape in Sequential
Order

In fact, usually when the size of the record system warrants, information on punched cards is transferred to magnetic tape for use with a computer by sending the cards through a card-to-tape converter. Coding by number would be a common requisite for data stored on magnetic tapes. The use of magnetic tape in electronic data processing systems is discussed later in this chapter.

SECTION 2. FILING OF MICRORECORDS

RECORDS IN MICROFORM

Both the storage and retrieval of information is greatly facilitated by the use of photographic equipment that reduces the size of the original document to very small (micro) form. Traditionally, this process has been labeled *"microfilming."* Today, however, there are many types of microrecords other than those which appear on rolls of film. Included along with roll film are film cartridges or magazines, aperture cards, microfiche, and the strip holder (a 14-inch-long molded plastic channel into which are inserted from one to ten strips of microfilm). Since there are now so many different "faces" of microrecords, it is more appropriate to refer to them as *microforms* than as microfilm. Although all appear on film, they are not necessarily sequential or continuous. Only microfilm, the aperture card, and microfiche will be discussed in detail in this chapter.

Microfilm. The microrecording operation involves photographing documents, usually on 16 or 35 millimeter film. Film sizes may range from 8mm to 70 or 105mm film, and records that are microphotographed may be reduced in size to varying degrees. If a record 10 inches by 10 inches were reduced to a microimage 1 inch by 1 inch, the reduction ratio would be 10:1. If this same original-size record were reduced to one-half inch, the reduction ratio would then become 20:1. The reduction ratios may vary from 5:1 to more than 50:1.

The tiny microimages, of course, are actual pictures of the original documents; but expensive, specialized equipment is required before they can be either photographed or later used. Although there is considerable variety in the type of this equipment, depending on specific needs, generally the microfilming operation includes these basic items of equipment:

1. The camera and film processor
2. The reader (either a reader-viewer or reader-printer) for magnifying the filmed image and projecting it for viewing
3. Photoprinting attachments
4. Special cabinets for microrecord storage

Several recent variations in this basic procedure should be noted. Usually when someone wishes to use a microrecord (the original of which has been destroyed or stored elsewhere), the microform on which the document appears is placed on a *reader-viewer* (Figure 11-5), which magnifies the image to its original readable size. A recent innovation to this piece of equipment enables a copy of any picture (called *hard copy*) to be printed out for subsequent use without the need for further magnification.

National Cash Register Co.

Figure 11-5
Microfilm Reader

Aperture Card. Although the most widespread use of micro-records is on reels of film, individual pictures (*frames*) are fre-quently clipped from the film roll and mounted on a special card that contains an opening (*aperture*) that fits the size of the frame. (See Figure 11-6). These aperture cards can then be handled manually or me-chanically in a manner similar to the method of processing or of sorting punched cards. Retrieval, therefore, can be mechanically performed on aperture cards just as the punched-card sorter is able to "select out" of a deck of cards those cards with prescribed identification on them. The microrecording operation then becomes an integral part of a mechanized data processing system. The most common use of aperture cards is for storing microimages of engineering drawings.

Figure 11-6
Aperture
Card

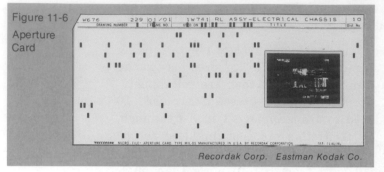

Recordak Corp. Eastman Kodak Co.

Figure 11-7
Microfiche

Microcard® Systems

Microfiche. While the most common microimages appear on rolls of film and aperture cards, another microfilm (called *microfiche*) is achieving widespread popularity. "*Fiche*" (pronounced "feesh") is a

French word meaning "card." Microfiche, therefore, represents a sheet of film the size of a standard index card on which microimages (microsize negatives of photographed records) are arranged in an orderly manner. (See Figure 11-7 on page 264.) Such microfiche sheets are usually produced in one of the popular standard card sizes, 5 x 3, 6 x 4, or 8 x 5, with either positive or negative images. The negative image serves as a master for photographing the images onto plates for offset printing where large quantities of hard copies (prints) are desired.

A microfiche card, therefore, represents a set of microimages of related documents. The images are easy to find, easy to read or reproduce in reader-printers (Figure 11-8), and can be mailed quickly and economically. This microform, too, is easily adaptable to coding signals. Since it is usually standard-card size, it can be manually indexed, filed, and retrieved as are cards. Usually microfiche carries eye-legible indexing data above the microfilmed frames at the top of the card, showing in a coded or abbreviated form the contents of the microfiche.

The largest user of microfiche is the Federal Government in the National Aeronautics and Space Administration and the Atomic Energy Commission. As a result, the Government and the National Microfilm Association have adopted the 105 x 148 mm. (or 6 x 4 card

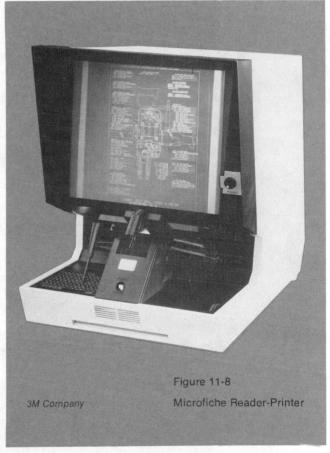

3M Company

Figure 11-8

Microfiche Reader-Printer

size) as the microfiche standard. Since one such microfiche may contain a maximum of 98 pages of records (originally 8½ x 11 in size) reduced to microimages, common applications tend to be collections of related documents such as automotive service and parts data and the Thomas Micro-Catalog (a seven-inch stack of 6 x 4 microfiche in which 60,000 industrial catalog pages are recorded and held ready for reference).

USE OF MICRORECORDS

Specialized office techniques, such as microrecords, have tended to become associated with large offices because of the high cost of the equipment and the technical knowledge required for their operation. Now, however, the small office can take advantage of microrecords. During the past few years many service centers have been organized to photograph the records of the nation's offices. For a stated fee, these service bureaus will handle all the technical details of photography and processing of the records and furnish advice on the storage and retrieval of the various microforms which they have developed.

But even in a very large office not all records should be converted to microform. Instead, the following criteria should be evaluated carefully to determine if it is feasible from the standpoint of cost and systems efficiency to convert the original records to microform.

General criteria. The following general points should be evaluated to determine the advisability of installing a microrecording system in an office:

1. Can considerable space be saved by converting to microrecords?

   Consider:

   Savings in space of 99 percent are reported when microrecording is used. For example, as many as 3,000 standard-size 8½ x 11 letters or 30,000 bank checks can be placed on 100 feet of 16 mm. film with obvious savings in floor space and filing equipment, ease of handling, and freeing of space for more productive use.

2. Can the paperwork system be rendered more efficient by using microrecords?

   Consider:

   Commercial banking check-return systems are facilitated by microrecording in that both sides of a customer's check are microrecorded after the check is charged against the customer's account and before the check is returned to the customer. Retail stores use microrecording in connection with monthly billing of customers. The beginning balance, monthly charges and payments, and the final balance are recorded on the statement form, and the statement is microrecorded, after which the original of the statement and the sales slips are mailed to the customer. In case of error or dispute, a full-size print (hard copy) can be made.

   Other bulky materials, such as engineering drawings and university research (theses and dissertations), which are difficult to store and transport through the mails, are now microrecorded. Duplicate copies of the film can be made on other film or transferred to aperture cards for use by engineers (in the case of drawings) or scholars (in the case of university research) and easily mailed.

3. Will microrecording properly protect and preserve the records?

Consider:

Microrecords may last as long as the best rag-content paper (100 to 300 years), but careful atmospheric conditions must be maintained.

Copies of important records can be microrecorded and stored in a safe place away from the original storage location to protect the records against fire, theft, opportunities for being misplaced in active file centers, and even hazards of war. Some equipment is available for double filming, in which case one copy can be made for storage and one for active use.

4. Is a large quantity of records to be stored for a long period?

Consider these rules of thumb:

   (a) If a record is to be retained only three years, or a shorter period of time, it costs less to keep the record than to photograph it.
   (b) If a record may be retained from 4 to 7 years, it may be less expensive to keep the record than to microrecord it.
   (c) Records kept from 7 to 15 years should be considered for micro-recording if the accessibility of the record and the cost of the "saved" storage space warrant.
   (d) Records kept on a permanent basis should be converted to microform unless they are frequently used and microrecording would render the record less convenient to use.

5. Can the cost of the microrecording operation be justified?

Consider:

Each of the preceding four criteria must be carefully weighed before a decision on microrecording can be made. Since the use of micro-records cannot be considered solely on a dollars-and-cents basis, the convenience of the system to the office personnel and to management must be given priority. Specific cost factors are outlined in the following section under "Specific Criteria."

Specific criteria. In addition to the general criteria just discussed, many specific criteria must be considered before a decision is made to microfilm records. The following are key points:

1. Are microrecords acceptable as evidence in courts of law?

Consider:

Microrecords are largely accepted in courts of law, but care must be taken to ensure that
—all governmental regulations concerning records retention have been observed.

—all microrecords have been properly certified as to their authenticity with certification "targets," which are included as a part of the microfilmed copy showing the reason for microrecording and method of record disposal.

—microrecording is a regular, standard procedure and not a sudden "coverup" to falsify or "manufacture" new filmed records.

Records such as government securities, licenses, citizenship papers, passports, and draft cards—along with others specified by the federal government—may not be microrecorded because of government prohibitions. The originals of these documents should be kept.

2. Are the specific costs involved low enough to permit microrecording?

Consider:

Microrecording is expensive and time consuming. The following specific costs are involved:

(a) Cameras—to photograph the original record
(b) Readers—to enlarge the miniature record for viewing
(c) Film—for photographing and storing the record
(d) Special storage files—for storing the microforms
(e) Floor space for storage; other overhead items, such as electricity, heat, insurance
(f) Labor in preparing records for microrecording (straightening out documents that are folded, removing staples or clips, etc.)
(g) Labor in operating the camera equipment
(h) Labor in managing the microrecords. Examples are:
　Inspecting the record for filming
　Indexing the record
　Editing the record
　Labeling containers, files, etc.
　Supervision in training workers, developing new procedures

3. Are security and protection of the records adequate in microrecording?

Consider:

(a) Has the original document been destroyed?
(b) Can a dispersal system be developed for storing two microimages of a record in two safe but different locations?
(c) Are all contingencies, such as fire, flood, temperature, theft, provided for? (Extreme heat, cold, dryness, or moisture subject a film to irreparable deterioration.)

4. Will the characteristics of the document to be microfilmed permit it to be photographed successfully?

Consider:

(a) Blurred carbon copies on white paper do not photograph well.

(b) Color problems frequently found include trying to photograph faint hectographed or mimeographed material, negative photostats, deep shades of colored paper and blurred carbon copies with "trees" of carbon on the sheets.

5. Will the microrecord contribute to the convenience and efficiency of the company's paperwork system? (Is the microrecord accessible for use?)

Consider:

(a) Microrecords are accurate, exact reproductions of original documents, but film images sometimes are poor and reproductions of film magnify defects in the original copy of the film.

(b) Reading from a viewer causes problems in group or conference study of records and in comparing with other microrecords.

(c) Since drawings are normally photographed separately from their supporting documents, coding problems arise in getting the two back together for use.

(d) Indexing difficulties may occur that make document location slow.

(e) The fixed location of the viewer is a handicap since the record user must go to the viewer. Recent improvements in making reprints of filmed records will tend to reduce this problem.

CODING, STORAGE, AND RETRIEVAL OF MICRORECORDS

When original records are stored, they must be identified and labeled in order to be found when needed. Similar techniques are used in the storing of microrecords. The indexing and coding operations, however, may be slightly different. Figure 11-9 contrasts regular filing procedures with the procedures used in filing microrecords.

Microimages, as well as original records, can be lost or misplaced so that it is imperative that proper coding be provided for all photographed records. Several related methods are used. The *targets* (frames of photographed signs identifying the form) and the *flashes* within the film assist the searcher in finding desired images. Frequently, a *microfilm roll record* form is used as an inventory of the entire contents of a film roll.

To illustrate, bulky reference materials, such as newspapers and periodicals, are frequently microfilmed in college and university libraries for later use by students. The *Wall Street Journal* is one

Procedures	Regular filing	Microrecord filing
1 Labeling the records container	Folders are labeled to show the names or the numbers under which documents are filed.	Indexes are placed on the front of the microrecord box, and targets (special markers identifying the microform e.g., roll number, name, etc.) are placed at the beginning and the end of each roll of film.
2 Dividing the storage space	Guides are used to subdivide sections of the file.	*Flashes* (special notation frames) are placed at intervals on the form to "subdivide" the microrecords.
3 Identifying the file drawer	File-drawer label identifies the contents of the file drawer.	At the top of each box are listed the microform number, the type of record, and other retrieval information.
4 Finding the record	Records to be retrieved are sought by the captions that appear on (1) the drawer, then (2) the guide, and then (3) the folder labels (in this order).	Records to be retrieved are located by caption code, which appear on (1) the filed film box; (2) the targets, (3) flashes, and (4) frame or record locations.
5 Notice of charge-out	Records taken from files are often replaced by OUT guides or OUT folders for follow-up and control purposes.	Microforms taken from the files may be replaced with an empty microform box (an OUT box) with a label on it showing the charge-out information.

Figure 11-9.
Comparison of the Storage and Retrieval of Regular Files and Microfiles

example. On a 35mm film with a 16 to 1 reduction in which one reel is stored in a cardboard carton, three months' copies of this daily newspaper may be photographed and stored. A student wishing to use this particular reel of film for, say, the February 14, 1943, issue, would consult the catalog cards in the library for location of the film. This film would, in all likelihood, be stored in special storage cartons on special shelves with the indexing appearing on the carton as shown in Figure 11-10 on page 271.

Once the proper reel was chosen, the film would be placed in a viewer after which the student-searcher would manually advance the frames until the February 14 issue (and the appropriate page of that issue) was found. At the beginning of the film, frequently an identifying frame or target appears which, in this case, might read as shown in Figure 11-11. With more complex equipment, a more detailed retrieval system to find the microfilmed records is necessary. Whenever business forms or contracts are photographed in their proper order, say by number or date, no separate index is required. The caption on the carton containing the film may serve as an index of the film in the same way that a file drawer label identifies the contents of the drawer. For example, student transcript records filed by student number could easily be located without referring to a separate index if they are photographed in numeric sequence.

An improved method of indexing and retrieving information from microfilm makes use of a pre-indexed film stored in reusable plastic cartridges or magazines which self-thread into the reader. (See Figure 11-12 on page 272.) Indexing of the film is keyed to coded symbols which appear on index scales on the side of the reader screen. The film contains code lines which flash across the screen at high speeds enabling the operator to find a desired image in a short length of time. Typical applications of

TITLE

WALL STREET JOURNAL
New York, New York

DATE

Jan. - March, 1943

Figure 11-10

Index of
Microfilm Carton

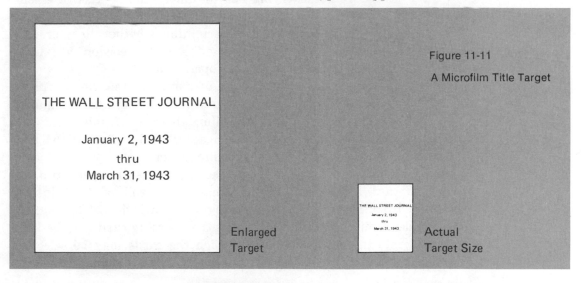

THE WALL STREET JOURNAL

January 2, 1943
thru
March 31, 1943

Enlarged
Target

Actual
Target Size

Figure 11-11

A Microfilm Title Target

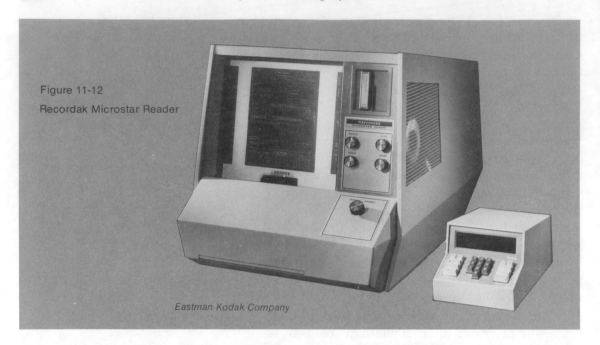

Figure 11-12

Recordak Microstar Reader

Eastman Kodak Company

such equipment include equipment and appliance parts lists, directories, pricing lists and guides, and rate and routing schedules of transportation companies.

TYPICAL MICROFILMING PROCEDURE

The procedure for carrying out the microfilming task is essentially simple and easy to understand. As a rule, the steps outlined on page 273 may be followed in determining whether to microfilm purchase orders and how, after an affirmative decision has been reached, to complete the microfilming operation.

To retrieve the microfilmed copy of a record, the files operator must know (1) the location of the stored film, (2) the flash number, and (3) targets or signs on that film. If reels of microfilm are used, they must first be located, then searched by placing the reel of film on a "reader" for rapid scanning until the proper frame image is located. However, when the frame is inserted into an aperture card for storage, rather than on a roll of film, it can be located like any other card in a regular punched-card file. Information describing the frame stored on the aperture card may be keypunched into the card itself after which the cards may be selected, sorted, or found by use of the sorter. Usually they are manually sorted.

Microfilming Procedure	Comments
1. Decision is made to microfilm purchase orders.	The decision depends upon retention and use requirements.
2. Request is made for microfilm; purchase orders are sent to the records management section.	Where necessary, personnel from the microfilm and requesting departments double-check on questions about the operation. The request is then approved or disapproved.
3. Microfilm personnel prepare the purchase orders, assign job or work order numbers, and prepare indexes.	This includes setting up "flashes" within the film as well as target information and planning the entire labeling or identification process to speed up reference to records when film is to be used.
4. Purchase orders are photographed on a reel of film.	Purchase orders must be in desired sequence; related (but seperate) documents, such as supporting requisitions, must be properly cross-referenced.
5. Films are checked, edited, and labeled.	Reader device used for this operation is operated either manually or mechanically to enlarge the filmed record for easy reading.
6. Films are submitted for approval to the requesting department; after approval, they are filed.	If the films are satisfactory, the original documents may be filed in another location or destroyed.
7. Reel of film is placed in a box, properly labeled, and stored in a specially designed cabinet.	

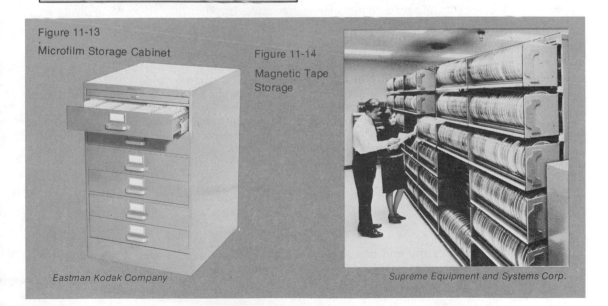

Figure 11-13
Microfilm Storage Cabinet

Figure 11-14

Magnetic Tape
Storage

Eastman Kodak Company

Supreme Equipment and Systems Corp.

In a computer system the contents of punched-card documents are frequently stored on magnetic tape (Figure 11-14 on page 273). In such cases the location of the reel of tape as well as the location of the record on the tape is required for rapid retrieval. Great advances have been made in coupling the computer system of processing, storing and retrieving information with the microrecording process. This topic is discussed in Section 3.

APPRAISAL OF MICRORECORDING

Indiscriminate use of microrecords is costly and unnecessary. In fact, recent studies tend to show that many such records should never have been photographed but rather retained in their original form. Frequently, hard (original) copies of the record can be stored up to forty years for the original cost of microrecording. In other areas, too, the businessman insists upon use of the original document rather than resorting to the "inconvenience" of using a reader. For example, parts lists, specifications, and personnel descriptions are used often and are more convenient in their original form. In any case, the decision to convert to microrecords should be made only after it can be determined that its use would result in greater cost advantages and systems efficiency than would the use of the original record.

The most common reason given for microrecording continues to be space saving. In the space-conscious age in which we live, however, other considerations are also important. Microrecording, as a rule, is usually feasible when the following conditions prevail:

1. Microrecords would result in little or no inconvenience to the record user to "come to" the reader, or when there is no need for two or more microrecords to be compared "side by side."
2. There is uniformity in the size of the records in a file (when records are not in varying sizes, unwieldy, or bulky).
3. There is little likelihood of a continuous reference to the record or re-entries of information on the record.
4. Only one side of a record is used.

SECTION 3. INFORMATION RETRIEVAL IN MANUAL AND MACHINE SYSTEMS

Time and usage have a strong effect on the meanings assigned to words. Initially, to "retrieve" information meant only to find it. Now, however, information retrieval has come to mean both the *method of storage* and the *system of reference* to the stored documents. Take, for example, a common storage and retrieval problem that all of us face: finding a name and telephone number in a metropolitan telephone directory. The *method of storage* is an alphabetic listing of names on the pages of a book; the *system of reference,* on the other hand, is a table search (scanning tabulated telephone lists) according to name. Similarly, nonfiction library books are stored on shelves in a sequential manner; the shelves are searched by reference number to locate a desired book.

The retrieval of information can take two forms: (1) manual retrieval—in which the worker goes to the file and extracts from it the document desired; or (2) mechanical retrieval—in which the physical record may not need to be retrieved, but the inquirer is only informed as to where it can be found. In the latter case, in effect, the machine scans an index to find the location of the record after which the original record itself may be found by hand or by machine.

MANUAL RETRIEVAL OF RECORDS

Where the record itself is retrieved manually by the file clerk, several new processes and updated versions of older ones have recently been developed. For example, the edge-notched card stores information in coded form along the edges of the card with the location of the notch indicating the information on it. In Figure 11-15, for example, the student name code (upper right-hand corner of the card) is "129" in three notch-coded numeric fields. In the hundreds or far left field, the "1" position is notched, in the tens or middle field the "2" position is notched, and in the far right or units digit field, both the "7" and the "2" positions ($7 + 2 = 9$) are notched. One or more cards may be separated from a deck of cards by passing a long needle through appropriate holes. All cards notched in that hole will fall free, that is, will be separated and retrieved from the deck. Notching and separating of cards and other types of records may be done by hand or by machine. Common applications of edge-notched cards include:

School report cards and registration forms
Sales analysis cards
Expense distribution
Payroll records
Employment records
Time-credit procedures

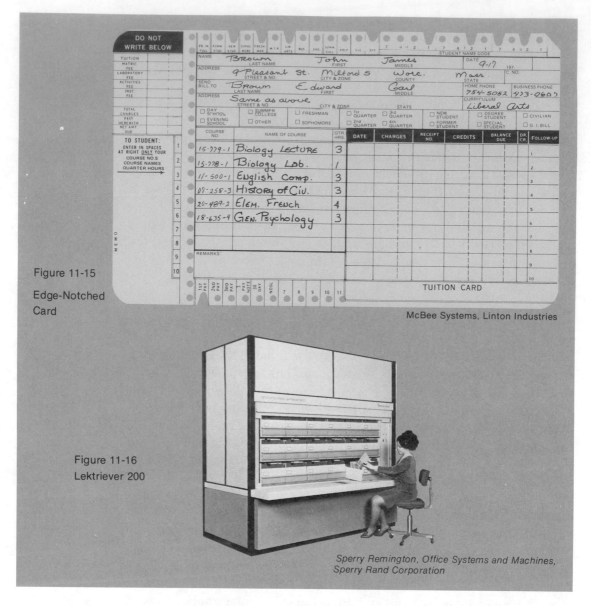

Figure 11-15

Edge-Notched Card

McBee Systems, Linton Industries

Figure 11-16

Lektriever 200

Sperry Remington, Office Systems and Machines, Sperry Rand Corporation

Another introduction of machinery into the manual retrieval process is the Lektriever 200 (Figure 11-16) manufactured by the Sperry Rand Corporation. Here card or letter-form records are stored in compact trays in tiers and mounted on chain tracks and carefully coded with a label on each "button" or tab. The operator sits at the control console, depresses the button describing the code of the stored document and its location, and the tray in which the record is stored is quickly turned on the track to the reference level (just above the lap) of the operator. One push-button "command" will bring one carrier tray to the reference level; an "all trays out" command will bring out an entire tier of trays for working with many records at one time.

MACHINE RETRIEVAL OF RECORDS

Punched-card and edge-notched cards may be located by hand or by machine while records stored on paper tape (Figure 11-17) will be stored and retrieved by hand. However, more advanced and complex records systems utilizing complete machine retrieval are now available. Several such modern systems will be briefly reviewed.

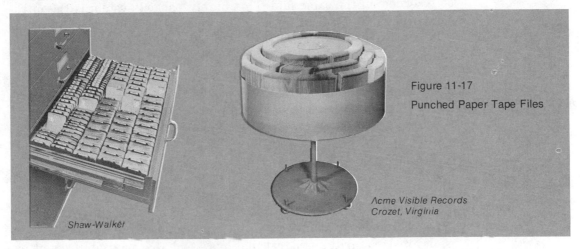

Figure 11-17
Punched Paper Tape Files

Acme Visible Records
Crozet, Virginia

Shaw-Walker

Miracode II. This automated film system by Kodak is used to store and retrieve records from microfilm. Along with the records, codes are recorded on 16mm film with a camera or computer-output-microfilm unit. The retrieval unit is a self-threading display terminal designed to operate with microfilm housed in magazines. When an operator registers in a keyboard console a coded request for a stored record, the system scans the roll film at a speed of 350 documents per second, comparing instructions from the operator against the code on the film. When the two codes match, the correct microrecord has been located and it can then be displayed or printed out. This system can also make dry copies of records selected for output.

Mosler 410. Rather than utilize film, the Mosler 410 system provides direct access to records stored on aperture cards or microfiche coded for retrieval purposes with 35 round holes along the bottom edge. Cards are held in 2,000 cartridges (100 cards per cartridge), with a total storage capacity of approximately 200,000 images. Several retrieval input commands are possible: through a keyboard, punched paper tape, or by computer command. Retrieval time is very fast, averaging less than 10 seconds from the time the request is made. After the particular card is located, it can be automatically withdrawn and presented to the console operator, held for viewing on the screen, or for hard copy printout. It takes about 3 seconds to refile the card.

Photochronic Micro-Image (PCMI). This system is a "high density" system, so called because many thousands of film images can be recorded on the same film. This highly packed system is the ultra-fiche system of NCR with contents reduced to a ratio of 150:1 as compared to a ratio of 24:1 to 40:1 in standard microfilm reductions. Each 6 x 4 in. ultrafiche has 3,200 possible page positions where standard fiche is limited to 98 pages per card. In one metropolitan bank, over 125,000 depositors' signatures are stored on 13 PCMI ultrafiche transparencies. When a teller wishes to verify a signature, he registers the passbook number into the bank's computer to obtain the correct ultrafiche card, column, and row location. Then the located ultrafiche card is placed in an NCR viewer, and the signature is visually verified by the operator.[3]

Retrieval by computer. As a rule, electronic computers have been used in business principally for the processing of data most of which is devoted to arithmetic calculations, such as payroll accounting, inventory control, and order processing. This is their most efficient use since they are basically "counting" machines.

Data in computer systems may be stored on several media, such as magnetic drums, cores, or disks as shown in Figure 11-18. Within the computer proper, data are stored in core locations which are identified by an address number, much like the street address of a home or business, or a file drawer in a manual system. To retrieve such information one must know the storage location number; or if this number is unknown, the computer must be instructed to search the stored data looking for certain specified attributes of the data. In principle, these two retrieval techniques are also employed in any manual filing system.

---

[3] Sam Bellotto, Jr., "Microfilm: Easy Access, Compact Systems," *Administrative Management*, July 1971, p. 45.

Drums and disks have certain retrieval advantages over magnetic tape since they provide fast, direct access to a record and do not require a search for a record in sequence. For this reason, disk storage and retrieval are commonly used for maintaining a large inventory system, such as spare parts for automobiles, where the parts number data will be needed on a random, rather than on a 1, 2, 3 basis. Magnetic tape, on the other hand, stores records sequentially. Data on 500 punched cards, arranged by number in 1-500 order, would be converted to magnetized spots on the tape in the original order of the deck. In order to locate the 486th record, then, it is necessary for the computer to scan all of the previous 485 records in sequence, rather than going immediately (direct access) to the desired record as would be true of disk storage.

Figure 11-18

Computer Storage Media: Cores, Drums, Disks

International Business Machines

A tape system is well suited to long-term storage and retrieval. Large amounts of data can be stored in a small area, and such tape is easily handled and stored. When using a magnetic tape system for retrieval, an operator usually follows two steps. First, it is necessary to locate the document or record code for the item sought; second, the abstract (or summary) of the desired document should be selected. (These abstracts are also maintained on magnetic tape.) The computer can then (1) search the tape for the document code location on the tape and (2) search the tape for the abstract of the document.

Increased use is being made of typewriter terminals for storing information in computer systems by simply registering information to be stored in the keyboard which is directly connected to the computer along with many other such terminals. This *time-sharing* concept permits many individuals to have simultaneous, immediate access to the computer file by storing and retrieving information from the same terminal.

Frequently *data display* units with both a keyboard and a screen cathode-ray tube (CRT) are used to project the retrieved information (Figure 11-19). If a hard copy of the displayed information is desired, it can be quickly produced. Meanwhile, the originally stored information remains undisturbed on the disk file.

With the continuous march of progress in computer systems, many unusual innovations will be made in record storage and retrieval. Even now it is possible to interrogate a computer file by "remote inquiry" where as many as 100 inquiries can be made of a computer and handled at one time from widely scattered locations.

One of the most widely heralded remote-inquiry systems is maintained by United Air Lines where nationwide reservations are made by contacting the reservation-computer system in Denver. The data center of the Strategic Air Command in Nebraska maintains a similar on-line relationship to its worldwide defense network. Large organizations like Westinghouse in its inventory-control system, or the state of Iowa in its Educational Information Center, maintain central computer processors in which information must be rapidly retrieved, updated, used, and stored again in its current form as it is disseminated to widely scattered areas of the regions they serve.

Computer-Output-Microfilm (COM). The computer and microfilming processes have been successfully combined in COM to provide a new and powerful tool for quickly handling information. The idea of

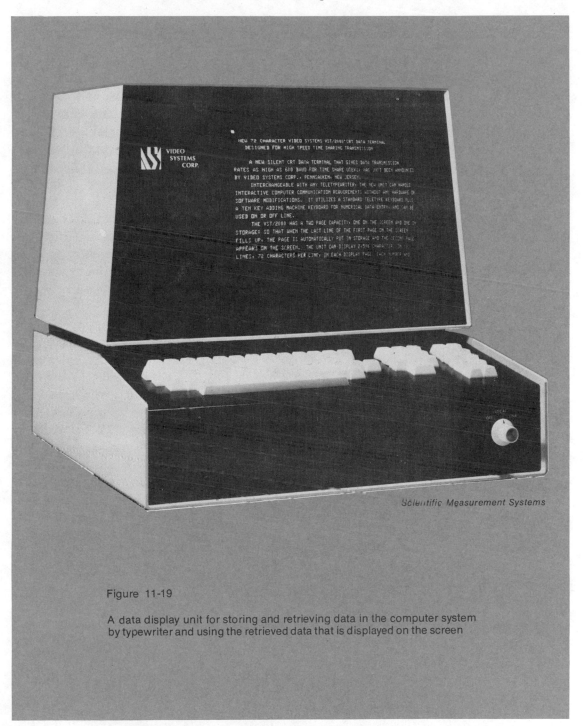

Scientific Measurement Systems

Figure 11-19

A data display unit for storing and retrieving data in the computer system by typewriter and using the retrieved data that is displayed on the screen

COM is simply this: a microfilm camera is "backed up" to a computer's output to microfilm the computer printout. COM can be used *on-line*, that is directly connected to the computer, or most commonly, *off-line* (Figure 11-20), not physically attached to the computer. In such an off-line operation, the COM unit converts data from magnetic tape into alphanumeric characters or graphics for projecting on a cathode-ray tube screen and then takes a picture of the contents of the screen. This filming is done at a rate 20 or 30 times faster than conventional line printers.

Some large firms maintain their own COM installations, while others subscribe to COM service centers. A minimum COM operation includes three pieces of equipment: (1) the COM recorder which converts magnetic tape data onto the film, (2) a processor that develops the film, and (3) a duplicator for making working copies.

With such equipment, one large firm, the Equitable Life Assurance Society of the United States, maintains many COM files. In its Individual Insurance Dividend History System, there are 800 inquiries processed daily and 2 million pages microprinted annually. Data are maintained on a magnetic tape file that is processed once a week to add new data and extract records for microfilming. Out of 3.5 million records, between 50,000 and 100,000 are updated in each weekly run with the record being written on an output tape and microprinted in policy number sequence.[4]

Aside from the fact that filming is faster, such firms find that space saving is substantial, costs have been reduced, record security

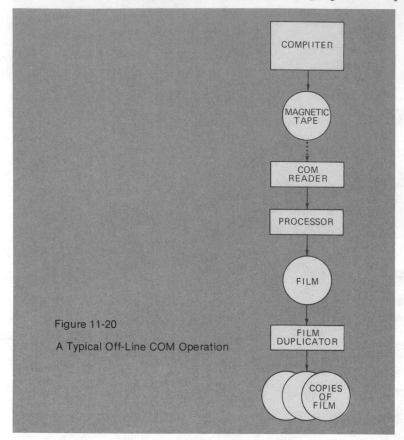

Figure 11-20

A Typical Off-Line COM Operation

---

[4] "COM at Equitable Life," *The Office*, May 1972, p. 80.

has been provided, and most important of all, access to the records has been vastly improved through computer indexing and automated filming operations.

For Review and Discussion

1. Explain the interdependence between the filing and finding cycles in controlling records.

2. What are the similarities and differences between large-office and small-office filing systems?

3. Of the two types of records in use (transaction and reference documents), which type would likely be more susceptible to automation? Discuss the reasons for your answer.

4. "Classifying is solely a mental process and cannot be assigned to a machine." Defend this statement using concrete examples to substantiate your point of view.

5. Explain clearly the ways in which rapid retrieval of information is dependent upon a careful classification system.

6. Is the idea of cross-referencing just another form of finding synonyms for key descriptors in a filing system? Discuss.

7. What factors would you consider in developing an effective coding system as you prepare data for storage?

8. How can color coding be used as a control device by the records manager?

9. In what respects does the KWIC method of indexing differ from the more traditional cross-referencing methods used in filing systems?

10. If your firm were converting from the standard 80-column IBM card as a storage medium to the newer System/3 90-column card, what would be some of the results of such a change from the standpoint of recordkeeping?

11. Since records stored on magnetic tape appear in invisible, magnetized form, how would these records be verified as to their accuracy?

12. What psychological shortcomings can be inferred for microfiles?

13. Compare microfilm, aperture cards, and microfiche in terms of the advantages, shortcomings, and potential applications of each.

14. What recommendations would you make to an office manager who has asked your advice about converting to microfilming for his office?

15. What basic differences *in principle* are involved in a manual and a mechanical information-retrieval system?

16. How does the edge-notched card, as a data storage-retrieval medium, differ from the IBM punched card?

17. Which is more important to records retrieval, speed or accuracy? Explain your response to this question.

18. What advantages do you see accruing to those office workers who have time-sharing equipment available for storing and retrieving data?

Learning Projects

1. In the latest December issue of the *Infosystems* magazine is a voluminous directory of firms that are involved in processing, storing, and retrieving data. Scan the section on information retrieval and select five leading sources of information on automated information retrieval. Contact each source asking for assistance and materials for a report on "Comparing manual and automated methods of information retrieval" which you will then develop for your records management class.

2. Either through the use of a technical manual, a systems reference, or through visits to a punched-card and computer department, review the use of coding systems in business. Justify the coding systems and identify possible shortcomings of each such code. A minimum of three coding systems is required.

3. Study the personnel, equipment, and related factors involved in a microfilming operation. (You may wish to contact a local microfilm service center to get additional information for this project.) Then develop a one-page checklist of (1) the cost factors involved in microfilming and (2) their relative importance to the company as it considers converting records to microfilm.

4. Collect two or three substantial lists of miscellaneous unclassified information (such as newspaper clippings of auctions). Then go on to classify the information into major and minor categories and assign a code to each classification. Type your classified list of items in outline form. Defend your choice of code(s) at the end of your report.

5. Several prominent organizations such as the National Records Management Council and the American Records Management Association have specialized in records management. Choose one of these organizations and investigate its historical development, the nature of its present program, and its educational activities. From your research (through a questionnaire or perhaps library research) write a 1000-word paper describing the functions of the organization and the services it provides management.

6. Chart the specific steps involved in storing and retrieving certain records of students in one of the following: (1) your college; (2) your sorority or fraternity; or (3) a club to which you belong. Use the informal charting symbols in Chapter 11, and secure the instructor's approval of the record system you chart so that each student will be charting a different system.

7. Collect ten original business letters. Carefully scan each letter to determine the keywords or descriptors by which each letter might be cross-indexed. Submit the letters and the outline of descriptors in typewritten form to your instructor.

8. Several national magazines, such as *Modern Office Procedures* and *The Office,* contain articles pertaining to micrographics—microfilm, microfiche, etc. Use the READER'S GUIDE TO PERIODICAL LITERATURE or the BUSINESS EDUCATION INDEX to identify current articles pertaining to trends in microrecord equipment and methods. Read several of these articles and be prepared to make an oral report to the class in which you will summarize the current trends relating to microrecord equipment and methods.

PART FOUR

MANAGING THE RECORDS SYSTEM

Chapter **12**

Control of the records
cycle: creation, retention,
transfer, and disposal

By walking through any office and observing carefully, the student of records management will quickly observe the great number and variety of records being used and stored. While each of these records differs either in construction or content from all others, generally each follows a common path or cycle along with other records. The cycle describing the route of the record from its creation until its disposal is the main focus of this chapter. Special attention is given to a set of controls that helps to assure the efficient operation of the records system.

NATURE AND EXTENT OF OFFICE RECORDS

The product of the office is *information,* and the medium for transmitting this information is the office record. Regardless of the level of the office worker—from messenger boy to secretary to purchasing agent to department head to chairman of the board— much of the working time of office personnel is occupied with office records.

The most common category of records maintained in the office consists of *business forms.* Invoices, orders, receipts, checks, contracts, and requisitions are common forms which fill and oftentimes clog the communication channels of the office. In addition to these records are the various types of communications usually referred to as *business correspondence.* Most office workers spend a great deal of time reading, analyzing, writing and summarizing business letters and interoffice memorandums as well as formal and informal reports.

These records may also include telegrams, printed matter (catalogs, pamphlets, brochures), and technical pieces (engineering specifications, advertising copy, galley proofs).

There is, of course, a heavy traffic in written communication between organizations, the typical buyer-seller and buyer-supplier relationships perhaps being the most notable examples of *external communication*. But there are also many related illustrations of *internal communications* such as between an organization and its employees (the payroll record system) or among an organization's departments (an inventory control system). Some records are created for public-service or public-relations purposes (as when a college student writes to the IBM Corporation for information on its latest small-scale computer). Even the telephone message, although in oral form, often is confirmed in writing by letter or on a message form so that a record of the call exists.

The computer age has not changed this strong trend toward maintaining records. In fact, the high-speed paper- and magnetic-tape machines that are an integral part of most computer installations magnify the record-keeping problem because they are capable of producing far greater volumes of information than their slower predecessors were able to do. As a result, more paperwork is created.

A common slogan seen in industry today is "Put It in Writing." Today's manager senses the critical need for more and more information. To be useful over a period of time, this information must be recorded. Records, therefore, must be made and managed.

THE RED TAPE PROBLEM

Historically, management has directed its primary attention toward the factory or plant. Usually the blue-collar work force was large compared to the white-collar staff in the office; and, it was reasoned that the factory rather than the office produced the tangible products from which profits came. Work control techniques developed by the industrial engineers were introduced into the factory including work sampling, time and motion studies, cost-accounting systems, and other processes designed to measure and control both the quality and quantity of the work.

Modern management prospers or fails on the basis of the soundness of the decisions it makes. In most cases, these decisions are made after a study of the up-to-date, accurate, relevant information that is contained in the company's records. Not too infrequently, the record-keeping systems get out of control and grow large and unwieldy with many unnecessary clerical operations involved. One colorful term used to describe the stranglehold that records have gained on the processing of information is the term *red tape*.

With the advent of the computer, a new emphasis has emerged stressing the need for controlling the information-production function. New areas of study, such as systems and procedures analysis, forms control, and records management, have been the result. Each of these new areas of work (discussed in Chapter 14) has the same general objective: to control or regulate the quantity and quality of record-keeping work in the office.

THE RECORD CYCLE

The life of any record—whether it is a simple one-copy payroll check or a complex, ten-copy purchase order— might be considered to parallel the birth-through-death cycle of man. The life span of the usual office record is shown in Figure 12-1.

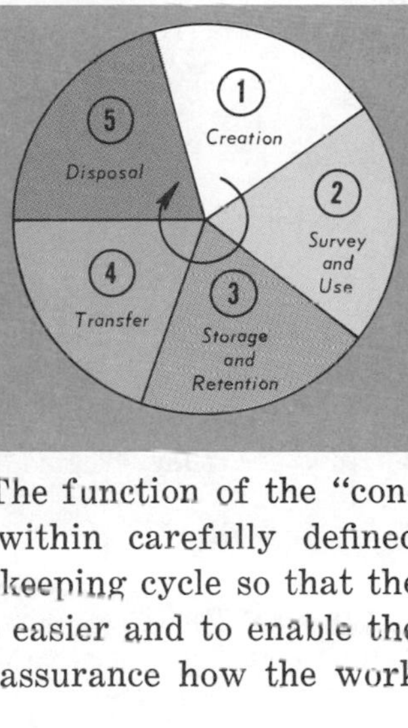

Management must have all the information needed at the right time, in the right location, in an accurate,

Figure 12-1

The Life Span of a Record

sufficiently complete, and economical form. The function of the "control" movement in offices is to regulate within carefully defined boundaries the various phases of the record-keeping cycle so that the job of using information to manage is made easier and to enable the decision-makers to predict with reasonable assurance how the work in the organization can be carried out.

SECTION 1. CREATION CONTROL

PROBLEMS IN RECORDS CONTROL

The old adage "an ounce of prevention is worth a pound of cure" may well apply to records control. Certainly the record that is not created will not need to have controls placed upon it. Obviously, then, the first line of attack in the battle against the unrestricted production of records is at the very beginning, the so-called *creation* stage itself. But this is not a simple task, for it involves many people at various levels with various backgrounds and attitudes, many with insufficient knowledge to understand the firm's overall record system. The complexity of such a task can be appreciated by a careful study of the following outline:

Key "Creation" Questions	*Typical Answers*
1. Who may create records?	1. All office employees. Usually, however, the forms and key documents (time cards, sales invoices, personnel requisition forms, etc.) that are used by several departments are created by the supervisors representing the departments. (Letters and memos are normally composed by all levels of office personnel.)
2. Where are records created?	2. In all offices or places where data are processed (including the factory).
3. When are they created?	3. At the discretion of any office or factory worker when he feels a need for a record. (If no approval is required [as from a records manager or forms control supervisor] before creating a record, many duplicate, unnecessary records result.)
4. How are they created?	4. Manually (with paper, pen, and typewriter) or mechanically (with duplicating machines, punched-card and computing machines).
5. Why are they created?	5. To transmit information from one person or business to another and to serve as a record of information vital to a business.
6. What has been the traditional records creation philosophy in business?	6. That the costs of creating and maintaining records are low compared to "blue-collar" work and, in too many instances, that records will tend to control themselves. (Programs to control paper work appear late in a company's history.)

In each office worker there exists the urge to be creative—to design and use your own office forms. In the small office, the receptionist designs, duplicates, uses, and stores the visitor's register or sign-in sheet and perhaps the forms for telephone messages and for other routine communications. No one is asked for approval as it is sensed that there is a need for the orderly system that the record provides.

The receptionist in a large office frequently does the same thing. In one large company employing 1,200 office workers, eight similar visitor's "logs" were found to have been created by receptionists at the eight entrances to the building, each of whom created the form without the approval or consultation of her supervisor. For all records that are used by two or more people or departments, however, usually the department managers or supervisors, who are familiar with all the interdepartmental needs for information, should first approve and then produce the form for use.

JUSTIFICATION OF RECORDS

The first and possibly the most basic requirement of any records control program is to determine and to justify the need for records that are being created or planned. In any forms management or communications program, therefore, a significant amount of attention must be given to investigating the need for the record. In creating a form, such basic questions as those shown in Figure 12-2, page 292, are asked.

Some of the difficulty encountered in determining the need for a record can be appreciated by considering that the word "record" is a vague term to many people. Since the term includes any piece of paper or its equivalent (such as a form, book, photograph, punched card or tape, computer printout, drawing, or other document regardless of its nature), the difficulty of fixing responsibility for the creation of such a multiplicity of documents is a persistent problem.

In the small office, the secretary *is* the filing department and usually is responsible for designing and filing records and sometimes also for creating them. In the larger organization, on the other hand, most office personnel seem to feel that the responsibility for all phases of records control rests with the central records section. Hence there is often little concern outside the filing unit to do anything about records control problems, even though all departments are responsible for creating them. Obviously, then, one of the first challenges facing the records manager is to show that the control of records is the responsibility of *every* department manager, who must, in turn, educate each member of the staff to the need for justifying each new record created. This dual cooperation—between

Form Name		Form No.	Requisition No.
Requested by Department		Telephone No.	Requisition Date
No. of Copies Required		Date Wanted	Department to Charge

	YES	NO
1. Purpose of the form.		
2. Other records or forms with which it is used.		
3. Can some other form be used instead?		
4. Can you combine this form with another? With what form?		
5. Are all copies necessary?		
6. Does the title clearly indicate the form's function?		
7. Are all items necessary and clear?		
8. Are all constant items preprinted?		
9. Is the sequence of items in agreement with related forms?		
10. Should this form be prenumbered?		
11. Is adequate spacing provided for manual or machine fill-in?		
12. Is the form size suitable for storage in standard-size cabinets?		
13. Have tabular stops been most effectively utilized for typewritten forms?		
14. Is check-off or box-style design used to advantage?		
15. For "external" forms to be mailed, has form been designed to be used in window envelope?		
16. Has the form been checked with actual users?		
17. Has the form been approved by the departmental supervisor?		
18. Has the form also been approved by the forms control unit for design, code number, etc.?		
19. Are all physical specifications (paper, ink, size, type face, color of paper and ink, and other features, such as punching, perforating. etc.) adequate?		
20. Is the quantity desired reasonable?		

Figure 12-2

Checklist for Forms Design

records manager and departmental manager—results in a well-balanced, well-controlled program for creating only *essential* records.

As a rule, the people who create the records want to maintain control over their records rather than conform to requirements set up by a records manager. Difficulties may, therefore, arise in achieving proper coordination between the program to control records and the operating needs of individual departments.

Probably the most effective way to stress the need for control over the creation of records is a *cost-accounting* approach, particularly since most people in business remain firmly impressed with the need to reduce costs. In a forms-control program, for example, it is important to show through a cost study that the decision to create a new form is costly, since the expenditure of $1 for forms, paper and printing ultimately results in from $20 to $25 or more in clerical handling and filing costs after its creation. When multiple-copy forms are considered, this figure may be even higher. To justify the creation of any form, therefore, the total costs of the *physical form* and its *functional use* must be considered along with any benefits anticipated from its use.

Business letters, like forms, generate information-production costs. This fact—with certain trends shown over the years—is evident from the annual studies conducted by the Dartnell Corporation showing the cost of creating an average business letter.[1]

Business-Letter-Writing Costs		
Cost Factors	Average Cost	
	1966	1972
1. Dictator's time	$ .42	$ .72
2. Stenographer's cost	.92	.94
3. Nonproductive labor (waiting time, vacations, etc.)	.20	.25
4. Fixed charges (overhead, rent, taxes, pensions, etc.)	.60	.83
5. Materials (stationery, envelopes, ribbons, etc.)	.07	.10
6. Mailing cost (postage, gathering, sealing, stamping, etc.)	.14	.20
7. Filing cost (clerk's time, cost of equipment, etc.)	.09	.16
Total costs	$2.44	$3.20

When you consider that a standard letter-size 26-inch file drawer holds from 3,500 to 5,000 sheets of correspondence (30 per cent of

[1] "'Average' Business Letter Costs $3.31," *Analysis and Staff Report*, (Chicago: The Dartnell Corporation), 1973.

which are usually carbon copies of original correspondence) in addition to the necessary guides and folders, considerable costs are incurred through creating correspondence alone.

To illustrate:

1. Cost of outgoing correspondence represented by carbons in one drawer:

1,500	carbons of original correspondence (30% of 5,000)
$\times$ $3.31	average letter cost
$4,965	cost of creating correspondence, the carbons of which are in one standard file drawer

2. Cost of outgoing correspondence represented by carbons in a standard four-drawer file:

$4,965	cost of creating correspondence, the carbons of which are in one drawer
$\times$ 4	number of drawers
$19,860	cost of creating correspondence, the carbons of which are in a four-drawer file

Additional costs of a more intangible nature are also involved, especially in connection with the time required by personnel to read and process the material. When the salary of a $25,000 a year executive and the secretary's salary (perhaps $125 to $150 a week) are considered as major costs in letter preparation, a figure exceeding 35 cents per minute (including salaries and other letter-cost factors) may be computed to produce a business letter, memorandum, or report. It soon becomes apparent that every effort must be made *not* to create a record in the first place if a reasonable substitute can be found for communicating essential information.

SECTION 2.   RECORDS SURVEY

PURPOSE OF SURVEY

In order to manage a department, large or small, a manager must be well acquainted with personnel, equipment, and information systems for which he or she is responsible. In much the same way, in order to manage the records of the organization, the records manager and the staff must be well acquainted with all the records of the organization, especially those important ones operating in the interdepartmental channels. A record manager's typical approach to understanding the scope of his or her responsibility is to survey all *key* company records.

It would be "penny wise and pound foolish" to try to locate all pieces of paper used in an organization. Many of the forms, slips, informal notes and messages used only by one or two clerks in one department do not clog the channels of an office. Such records need not become a part of the important records to be surveyed in the records management program.

Basically, the records survey is made at the start of the program in order to determine the location, the volume, the frequency of use, and the types of records that presently exist. Some companies use a follow-up every two years to uncover other "bootleg" records that have not been reported. Since the initial survey is a difficult task, it must be approached with care; without a proper inventory of the organization's present records, no adequate attention can be given to such important matters as locating duplications in records, determining how long to keep records, deciding when to transfer them to less expensive storage, or when to destroy them.

Any thorough records survey should include every possible type of record within the office. Frequently, however, only the active file cabinets and storage areas are initially surveyed with the result that shelves, working files, and desk drawers as well as bookcases are overlooked. To circumvent this problem, some records management authorities suggest starting the inventory with the records in the storage areas and progressing back toward the active records. The information thus surveyed would then be used as a nucleus for further development of the records management program.

Other authorities prefer determining the types of records presently being created, assigning retention codes to them (a symbol telling how long each type of record should be kept), and destroying records no longer useful (including those in inactive storage).

Usually, however, some type of survey is made using a questionnaire, a personal interview, or a combination of both in order to gather copies of each record and information about its use. When the questionnaire is issued, all departments can be contacted at once, a definite deadline for compliance with the survey request may be set, and normal office procedures in the surveyed departments are not disrupted. On the other hand, several disadvantages accrue to this survey method. Clerical personnel do not generally look with favor on another questionnaire to fill out, since it adds another burden to their daily tasks. Furthermore, difficulty is often encountered in interpreting the instructions on the questionnaire. When the personal interview is used, more perspective by the interviewer can be gained and greater attention to detail provided although considerably more personnel time is involved.

From a practical standpoint, the records management staff will usually survey one department at a time rather than all departments at once. Such a stepping-stone approach permits a person to complete one unit's inventory, study the results, develop the retention schedule, and get approval before proceeding to the next department.

SCOPE OF THE SURVEY

Typical information to be gathered in the survey includes:

1. Identification (name and number) of the record
2. Purpose of the record: use of each copy
3. The department having primary custody or control of the record
4. Nature of the copy: original, carbon, typed, handwritten, photographed, with color specified
5. What kinds of information are filed together
6. How the record is filed (by customer name, by number, etc.)
7. Quantity in cubic feet, number of file drawers, or lineal inches
8. Inclusive dates of batching or accumulating the records
9. Where other copies of the record are distributed and filed (This information is useful for systems analysis purposes.)
10. Frequency of reference
11. Suggested classification of record: vital, important, useful, or nonessential
12. Suggested period of time to retain record
13. Name of person taking the inventory and date of inventory

From the data gathered, the records management personnel will be able to develop the remaining phases of the program for controlling records. A combined inventory-retention card [2] that is used to survey records by the Bankers Box Company is shown on page 297. With such a form, one person can survey about 1,000 cubic feet of records per week.

SECTION 3. RETENTION CONTROL

With our present capability for creating records, one can easily understand why unrestricted record growth quickly leads to storage problems. Complicating the picture is the rising cost of office space, ranging from $5 per square foot in smaller cities to as high as $35 a square foot in metropolitan centers.

---

[2] *Records Control and Storage Handbook*, Handbook 1680 (Franklin Park, Illinois: Bankers Box Company, 1963), pp. 4, 5.

RECORD TITLE *General Correspondence*					
INVENTORY			**RETENTION**		
DEPARTMENT *Sales*			APPROVALS		YEARS
RECORD COPY [X] DUPLICATE COPY [ ]			RECOMMENDED (SPECIFY SOURCE) *Sales July '73 article in Management*		*4*
VOLUME			ADMINISTRATIVE BY *W. M. Smith Mgt.* DATE *2/15/74*		*5*
INCLUSIVE DATES	LOCATION	QUANTITY	*NO REQUIREMENT* LEGAL COUNSEL BY *J. O. Sanders* DATE *2/16/74*		*X*
1970-1973	OFFICE	*90 cu. ft.*	EXECUTIVE BY *R. L. Douglas* DATE *3/2/74*		*4*
1963-1969	STORAGE	*125 " "*	FINALIZED SCHEDULE		
REMARKS			IN OFFICE *1 year*	IN STORAGE *4 years*	DESTROY *after 5 years*
			BY *S. L. Moore, Comptroller* DATE *4/10/74*		
COUNTED BY *Harry Mills* DATE *4/11/73*			SPECIAL INSTRUCTIONS *Note: 10 four drawer cabinets will be released by Sales Dept.*		
FORM 1606 RECORDS INVENTORY AND RETENTION CONTROL CARD			COPYRIGHT 1963 BANKERS BOX COMPANY FRANKLIN PARK, ILLINOIS		

Storing records costs considerable money; yet indiscriminate discarding of records is not necessarily the answer to this problem. Therefore, one of the vital elements of any records management program involves *records retention control,* the set of activities involved in deciding how long records should be kept and in what locations these records should be stored.

THE REAL RETENTION PROBLEM

It seems to be human nature for many office workers to keep almost every piece of paper with which they deal. There are various explanations for this situation. For one thing, job security is involved. The typical reaction seems to be that the executive feels the need to keep every important record he creates; and as a rule, every record he creates he considers important! So the problem of deciding what records to retain must be approached with caution for it involves certain basic aspects of job psychology.

Studies repeatedly show that the office that does not control its records will quickly assume a "cluttered-attic" appearance. Valuable documents become needles in a haystack of limited-value, out-of-date records. In such a setting, systems breakdowns occur, records are difficult to retrieve or locate when needed, and the overall work efficiency of the personnel is reduced. Filing and finding difficulties arise, decision making is delayed, space becomes limited, and fire hazards multiply.

A limited number of executives form the habit of discarding everything not of current value. Should their companies be sued and be unable to produce a certain document as evidence, legal problems might ensue. A middle-of-the-road approach—retaining only essential records—is the best approach. However, the biggest problem is in getting agreement on the meaning of the word "essential."

THE RECORDS RETENTION SCHEDULE

To classify records as to their value, as well as to control the time period during which the records are maintained in storage, requires the combined effort of all record users as well as other specialists within the firm. The results of their efforts usually culminate in the development of a timetable or *records retention schedule* showing how long each record should be kept.

As a rule, these steps develop the retention schedule:

1. Identify those personnel to be assigned the responsibility for developing the retention schedule
2. Classify records according to their relative value
3. Assign a time period for retaining the record
4. Get approval of departmental executives for the proposed retention schedule

Records Retention Responsibility. In today's complex organization, the information system which the records serve involves the interdepartmental flow of forms and other communication media such as letters, orders, requisitions, directives, and reports. In order to evaluate such records and assign the correct retention classification, a broad knowledge of company information requirements is essential. Such a task is usually too large and complicated for one man to handle. Since most departments of a firm are involved in creating and using records, they should also have a voice in their retention.

The most expeditious way of developing a sound records-retention schedule is to form a working committee of key staff and line personnel representing each of the major organizational units of the firm. Such a group might include representatives from the following:

Accounting Department	Records Management Department
General Management	Research and Development Depart-
Legal Staff	ment
Personnel Department	Sales Department
Purchasing Department	

From such a group considerable combined experience and background can be brought to bear upon the importance of each of the key records. A committee of this type can also be expected to make a fair and impartial appraisal of the net value of all the records it reviews for retention purposes.

Classification of Records. While it is difficult to determine with mathematical precision the monetary value of information on records, it is still possible through group study to predict the general utility of most basic records. By realistically facing the question "What would I do if my basic records were destroyed?" a manager can classify reasonably well the relative value of most records.

Most office records can be classified in one of these four ways:

1. Vital records

    a. Definition: Records that cannot be replaced and hence should never be destroyed. These records are essential to the effective, continued operation of the organization and should not be transferred from the active section of the storage area (usually the general office area).

    b. Examples: Corporate charter
Major contracts
Accounts receivable records
Accounts payable records
Inventory records
Deeds and other legal documents
Tax returns

    c. Protection: Safes and vaults

2. Important records

    a. Definition: Records that are necessary to an orderly continuation of the business and are replaceable only with considerable expenditure of time and money. Such records may sometimes be transferred to inactive storage but are usually *not* destroyed.

    b. Examples: Financial statements
Sales data
Credit histories
Some purchasing data
Specifications and drawings
Operating and statistical records

    c. Protection: Safes and vaults

3. Useful records

a. Definition: Records that are useful for the smooth, effective operation of the organization. Such records are replaceable, but their loss would involve some delay or inconvenience to the firm.

b. Examples: Business letters (active files)
Interoffice memorandums
Business reports
Bank statements

c. Protection: No special forms of protection, but they should be housed in closed steel containers and not be exposed to combustibles.

4. Nonessential records

a. Definition: Records that have no predictable value to the organization. Since the purpose for which they were created has been fulfilled, they may be destroyed.

b. Examples: Routine inquiries completed
Simple acknowledgments
Bulletin-board announcements
Seasonal publications
Temporary, extra-copy pieces

c. Protection: None after the use of the record is gone.

Retention considerations. A widely known consultant [3] in records management suggests seven key values of records to help develop a records-retention schedule:

1. Administrative use
2. Legal use
3. Fiscal use
4. Policy use
5. Operating use
6. Historical use
7. Research use

While most of these record values are obvious to the reader, several points seem worthy of comment regarding this list.

With government, business, and industry devoting greater amounts of money to research and development, the values of records for research purposes such as developing new and improved products should not be minimized. And with the ability of data-processing machines to utilize greater amounts of information for research and operating purposes, the importance of maintaining adequate records becomes evident. The most definite, exacting requirements made of records managers come from the legal and governmental

---

[3] Victor Lazzaro (Editor), *Systems and Procedures: A Handbook*, 2d ed., (Englewood Cliffs, New Jersey: Prentice-Hall, 1968), p. 235.

decrees that describe in detail how long certain types of records should be kept. However, less than 10 percent of all records created must be retained to satisfy legal requirements.

The National Records Management Council publishes a list of federal record-keeping requirements for commercial firms. In addition, the U. S. Government Printing Office annually publishes a *Guide to Records Retention Requirements,* in which the records by governmental departments (such as Department of Agriculture; Department of Commerce; Department of Labor; Department of Treasury, which includes the Internal Revenue Service; and the Interstate Commerce Commission) are listed with the recommended periods of time the records should be kept. Of special interest to the federal government is the fact that a business maintain an adequate recording system for determining income and expense. In general the government's interest in such a system continues for "so long as the contents thereof may become material in the administration of any Internal Revenue Law."

Statutes of Limitations. Each of the fifty states has developed statutes of limitations, which specify the time after which legal rights cannot be enforced by civil action in the courts. What this means is that once a record reaches an age beyond which the Statute of Limitations applies, the record is valueless as evidence in a court of law. Through common practice many states will usually audit the records of business within a period of three years. Such audited records can then be considered for destruction, especially such valueless records as time cards and cancelled payroll checks, completed sales and accounts receivable documents, and paid-up accounts payable files.

Each of the statutes must be considered (along with other factors) by the records retention committee. A list of these statutes for the various states is shown on page 302.

Recommended Retention Periods. Each type of record must be evaluated in terms of its contribution to the functions of the organization. Records, such as out-of-date payroll registers, that transmit information that is of no immediate or future value to the organization should be destroyed. Records, such as production control orders, current inspection reports, and social security literature, that contain information actively referred to should be kept in the active, easily accessible work areas. And those records only occasionally referred to, such as obsolete sales reports, should be transferred to inexpensive storage centers as soon as possible.

Statutes of Limitations

State	Open Accounts	Written Contracts	Judgments of Record
Alabama	3 years	6 years	20 years
Alaska	6 years	6 years	10 years
Arizona	3 years	6 years	5 years
Arkansas	3 years	5 years	10 years
California	4 years	4 years	5 years
Colorado	6 years	6 years	20 years
Connecticut	6 years	6 years	No limit
Delaware	3 years	3 years	10 years
Dist. of Columbia	3 years	3 years	12 years
Florida	3 years	5 years	20 years
Georgia	4 years	6 years	10 years
Hawaii	6 years	6 years	10 years
Idaho	4 years	5 years	6 years
Illinois	5 years	10 years	20 years
Indiana	6 years	20 years	20 years
Iowa *	5 years	10 years	20 years
Kansas	3 years	5 years	5 years
Kentucky	5 years	15 years	15 years
Louisiana	3 years	10 years	10 years
Maine	6 years	6 years	20 years
Maryland	3 years	3 years	12 years
Massachusetts	6 years	6 years	20 years
Michigan	6 years	6 years	10 years
Minnesota	6 years	6 years	10 years
Mississippi	3 years	6 years	7 years
Missouri	5 years	10 years	10 years
Montana	5 years	8 years	10 years
Nebraska	4 years	5 years	5 years
Nevada	4 years	6 years	6 years
New Hampshire	6 years	6 years	20 years
New Jersey	6 years	6 years	20 years
New Mexico	4 years	6 years	7 years
New York	6 years	6 years	20 years
North Carolina	3 years	3 years	10 years
North Dakota	6 years	6 years	10 years
Ohio	6 years	15 years	21 years
Oklahoma	3 years	5 years	5 years
Oregon	6 years	6 years	10 years
Pennsylvania	6 years	6 years	20 years
Rhode Island	6 years	6 years	20 years
South Carolina	6 years	6 years	10 years
South Dakota	6 years	6 years	20 years
Tennessee	6 years	6 years	10 years
Texas	2 years	4 years	10 years
Utah	4 years	6 years	8 years
Vermont	6 years	6 years	8 years
Virginia	3 years	5 years	20 years
Washington	3 years	6 years	6 years
West Virginia	5 years	10 years	10 years
Wisconsin	6 years	6 years	20 years
Wyoming	8 years	10 years	5 years

* For more detailed information concerning the Statute of Limitations in Iowa, consult George A. Arvidson, Jr., Indexer, *Index to the Code of Iowa*, State of Iowa, 1971. Similar references can be found in each of the other states.

In developing the schedule, the retention committee must take into careful consideration the following points regarding each important *type* of record:

1. The frequency of reference to the record
2. Whether the record or an equivalent exists elsewhere
3. Whether the record is used indirectly or with other records for a period of time
4. Legal requirements for retaining the form, for example, the Statute of Limitations or Government regulations
5. The number of copies of the record and the anticipated costs of maintaining them in active, as opposed to inactive, storage space
6. The usefulness of the record in systems studies as well as for historical purposes and for analyzing future organizational needs

One basic yardstick is: If there is any doubt as to the record's value, keep it!

Through the years, common practices have developed in offices of all sizes and types regarding the length of time certain routine documents should be kept in the files. A survey of record-keeping practices [4] indicates that the following rules of thumb often apply to retention periods of records:

Destroy immediately (after use):	Routine memos (after action has been taken) Incoming mail of no importance (form letters, announcements, 3rd-class mail) Pencil notations such as telephone messages
File three months:	Incoming and outgoing routine correspondence with customers and vendors Stenographers' notebooks Purchase requisitions (originator's duplicate) Bank statements Expired insurance policies
File the number of years necessary according to the Statute of Limitations:	Cancelled payroll checks Invoices to customers and from vendors Duplicate deposit tickets Accident reports Time cards and tickets Cost compilations Audit reports
File permanently:	Minutes of meetings Books of account Capital stock ledgers and transfer records Deeds, mortgages, and other conveyances Tax returns and related papers Property records, insurance in force Reports to stockholders

---

[4] *Office Standards and Planning Book* (New York: Art Metal Construction Co., 1954), pp. 25-26.

Records Retention Alternatives. The *value* of the record and the *frequency* of its use have a strong impact upon the decision that is made as to its disposal. For example, a corporation's charter is one of the corporation's most valued possessions, yet it is rarely, if ever, referred to. Because of its high value, however, it is kept in well-protected, accessible storage. On the other hand, accounts receivable records that are active but that date back several years are valuable but need not be kept in their entirety in expensive active storage. The nature of the document and the frequency of its use should determine its retention and location.

As a rule, there are several alternatives which the retention committee faces as it reviews the inventory of collected records:

1. Transfer the record to inactive storage and retain it permanently.
2. Transfer the record to inactive storage and destroy it within a stipulated period of time.
3. Keep the record in active storage and transfer it to inactive (less expensive) storage at a later time.
4. Keep the record in active (expensive) storage permanently.
5. Destroy the record immediately.

Since many records must be kept even though they are not current in nature or are not referred to frequently, they should be transferred from the limited, expensive, active storage to inactive storage somewhere outside of the office area. Many record analysts agree that a record should be considered *inactive* if it is referred to less than 15 times a year. If a record is used twice a month (24 times a year), it can be considered *semiactive* and stored in the less accessible drawers or cabinets in the active storage area. If a record is used three or more times a month, the record is considered to be *active*.

PERSONAL FILES

Regardless of how thorough the records inventory is, there is at least one "privileged sanctuary" whose records are usually successfully withheld from the control of the records manager. This sanctuary is the executive's *private file*.

In today's business world, there are many executives who have charge of confidential matters. These transactions may vary from simple contracts made on a personal basis with vendors to complex subcontractors' agreements and various other types of transactions that should be kept from other employees or from outsiders in general. Often highly restricted competitive information is involved.

Still another type of information adds to the record-keeping problem. Today's businessmen are community-minded and, therefore, willing, avid workers in business and trade associations, as well as in civic and service groups such as the Rotary International, Kiwanis, the Optimists, and the United Fund. As a result, a considerable amount of correspondence and record keeping finds its way into the organization's files. Obviously, the contents of these files should be maintained separate from those controlled by the records manager. Nevertheless, they should be organized in an efficient, orderly fashion so that their use does not hamper the efficiency of the executive.

SECTION 4. TRANSFER CONTROL

By using the approved records retention schedule, records management personnel can evaluate each record in terms of its status: to be retained (and if so, where and for how long) or to be destroyed. A logical follow through, therefore, on the retention schedule is a plan of *transfer control* in which all records slated to be moved from active to inactive storage or to final destruction. The cost of maintaining a typical 4-drawer file in active storage for one year is conservatively estimated at $180, whereas the same files can be maintained in inactive storage for approximately $5 to $12, depending upon the cost of floor space. In most cases, experience has shown that the current year's records plus those of the past year are all that is needed in active files. However, there are many factors to consider which require an individual approach to each transfer situation.

Although the transfer of records takes time and requires the setting aside of space for a records storage center, there are several obvious advantages to the transfer plan. First of all, it helps to reduce equipment costs, since transfer materials may be stored in less expensive containers than those used for storage of active materials. Second, the filing drawers and cabinets formerly used by the transferred files provide additional space for the active files. Finally, the ease of filing is improved because the crowding of the file drawers has been eliminated; and, as a result, the work space in the file drawers or shelves has been increased.

METHODS OF RECORDS TRANSFER

Two methods of transferring files from active to inactive storage are used: (1) the *perpetual method,* which provides for the constant transfer of materials from active to inactive files, and (2) the *periodic method,* which provides for the transfer of materials from active to inactive storage at stated intervals. The perpetual transfer method is the simpler in concept and is described in the following outline.

Perpetual Transfer Method	
Definition	Continuous transfer of stored materials from active to inactive files.
Advantage	The files are kept current because this method of transfer is used in offices that complete the work in well-defined segments or units. When a unit is completed, it can be transferred in its entirety to the inactive files.
Disadvantage	The method is not good for business correspondence or routine documents of more or less continuous nature.
Examples of use	Lawyers' cases, architects' projects, terminal cases in surgeons' offices, prison records.

The periodic transfer method is more complex, usually taking one of three different forms. Each of these forms is defined and compared in the chart on pages 307 and 308. A graphic illustration of the periodic transfer (Figure 12-4, page 308) shows both 4- and 5-drawer files in operation in the transfer system as used by a filing equipment manufacturer.

By studying both transfer methods, it soon becomes obvious that the perpetual transfer method is not practical for most offices since it requires continuous attention to the transfer of files. Rather, in most instances, it appears that the periodic transfer is more satisfactory since it keeps together all records for a certain time period. Under such conditions, there is one definite place in which to conduct a search for materials in a file. In the periodic plan, even though records on one subject that cross two time periods may be separated, the majority of references are made to active files.

When the perpetual transfer method is used, records that are semiactive may already have been transferred to inactive storage. Thus, there may be considerable confusion and delay in reassembling all related records in active storage.

Periodic Transfer Method

	One-Period Method	Two-Period Method (Duplicate-Equipment Method)	Maximum-Minimum Method
Definition	All materials are removed from the active files at least once or twice a year and are placed in an inactive file.	Duplicate files (one active; one inactive) are maintained in the department. They may be located side by side, or the lower drawers of each filing cabinet may be for inactive materials while the upper drawers are for active materials. At stated intervals, all the inactive files are removed to the records storage center; the active files are transferred to the inactive drawer space; and new files are set up in the active drawers at the beginning of the new period.	Active materials (six months old or less) are kept in the active files; all materials for the year preceding the last six months are transferred to the inactive files. For example, if the transfer date is June 30, all materials dated in the preceding year are transferred. Thus, transferred material varies in age at the time of transfer from six to eighteen months (that is, the minimum to maximum age of the records at time of transfer).
Advantages	Ease of operation. When space is limited, reference to files of previous period is infrequent.	Suitable for a small office where office file space is limited. In a large office it may be useful by reducing the length of the transfer period. It keeps the records of two periods accessible even though they are separated.	Elimination of the objectionable features of the one- and two-period methods since the most recent files are retained in the active files.

(Continued on page 308)

	One-Period Method	Two-Period Method (Duplicate-Equipment Method)	Maximum-Minimum Method
Disadvantages	Time is lost in making frequent trips to the storage center. Recent materials are usually needed for one to three months, but they are not available for immediate reference.	This method is especially geared to large-scale offices where the active files alone account for considerable space needs. Some inconvenience and extra expense are involved in maintaining both active and semiactive files in one location.	There is some slight inconvenience of separating the records at transfer time to provide for the correct maximum-minimum time period.

In 4- drawer files the upper two rows hold active papers, and the two drawers below, inactive records

A-E ACTIVE	L-R ACTIVE
F-K ACTIVE	S-Z ACTIVE
A-E INACTIVE	L-R INACTIVE
F-K INACTIVE	S-Z INACTIVE

This arrangement of active and inactive papers in 5-drawer files allows current reference to drawers most easily reached, and easy reference to inactive papers located in equal, if less convenient space.

A-B INACTIVE	D-E INACTIVE	K-L INACTIVE	O-R INACTIVE
A-B ACTIVE	F-G ACTIVE	K-L ACTIVE	S ACTIVE
C ACTIVE	H-J ACTIVE	M-N ACTIVE	T-Z ACTIVE
D-E ACTIVE	F-G INACTIVE	O-R ACTIVE	S INACTIVE
C INACTIVE	H-J INACTIVE	M-N INACTIVE	T-Z INACTIVE

In 5-drawer files, inactive files often may be contracted to fit less accessible space.

A-E INACTIVE	I-Q INACTIVE
A-B ACTIVE	M-N ACTIVE
C-F ACTIVE	O-S ACTIVE
G-L ACTIVE	T-Z ACTIVE
F-H INACTIVE	B-Z INACTIVE

The "double-spread" plan for 5-drawer files need not involve drawer shifts at the time of transfer. The sketch illustrates a "side-by-side" treatment which saves end-of-year labor.

A-B ACTIVE	A-B INACTIVE	K-L ACTIVE	K-L INACTIVE
C ACTIVE	C INACTIVE	M-N ACTIVE	M-N INACTIVE
D-E ACTIVE	D-E INACTIVE	O-R ACTIVE	O-R INACTIVE
F-G ACTIVE	F-G INACTIVE	S ACTIVE	S INACTIVE
H-J ACTIVE	H-J INACTIVE	T-Z ACTIVE	T-Z INACTIVE

Figure 12-4

Periodic Transfer Plans

Sperry Remington, Office Systems and Machines, Sperry Rand Corporation

EXECUTION OF RECORDS TRANSFER

After the initial transfer plan has been set up for all records, several remaining management considerations must be handled before any physical transfer of records can be executed. These considerations include (1) setting aside or procuring of transfer equipment and supplies, (2) setting up the records storage center (or archives), or (3) taking the inactive records from the office to a commercial records center. Each of these considerations will be briefly discussed.

Records Transfer Equipment and Supplies. The size and complexity of the record-keeping operation usually influence the expense and detail connected with procuring transfer equipment and supplies. In general, however, the following items may be considered as basic needs of any records storage center:

1. Steel shelving or a substitute that will accommodate heavy boxes or cartons
2. Special heavy cardboard cartons for storage of the transferred records
3. Card files describing the contents of the transfer files and indicating the dates on which the papers may be destroyed
4. Transfer file accessories, such as labels, dividers, and other miscellaneous minor items commonly associated with file maintenance

Bankers Box Company

Figure 12-5   Storage Files for Inactive Records

5. Special files for miscellaneous records, such as tabulating or punched cards, microfilmed documents, and records of nonstandard sizes.
6. Carts (and, if needed, dollies) for moving heavy files and filing equipment into the records center.

Figure 12-5 on page 309 shows two types of the basic archival equipment used in large records centers. As a rule, this equipment as well as the space it occupies is considerably less expensive than that utilized in the active office area.

The Storage Center. The storage center or *archives* is the central part of the transfer and retention program. This center houses all records that are no longer actively (that is frequently) used in the office. All files sent to the records center will be stored there permanently or temporarily until destroyed as specified by the records retention schedule. And since the number of records tends to multiply rapidly, it is necessary that the center be operated in an orderly, systematic manner.

From the standpoint of good management, a records storage center should encompass all of the following characteristics:

1. A location for the center that is accessible to the records-using personnel in the organization.
2. Low-cost storage space.
3. Housing (cabinets, boxes, cartons for the records) that is inexpensive but that provides maximum utilization of space along with appropriate shelving.
4. An area that provides normal protection from such hazards as acts of God (fire, flood, storm), acts of man (theft, arson, and the like), and the elements (dust, insects, mildew).
5. A layout that can accommodate the stresses of heavy weight since stacked file cartons or cabinets are very heavy.
6. Proper environmental controls, including humidity controls and temperature regulation (from 65° to 75°), lighting and plumbing facilities; and general receiving and dispatching space for the distribution of records.
7. Proper utilization of floor space with provision for wide enough aisles to maintain an efficient traffic pattern.
8. A card index system on which this information should be entered:
   a. title of the record
   b. department sending the record
   c. date the container is received in storage
   d. container number
   e. description of the contents
   f. inclusive dates of the contents
   g. specific location of the container in the storage area
   h. destruction date
9. An efficient system for filing and finding the inactive records with proper provisions for cross-referencing and charge-out.

10. Miscellaneous equipment such as work tables for sorting, staplers, moving equipment, etc.
11. A security system that will restrict the records center to authorized personnel only.

Commercial Records Center. Since World War II there has been a noticeable trend among firms to subcontract the storage of their inactive records to commercial records centers. Such a service is provided for a relatively low storage cost (compared to storing the records on the firm's premises) with many other recordkeeping services provided. Some centers, for example, offer assistance in developing retention schedules, in setting up records management programs and policies, and in the selection of effective storage and retrieval systems.

The principal advantages of using a commercial records center are: (1) low-cost storage with many estimates for such storage as low as 1/10 of storage costs on the firm's premises; (2) greater protection and security (sometimes utilizing underground security vaults for special records); (3) fast, accurate, and low-cost retrieval, with telephone retrieval of information or messenger-dispatch services available; (4) elimination of long-range storage space planning considerations for a client; and (5) the availability of expert consultation.[5]

The selection of such a center must be done in a careful manner. To assure that the best available center is obtained, management should personally visit the center and evaluate its services and its space facilities, as well as the overall capabilities provided by the staff. Of special importance are answers to these questions:

1. Does the facility really have the capability to store and protect records adequately?
2. Can the center provide efficient retrieval at reasonable cost?
3. Does the center assure adequate space for future storage needs?
4. Is the facility's security, including fire control equipment, adequate?

SECTION 5. DISPOSAL CONTROL

MEANING OF "DISPOSAL"

The term *disposal* (sometimes used synonymously with *disposition* of a record) has several connotations as it is used in connection with records management. In a specific, precise way, "disposal" is used

---

[5] Cameron, Christopher A., "Records Storage Centers," *Information and Records Management Annual Guide Book 1969*, pp. 62, 64.

to indicate the final action that has been recommended on the retention schedule for a record. To illustrate, if accounts receivable records were classified as being "vital," the following conditions might apply to these records:

Name of records:	Accounts receivable journals
Date of records:	1962-1965
Classification of records:	Vital
Retention of records:	Permanently
Transfer:	To inactive storage after records are 2 years old
Disposal of records:	Filed by customer names in archives

In this sense, "disposal" means in essence "what finally happens to the record."

Far more frequently, however, the term "disposal" has come to mean the destruction of the records. The most common, though risky, method of records disposal is discarding in the wastebasket (called facetiously "the circular file" or "file 13") records that are no longer needed. The safe way to dispose of records is to keep them in the transfer file until authorization has been received by the archivist stating that the records no longer have any value and should be destroyed.

METHODS OF DISPOSAL

When records are transferred to the storage center, the disposal date for the records within the storage carton is clearly printed on the box. In such cases, records have been previously segregated so that those with temporary value will not be stored with those requiring permanent retention. However, for purposes of orderly destruction and to provide a record of all those destroyed, modern records managers tend to prefer the use of an authorization form. This form serves as evidence that management has released certain identified obsolete records for destruction. A copy of such a form is shown in Figure 12-6 on page 313.

Various methods are used to destroy records. These range from the simple crushing of records and throwing them into the wastebasket to the use of complex, expensive machines. Many records are easily destroyed by macerating, burning, or shredding. In an increasing number of instances in modern times, however, stocks of paper may be sold to paper purchasers as waste paper or possibly donated to paper-collection agencies such as the Salvation Army for "recycling" purposes. However, where records have confidential content, they should be carefully "dismantled" or "disfigured" through shredding so that their utility is completely destroyed. The electric wastebasket was designed for this purpose.

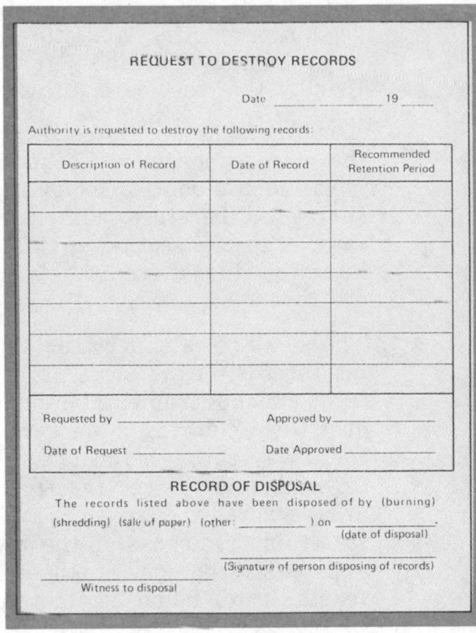

REQUEST TO DESTROY RECORDS

Date _____ 19 ___

Authority is requested to destroy the following records:

Description of Record	Date of Record	Recommended Retention Period

Requested by _____   Approved by _____

Date of Request _____   Date Approved _____

RECORD OF DISPOSAL

The records listed above have been disposed of by (burning) (shredding) (sale of paper) (other: _____) on _____ .
(date of disposal)

(Signature of person disposing of records)

Witness to disposal

Figure 12-6

Authorization Form for Destroying Records

SECTION 6. THE RECORDS CYCLE IN THE SMALL OFFICE

The principles outlined in this chapter apply to all offices regardless of size. Implied in this chapter, however, is the fact that the formal "machinery" for controlling the records cycle is a function of a large organization capable of having a specialized records management staff to handle each of the steps in the cycle.

But the small office, too, must control the records it creates and, in effect, must develop its own control techniques. Each of the cyclical steps must, of course, be managed by the small-office supervisor although in a less formal way than in the large firm. Some of the ways in which the smaller office can adapt the principles of controlling the records cycle discussed in this chapter are as follows:

1. Probably no full-time files operator will be available in the small (say 5-person) office. Nevertheless, the responsibility for managing records should be assigned to one or two persons who have the greatest knowledge of the firm's information system as well as the best aptitude (accuracy, patience, and knowledge of filing procedures) for this type of work. Others in the office should be discouraged from direct use of the files.

2. All records created should be approved by a designated person who can analyze the justification for such records. Assistance on records design, production, and storage can be obtained from printing firms or systems and business forms salesmen specializing in this work. Usually this service is provided without a charge.

3. A copy of all records used by the office should be centrally filed by the office supervisor. Frequently a three-ring notebook is used to house such a control set of records. The need for a time-consuming survey is, therefore, eliminated; but continuous follow-up is necessary. A special section of this manual should be devoted to a chronological listing of records by time periods showing when they can be destroyed.

4. The small-office supervisor should be aware of the need to classify his records on the basis of (1) the frequency of their use and (2) legal and governmental requirements for retaining them. At least once a year during a slack work period, the office staff should work their way through the files in an effort to remove all "deadwood." In some small offices inactive records are transferred to storeroom areas where extra space is available. In such offices, too, the decision to retain or dispose of the record can be quickly secured from the appropriate person. Small offices, especially, should investigate the feasibility of using commercial records centers.

5. Disposal of records, while handled informally, should nevertheless be done with caution so that all records destroyed have been so authorized and a record kept of the files and the time when they were destroyed.

6. Small-office files personnel should be encouraged to participate in professional activities and programs (such as those provided by the National Secretaries Association) which increase their understanding of modern storage and retrieval systems. Many of these systems have great value to both small and large office alike.

For Review and Discussion

1. How is the growth of red tape affected by economic and social conditions in this country?

2. What reasons underlie the fact that data processing records relate more directly to business forms than to business correspondence?

3. Outline the records cycle and the means that are available for controlling each step in the cycle.

4. Suppose you are an office manager responsible for deciding on the need for a new multi-copy office form. You are aware that the form is not needed, although it would be convenient for the requester to have it. Defend your decision to reject the request for creating the new form. Use a concrete example to answer this question.

5. In a small office it would probably be impossible to set up a full-fledged records retention schedule even though such a retention program is

needed in all such offices. How would you practice good retention principles when you do not have the specialization for such a program?

6. What sources—both local and beyond—would you consult in order to ensure that all records in your office are retained for an adequate period of time?

7. Why is special consideration given to income and expense records of a business firm when the government sets up its records retention requirements? Does this mean that other types of records are secondary in importance? Discuss.

8. What would be the contribution of each of the following business executives who might be members of a records retention committee:

> The patent attorney
> The controller
> The sales manager
> The assistant to the general manager
> The purchasing agent
> The records manager

9. Which methods of transfer might be recommended for each of these files?

(a) Divorce suits
(b) Clients' files (long term)
(c) Purchase orders
(d) Personnel applications

10. Concerning each of the following requisites of good records management, compare an active storage area to an inactive storage area:

(a) The equipment
(b) The storage location
(c) Filing procedures utilized

11. Assume you are working in a 10-person office and are considering setting up an inactive file. How would you decide (and later document the fact) on the contents of the inactive file?

12. Under what circumstances do you feel that a perpetual transfer plan is warranted?

Learning Projects

1. The local city association of independent insurance agents has arranged a meeting with you to discuss their overall records operations. As intermediaries between the home offices of the insurance companies they serve and the customers they handle, these agents have a growing record problem largely involving premium forms, notices of premiums due, contracts and policies, and correspondence. Basically they are interested in knowing how they can control their records with greater efficiency.

Outline what your report to these agents should include. Mention, wherever necessary, outside services that may help alleviate their problems.

2. You are employed during the summer months by a busy, successful young lawyer. His files include the usual legal records (abstracts, title search records and other property and real estate files as well as records of law which he has handled) and a growing number of private files due to the fact that he is now a very active member of a political party and is running for election to the state senate. You notice potentially dangerous records problems, an unwieldy private file system (or lack of system), and a serious lack of space. Furthermore, there are no obvious controls at any point in the records cycle. Draft a report to your employer pointing out the problems and making some realistic suggestions for circumventing the problems you sense; but also consider the fact that such a report could reflect negatively on his long-time secretary, Miss Batterson, who has complete charge of the office.

3. The records transfer-retention disposal plan for a company usually involves considerable detail and complexity. As such, it is difficult to understand and explain to personnel who may be involved in the program.

   Arrange, if possible, to visit a prominent, up-to-date bank or office that has a large records department. Tour the installation. Wherever possible, obtain a copy of the principal control forms (e.g., the disposal authorization form, the records survey form, etc.) and written retention procedures that have been developed for such a program. After you have had an opportunity to study all those routines related to transfer, retention, and disposal, draw a flow chart (a graphic picture) of the routines and explain in a written report to your instructor the entire retention system in a clear, concise, and complete manner. Consult a reliable office management reference for suggestions in drawing the flow chart and explaining its symbols.

4. To transfer records from active storage to an inactive type of storage physically removed from the active office operation, new organizational and operational needs must be met. From your study of Chapter 12, outline in writing relevant answers to the following questions:

   (a) To plan an inactive storage operation, what organizational considerations must be analyzed?

   (b) What new communications channels must be set up? Give an example of one type of written communication that might be devised to requisition a record from inactive storage.

   (c) Within the inactive records storage center, what are three major routines that must be set up?

Chapter 13

Procurement and use of equipment and supplies

In the management and control of the records system, the records manager or the one in charge of procurement of supplies and equipment should be knowledgeable about the kinds available. Factors of efficiency of use and overall cost are of prime importance.

Economies result when the right size, quality, and number of storage equipment items and supplies are used. Competition among filing equipment manufacturers to improve the efficiency of storage by improving equipment and supplies has been an important factor in helping to make filing the indispensable tool of office management that it is today.

The equipment and supplies that are best for a particular office are those that are best suited to the needs of that office. The most efficient filing departments are not necessarily those that have the costliest equipment and supplies. The records manager should welcome information furnished by the office equipment and office supply manufacturers; and he should consult with the dealers who sell equipment and supplies in his locality, all of whom have consultants available to work with the records manager in determining his or her needs.

To help the records manager plan wisely and carefully, this chapter is divided into seven sections. Section 1 presents a discussion of the basic considerations for the selection of equipment and supplies. In Section 2, features of a well-constructed file are discussed and information is given pertaining to standard and special features of filing cabinets. Section 3 presents facets of various types of guides and folders. Sections 4 and 5 present information pertaining to card files and visible records, open-shelf files, side files, and lateral filing. In Section 6, the storage equipment for inactive files is discussed; and in Section 7 is found discussion of miscellaneous equipment and supplies which are valuable aids in maintaining and controlling a records system.

Some of the information contained in this chapter has been mentioned previously in this textbook in connection with the methods and systems of filing. Here, an attempt is made to draw together in one place, for the benefit of the records manager, the many details pertaining to equipment and supplies. Because electronic data processing and microrecords are specialized areas of knowledge, the discussion of equipment and supplies pertaining to them, contained in Chapter 11, is not repeated here.

SECTION 1. BASIC CONSIDERATIONS FOR THE SELECTION OF EQUIPMENT AND SUPPLIES

The needs of each office differ from those of other offices. The records manager must know the answers to the following questions before he can plan his filing needs:

1. What kinds of records will be stored?
2. What volume of materials will be stored during a specified period— a month, six months, a year?
3. How frequently are the records called for?
4. How many people ordinarily refer to one record that is taken; i.e., how extensively does one record travel?
5. How many people have access to the files?
6. What methods of storage are best for the records to be filed?
7. What methods of charge-out and follow-up are best suited to the operation of the filing department?
8. Are the records kept in a central location? Are they departmentalized? Or are they a combination of central files and department files? Why?
9. What are the policies of top management toward transfer, retention, and disposal of the filed records?
10. What kinds of equipment are on hand?
11. How much space is now available for the records? How much additional room is available for expansion?
12. Has the layout of the office been studied to provide for the most efficient use of space and flow of work and records? If not, can this be done and changes be made?
13. Are economic factors taking precedence over efficiency factors? (Equipment and supplies are the tools of efficient storage, and rigid economies can seriously hinder that efficiency.)

14. What types of equipment and supplies are locally available without special order?
15. What services do local equipment and supply firms offer in connection with filing needs?

A records manager who knows the answers to these questions will know what he wants and why he needs it. He will see that efficient practices are followed in order to keep a minimum number of records in the active files, for not every paper that is received should be filed nor should every paper be transferred and retained. A records manager keeps up to date on new and improved products through the reading of business periodicals, trade magazines, and catalogs; by attending special business shows; by visiting the showrooms of office equipment dealers and stationers; and by participation in professional records management society meetings.

SECTION 2. FILING CABINETS

Thomas' Register of Manufacturers lists numerous manufacturers of filing cabinets, supplies, and special equipment. Their types, sizes, prices, and special features vary greatly. They range in quality from files little better than tin boxes to heavily insulated, combination-locked cabinets. As is true with most purchases, quality equipment costs more, withstands heavier use, and lasts longer—one gets what he pays for! Using high-quality equipment for active files and less expensive equipment for inactive files is a proven workable practice.

Almost without exception, files purchased today to house correspondence are made of heavy-gauge furniture steel, with vertical reinforcements and spot welding in many places to give strength and rigidity. *Letter size* and *legal size* are the commonly used terms for designating file drawer cabinets. Some manufacturers indicate legal size by the term *cap size*. Combinations of card- and letter-size drawers, blueprint cabinets, fingerprint files, invoice files, document files, ledger files, combination safe and letter files, jumbo drawers to house X-rays, art work, large forms or plans, and many others are available from leading manufacturers.

The features of a well-constructed file drawer are shown in Figure 13-1 on page 320. They include (1) no-rust hardware (usually of anodized aluminum) for long-lasting beauty, with drawer pulls large enough to allow a firm grip by the hand and a card label holder rigidly affixed so that the card will be securely held in it; (2) a compressor or follower-block that locks firmly in place yet is simple and easy to move and takes a minimum of space; (3) a locking device (plunger type, called *paracentric*, or vertical locking bar) which is available at extra cost; (4) finish that does not absorb light but reflects it without glare (the range of colors available at the present time is large—grays, greens, beiges, wood grains of many kinds, and special decorator finishes); (5) heavy-gauge construction so that the drawer channels will carry great weight without sagging or distortion; (6) rigid construction permitting even distribution of weight when the drawers are opened at any position; (7) enclosed bottom plate for cleanliness; (8) base reinforcing cross brace for rigidity; (9) ladder-type construction that permits the substitution of drawers—two card drawers, for instance, in the space formerly occupied by one letter-size drawer; (10) a roller-bearing or ball-bearing suspension system allowing each drawer to open smoothly and easily because of a telescoping slide mechanism on either side operating on ball bearings; (11) a safety latch near the drawer handle for anti-rebound action; (12) a trigger or other stop mechanism on the drawer to brake the drawer as it glides open; and (13) a rod running from front to back at the bottom of each drawer, on which the guides are threaded and which can be easily removed by snapping or screwing slightly.

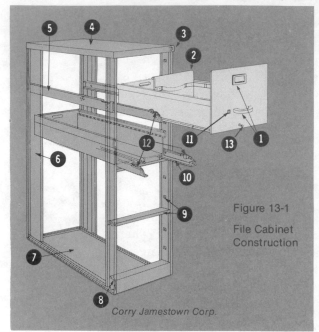

Figure 13-1

File Cabinet Construction

Corry Jamestown Corp.

Height, width, and depth dimensions vary slightly from manufacturer to manufacturer. Special-dimension cabinets can be built to special order. Equipment is manufactured to conform to standard sizes of stationery and printed forms that have been cut economically from standard-size sheets. When nonstandard items are used, the cost is inevitably increased.

A cabinet containing drawers with rods is about one inch higher per drawer than is a cabinet composed of drawers without rods, to allow space for the channel at the bottom of each drawer into which the rod must go. Files with special insulation for fire protection are necessarliy heavier, higher, and thicker in construction than are noninsulated files. Insulated file cabinets can be obtained to withstand ½ to 4 hours of extreme exposure. Such files are usually built to withstand the impact of falling debris or the sudden dropping through a collapsing floor, equal to a drop of 30 feet onto a rock surface. Papers can be protected in noninsulated cabinets from severe fire damage if compressors are moved forward so that they compress the papers within the drawer as tightly as possible when the drawer is closed. Paper will char at a temperature of about 350° F. even though untouched by flames, but tightly bound bundles of paper will char only around the edges.

The number of drawers in filing cabinets varies from one to the number required to reach the ceiling. One-drawer files are usually on caster bases and may be called *file caddies* (Figure 13-2)—a drawer on legs with rollers, a sliding top cover, and a key lock, to be taken from place to place in the office as needed. Two-drawer files are usually found in executive offices or as part of a modular desk unit. A three-drawer file is often counter height and may be used to separate the working space from the reception area. When files are used as counters, toe space should be allowed at the base for ease in working at the counter. Counter files are often kept together with a custom-built top cover usually made of linoleum or one of the newer plastic laminates. The cover may be made with or without an overhang and may have metal binding on the edges. Covers are sometimes provided for higher-than-counter files to keep them from creeping apart as they are used.

Oxford
Pendaflex
Corporation

Figure 13-2
File Caddy

Four-, five-, and six-drawer files serve as area dividers where ventilation and light are not affected. Some five-drawer units are now manufactured to fit the space formerly used by four-drawer units. The base has been lowered and the space between drawers lessened to expand file room capacity and save valuable floor space. They are also used in banks or batteries along walls. A file cabinet with more than six drawers requires a movable ladder for access to the higher drawers. Such an arrangement is not commonly used for active files but can be found with inactive or storage files.

Although the depth of filing equipment varies, 28 inches has become almost standard. (This means that a file drawer is 28 inches from front to back.) Manufacturers and files operators have found that any greater depth causes fatigue to anyone who is working with the extreme back folders in the drawer. In the standard file drawer, 3,500 to 5,000 papers may be housed in addition to the necessary guides and folders. The varying thicknesses of papers filed necessitates the variance in the figure just stated. To estimate the number of file drawers necessary for the volume of papers to be filed, authorities figure on 150 to 180 sheets to the inch.

Special features available in filing cabinets include corner units usually found in counter files, drawer inserts to convert regular letter- or legal-size drawers into card trays horizontally or vertically, and false-bottom equipment to convert regular correspondence depth drawers to check or card file depth. Swing-front drawers have an automatic latch arrangement that gives needed working space in the drawer (4 inches of working space should be allowed for easy access to the contents of the folders). As the drawer is pulled open, the front automatically swings forward at the top edge (Figure 13-3); in some equipment, the back edge of the drawer slants backward to create a supported natural reading angle spread when the contents of the file are parted at any spot. When the drawer is closed, the compression is automatic. To match modular furniture, file cabinets can be purchased with rounded front corners.

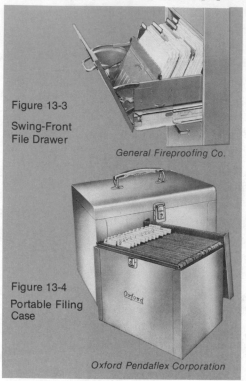

Figure 13-3

Swing-Front File Drawer

General Fireproofing Co.

Figure 13-4

Portable Filing Case

Oxford Pendaflex Corporation

Portable filing cases for field work and sales purposes have a cover and may have a handle on top for ease in carrying (Figure 13-4).

With the many styles and sizes of filing cabinets available, the records manager must accurately estimate both the present and the future needs of the office before making any recommendation for the procurement of equipment.

SECTION 3. GUIDES AND FOLDERS

A simple and uncomplicated set of logically arranged, high-quality guides and folders is an indispensable aid to anyone who understands the basic rules of file operation.

GUIDES

Finding a paper in a file is like finding a certain house on a certain street. Signposts are needed; guides are filing signposts.

For top efficiency in filing and finding, authorities suggest one guide for every 8 to 10 folders or about 20 to 25 guides in each drawer. A guiding system that permits the files operator to find a folder quickly is a system that has guide captions that lead the eye and the hand to a spot within about 10 folders of the one desired.

Filing equipment manufacturers stock sizes of guides for letter- and legal-size correspondence, ledger sheets, bills and invoices, checks, notes, and documents. Guides may be printed with alphabetic divisions, days (numbered 1 to 31), combinations of dates (Jan-June and July-Dec; Jan-Apr, May-Aug, Sept-Dec; Jan-Mar, Apr-June, July-Sept, Oct-Dec; bimonthly; monthly; semi-monthly; Jan. 1-10, 11-20, etc.; Jan. 1-7, 8-15, etc.) consecutive or skip numbering. They are available also with blank tabs.

Body size is the size *exclusive* of the tab and the bottom projection (on guides that have the projection). *Overall size* is the size *including* tab and bottom projection. Guides for letter-size drawers are approximately 10 inches high, including the tab, and 11¾ inches wide; for legal-size drawers, they are 10 inches high, including the tab, and 14¾ inches wide. Because the sizes vary among manufacturers, guides should always be purchased from the same source and always ordered by specific size. Guides are purchased by the set except for blank guides that can be bought separately. Special orders can always be placed for any quantity and type.

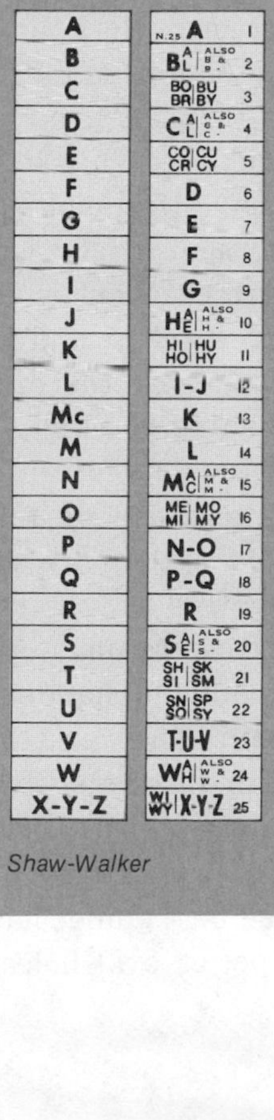

Figure 13-5

Two 25-Division Guide Sets

Shaw-Walker

Guides for alphabetic filing are available in printed sets of 25 divisions of the alphabet to 10,000 divisions. Manufacturers vary even in their methods of dividing the letters *A* to *Z* into 25 divisions. Figure 13-5 shows two 25-division breakdowns. A 100-division set is not made up just by dividing into four parts each of the 25 parts of a 25-division index. The letters of the alphabet do not occur in names with equal frequency. Research has shown that *B, C, H, S, M,* and *W* require about 51 percent of the space in the files. The letter "S" is the largest consumer of filing space, while *Q* requires the least space. In planning the divisions in their sets, manufacturers have taken into account this unequal distribution of the letters.

The thickness of guide stock is referred to in *points,* a point being 1/1000 of an inch. A helpful chart is as follows:

8 points = lightweight	14 points = extra heavyweight
9½ points = medium weight	25 points = pressboard (heavyweight)
11 points = heavyweight	

Guides may be obtained in manila (18 point, usually 100 percent sulphite bleached Kraft), Kraft (similar to the foregoing but not bleached), bristol (15 and 17 point), pressboard (20 or 25 point in various colors, or red in 30 point), fibreboard (25 to 35 point), and aluminum. Manila and Kraft guides should be of long-fiber stock cut so that the grain runs from top to bottom to assure a minimum of buckling. This stock is designed for use in files that are referred to very infrequently and for inactive files that have been put into storage. Bristol is a heavy body stock that is tough and long wearing with excellent writing surface. Pressboard guides are hard and dense for rigidity and strength—the best stock for long wear and hard usage and the most widely used guide. They stand up under daily pushing, pulling, and thumbing. Fibreboard guides, constructed of heavy-duty granite fibreboard, absorb the wear and tear of moving large bulks of folders back and forth. Sometimes called *throwing guides,* they are usually placed in the front, center, and rear of filing drawers to take the load from the standard guides and folders used. Stronger than pressboard, aluminum guides can withstand any amount of handling and therefore cut replacement costs to a minimum. They are thin, light, and easy to handle; and they have tabs with insertable labels. Many tab cuts and positions are available—halves, thirds, fourths, and fifths being the most common.

Guides may be secured with or without bottom rod projections. The best guides have a metal reinforced projection with round, tunnel type, or oval holes through which the rod will pass. Guides such as these prevent folders from slipping under guides and becoming hidden in the files. Guides used with rods also eliminate the possibility of their being removed from the drawer and being misplaced. They also will not slide up and become damaged when the file drawer is closed hurriedly.

The tab of the guide may be an extension of the same material of which the guide is made (with no reinforcement—usually used only with inactive materials because they will not stand a great deal of use). Tabs of clear acetate may be welded on the front and back surfaces of the self tab, or a plastic coating may be placed across the entire top of the guide (usually used for comparatively inactive files because they will not stand excessive use). Flat or angled metal tabs into which labels may be inserted may be attached to the guides (heavy-duty guides for use with active files). Metal tabs usually have dull black or green enamel finish to prevent eye strain by removing glare. Their beveled edges and round corners protect fingers, and papers do not catch. Large windows permit the use of inserts with large type; since the inserts can be changed, expansion is easy. The labels and the transparent protective covering that fit some metal tabs are held securely by small indentations, yet are easily inserted and removed because of a finger opening in the back.

Some metal tabs are made with triangular bases that grip deep into the pressboard body to increase the strength of the tab and prevent its breaking from the guide. If eyelets are used to bond the metal to the pressboard, those drawn out of the metal of the tab are more compact than if separate eyelets are used. Some metal tabs are placed over the pressboard tab, the pressboard extending out on either side to give added strength. Steel tabs which are positioned above the height of the papers (or cards) included in the file allow for even distribution of material between the guides (Figure 13-6).

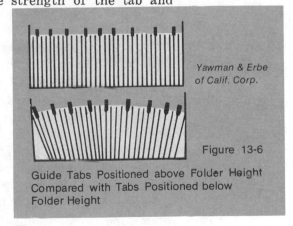

Yawman & Erbe
of Calif. Corp.

Figure 13-6

Guide Tabs Positioned above Folder Height Compared with Tabs Positioned below Folder Height

OUT GUIDES

OUT guides are usually of a distinctive color and may have plastic pockets for insertable cards or may contain lines on both sides on which information is recorded (Figure 5-6, page 114). OUT guides 5 inches by 8 inches or 6 inches by 8 inches may be secured with a celluloid tab at the right or offset at the right corner (Figure 13-7).

Figure 13-7
OUT Guides

The size of most OUT guides corresponds to the size of regular letter- or legal-size guides. Plastic OUT guides in brilliant colors are also commonly used; some have see-through pockets in which to house requisition slips.

FOLDERS

The proper grade and the weight of folders used have much to do with the efficiency of the filing system. A folder that is too light in weight will not withstand wear; one that is too heavy wastes needed space in the files. Legal-size and letter-size folders usually mean a standard size to manufacturers, although there is a variance in manufacturers' specifications. For that reason, folders should be carefully specified as to kind and size and should be purchased from the same source or a comparable source at all times.

The size of folders is the same as the size of guides in most systems. Blank manila folders of 100 percent sulphite (bleached Kraft) are available in at least four weights (8, 9½, 11, and 14 point) in various colors. Orders of 100 are the usual minimum with special prices beginning at the quantity of 500. Red fibre (11 point) and tan stock (18 point) folders are also available. Pressboard folders (25 point) for heavier use may be secured with cloth-bound bottoms and linen expansions. Pressboard folders are usually ordered in lots of 25 with special prices beginning at 500 and over.

Manila or Kraft folders are manufactured with tabs positioned in the usual half-, third-, fourth-, and fifth-cut positions. Tabs are printed to agree with the guide set purchased. Follow-up information may also be printed across the top of a folder for use with purchase orders, collections, insurance due dates, quotation due dates, contracts, and the like. (See Figure 5-14, page 124.) Folders with double or triple thick tops provide protection where wear is greatest while permitting use of lighter-weight folders, saving cost and file space. Folders with front flaps undercut (Figure 2-3, page 17) increase the visibility of the tab heading area. Color tinting may be secured in almost any shade along the entire top edge of a self-tab folder, as an aid to filing and to eliminate the need for colored labels. Clear plastic flat or angular label holders are available on pressboard folders, into which are inserted labels as needed. Some angled tabs have magnifying power to increase readability. The flat metal tabs and angled metal tabs that are available on pressboard folders often have colored inserts used to call special attention to their position.

Very durable all-plastic folders are available in many bright colors. They have clear plastic tabs into which typed labels may be inserted.

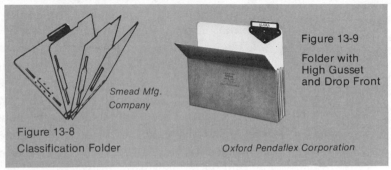

Figure 13-9

Folder with High Gusset and Drop Front

Smead Mfg. Company

Figure 13-8
Classification Folder

Oxford Pendaflex Corporation

Special folders include the following:

1. Classification folders, used to organize a group of papers within a folder—such as contracts, personnel records, case histories, and the like. A personnel classification folder might contain sections for (a) employment applications and letters of reference, (b) employment documents, (c) supplemental papers, (d) performance records, (e) correspondence, and (f) leave and payroll slips (Figure 13-8).
2. Bellows folders for bulky correspondence, with high gussets of manila or cloth on the sides and drop fronts (Figure 13-9).
3. Binder folders used for security and orderliness (Figure 4-6, page 85).
4. Box-bottom suspension folders, for use with hanging folder arrangements, with 2-, 3-, and 4-inch expansions (Figure 13-11).

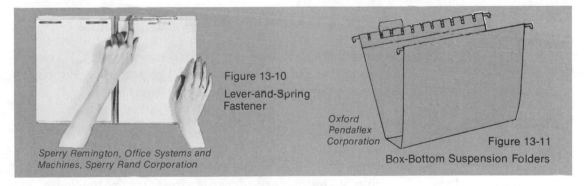

Figure 13-10
Lever-and-Spring Fastener

Oxford Pendaflex Corporation

Figure 13-11
Box-Bottom Suspension Folders

Sperry Remington, Office Systems and Machines, Sperry Rand Corporation

File fasteners of steel, brass, plastic, or nylon prongs may be positioned at any of eight places in a binder folder. Prongs that bend outward need no compressors, resulting in less bulk in the files. Prongs that are compressed into the folders will not scratch or catch desk, fingers, or other papers. A one-hole prong fastener provides security but allows papers to slide askew. A much-used fastener is that consisting of two prongs with a compressor bar that fits across them; the prongs are then folded and secured over the bar. To fasten papers that cannot be punched or clipped together, a combination of lever and spring is used (Figure 13-10, page 327).

The most useful and most often recommended folders have score marks at ¼-inch or ⅜-inch intervals along the bottom edge to allow for expansion of the folder to a flat base upon which to rest. Most folders expand ¾ inch to 1 inch and will easily hold 150 to 180 pieces of paper, depending on the thickness of the paper. When the bulk of correspondence causes a folder to bulge, *period folders* may be needed—semiyearly, quarterly, bimonthly, monthly, or semi-monthly (Figure 2-9, page 23).

High-quality folders are made with the grain of the stock running vertically for greater rigidity in the file. They resist tearing and have a smooth surface for easy removal from and replacement in the file. Top corners are rounded to eliminate dog-earing and to add to the life of the folder.

OUT folders are usually made of manila, with their tabs extending to guide height for easy visibility. They are either of a distinctive color or have "OUT" printed in a brilliant color. (See Figures 5-7 and 5-8, page 115.) Plastic OUT folders in brilliant colors are available, some of which have one side of clear plastic so that papers stored temporarily in them can be quickly seen.

SECTION 4. CARD FILES AND VISIBLE RECORDS

The arrangement of drawers, trays, compartments, frames, panels, books, and the like in card and visible record filing equipment is as varied as are the manufacturers of the equipment.

CARD RECORDS

Cards filed vertically are estimated at 100 to 150 to the inch depending on the thickness of the cards and the guides used with them. To estimate the number of cards presently in the office file, the number in one inch should be counted and multiplied by the total inches in the card records. To estimate capacity of drawers in a new piece of equipment, the clear filing area inside one drawer should be multiplied by the number of cards found to be in one inch; that figure should then be multiplied by the number of empty drawers in the equipment. If a card file is to be newly set up, equipment capacity may be estimated by multiplying the number of inches in the clear filing area inside one drawer by 100; that figure obtained should then be multiplied by the number of drawers in the equipment.

Authorities vary in their recommendations, from one guide for every 20-25 cards to one guide for every 35-40 cards. Guides for use in card files are similar to those used in correspondence files, varying only in size. Vinyl guides (15 point) in opaque colors are available for card files. Washable vinyl guides will not warp, crack, or become dog-eared.

The records manager, when ordering cards, ordinarily gives the width dimension first. However, manufacturers vary in their expression of card size; the better practice, therefore, is to indicate specifically on the order which figure refers to width and which to depth. Dimensions given here state width first.

The common sizes are those used with 5″ by 3″, 6″ by 4″, 8″ by 5″, and 9″ by 6″ cards. Guides for tab cards, that is, cards used with tabulating equipment ($7\frac{3}{8}$″ by $3\frac{1}{4}$″ and $7\frac{1}{2}$″ by $3\frac{1}{4}$″), for checks (9″ by 4″ and $8\frac{3}{4}$″ by $3\frac{1}{2}$″), and for documents ($4\frac{1}{2}$″ by $9\frac{1}{2}$″) are also available. Bristol board or pressboard is usually used for guides in card files. The various printed sets of guides available include 25- to 100-division alphabetic, consecutive or skip numbered, daily 1-31, states, weekly, counties, cities over 1,000 population, and blank.

Cards can be purchased with horizontal rulings or with horizontal and vertical rules, for journals, sales department quotations, salesmen's follow-ups, perpetual inventory, Social Security tax records, employees' Social Security history, insurance expiration, insurance line or record, diagnosis information, associated condition information, operation information, bank cards, membership/subscription, plant asset records, price and material records, lawyer's follow-up for cases and claims, assured records, abstract of policies.

Hinge clips can be attached to existing vertically filed cards to convert them for use in a visible card file. No copying of records is necessary. A punch notches and slots plain cards to permit use of the hinge clips (Figure 13-12, page 330). If the present card has no room for a visible index margin, a gummed strip can be attached to the card edge to provide the needed space.

Card characteristics are body (stiffness), surface quality, cutting, and color. Cards may be cut from 16-, 20-, 24-, and 28-pound

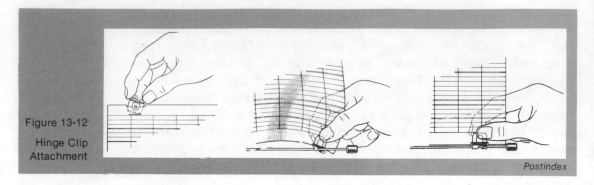

Figure 13-12

Hinge Clip
Attachment

Postindex

bond stock, 110-pound bristol stock, 7½-point bristol stock, and 32-pound ledger stock. Straight-cut cards should lie flat, should not tear easily, and should return to their flat shape after bending slightly such as would occur if they were put into the typewriter for a short time. For permanence and lasting wearing quality, 100 percent new rag content is recommended, as the card will not discolor with age. A high-quality card, good for 25 years, is made of 50 to 60 percent rag; sulphite content is acceptable for cards that are to be filed flat with an anticipated life of 15 years. Cards made of wood pulp should be avoided because they are difficult to write on and do not wear well. The surface of a good grade of card should be smooth, suitable for penned entries, and easily erased without ruffing up. Self-tab cards, on which information is typed or is lettered by hand, make card systems flexible. Such tabs can show dates, initials, numbers, or subject arrangements; and the system can be added to very quickly. These tabbed cards, because of their use as guides, should be of a relatively better grade than are straight-cut cards. Brittle stock must be avoided as the tabs snap off easily, making records worthless. Excessive sizing gives a sticky touch to the card and causes rapid deterioration.

The color should be suited to the purpose for which the card is to be used. Color can separate sections, designate special characteristics, be used for guiding purposes, or indicate recent additions to the file. Because cheaper material content can be disguised with color, the quality of the colored card should be carefully checked. A good percentage of rag in the card stock should be adhered to even with colored cards.

The two most frequently used methods of cutting paper and card stock are (1) knife cutting and (2) rotary cutting. Knife cutting is done by most printers, who use a paper cutter consisting of a knife blade operated manually or by power. Papers to be cut are held in position by pressure while the knife cuts through the entire pack. The prevention of variations in size of the finished pieces when knife cutting is used is very difficult because the stock "gives" no matter how heavy the pressure that is applied. Since there is only one edge to the knife, it is easily dulled by the foreign substances found in low grades of stock—sand, grit, etc. Ravels or slivers of paper and almost imperceptible nicks at the edge of the cut stock are the results of knife cutting.

Rotary cutting takes place on a machine with two horizontally revolving shafts on which are mounted hardened steel disks. The upper and lower discs are in snug contact at all times and insure a smooth cutting edge and uniform size since only one sheet is fed through the discs at a time. The best cards are rotary cut on all sides; rotary cutting to height alone insures uniform size which is important when quick fingering in a file is expected.

Every order for card stock should specify the punching or die cuts necessary—corner cuts, bottom notches, eyelets, slots for locking-in cards, hinge slots, side slots, side cuts for overriding sheets, and the like.

When printing is specified on the cards, proofs should be ordered so that the records manager will be sure that the finished card is exactly like the correct copy that was submitted. The best economy requires the use of the smallest card that will serve the purpose for which it is to be used.

VISIBLE RECORDS

Cabinets for visible records are made in various widths to accommodate standard sizes of cards and pockets. They may be secured with single or double panels for single filing of cards or side-by-side arrangement. The number of items that can be housed in the various kinds of equipment will vary according to the size and bulk of the card stock used or the width of the visible strip to be accommodated. The depth of the trays (slides) and the size of the material to be housed govern the number of cards, inserts, signals, or build-up of material that is possible in each pocket.

Record equipment manufacturers have charts showing the number of frames required and holding devices needed for varying capacities of visible references. To estimate the equipment needed for strip reference, for instance, it is necessary to know the desired number of lines for each visible insert, the length of strip desired, the type of strip to be used (flexible, tube, folded), the height of the equipment, accessibility desired (from certain sides only, or in rotating arrangement), and location of the stand. An index of over half a million names may be kept in a space no larger than that needed by the average office desk. The capacity of a single-tier rotary visible file, for example, is from 14,400 to 72,000 names; of a double-tier, 28,800 to 144,000 names. Equipment is available in a wide variety of sizes from that for storing only 300 names up to that for storing a million reference names.

The illustrations in this chapter show only two of the possible variations in equipment. Other features include a locking disappearing door that can be pulled down or up to cover the card trays; stands with removable end panels to allow them to be fitted together in groups to support visible card trays; drawer depths of different sizes to accommodate varying numbers of trays; steel dividers between trays that prevent one slide from injuring cards in adjoining slides; backward tilting stands that allow frames to stay open without being held; "lazy susan" desk or table-top arrangements; and insulated cabinets or double-walled cabinets with dead air space for fire protection certified at 1700° F. for one hour.

The features of well-constructed visible record equipment include glare-free finishes; trays on nylon or ball-bearing rollers for quick, effortless gliding; easy hand grips on the front of the trays; large label holders on the trays for easy visibility and quick reference; low side edges on the trays for nominal interference in posting activities; almost flat lay-back angle of posting-record equipment (Figure 13-13) ; ¼-inch to ½-inch visible margin exposure on cards;

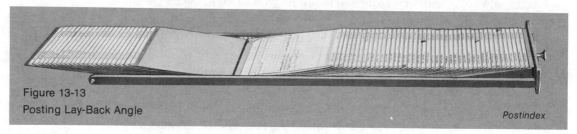

Figure 13-13
Posting Lay-Back Angle

Postindex

and protection on the bases of desk-top equipment to prevent marring and slipping (thick corrugated rubber pads or small rubber "bumpers" or knobs attached to the equipment). If a table is used as the base for posting cabinets, a ¼-inch upright on the back edge of the table insures alignment of the cabinets and prevents them from being pushed off or working off because of the constant jarring that results from opening and closing trays of cards. Upright frames used for constant reference should have several places for label holders along their edges so that the information may be read from both sides (Figure 13-14).

A loading device is useful to insert an entire set of strips into a visible frame at one time. The paper backing must be removed from the strips; without it, each strip would come apart from all others, making insertion into the frame very tedious (Figure 13-15).

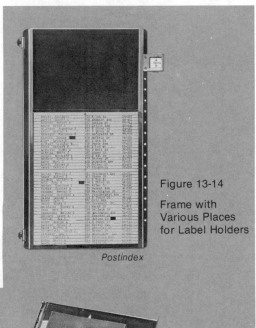

Figure 13-14

Frame with Various Places for Label Holders

Postindex

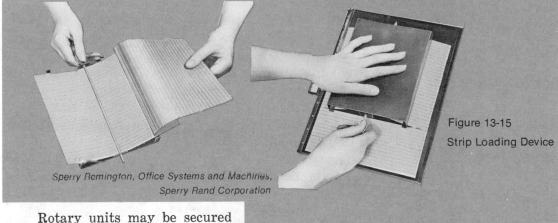

Figure 13-15

Strip Loading Device

Sperry Remington, Office Systems and Machines, Sperry Rand Corporation

Rotary units may be secured that provide four reference sides at once. (With round rotaries, when one frame is in use, all other frames are automatically compressed.) Convenient corner turning handles bring the records to the operator. (Figure 13-16). Tilted angle construction makes reference easier, and the square flat top of the rotary furnishes a working surface for standing clerks.

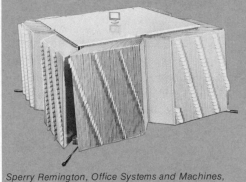

Figure 13-16

Rotary Reference Stand

Sperry Remington, Office Systems and Machines, Sperry Rand Corporation

SECTION 5. OPEN-SHELF FILES, SIDE FILES,
AND LATERAL FILING

OPEN-SHELF FILES

The growing tide of papers to be filed and the resulting demand for more filing space, more equipment, and new methods have resulted in the increased use of open-shelf filing.

Open-shelf filing is recommended only for material that is filed and removed in complete folders, not for use in offices where individual sheets are removed and refiled constantly. Open-shelf filing is used for active materials as well as for inactive storage. It is particularly adapted to terminal- or middle-digit filing methods, combining numerical coding with color coding (also called color keying, color checking, tinting, and blocking).

As its name implies, open-shelf filing consists of materials filed on open shelving tiered horizontally. Tabs on the guides and folders permit access from either the left or the right. Some equipment is constructed so that the folders may be removed from either side of the free-standing shelves, although the majority of open-shelf filing is done from only one open side.

Shelves are adjustable to accommodate different heights of papers. Uprights that divide the shelving units are movable or adjustable and give support to the folders placed on the shelves.

Units may be purchased with or without retractable doors that open and slide over or under the shelf. Large sliding doors, similar to sliding closet doors, may be secured that cover all shelves during the nonworking hours. Doors may be obtained with locking devices for security purposes.

The advantages claimed for open-shelf filing over drawer filing include (1) faster filing and finding—time studies have shown that removing folders is as much as 40 percent faster and refiling is approximately 50 percent faster since time is not needed for opening and closing drawers, and folders are not lifted for removal but are slid horizontally out of and into the shelves; (2) fewer errors—misfiles are not as common since folder edges are always visible and color coding is common; (3) lower cost—the first cost for equipment is much less, maintenance is almost nonexistent, less aisle space is required than for standard filing cabinets, fewer files operators are required to handle a greater volume of records; (4) easier operation—expansion is quick, and compactness reduces walking time and minimizes fatigue; and (5) better lighting.

The disadvantages of open-shelf filing include (1) dust and dirt accumulation, where no covers or doors are provided (even if they are used, the files are usually open during the day) ; (2) inaccessibility to top and bottom tiers, necessitating ladders and stools to reach the highest and lowest shelves; (3) unattractive appearance because folders vary in size and bulk and cannot be arranged at identical angles on the shelves.

The Spacefinder Unit (Figure 13-17 and illustration D of the colored inserts preceding Chapter 2), an open-shelf filing concept, uses boxes or shelves tilted for quick visibility. The boxes slide along rails and may be secured in various sizes to hold office correspondence, cards, microrecords, books, blueprints, and computer print-outs. Cabinets with retractible doors may be purchased to take the place of the open shelf arrangement shown here. Folders are housed in the boxes which keep the contents from slumping and the boxes are portable so that they may be easily carried to a working area.

Movable open-shelf storage units (Figure 13-18) are designed to increase the existing capacity of any storage area by reclaiming aisle space. They also usually increase operating efficiency by reducing the distance normally traveled to a fixed layout. A shelf is accessible only when it has been exposed by pushing aside (manually or by push-button) the shelves in front of it. The manually operated units glide easily even when fully loaded since each is mounted

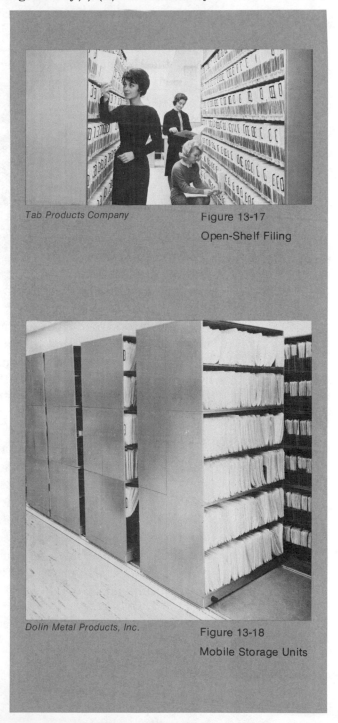

Tab Products Company

Figure 13-17
Open-Shelf Filing

Dolin Metal Products, Inc.

Figure 13-18
Mobile Storage Units

on moving bases with ball-bearing wheel assemblies that roll on tracks laid on the floor and leveled. Names of commercially manufactured mobile units include "Power Glide," "Roll Shelf," "Space-finder," "Magic Aisle," "Roll-Away," "Stor-Trac," and "NO WALK."

This type of movable shelf storage is not recommended for extremely active files but may be very useful for storage of relatively inactive materials to which infrequent reference is made.

Conveyer files (Figure 13-19) are also open shelf, using hanging folders or compartments, as illustrated in Figure 10-6 on page 243. The operator at his desk dials a "number" which corresponds to a location on the conveyor. It starts revolving and stops automatically when the desired number reaches the desk.

Figure 13-19
Conveyer Files

White

Mobile desk-and-chair units at which files operators sit can be mounted on rails in front of shelf files. These mobile units are often equipped with telephones because continual reference is made to the files and the information can be relayed to the requester at the moment it is found.

A rotary shelf file (Figure 13-20) is another type of open-shelf filing. Each independently rotating shelf holds the typical contents of three or more ordinary file drawers. Several operators can use the file at one time and much walking and aisle space is frequently eliminated.

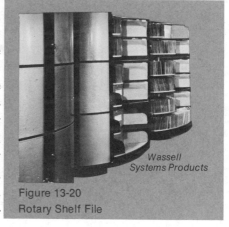

Figure 13-20
Rotary Shelf File

*Wassell
Systems Products*

SIDE FILES AND LATERAL FILING

Side files and lateral filing are two terms used to describe drawer files whose arrangement appears to be that of a book shelf with doors. Supreme Steel's "Conserv-a-File" (Figure 13-21) illustrates the principle of drawers that roll out from the side of the cabinets. Figure 13-21 shows a 3-drawer cabinet with two drawers closed and one opened. Figure 13-22 shows a 5-drawer cabinet with a variety of drawer heights that may be purchased. Such files will handle

Figure 13-21
"Conserv-a-File"

Supreme Equipment and Systems Corp.

letter and legal end-tab or top-tab folders, binders, computer printouts, tapes, disc packs, cards, etc. Combinations of letter- and legal-size folders may be arranged in the same drawer (the legal sizes perpendicularly and the letter sizes horizontally to the front, for instance). A safety interlocking system can be secured which will not permit a drawer to be opened while another is extended.

Figure 13-22
Lateral Filing Cabinet

A type of side file in use in some businesses is a tilting drawer. When the drawer front is tilted open, the entire contents of the drawer are visible. When the drawer is closed, all folders rest on a side edge—not on the bottom edge of the folder as is the case with conventional drawer files. The space required to open a complete drawer is one-fourth the distance of that required to open a complete drawer of a standard file cabinet. Folders slip in and out in the manner of open-shelf filing and no effort is required to lift them.

The lateral file is particularly suited to use in narrow spaces, such as between pillars or behind desks where aisle space is limited, or in offices where the appearance of a chest of drawers is preferred over that of conventional pull-drawer files. Because the long side of the cabinet opens out, lateral cabinets take up less depth than do regular drawer files. The guides and folders inside the lateral drawer can be arranged to face

Figure 13-23

Lateral Filing Cabinets in Use

Oxford Pendaflex Corporation

front or to face perpendicular to the front of the drawer. A 3-drawer unit has space for over 100 inches of filed materials—approximately 20 inches more than the space available in the typical 3-drawer front-opening cabinet. Figure 13-23 is an illustration of an executive using lateral filing equipment arranged in three rows of guides and folders.

SUPPLIES FOR OPEN-SHELF AND SIDE-FILING EQUIPMENT

Having the right folders, guides, and supplies is just as important to efficient open-shelf and side filing as it is to efficient filing in drawer cabinets. Materials filed in open-shelf and side-file equipment are visible at one edge instead of across the entire top (as is true in drawer files). For that reason, supplies used with side-filing equipment differ generally from the supplies formerly described.

Guides. Some guides are made with a metal hook on the back that fits over the shelf riser at the rear, slides along it, yet cannot be pulled from the shelf with the folders. Guides without the metal hook may also be purchased but are not recommended because they work out of the files and are easily misplaced or damaged. Letter-size (11¾ by 9½ inches not including tab or hook) and legal-size (14¾ by

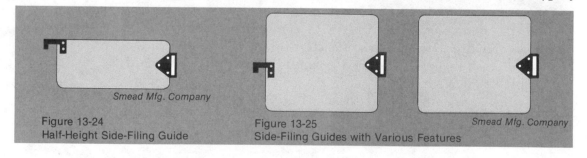

Smead Mfg. Company

Figure 13-24
Half-Height Side-Filing Guide

Figure 13-25
Side-Filing Guides with Various Features

Smead Mfg. Company

9½ inches) guides are commonly used; half-height (letter- or legal-length and 6 inches high) guides are available with flat or hook backs and with vertical or angled tabs (Figure 13-24).

Guide tabs are usually made of metal with insertable captions and may be either vertical or horizontal. Acetate-covered tabs are also available for use in less active files. Indexed guide sets are available on special order. Two styles of guides are illustrated in Figure 13-25.

The captions on the guide tabs can be read from either side. Guide bodies are usually made of 25-point pressboard to give support to the material filed and to provide for long wear.

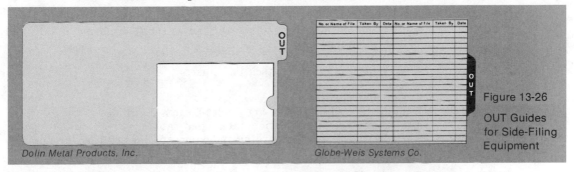

Dolin Metal Products, Inc.   Globe-Weis Systems Co.

Figure 13-26

OUT Guides for Side-Filing Equipment

OUT guides are made to house requisition slips in a plastic pocket on the guide or are lined to take writing on both sides. Sturdy pressboard is recommended although manila OUT guides are also available. OUT-Wanted guides are also made of pressboard with transparent card holders. Tabs of self material or of metal are prominently labeled "OUT" so that they can be seen instantly by anyone using the files. Figure 13-26 shows two types of OUT guides for use in side-filing equipment.

Folders. Straight-edge, side-tabbed, and any regular folder with its tab at the extreme right may be used in side files. The most used and recommended folders have straight edges. Labeling is printed on the outside of the folder at the lower right corner as well as on the outside right top corner. When a folder is filed on a shelf, therefore, the indexing can be conveniently read whether it is on a lower or an upper shelf. Folders formerly used for drawer filing may be used for side filing if the tab is third-cut, third position or fifth-cut, fifth position and the information on the label is copied to the back of the folder label. Reference to the files may occur from either right or left.

Pocket folders, with cloth reinforcing hinges and drop front flap or with half-height gussets on both sides, are made to contain especially bulky records. They may be of manila, Kraft, pressboard, or red-rope construction. Self tabs are used on manila and Kraft folders; self tabs or metal tabs are available on all heavier-weight folders.

Because of the variety in sizes, hook placement, materials, printing, and tab positions, the records manager must be specific when ordering guides and folders for use with open-shelf or side files. The following information must be specified on orders for guides and folders:

1. Quantity
2. Body height measurements (specified as such) exclusive of tabs and bottom projections
3. Width
4. Weight and grade of stock to be used
5. Color
6. Cut and position of tab
7. Plain bottom or tongue-and-eyelet bottom on guides
8. Size and color designations of angled tabs
9. Exact information regarding indexing, special printing, or numbering

Other equipment. Other equipment especially designed to make shelf filing easier includes a sliding reference shelf for attachment under any shelf; a movable hook-on shelf that attaches under the front flange of any shelf; a filing truck that moves on rollers and provides a complete filing work station (an automatic step locking device assures safety when the truck is not moving); range finders that are attached to the aisle ends of the filing shelves, showing the range of materials filed in the shelves; card holders for finished or open ends of shelves to be used to further identify the contents of a row of shelves; label holders to be attached along the bottom edges of shelves to indicate their contents.

Canopy tops improve the appearance of the open-shelf units, as well as protect the material on the top shelf that would otherwise be exposed if the shelving were not constructed from floor to ceiling.

SECTION 6. STORAGE EQUIPMENT FOR INACTIVE FILES

Chapter 12 contains a comprehensive discussion of the storage of inactive files and some illustrations of the equipment used to house these records. Most storage space is relatively low-rental property or somewhat inaccessible; for that reason, all usable square feet houses records. A floor-to-ceiling arrangement is commonly found, with ladders needed to reach the higher levels. Because inactive records are not often referred to, they can be packed more tightly in storage than they were in the regular files. Whereas one guide for approximately every 10 folders is considered necessary for active files, one guide for every 15 to 20 folders is considered sufficient for inactive materials. In many transfer or storage files, the miscellaneous folders are moved to the front of their sections and become the guides.

The number and kinds of transfer equipment available are limited only by the number of manufacturers in the field. Storage equipment can be purchased for letter- and legal-size records, invoices, checks and vouchers, tabulating machine cards, other card records, deposit slips, forms, and ledger sheets. Heavy cardboard containers may be purchased folded flat. They are easily unfolded to set up with no taped flaps to catch, and they are dustproof. An aluminum top plate with a cord closure provides extra rigidity. Double-wall construction of some boxes assures better storage of heavy loads (Figure 13-27). Side-opening boxes of similar construction are available for the transfer of side-tabbed shelf-filing folders; a vertical divider keeps folders upright and reinforces the box (Figure 13-28).

Pull-drawer boxes are recommended for storage of records to which reference may be made. Boxes are available in white marble-finish corrugated board, natural color corrugated board, and juteboard, and are made of wood covered with paper and reinforced with

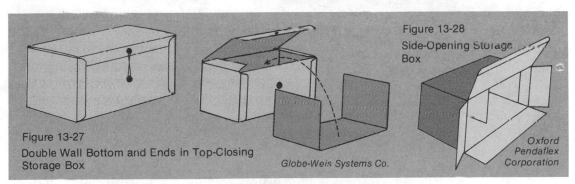

Figure 13-28
Side-Opening Storage Box

Figure 13-27
Double Wall Bottom and Ends in Top-Closing Storage Box

Globe-Weis Systems Co.

Oxford Pendaflex Corporation

cambric. Most drawer-type storage units can be fastened together vertically. At the time of destruction in the future, box and contents can be destroyed together.

Removable identification cards and tapered side and rear panels on the drawers, for easy pull, are special features obtainable from some manufacturers. Tape pulls, leather pulls, metal pull rings, and finger holes on the front of drawers eliminate protruding handles yet allow for easy opening of the drawers.

For temporary current filing and for heavy-duty transfer filing, steel-front or steel-clad files may be purchased. Both have a steel collar fastened securely to the shell and may be horizontally or vertically interlocked without the need of shelving. A steel front on the drawer gives the illusion of expensive filing cabinets. The double-thick gray fibreboard front of the steel-clad drawer gives long, hard service. Steel rods securely connecting back and front masonite panels also provide sturdiness that resists buckling and sagging when drawers are stacked.

Top-opening boxes are useful for storing records to which reference is not expected to be made. The effort required to remove the boxes from their shelves is such that these boxes are recommended only for "dead" storage. Some of these boxes are metal-stitched for long life; others have flip tops; many have hand holes on the ends for ease in carrying; most have index panels printed on both ends for easy identification.

Although card files are infrequently transferred and stored, drawer-type card transfer boxes are available in 100-point fibreboard. Stacking, interlocking, and labeling features are similar to those found in correspondence file storage equipment.

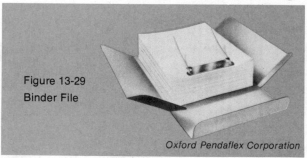

Figure 13-29
Binder File

Oxford Pendaflex Corporation

Sales checks, deposit slips, delivery records, invoices, voucher checks, snap-out forms, and the like may be stored in binder files (Figure 13-29). The binders become drawers that may be stacked and interlocked for easy accessibility. No shelving is needed as the binder files become self-supporting units.

SECTION 7. MISCELLANEOUS EQUIPMENT AND SUPPLIES

CROSS-REFERENCE SHEETS

Printed cross-reference sheets (a stock item or printed to special order) are available in various colors in pad form or in packages of letter-size sheets, usually 100 to the pad or package.

LABELS

Plain or colored, printed, lined, or color-striped (with narrow or wide bands and with single or double stripes) labels can be purchased in many colors and hues. They are stocked by the pad, box, or package, in roll form, packed flat in sheets, or in fanfold arrangement. Labels may be gummed on the back, requiring moistening and pressure, or they may have adhesive backs to be peeled from a protective sheet, after typing, and pressed on tabs.

FILEBACKS

Figure 13-30
Fileback

Sperry Remington, Office
Systems and Machines,
Sperry Rand Corporation

Especially in the insurance field, many companies prefer to file papers unprotected by folders yet fastened together on a fileback. Filebacks are made in several grades of stock with many fastening forms (Figure 13-30).

FOLLOW-FILE STICKERS

Brilliantly colored gummed stickers, purchased in pads, may be attached to papers wanted at a later date. A tickler file notation calls to the attention of the files operator the need for a filed paper; he goes to the file and easily and quickly finds the paper wanted because a follow-file sticker had been attached to it at the time it was filed. The sticker peels off the paper easily, leaving no mark.

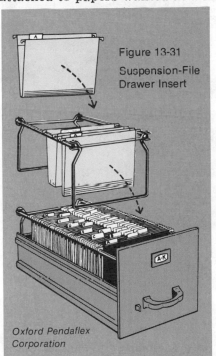

Figure 13-31
Suspension-File
Drawer Insert

Oxford Pendaflex
Corporation

KEY FOLDERS

Key folders, made of heavy pressboard, have tangs on which keys may be hung; the folder is inserted into a vertical file drawer.

SUSPENSION-FILE DRAWER INSERTS

Metal framework may be purchased to convert a regular drawer file into suspension-folder equipment (Figure 13-31).

LINKS

Folders that are suspended in a drawer may be linked together accordion style by the use of clips or links especially manufactured for this purpose.

SORTERS

A general-purpose sorter will accommodate papers with one dimension of 10 inches or less (checks, sales slips, time cards, correspondence, ledger sheets). The sorter has six means of classification: alphabetic sections, numbers 1 to 31, days of the week, months

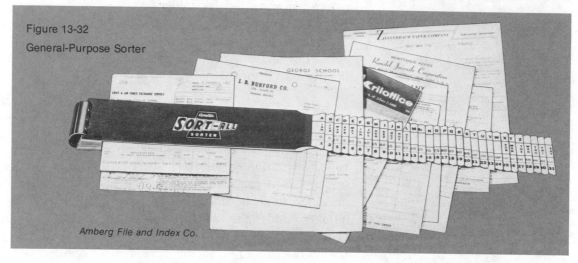

Figure 13-32
General-Purpose Sorter

Amberg File and Index Co.

of the year, numbers in groups of 5, and space on the center panel of the tabs for special captions that may be typed and taped where desired (Figure 13-32).

Card and ticket sorters have aluminum dividers that swing in either direction to the base. Each side has two systems or types of sorts. On one side are the numbers 1 to 31 and a subdivided alphabetical index; on the other side the first 12 dividers are designated with the names of the months, and the other 19 dividers are labeled with numbers in intervals of 5 (from 5 to 95) for numerical sorting.

FILE SHELF

A portable filing shelf fits on a drawer handle, on the side of an opened drawer, or under the edge of a shelf file and can be moved from place to place as the files operator needs it. The shelf should have a clip, a hood, or raised edges on two sides to keep papers from falling or being blown off (Figure 13-33).

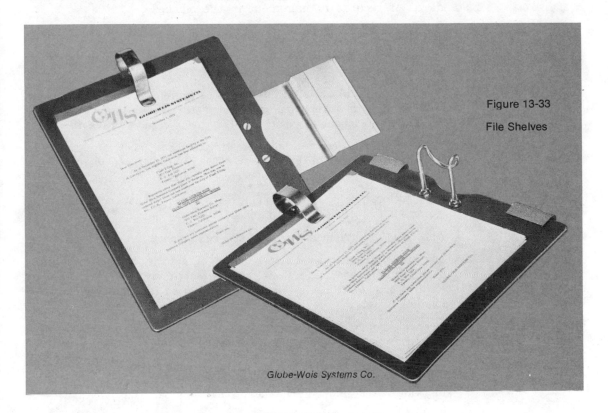

Figure 13-33

File Shelves

Globe-Wois Systems Co.

FILING STOOL

A filing stool, used when filing papers in the lower drawers of equipment, will help the files operator to avoid fatigue. Often filing is done hurriedly in an area that is difficult to reach and, as a result, errors increase. For safety, the stool should be painted a brilliant color, or the top should have a vivid cushion or bright tape attached to call attention to its presence. One may be purchased that moves freely until weight is put on it, at which time it locks in place.

The equipment and supplies mentioned in this chapter are indicative of the vast variety on the market. Each year improvements are made and innovations are manufactured. The records manager must constantly consult catalogs, read current office administration literature, attend meetings, and seek the counsel of filing experts in order to be up to date in this fast-changing, professional field. As his knowledge increases, so will his effectiveness increase in the selection of personnel, in their supervision, and in the maintenance of high standards of records management in the office.

For Review and Discussion

1. Give specific examples of types of records and papers that might be received in an office but should never be filed.

2. Of what value will consultation with office equipment and supply manufacturers and their representatives be to the records manager who is planning replacement of some or all of the records storage facilities?

3. What would you need to know to estimate the number, size, and type of equipment needed to house your office records if you were contemplating complete revision of your records storage facilities?

4. What factors might have a bearing on whether or not motorized filing equipment is installed in your office?

5. What kind of equipment is "cap" size equipment?

6. You are contemplating the installation of a bank of files to be used as a counter separating workers from office visitors. What certain features or characteristics should be secured on the equipment ordered for these files?

7. If you do not have insulated file cabinets to house your records, what precautions can you and other office personnel take to resist damage to the records in case of fire?

8. What may be an advantage of using half-width OUT guides instead of full-width OUT guides in the files? What may be a disadvantage?

9. With reference to file folders, what is the meaning of the term "front flap undercut"? of "gusset"?

10. Mention as many uses as you can for colored cards in a card vertical filing system.

11. Is the lay-back angle important for equipment housing posted-card records? If so, why? If not, why not?

12. In offices where individual sheets of paper are removed and refiled constantly, what are the advantages and disadvantages of open-shelf filing? of drawer files? of side or lateral files?

13. What is the main difference between supplies used with side-filing equipment and those used with conventional drawer files?

14. The sorter pictured on page 344, Figure 13-32, has printed information on its tabs to take care of five kinds of sorts. What type of stick-on captions can you think of that might be used for a sixth kind of sort? Be specific.

15. How can you, the records manager, keep up to date on systems, products, and procedures related to records management and control?

Learning Projects

1. (a) Secure the yellow pages section of the telephone book of your city (if it is over 75,000 population) or of the largest metropolitan area near your city. Look under the heading of "Files—Office" or something similar. Make a list of the trade names and manufacturers of filing supplies and equipment found there.

   (b) Locate *Thomas' Register of Manufacturers* in the library. Look for manufacturers of filing equipment and supplies for the office. Compare your list made from the telephone book with the list of manufacturers of filing supplies and equipment in this reference book. What comments can you make concerning each listing?

   (c) Be prepared to tell the class what value each of these reference sources might be to you as an office worker charged with records management responsibilities.

2. Examine for construction details any file cabinets your instructor specifies. Make notes on special bracing, reinforcements, insulation, locking devices, bases, welding, suspension or nonsuspension drawers, hardware, compressors, finish, etc. Compare your findings with those of other students in small group discussions, to see where you agree or disagree.

3. Secure several folders, guides, and cards (at least two of each). Test each of them in the following ways and write your findings on the pieces tested.

   (a) Snap the stock—the sharper the ring, the better the stock.

   (b) Inspect under strong light—short fibers evenly distributed give a clear surface; a poor mixture of fibers gives a cloudy surface.

   (c) Erase—a fine powder indicates well-made stock; rough, ragged edges indicate poorly made stock.

   (d) Fold each piece—breakage at the fold usually indicates short fibers that stand erasure and hard usage; long fibers will not break but generally will not withstand hard usage.

   (e) Ask your instructor if it is permissible to burn a portion of the cards. If so, rub a bit of the ash between your fingers. A greasy ash indicates the presence of clay or other fillers. Look for layers—genuine pressboard will not show layers when burned.

   (f) Inspect the edges—rotary cutting results in a sharp edge; knife cutting shows frays and nicks.

   (g) Tear a short distance both ways—note which is "with" the grain and which is "against" the grain.

   (h) Inspect the fibers at the torn edges—if the edges are hard and sharp, the fibers are short; if the edges are soft and fuzzy, the fibers are long.

   (i) Write several words with ink on each item. Ink will not spread or blot on high-grade stock; ink spreads and "feathers" on poorly made paper.

Exchange your materials with those of another student and test his pieces to see if you agree with the comments he made. If you do not, discuss your findings with him to see if you can resolve your differences.

4. Locate a shelf-filing installation. Discuss with the files operator his opinions about shelf filing and write a report of your conversation. Duplicate it so that the class may share your visit.

Chapter **14**

Organization and operation
of a records
management program

While primary emphasis in this book has been on filing systems and procedures, the effective use of the systems approach in records management points to the fact that filing is but one aspect of the whole system of records. Other components such as the creation, use, retention, and disposal subsystems have been discussed.

The *systems approach* represents a method of thinking about systems and their parts that is widely used by management to solve problems connected with the operation of their firms. Each of the firm's systems is made up of sets of components (such as people, equipment, space, procedures, and data) that work together to satisfy the overall goals of the firm. With the systems approach the firm may be considered as the *total system* and then further subdivided into parts or *subsystems*.

The records subsystem represents an important component or part of the organizational system. It is often referred to as management's memory from which information is called to help management in its decision-making functions.

A records manager, like any manager, must understand the entire system over which his jurisdiction extends—the whole (or total system) as well as the parts (or subsystems). It is important, therefore, that the reader turn his attention to the overall organization and operation of the records management program.

SECTION 1. THE BUSINESS INFORMATION SYSTEM

Information is widely regarded today as a valuable economic resource like real estate, equipment, and labor. This means that to be informed (or to know something) has value and power. Business management through its system staff now spends millions of dollars annually to set up communication and records systems through which information passes to processors and users.

Although this business generation has been labeled the age of automation, it should be emphasized that the bulk of all information appears in paper form. Today's business functions on paper to an extent almost impossible to understand. One source [1] roughly estimates that over 15 trillion (15,000,000,000,000) pieces of paper are now being circulated in U. S. business offices and, furthermore, that each minute of each working day a million new pages are added. This huge volume of records represents the raw materials that must be controlled by the records management program, along with other new and changing office functions.

To illustrate some of the changing concepts of the office, compare the new terms below (now commonly used in modern offices) with the older more traditional forms:

CHANGING OFFICE CONCEPTS

The old, narrower term	*The new, broader concept*
The record	Information on the record
Office work	Information handling
Filing procedures	Storage systems
Finding procedures	Retrieval systems
Microfilm	Microrecords
Files supervision	Records management
Office management	Information management

Emphasis has, therefore, shifted from a restricted view of office work to broader systems for managing information. In simple terms, therefore, an *information system* may be defined as "any means that communicates knowledge from one person to another. It can take many shapes—simple verbal communication . . . punched card (and on to) computerized means for storage . . . retrieval." [2] In most cases, paper records are involved.

---

[1] Morton F. Meltzer, *The Information Imperative* (New York: American Management Association, 1971), p. 3.

[2] Walter A. Kleinschrod, "Finding the 'IR' System for You," *Administrative Management* (April, 1965), p. 63.

Information systems in business may be of two types:

1. External information systems (from the outside to the firm)
                                 (from the firm to the outside)
    Examples: Intercompany relationships of buyers and vendors
              Business—general public communication
2. Internal information systems (within the firm)
    Examples: Purchase requisition system
              Main office-branch office communication

All business organizations deal extensively with individuals and firms on the outside and, accordingly, maintain many records of these transactions. Such *external information systems* must be coordinated properly within the firm's office, for the firm relies on the records of such transactions for such important functions as obtaining essential materials and supplies, maintaining and retaining customer sales and goodwill, and promoting good public relations for the firm.

The *internal information systems* are subsystems that serve as a basis for much external communication. For example, if a supervisor requests a new typewriter by filling out a purchase requisition, this form serves as the basis for initiating the purchase order form that is sent to the supplier. Such systems frequently follow a common pattern and are useful for illustrating the broad scope of the records management program in business. Typical of the unlimited amount of business data to be preserved on records as the business "memory" are the following:

Information Required	*Types of Source Records*
1. Ownership	Stock ledgers; minutes of meetings
2. Management	Organization charts; annual department reports; comparative periodic reports
3. Finance	Prospectus for stock issuance; balance sheet and statements; income and expenditure statements
4. Production operations	Production reports by physical and dollar value; annual inventories; plant layouts; time schedules; machine specifications and engineering drawings; depreciation records; expense ledgers; cost studies; training manuals; personnel bulletins
5. Products—research and development	Engineering reports; sales catalogs; product development reports
6. Marketing	Price lists; catalogs; annual sales budgets and expense budgets; sales reports by area and product

Information Required	*Types of Source Records*
7. Community relations	Samples of materials or methods used; copies of speeches by executives; newspaper clippings; publications; correspondence.[3]

In the past few years, a number of conditions have developed which have affected the *nature* and *volume* of records. In the first place, there have been increased records requirements for several reasons: additional Federal, state, and local government regulations; decided changes in economic activity accounting for expansion, contraction, and diversification in industry; and other economic practices such as increased credit buying, subcontracting, and installment purchasing as well as the use of more business and professional services (banks, medical and insurance services). In the second place, man has expanded upon his ability to produce records by advances in office mechanization and automation. There are, for instance, more typewriters, adding and calculating machines, more duplicators and photocopying devices, than ever before. The multiple-copy "disease" is firmly entrenched in most business offices. During this time, the office managers have failed to develop adequate cost and efficiency controls to keep pace with their ability to produce records. The result is a serious accumulation of unnecessary, nonstandardized, unregulated, ill-designed, and consequently ineffective records that clog the communication channels of business and impede the flow of useful information.

PAPERWORK MANAGEMENT

One of the recent programs designed to assist the businessman in controlling his clerical operations more effectively is *records management,* a term which was defined in Chapter 1 as ". . . [the control of] the life cycle of a record from its creation, through processing, checking, maintenance, and protection, to its destruction." While this term is used in a more restricted sense in many business offices to mean the transfer and retention of records with primary emphasis on filing, the broader definition stressing all phases of paperwork is more indicative of the types of records management programs in large organizations. The U. S. Government, for example, frequently substitutes for "records management" the term *paperwork*

---

[3] Robert A. Shiff, "Can Your Records Go to Washington?" *The Controller,* Vol. XXX, No. 11 (November, 1962), pp. 554, 555.

management [4] to mean a functional approach that aims to achieve companywide, integrated control of all links so that an orderly and efficient flow of paperwork is provided from creation to ultimate disposition. For all practical purposes, paperwork management and records management may be considered as being synonymous.

The larger the organization, the more likely it is to define and to change adaptively its records management program. Considerable variation is found between the all-inclusive records control programs of the federal agencies and those reported by private businesses.

Records management in Government. In the General Services Administration, a branch of the U. S. Government, a complex records management program and series of workshops are conducted by systems specialists on a continuing basis throughout the country. Included in these programs are the following topics: [5]

Organization and administration of a records management program
Government legislation on records
Staffing and supervision of a records program
Filing and finding systems
Correspondence, reports, and directives
Mail management
Forms management
Records control (disposal, archives, etc.)
Space and equipment management
Records protection
Records manuals

Besides the Federal Government, many state governments are starting paperwork simplification programs. In addition, metropolitan areas such as New York City and Los Angeles County have long maintained well-developed programs to control paperwork.

Records management practices in business and industry. Through a survey of 429 of its member firms, the Administrative Management Society (formerly the National Office Management Association) showed a rather consistent pattern in practices in record

---

[4] Irene Place, "From Filing to Records and Paperwork Management," *The Clerical Program in Business Education,* American Business Education Yearbook, Vol. XVI (New York: The Eastern Business Teachers Association and the National Business Teachers Association, 1959), p. 148.

[5] Adapted from materials prepared by Pomrenze, Seymour J., "54.545 Planning and Administration of a Records Program: CREATION," (Washington, D.C.: The American University, 1962).

management practices. Most programs studied had these characteristics (percentages are approximate) : [6]

1. They are centralized (70%).
2. Responsibility for control rested with the Accounting Department
   in the small office and with Office Services in the large office, (71%,
   71%).
3. Principal program attention was focused on records retention, 98%;
   records center for inactive records, 97%; protection of vital records,
   97%.
4. Operating responsibilities included purchase of record filing equipment, 67%.
5. Centralized programs maintained vital records centers, 80%.

Since more than half of the offices responding to this survey (53
percent) represented firms having fewer than 500 employees, the
rather narrow scope of their programs (No. 3 above), compared with
the governmental programs, is easily seen.

SECTION 2. ORGANIZATION OF THE RECORDS
MANAGEMENT PROGRAM

To manage any program well requires proper organization, planning, the procurement of adequate personnel at all levels, and the
development of proper operating controls. In the case of records
management, the program must be properly integrated with the
existing paperwork or information systems that are already functioning in the firm.

A major task facing top management is the elimination and
simplification of its growing paperwork burdens in order to:

Release management time for creative thinking.
Promote the opportunity for more effective decision-making.
Increase the efficiency of the clerical work force.
Reduce clerical costs.
Retain for future use only essential information.

MANAGEMENT SUPPORT

To get the support of management needed for adopting a records
management program, carefully documented information on records
problems must be gathered on a *company-wide* basis. Actual examples
of the kinds of problems found in such a survey are listed on page 355
and are definite symptoms of faulty records-control practices:

------

[6] *Records Management Practices* (Willow Grove, Pennsylvania: The Administrative Management Society, undated).

1. Persistent delays in finding requested information.
2. Frequent loss (temporary or permanent) of important documents.
3. Shortage of space in which to file records.
4. Duplication in records maintained in various divisions.
5. Poor organization of active and inactive files.
6. Lack of standards and controls over files, forms, and correspondence.
7. Continual purchase of new filing equipment.
8. Lack of creation, retention, and disposal policies for records.
9. Poor work methods by file clerks.
10. Absence of a training program for the clerical staff.
11. Lack of a program for records transfer or a records storage center.
12. Messy, cluttered file folders and file drawers.
13. Lack of appreciation of the multiple roles records serve and the total dependence of the organization upon well-controlled records.

When management is shown how such problems can be solved and what the savings in convenience, goodwill, time, and cost will be, it becomes less reluctant to give its approval to the organization of a company-wide program for controlling paperwork.

PRINCIPLES FOR ORGANIZATION OF THE PROGRAM

In the small office the filing work will be done by clerks having many other duties. In the large office, on the other hand, the same control over records may be centralized in one or more persons as their full-time responsibility. In either case, however, the well-planned program in records management should include these fundamentals of good organization:

1. Lines of authority and responsibility should be drawn running upward and downward through the several levels with a broad base at the bottom and a single head at the top. (This single head is the *records manager* or *records administrator;* the base represents the clerical staff.)
2. Each person or unit in the organization should understand the organizational breakdown and know to whom he or she is answerable and who is accountable to him or her.
3. No member of the organization should report to more than one supervisor.
4. Every necessary function must be assigned, according to the mission of the unit, with no function being assigned to more than one unit at one time. At the same time, there should be a fair distribution of all work assigned.
5. Whenever responsibility for a function is fixed in an individual or a unit, commensurate authority necessary to perform that function must accompany it.
6. The number of individuals reporting directly to a supervisor should not exceed the number that can be well coordinated and directed by that supervisor (concept of "span of control").

7. Authority and responsibility for action are decentralized to the individuals and units responsible for actual performance of work to the greatest possible extent so long as this does not hamper control over the work.

8. The primary goal of management is to exercise control over policy problems of *exceptional* importance rather than through giving constant close attention to routine actions of subordinates (concept of "management by exception").

9. The policies as well as the operating procedures of the unit should be distributed and used by the entire staff. (A definite written plan for handling all phases of the records program frequently appears in the *records manual*.)

10. Adequate orientation and training must be provided for all levels of managerial and operating personnel.

11. The working environment must be conducive to efficient motion, comfortable areas of work, and convenience to worker and customer alike. This would involve correct layout of files, including adequate space, proper equipment and supplies, good lighting and noise control, and a clean and attractive work area.

12. Provision must be made for periodic follow-up of the unit to evaluate its effectiveness, to take corrective steps if necessary, and to make plans for the future responsibilities to which the unit may be assigned.

The ideal form of organization, according to a leading records management authority,[7] is to control the flow of information and paperwork in an organization from a centralized location. Over two thirds of all companies with formal records management programs exercise a centralized control over their programs. Of course, physical passage of all paper through such a monitoring point is not necessary. Such centralized control, however, has these advantages:

1. It enhances the speed of controlling records.
2. It reduces the opportunities for "bootleg" records.
3. It permits current ideas and methods to be "broadcast" to all parts of the firm.
4. It makes the development, testing, and application of standards more feasible.
5. It promotes the advantages of specialization of labor.

PLAN AND SET-UP FOR THE RECORDS MANAGEMENT PROGRAM

In the final analysis, business as a social institution is composed of *people*. No matter how good the organizing phase of the program, personnel must be selected to administer all activities. Records

---

[7] Lyle R. Clark, "Records Management," Chapter 8, *Business Systems* (Cleveland: Association for Systems Management, 1970), p. 260.

problems differ from industry to industry so that the decision on how to staff the program must be an individual matter. Several alternative approaches are available.

Committee approach. Often a committee made up of managerial personnel from key departments such as accounting, personnel, production, purchasing, and the legal staff is formed to study the need for records control and, if necessary, to organize and administer a records management program. Such a committee brings company-wide experience and group thinking and flexibility to the program and the benefits of standardizing operating policies and procedures. Potential disadvantages of such an approach typically include the "slowness" of the committee process, lack of decisive action, and passing the buck. In actual practice, a steering committee often functions to develop policy, leaving the administration of the program to the specialized records management staff.

"Inside" consultants. Some large companies, such as General Electric and Metropolitan Life Insurance Company, use the present personnel of the organization to develop the program. Such personnel, specialized in information systems, are familiar with their firm's organizational structure, its paperwork flows, and key operating personnel. As a result, they may have a common ground with their associates and can help not only to install but also to follow-up on a day-to-day basis all of the details of the records management program. Often, both "inside" and "outside" consultants work together to get the program started and choose the personnel required to operate the program.

"Outside" consultants. In today's paperwork world, many new consulting services are appearing. In data processing, for example, systems engineers and management scientists help a firm to improve its understanding and use of computers; in personnel work, specialists in manpower utilization are now functioning; in forms control, in correspondence management, in general systems and procedures as well as in records management, professional analysts are available to improve all phases of a paperwork system.

Some consultants operate in independent consulting firms; others, such as the filing systems authorities of Sperry Remington, are furnished as a system consulting service of the manufacturer. Such outside consultants bring new ideas and the experiences of many previous clients with them to the job. Furthermore, they are not restricted by knowledge of present company personnel biases but can give full time and the benefit of their specialized skills to the program. Experience has shown that the "outsider" is often very successful in helping the organization's office staff to accept change and train them adequately in the new techniques.

On the other hand, such consultants may bring some weaknesses along with them. At times they tend to hurry into "obvious" solutions similar to previous solutions; they may not fully prepare all levels of the staff for implementing their recommendations and hence may incur the wrath of the staff and cause the program to falter. Data-processing consultants have been known to be ready with the "quick" solution—the purchase of an expensive machine—before investigating all the real information needs of the firm. A hasty decision on a transfer and retention program, without regard to all record references, illustrates one potential danger of the outside consultant.

ORGANIZATIONAL PLACEMENT OF THE PROGRAM

If the records management program is to function both adequately and objectively, it should not be organized as a part of any operating department, such as accounting. Rather, it should be a staff unit that is responsible for advising all departments on their records management problems, operating across department lines, with one man responsible for maintaining centralized controls over the creation, retention, and disposal of all records.

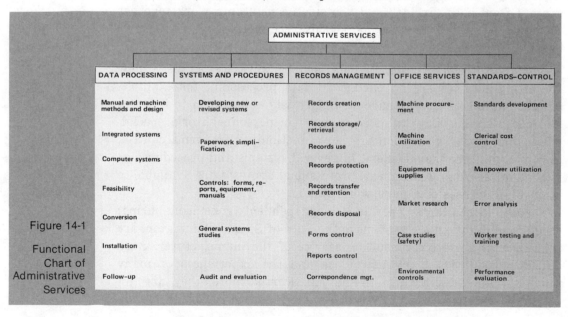

Figure 14-1

Functional Chart of Administrative Services

ADMINISTRATIVE SERVICES				
DATA PROCESSING	**SYSTEMS AND PROCEDURES**	**RECORDS MANAGEMENT**	**OFFICE SERVICES**	**STANDARDS–CONTROL**
Manual and machine methods and design	Developing new or revised systems	Records creation	Machine procurement	Standards development
Integrated systems	Paperwork simplification	Records storage/ retrieval	Machine utilization	Clerical cost control
Computer systems		Records use		
		Records protection	Equipment and supplies	Manpower utilization
Feasibility	Controls: forms, reports, equipment, manuals	Records transfer and retention	Market research	Error analysis
Conversion	General systems studies	Records disposal		
Installation		Forms control	Case studies (safety)	Worker testing and training
		Reports control		
Follow-up	Audit and evaluation	Correspondence mgt.	Environmental controls	Performance evaluation

Records management is frequently considered as one specialized area of office management. With the current trends, more office automation, integrated related office systems, diversified training of office executives, and greater reliance on office services (that have given more breadth to the office function—to the point where it is often headed by a Vice President of Administration), a new concept of office management has evolved. Today it is considered as the area of *administrative services* in which the subdivisions in Figure 14-1 might appear with planned and useful duplication in several sections.

QUALIFICATIONS OF THE RECORDS MANAGER

Broad administrative experience and a sound knowledge of the entire company's operating needs are basic qualifications for the records manager. Management must examine carefully its needs concerning business records and seek to find a person who can effectively manage the records program. Specific qualifications for this type of position are shown in Figure 14-2. In addition to these specific duties and responsibilities, most records managers' positions require considerable background knowledge of business administration, especially accounting, business management, and economics; a knowledge of systems analysis techniques and the ability to sell new ideas; as well as the administrative ability to organize, plan, and implement the type of program which is covered in this book.

Other titles used for "records manager" include the following:

Records administrator	Information engineer
Records officer	Information manager
Records controller	Chief records analyst

The mistaken notion that "anyone can manage the records" should be quickly dispelled. The success of the program hinges upon how well the records manager carries out his responsibilities and organizes his staff to carry out, in turn, the policies and procedures he has set up. Special problems relating to the operating personnel (records supervisors, file clerks, tape librarians, records analysts, etc.) will be discussed in the next section.

QUALIFICATIONS OF THE OPERATING PERSONNEL

In a small office, a file clerk may be her own files supervisor; but in the large office, many levels of workers may be found. Normally

Position (Job Title)	Reports to	Typical Duties	Minimum Qualifications
Tape Librarian	Supervisor, Center Tape Library	Maintains indexed file of all tapes. Assists in setting up tape retention periods and locations of tapes for new jobs; maintains manuals of application procedures and flow diagrams; releases tapes from files for reuse at conclusion of a retention period; assists in screening new programs to insure complete coverage, per established schedules. Receives listings of computer applications to be processed, per established schedules. Locates applicable tapes and arranges in proper sequence for release. Inspects tape identification to determine if replacement is necessary because of wear and tear. Transcribes tape identification to record card and files in proper location. Maintains record of magnetic tape usage, indexed record of tape assignments, and records all changes made to the tapes. Checks labels on all tapes to verify complete and proper identification.	High school graduate with one year general office experience or 6 months' experience in computer-related fields.
Central Files Storage Clerk	Supervisor, Records Management Section	Plans and schedules space requirements for received records and records transferred from semiactive to inactive storage, considering quality, size, activity, and importance. Also assigns location number and marks with date of destruction in accordance with retention schedule. Handles records for Records Management; transfers records unloaded at dock with aid of fork lift and skids. Stores records within storage areas, and removes them for burning or sale as scrap. Stores surplus furniture and office machines. Maintains storage area in a neat, orderly manner to provide safety to records and efficient record retrieval service. Locates and issues records or information from central files according to requests received. Maintains supply of materials used in storage of records. Distributes boxes and other materials to enable departments to forward records for retention.	High school graduate. Must be capable of heavy lifting.
Records Clerk and Indexer	Supervisor, Records Management Section	Receives company records for filing and storage. Inspects contents to determine filing method and to establish suitable filing captions. May recommend changes in contents or methods of filing. Selects information necessary to originate entry on detailed indexes and cross-reference files. Assists supervisor in organizing and reorganizing records, filing methods, and procedures to maintain efficient service. Maintains Central File Storage date for destruction in accordance with retention schedules. Furnishes Central File Storage clerks with information covering destruction of records in accordance with retention schedules. Locates and issues records or information from central files in accord with specific telephone or personal requests. Maintains location and "records detail" indexes showing contents of the file, shelf or drawer number, date of records, and required retention. Furnishes instructions as to labeling of records, showing names of department, description of the contents, inclusive dates covered, alphabetical or numerical sequence and date of destruction as determined by retention schedule.	High school graduate, with high clerical ability. Must have at least two years' filing experience, preferably in a central files system or four years of varied office experience.
Program Library Records Clerk	Supervisor, Center Program Library	Prepares prints of documents from microfilm cards, operating Xerox print machine. Prepares prints for daily computer operations as indicated by daily schedule. Prepares library documents for microfilming including application of serial number, date/time number, document control code, and entry in log. Handles check out and return of material from files, recording all transactions. Assists in other library functions such as cataloging, operating teletype machine, and updating library records.	High school graduate; capable typist.
Supervisor, Records Management Section	Manager, Adm. Services Dept.	Originates and maintains records retention schedules on all active and inactive records by examining each record to determine use, reference frequency, duplication of similar or derivative records, legal retention requirements, and historical value. Secures management approval of record retention and presents to Records Retention Committee for final approval. Coordinates inactive record processing and responsible for permanent inactive record classification (indexing) and filing record systems. Plans and schedules general space and equipment requirements for storage of inactive records. Determines whether obsolete records should be destroyed or scrapped and supervises records disposal. Reviews status of inactive records periodically and determines need for microfilming of specified records. Responsible for general classification, filing, and storage of microform records. Responsible for processing of incoming company mail. Establishes and maintains surveillance of mail distribution systems. Assists department heads in planning filing and storage methods and procedures. Recommends system changes to promote uniformity in handling company records. Supervises employees assigned to Section and assists in administration of Company personnel policies.	High school graduate with two years' college training and two years' business experience, preferably involving records administration.

Figure 14-2.
Job Descriptions of Key Records Management Positions

there are two levels of workers under the control of the records manager:

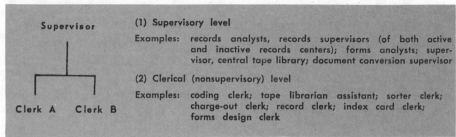

Supervisor

Clerk A   Clerk B

(1) **Supervisory level**

Examples: records analysts, records supervisors (of both active and inactive records centers); forms analysts; supervisor, central tape library; document conversion supervisor

(2) **Clerical (nonsupervisory) level**

Examples: coding clerk; tape librarian assistant; sorter clerk; charge-out clerk; record clerk; index card clerk; forms design clerk

Both of these levels are described in Figure 14-2. Of special note is the fact that positions relating to automation (such as tape librarian and program library records clerk) are assuming greater frequency and importance in large offices, such as banks, insurance companies, and utilities. Sometimes, too, related departments, such as printing or duplicating and the mailing department, are coordinated with filing duties, giving more diversification of tasks to the workers and utilizing the clerical staff more completely.

Qualifications required for operating personnel in records management work will depend upon the level and nature of work done. As a rule, the following are minimum qualifications for supervisors:

The Supervisory Level

Skills and knowledges:

Knowledge of business forms use and design
Knowledge of various record systems and their relative advantages
Considerable accuracy in working with records
Manual dexterity and speed in work methods
Basic recording skills: handwriting, typewriting skills
Exercise of judgment in classifying records
Capacity for considerable detailed work and a good memory
Steady work at routine level
Comprehension of technological and mechanical techniques related to records management (i.e., automated information retrieval)
Facility in systems tools such as work measurement, flow charting, duplicating, microfilming, systems and procedures, data processing, and information retrieval

Related needs:

Ability to plan, organize, and administer a program
Ability to supervise, train, and direct the work of others
Ability to get along well with superiors, subordinates, and peers

Supervisory workers should never be selected if they have not had previous experience in their area of responsibility (a point which is sometimes overlooked). Those full-time workers dealing with the filing phase of records management must be content to work in a setting which often has little variety (and hence may become monotonous), in which the pay is sometimes below average, in which the work requires intensive concentration, with perhaps little hope of advancing. Beyond the general area of filing, however, with the advent of automation and the broadening of the administrative services area, new horizons are appearing for the records management person with the potential to reach supervisory and managerial levels.

A more specific set of qualifications would be found for the nonsupervisory personnel. Demonstrating these qualifications are some findings of a study by Erickson [8] of more than 300 office jobs in the Los Angeles-Long Beach area. For nonsupervisory office personnel responsibile for sorting, filing, and retrieving duties, these qualifications were mentioned:

Skills and knowledges:

Accuracy in working with records
Scanning and reading skills
Ability to distinguish names, numbers, and colors
Knowledge of filing systems and departmental functions
Ability to set up a filing system or to adhere to an established one
Manual speed and dexterity
Ability to use coding systems or to establish coding systems
Recording skills; handwriting, typewriting, and logging of data
Good alphabetizing skills
Good technical vocabulary
Ability to match the same or similar item in a variety of source data
Working knowledge of a wide variety of forms, catalogs, and manuals
Good memory
Physical strength (for movement of files and equipment)
Knowledge of material filed

Related needs:

Strong interest in and aptitude for clerical work
Systematic worker
Ability to organize time and work tasks
Effectively handling pressure of time, work flow, and deadlines

An interest in filing work seems to be a key qualification, especially since it affects both the speed and accuracy with which the work is done. Primary attention should be given to this factor in selecting nonsupervisory filing personnel.

---

[8] Lawrence W. Erickson, *Basic Components of Office Work—An Analysis of 300 Office Jobs*, Monograph 123 (Cincinnati: South-Western Publishing Company, 1971), p. 9.

A records management manual is an essential part of the program for the control of records. It should be developed to show in detail the scope of the entire program as well as to provide instructions for carrying out individual phases of the program. Large organizations that are able to specialize in paperwork control maintain such a complete manual, although even small offices should have a simple written record of their records control procedures.

All major segments of the records management program are included in the manual. Information to be included would be:

1. Introduction
   a. Title, foreword, table of contents
   b. Organizational structure
2. The records management program
   a. Statement of objectives, scope, and responsibilities
   b. Definitions and vocabulary
   c. Functions, personnel, job descriptions
3. Records control cycle
   a. Creation through disposal
   b. Active and inactive storage
   c. Vital records centers
4. Records management methods
   a. Files management: active, inactive
   b. Records retention and disposal
   c. Correspondence and directives management
   d. Forms management
   e. Reports management
   f. Mail management
   g. Mechanization and records controls
      (1) Microphotography of records
      (2) Document retrieval
      (3) Managing computer system records

SECTION 3. OPERATION OF THE RECORDS MANAGEMENT PROGRAM

If you were to interview the head of a full-fledged records management program, he would likely describe his chief administrative responsibilities as:

Planning (what is to be done)
Supervising (directing the personnel in their work)
Controlling (working in accordance with established plans and standards)

Generally people tend to think of filing when records controls are mentioned and hence view the chief responsibilities of the records manager as those dealing with filing routines (already discussed), training of the workers (discussed in the next section), coordination of the filing in all departments, studying the filing systems and analyzing the workers' production, and reducing filing cost and inefficiency. Since records management is broader than filing, it should include some or all of the elements of paperwork management which are briefly described near the end of this chapter.

RECORDS PERSONNEL TRAINING

A progressive manager provides instruction and training continuously in accordance with the needs of his group. In the filing department, for example, several possibilities exist regarding the nature of training. One approach is to train filing personnel on one operation—such as sorting, indexing, charging-out, or cross-referencing. After an extended period of time (2 to 3 months), the worker may progress to another operation for training or choose one in which he or she has shown an aptitude and indicated an interest.

Another approach, in part the reverse of the first, is to train the filing personnel in all file-room operations, a form of *job enlargement*. This popular concept enables a worker to learn many jobs and to move from one operation to another with the result that broader training is provided, a staff is trained for many emergencies, and single-job monotony is minimized.

To ensure efficient filing operations, training may be carried on at various times. When a new file clerk comes to the filing department, the clerk must be oriented to the company and to the filing unit in addition to the specific filing procedures necessary to perform the job. Similarly, any good supervisor will conduct follow-up training periodically to ensure that the personnel are performing satisfactorily. Some companies make use of spot checks by randomly examining several dozen folders to determine if all the records they contain are correctly classified and filed and if the labels, tabs, and guides are properly identified and placed. Other offices make a personal audit of the files at irregular, unannounced times instead of at regular times.

The contents of one well-known training program maintained by a major western public utility includes the topics following on page 365.

Basic orientation:

> Company history
> Records systems in the company
> Mutual understanding of records importance and
> use
> Proper disposal of noncurrent files
> Reduction of recordkeeping costs
> Knowledge of major job responsibilities

Specific training:

> Daily and periodic duties
> Examples:
>
>> How to pull follow-ups
>> How to check out a file
>> How to secure a requested file already checked
>> out to someone else
>> How to place folders back in file
>> How to cross-reference
>> How to identify and label files, folders, guides
>> How to set up a new file
>> How to deactivate a current file
>> How to reactivate an inactive file
>> How to obtain an inactive file from the archives
>> How to control confidential records
>> How to use the equipment and machines

The importance of good filing operations is underscored, in one firm, by the slogan, *"Filing time is operator's time. Finding time is executive's time."* [9]

STANDARDS OF EFFICIENCY, COST, AND CONTROL

For several decades industrial engineers have applied measurement techniques to control both quality and quantity of the factory product. These same techniques, through the encouragement of the Administrative Management Society and other groups interested in office work, are now being applied to paper processing as well as to factory work.

In general, *quantity control* is much more objective and easier to develop and apply than quality control since it usually involves counting the number of routine, repetitive units (checks sorted, invoices extended, etc.) processed. As a result, quantity control operations are relatively common in large offices.

---

[9] Adelle Whitt, "Training Filing Personnel," *Records Management Journal,* Vol. I, No. 3 (Autumn, 1963), p. 24.

On the other hand, *quality control* programs in office management are more subjective and are harder to define, to develop, and to apply since they are concerned with judging the presence or absence of certain characteristics such as accuracy (an error-free letter) or meticulous appearance (a smudgeless typed contract) of records. In summary, quantity control is concerned with "how many" while quality control is concerned with "how good" or "how bad."

The usual means for controlling either quantity or quality of production is to develop standards relating to these factors. Such standards are developed on the basis of (a) past experience, (b) time and motion studies, and (c) standard-time data (basic motions common to many tasks) in which only the best performances in an office are measured.

Among the many benefits to be derived from work standards, Neuner [10] lists the following points as the most important:

1. Standards aid in determining the number of employees required to perform various office activities. Thus the office manager is able to determine the volume of work that each employee should complete and to indicate the meaning of a "fair day's work."
2. Frequently standards permit reductions in the number of employees as a result of work measurement programs upon which the standards are based.
3. Standards aid in determining the cost of the work performed which, in turn, helps in preparing budgets and in measuring the effectiveness of forecasts.
4. Standards also aid in performance evaluation and should result in improved morale due to the workers' knowing what is expected of them, and what their reward will be for a good performance.
5. Standards are helpful in installing incentive wage systems where management deems them desirable. Usually more production is the result, as was found in a large mail-order firm where quantity control standards helped to reduce the personnel in the mailing and filing department by 40 percent.
6. Standards may be used as guides in suggesting the need for newer or more efficient office systems and procedures.
7. Standards serve as a basis for measuring the effectiveness of any department in the office by indicating the achievements as compared with the standards. This, then, measures "what is" against "what ought to be" (the standard).
8. Standards help a supervisor to measure the effectiveness of a new employee and the rate of the learning that has taken place.

A standard should be considered as a *guide* or yardstick rather than as a precise form of measurement. This is true because it is

---

[10] John J. W. Neuner, B. Lewis Keeling, and Norman F. Kallaus, *Administrative Office Management* (6th ed.; Cincinnati: South-Western Publishing Company, 1972), pp. 604-607.

almost impossible to achieve accurate measurement of office work for these reasons:

1. There is wide variation in type of work from company to company.
2. Working conditions, especially relating to worker training, methods, and environment, differ from one office or one community to another.
3. Most businessmen do not have the knowledge or time to develop standards or appreciate their value and hence do not develop them.
4. Workflows are often not constant.
5. Too much intellectual reasoning, not easily measured, is involved.

Standards relating to quality and quantity may be applied to all phases of records management, including forms, correspondence, reports, space, and the methods and motions of the workers. However, they are most commonly found in such "paper-conscious" firms as insurance companies and banks, especially in the filing department.

ILLUSTRATIONS OF FILING STANDARDS

The job of developing standards of worker performance has never been easy. With the number of positions related to records management and filing growing, the problem of developing standards for this area becomes even more difficult.

An example of factors established as standards can be illustrated in the analysis of the work of a file clerk. The total duties of a file clerk are studied; these typical tasks are selected as the basis for the development of standards of performance of filing clerks.

Task	*Potential Work Count*
1. Selecting cards from file	cards
2. Filling in form letters	forms
3. Filing invoices after posting	invoices
4. Searching file for missing cards	cards
5. Sorting sales reports by salesman number	forms

The work measurement engineer, on the basis of the number of work pieces completed accurately per hour, is then able to construct a standard time for each task. By accumulating each standard task time for each employee and giving due allowance for nonproductive periods of activity, a total standard for each employee can be created. The standards shown in Figure 14-3 have been obtained from several nationwide surveys of filing operations [11] and serve as reliable guidelines by which the work of operating personnel can be evaluated.

---

[11] Marian J. Collins, *Handbook for Office Practice Teachers*, Monograph 91 (Cincinnati: South-Western Publishing Company, December, 1954), p. 11.

Whenever such performance standards are tabulated, the reader must remember that these standards were developed on the basis of certain controlled conditions. If an office manager wishes to compare

FILING PERFORMANCE STANDARDS

Operation	Measurement Unit	Rate	Additional Details	Source
Alphabetizing 5 x 3 cards	cards per hour	150	with approx. one guide for each 30 cards	NOMA [7]
Alphabetizing 8½ x 11 sheets	sheets per hour	100	with approx. 24 guides per drawer	NOMA [7]
Filing (all operations) 8½ x 11 sheets	pieces per 8-hour day	600-833	coding, marking, sorting, filing, look-ups and charge-outs; alphabetic systems	Odell and Strong [8]
Filing 5 x 3 cards	cards per minute	1.9-5.16	cards previously sorted and arranged in alphabetic sequence	Odell and Strong [8]
Sorting and arranging 5 x 3 cards	cards per hour	268	using table top	Odell and Strong [8]
Typing gummed labels	labels per hour	85	for use on the file folder	Odell and Strong [8]
Pasting gummed labels	labels per hour	60	on file folder	Odell and Strong [8]
Inspect, sort, and file	pieces per day	200	alphabetically	NORS [9]
Find correspondence	pieces per hour	22	in an alphabetic file	NORS [9]
Search for particular piece of information	pieces per hour	6-8	in several possible places in the file	NORS [9]
Make preliminary sort of correspondence	pieces per hour	250	into specified dimensions	NORS [9]
Sort in distributor; remove; re-sort in main file	pieces per hour	275	alphabetic	NORS [9]
Look up references	pieces per hour	50	in alphabetic file	NORS [9]
File 8½ x 11 letters	pieces per hour	300	in alphabetic file	NORS [9]
File account cards	pieces per hour	225	in alphabetic file	NORS [9]

Figure 14-3. Nationwide Performance Standards of Filing Operations

[7] National Office Management Association, *"Survey Summary No. 10,"* as cited in *Curriculum Construction and Schedule Planning for Continuation Schools,* Florida State Department of Education (Tallahassee: 1950), pp. 4-5.

[8] Margaret K. Odell and Earl P. Strong, *"Management and Filing Operations"* (New York: McGraw-Hill Book Company, Inc., 1947), pp. 301-306.

[9] *National Office Ratio Survey,* as cited by Margaret K. Odell and Earl P. Strong, *ibid.,* p. 306.

his workers' performance with such standards, the circumstances in each office should be identical with the original.

RATIOS OF FILING AND FINDING EFFICIENCY

To determine both quality and quantity standards in filing work, work counts are required (see Figure 14-3, "Measurement Unit" and "Rate" columns). Two additional measures of filing and finding efficiency are often used. The *activity ratio* represents a form of quantity standard and the *accuracy* (of finding) *ratio* a type of quality standard. The nature and purpose of each ratio is described in detail:

1. *Activity ratio:*
   a. What it does: Measures amount of reference to files.
   b. What it shows: Firm's needs for analyzing files, developing retention, transfer, and disposal procedures for records.
   c. How it is computed:
   $$\frac{\text{No. of references requested}}{\text{No. of records filed}} = \text{activity ratio}$$
   d. Example:
   $$\frac{2,000 \text{ references requested}}{6,000 \text{ references filed}} = 33\tfrac{1}{3}\% \text{ activity ratio}$$
   e. Guidelines: If the ratio is greater than 20%—filed records are useful.
   If the ratio is from 10% to 20%—files need improvement.
   If the ratio is below 10%—separate files may exist.
   If the ratio is below 1%—files are inactive.

2. *Accuracy ratio:*
   a. What it does: Measures the efficiency of filing personnel and the filing system.
   b. What it shows: How accurately records have been filed.
   How well the file clerks can use the file.
   How faithfully charge-out and follow-up have been carried out.
   How much material may be retained in private files (hence cannot be found in the regular files).
   c. How is it computed:
   $$\frac{\text{No. of records found}}{\text{No. of records requested}} = \text{accuracy ratio}$$
   d. Example:
   $$\frac{5,950 \text{ records found}}{6,000 \text{ records requested}} = 99.17\% \text{ accuracy ratio}$$

e. Guidelines: If the ratio is more than 99.5%—files are in excellent operating condition.

If the ratio is between 97% and 99.5%—files are in satisfactory condition.

If the ratio is below 97%—files should be studied for these "symptoms" of poor filing techniques:
Improper indexing and coding
Poor charge-out procedures
Insufficient cross-referencing
Cluttered files (e.g., too much material in folders)
Too many private files

Through the years another activity guideline has been developed in company records centers in which record volume is measured in terms of cubic feet of space occupied by the documents. Good operating practice has pointed to the fact that there should be one reference for each two cubic feet of records housed. Therefore, minimal "activity" efficiency would require 50,000 references per year for a storage center having 100,000 records housed. Such references can come from various sources: by telephone call or by a personal visit from a requester, having the file clerk withdraw a record and mail it or a photocopy of it to the requester, and by adding additional records. Furthermore, this ratio can be *increased* (and efficiency improved) by *decreasing* the number of records stored. Regardless of which method of measurement of efficiency is used, a record of the activity is required to appraise the records system. In such an appraisal it must not be forgotton that essentially management wants:

(1) every requested record located
(2) the record search to be minimal—that is, immediate records access
(3) the cost of filing and finding to be low
(4) the methods of the personnel to be efficient
(5) only required machines and equipment to be used

A files supervisor should provide periodic reports on the status of the filing system. Included in such a report would be the volume of records received (either in number of records or in cubic feet of space occupied); how much space is available as of the reporting date; what kind of reference activity has been noted; an inventory of filled and unused file housing; and other activities such as files destroyed, files transferred to inactive storage, and the like. The checklist shown in Figure 14-4 [15] will help to evaluate the overall filing operation as well as to develop solutions to the major problems uncovered.

---

[15] "How to Measure Your Filing Costs and Efficiency," Pamphlet LBV804A Rev. 2, Remington Rand, p. 18.

EVALUATION OF YOUR FILING OPERATION

1. Is there a centralized or decentralized file plan? Does it afford necessary control over files?
2. Is the proper file system used for each record function? Is it simple or complicated?
3. Is there misfiling?
4. Are related records together to provide cumulative information or is information split and segrated?
5. Are folders and guides used properly?
6. Is equipment used properly or wasted?
7. Do files contain useless and obsolete information or is there a continuous plan to eliminate such material through proper transfer and disposal procedures?
8. Are drawers overcrowded? Are file areas congested or neat?
9. Is there a place to file everything or is information kept from files?
10. Is the sorting operation slow?
11. Are standard filing and indexing methods and procedures practiced?
12. Are records afforded required protection?
13. Is the follow-up system reliable?
14. Are records charged out?
15. Is the file personnel salary budget increasing?
16. Are file personnel adequately trained?
17. Is there an organized storage area?
18. Is authority and responsibility for filing properly delegated?
19. Is there a file operating manual?
20. Do you know: how many documents you have filed?
    how many requested documents are not found?
    how many requests are made for filed documents?
    how many file clerks and other personnel you have?
    how many file drawers you are maintaining?

Sperry Remington, Office Systems and Machines,
Sperry Rand Corporation

Figure 14-4.
Checklist to Evaluate the Filing Operations

CONTROL OF RECORDS COSTS

Today's records manager, as is true of all members of management, must maintain close control over costs. He must know the cost components, both *direct* costs such as salaries and *indirect* costs such as telephone and insurance. Such cost accounting information should be derived from reliable cost accounting references as well as from assistance provided by the firm's accounting staff.

To understand the cost factors involved in records systems maintenance, consider Figure 14-5 on page 372, which shows how today's records "dollar" is spent.

Salaries comprise the greatest percentage of the money spent for keeping records. In some cases this factor comprises as much as 80 percent of clerical work. Involved in this category are clerical salaries (file clerk, secretary, typist, keypunch operator, etc.),

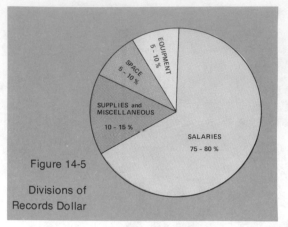

Figure 14-5

Divisions of
Records Dollar

supervisory salaries (records room supervisor, stenographer pool supervisor, keypunch supervisor), and that portion of executive salaries engaged part time in paperwork. The principal opportunity for cutting records salary costs is achieved through establishing performance standards, developing a cost-consciousness among all the workers, and increasing their efficiency on the job. Company records centers that measure their efficiency in terms of number of references to records per cubic feet of records housed use this same ratio for determining the need for personnel. For example, sound business practice may show that a total of 25,000 reference requests per year requires three full-time files operators.[16]

The nonsalary filing costs, though small by comparison to salaries, nevertheless "eat up" about one-fifth of the filing dollar and many of these costs are easy to overlook. In the following outline each of these costs is identified with some suggestion made for control.

Nonsalary Cost Items

A. Equipment: Machines and Furniture

   1. Costs

      a. Machines for processing records (keypunch, typewriting, and duplicating machines)

      b. Housing of records (such as cabinets, shelving, etc.)

      c. Furniture for processing and for administration

      d. Purchase, lease, or rental costs of equipment

      e. Maintenance agreement costs for equipment

      f. Depreciation costs on purchased equipment

   2. Cost-reduction possibilities

      a. Eliminate unnecessary operations

      b. Reduce files size

      c. Improve worker efficiency

      d. Install preventive maintenance program for machines

B. Supplies and Miscellaneous Items

   1. Costs

      a. Stationery, carbon paper, cards, envelopes for correspondence

      b. Business forms and keypunch cards

---

[16] For a comprehensive analysis of the operation of a company records center, the reader should consult William Benedon, *Records Management* (Englewood Cliffs: Prentice-Hall, Inc., 1969).

      c. Duplicating machine supplies (masters, copy paper, and working tools)

      d. Printing expense

      e. Telephone, telegraph and postage expense

    2. Cost-reduction possibilities

      a. Eliminate or reduce number of records filed

      b. Tighten controls over dispensing and use of supplies

      c. Maintain close inventory over all supplies stocked

C. Space

    1. Costs

      a. Space

        (1) Active storage: (cost averages from $5 to $10 per square foot per year)

        (2) Inactive storage: may represent but one-fifth of cost of active storage

      b. Maintenance costs

        (1) Lights, heat, air-conditioning

        (2) Custodial costs

        (3) Telephone expense

    2. Cost-reduction possibilities

      a. Eliminate useless files

      b. Transfer inactive files from active to inactive storage

      c. Provide better space layout to gain more efficient use of the storage area

When records costs are translated into concrete figures (dollars and cents, space requirements, etc.), a better appreciation of the need for cost control can be achieved. Such a breakdown—by equipment, retrieval times, space and amortization tables, as well as a total files summary—is provided in Figure 14-6 [17] on page 374. Combining all these work factors results in a high cost of the filing operation. One recent estimate places the annual operating cost for maintaining a 5-drawer file at approximately $536.[18]

SECTION 4. METHODS OF RECORDS CONTROL

While large organizations will usually maintain complex systems for controlling their paperwork, the small office has many of the same needs but is without the specialized means to effect such controls. In this section selected methods of achieving control over records in all

---

[17] Elmer W. Blankmann, "Information and Records Retrieval Systems," *Records Management Quarterly* (October, 1971), p. 18.

[18] From a letter written by H. M. Workman, Manager, Systems & Supplies Division, Shaw-Walker, Muskegon, Michigan, to the authors, April 25, 1972.

EQUIPMENT—COST PER FILE INCH

File Cabinets
Conventional ....$ .50 - 1.25
Lateral 1.50

Shelf Filing
Manual Fixed .... .40
Manual Movable ....,. .... .80
Mechanized 1.50

Automated Retrieval Devices
Rotating Shelves
Lateral 3.50
Front to Back 5.00

Advanced Automated
Retrieval Devices 2.50
                                  to
Individual Container   5.00
Selection ....

There are others but these are
the most widely used today.

SPACE

	Files	Rotating Shelves	Individual Container Selection
Equipment/Square Feet	120	80	60
Personnel	50	..	..
Misc. Work Area ...	20	20	20
Total	190	100	80
Height	52''	120''	1200
Space Cost Per Sq. Ft. ....$	10.00 $	10.00 $	10.00
Annual Space Cost	$1900.00	$1000.00	$800.00

AVERAGE RETRIEVAL TIMES

	Files	Rotating Shelves	Individual Container Selection
Filing Inches	3000	2800	3000
Cost Per File Inch	1.00	3.50	2.50
Equipment Cost	3000	9800	7500
Time Per Retrieval	60 Sec.	15 Sec.	40 Sec.
Daily Retrievals (A)	1000	1000	1000
Required Time	17 Hrs.	4 Hrs.	12 Hrs.
Clerks Required (7 Hr. Day)	2 1/2	2/3	1 3/4
Daily Retrievals (B)	500	500	500
Clerks Required (7 Hr. Day)	1 1/4	1/3	1
Personnel Costs Year ..	5200.	5200.	5200.
Fringes	800.	800.	800.
Total	6000.	6000.	6000.
Annualized (A)	15000.	4000.	10500.
Annualized (B)	7500.	2000.	5250.

SUMMARY

	Files	Rotating Shelves	Individual Container Selection
Personnel	$15000	$4000	$1050
Equipment	3000	9800	750
Space	1900	1000	80
Total	$19900	$14800	$1880

AMORTIZE EQUIPMENT—5 YEARS

	Files		Rotating Shelves		Individual Container Selection	
Personnel	$15,000	85%	$ 4,000	56%	$10,500	82%
Equipment	600	4%	1,960	29%	1,500	12%
Space	1,900	11%	1,000	15%	800	6%
Cost Per Year	$17,650	100%	$ 6,960	100%	$12,800	100%
Cost 5 Years	$88.250		$34,800		$64,000	

Figure 14-6

Physical Factors and Costs Involved in the Filing Operation

sizes and types of offices are discussed. Such topics as paperwork simplification, forms control, reports and space management are outlined. Their application to all offices should be apparent.

PAPERWORK SIMPLIFICATION

The philosophy of paperwork simplification—as is true of all work simplification—rests upon these basic tenets: (1) that all work can be improved; (2) that there is always a better way to do a job; and (3) that the one best way will probably never be found. Its main thrust is to *eliminate* unnecessary paper wherever found; if elimination is not possible, then to *simplify* wherever possible; and if this cannot be done, then to *change sequence* or *further improve* the overall nature of the paperwork operation.

Paperwork simplification as such is an extension of the principles of scientific management begun in the late 19th century by Frederick W. Taylor and later applied to the office. Its principles are directly used in the records control methods which follow.

FORMS MANAGEMENT

The business form has been called the common denominator of all offices. In executive offices, correspondence and reports may, of course, outnumber the business form; but in all other offices three out of every four records will be business forms, serving as the chief means of communicating information in a standardized, repetitive manner. As such, the business form represents a paper record composed of *static* (fixed) data (such as date ....) and *variable data* (those which change each time the form is filled in).

To manage forms, office administrators have usually set up forms control programs involving routines for *ordering, designing, procuring, storing, distributing, reordering, reviewing,* and *disposing of the form.* Each of these control phases represents an area of specialization in today's office.

Two specific phases of forms management briefly demand attention: the *functional analysis* of forms and *physical design,* both areas in which the college-trained office worker can participate.

Functional analysis. Because the cost of paper and printing is tangible, it is usually emphasized in a discussion of forms cost. Actually, however, the cost of the forms *function* or use ranges from 20 to 30 times more than these tangible physical costs. In fact, paperwork studies in both government and industry show the following costs:[19]

> 4.4% for printing (the main physical costs)
> 11.2% for file maintenance
> 84.4% for clerical processing (the main functional costs)

It is in this processed form cost (representing the paper, clerical salary, and overhead costs) that the greatest savings can be achieved. For example, in one West Coast oil company a costly problem was discovered in which one clerk typed a standard five-part sales invoice form (original and 4 carbons) and wasted considerable time. After a study of the typist's motions and the uses to be made of the information, the form was changed to a five-copy, snap-out, one-time carbon pack in which the form itself cost more, but labor time and cost were reduced 50 percent. Frequently a functional file is set up into which all records are stored by type of function. Using this filing technique, duplicate-function forms can be quickly spotted and eliminated.

Physical Design. From a functional analysis of the form, the records manager knows how the form is used and is then in a position to provide efficient physical design of the form. In such a design task the objective is to make the form easy to read and understand, easy to fill in, and easy to store. This can be done only by questioning the form in its entirety and then applying these forms design principles:

Principle 1. Study the purpose (or intended purpose) of the form and design it with the user in mind.

> Illustration: If the form is to be used out of doors, use heavy card stock.
>   If multiple copies are prepared, use various colors for ease in distribution of copies.

Principle 2. Keep the design simple, eliminating unnecessary information and lines.

> Illustration: Do not ask for "age," *and* "date of birth."
>   Keep instructions for filling in form at top and instructions for distributing the form at the bottom.

---

[19] William Benedon, *Records Management* (Englewood Cliffs: Prentice-Hall, Inc., 1969), p. 125.

Principle 3. Give each form a proper identification:

    a. *A name which designates the form's function.*

    b. *A number with properly coded, flexible features.*

Illustration: Name: Employee Requisition (not Employee Request *Card*)

                Number: P-12 (e.g., 12th form in the personnel section)

Principle 4. Use standardized size and type faces, where practicable, and a standardized terminology.

Illustration: Use card/paper sizes that may be cut from standard 17 x 22-inch mill-size stock without waste of paper.

                Such sizes as 5 x 3, 8 x 5, 6 x 4, 8½ x 11 are economical to buy, use, and store.

Principle 5. Arrange items on the form in the same sequence in which they will be filled in or extracted from the form, thus eliminating waste motions.

Illustration: Information on purchase orders is usually copied directly from approved purchase requisitions. In designing the purchase-order form, maintain the same sequence of data as appeared on the purchase-requisition form.

Principle 6. Preprint constant data so as to keep fill-in (variable data) to a minimum and allow fill-in to stand out clearly.

Illustration: Brown-colored printing on a form to be filled-in with black-colored typewriting will permit the fill-in to be stressed.

                Print size smaller than elite spacing on a standard typewriter will draw the reader-user's attention to the fill-in, making it easier to read.

Principle 7. Adapt spacing to the method of fill-in (manual or machine) allowing sufficient space.

Illustration: For handwriting: ¼" vertical spacing is satisfactory.

                Caution: Handwriting of nonclerical workers is often large and unpredictable and requires at least ⅓".

                For typewriting: Allow double spacing (⅜")

                For handwriting or typewriting: Same as for typewriting.

On typewritten * forms only:

Know the *pitch* (12 spaces to horizontal inch on elite typewriters; 10 for pica).

Know the *throw* (6 line spaces to vertical inch on standard typewriters).

Keep writing lines to a minimum.

Ensure that each line commences immediately below the previous one to reduce number of tabular stops.

Omit ruled lines (horizontal) to increase legibility and permit single-spaced typing.

(Also see Illustration, Principle 8.)

Principle 8. Use box design for variable data, if possible, but do not compel writing if a check mark can be substituted.

Poor: Marital Status: _____

Good: ☐ Married
        ☐ Single

Poor: Name JAMES B. CARNEY   Age 42
        Address 2617 W. Ambrose St., Detroit

Good:

Name	Age
JAMES B. CARNEY	42
Address	
2617 W. Ambrose St., Detroit	

Principle 9. Locate filing information so as to facilitate rapid retrieval of the form.

Illustration: For visible (Kardex) files: Place filing information on the bottom of the form.

For prenumbered purchase order form: Locate file number in upper right-hand corner.

Principle 10. Provide for effective esthetics (or appearance) by proper combinations of type and lines in forms design.

Suggestion: Check with a reputable printer regarding the use of hairlines, double hairlines, one-half point and one-point lines, and broken or dotted lines for improving the appearance and use of the form.

Figure 14-7 illustrates a simple 5 x 3 personnel card that is maintained by a personnel department and completed on the typewriter. This form is a 5 x 3 card vertically filed as a typewritten

---

* The rules for typewritten forms relate only to the use of standard-size type. Machines having nonstandard type (such as microtype or proportional spacing) are, therefore, excluded.

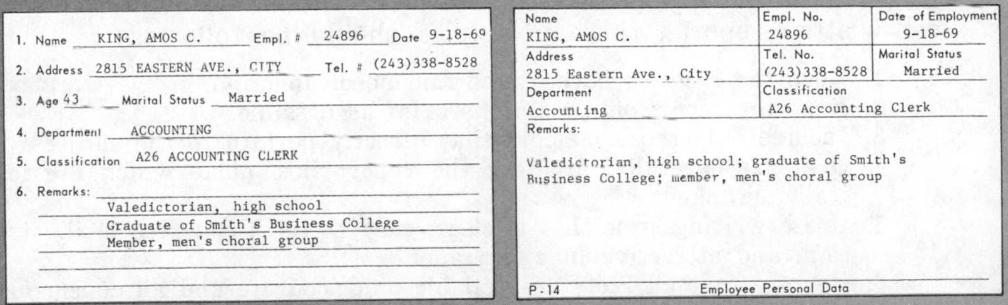

Figure 14-7

Comparing Forms Designs

Left: old form, inefficient to use.
Right: new form, efficiently designed according to rules in Chapter 14.

record of employee personal information in a public relations department of a large insurance company. Information from the card is requested by employee name and number.

For forms to be used in data-processing machines, such as tabulating cards and reports, additional specialized knowledge of the equipment is required. The frequent difficulties in using more complex data-processing forms experienced by every worker are expressed in this poem:

Let's Sing a Song of Forms Design [20]

For printed instructions I had great regard
Until, in the mail came a tab card
With a written command not to crease it or fold it
And a stamped, return envelope too small to hold it.

REPORTS MANAGEMENT

Forms are the feeder records from which reports are prepared. And in the age of data processing, the report is usually defined as the final goal of any processing system, for it represents a summary of data previously collected and processed. The report then serves as an "information feedback" upon which management policies and decisions are based. Typical reports on product sales are prepared by product, by region, by sales territory, or even by salesmen to evaluate the effectiveness of sales policies. Other common reports involve monthly, semiannual, and annual accounting statements; credit reports on prospective customers; scheduling data-processing work loads; and reports on personnel problems, such as absenteeism and labor turnover.

---

[20] *Records Management Journal* (Spring 1965), Vol. III, Number 1, p. 32.

Like all other records, reports must be controlled. To assure well-written reports, these principles should be followed:

1. Keep the reader's background and needs in mind.
2. Keep the report simple and as brief as possible.
3. Include only those matters that directly pertain to the subject.
4. Organize carefully, dividing the report into parts which are logically arranged.
5. Use a writing style that is clear, easy to read, concrete in illustration, and attractive in appearance.
6. Be sure that all facts are reliable and accurate and all conclusions soundly drawn.
7. Keep personal bias and conjecture out of the report unless they are clearly identified as such.
8. Use visual displays (charts, pictures, diagrams, graphs) freely to promote variety and ease of understanding and thereby add to the reading interest.

MAIL MANAGEMENT

Recently one small midwestern electrical cooperative prepared a large first-class quarterly mailing of 10,000 items. The clerk weighed a sample letter and prepared to affix 16 cents postage on each letter since the sample letter weighed slightly more than one ounce. By coincidence, however, a supervisor suggested that the old postal scale be tested for accuracy. The scale was found to be weighing "heavy," with the result that each letter in the mailing of 10,000 items required only 8 cents postage; the saving in this case was $800. Since this was a routine quarterly mailing, approximately $3,200 could have been wasted in one year because of a faulty postal scale!

Mail management, attempts to cut mail costs and improve mailing efficiency by giving attention to these points:

1. Good organization of the mailing function.
2. Consolidation of mail and related functions, such as filing, if profitable.
3. Setting up controls for routing incoming and outgoing mails.
4. Adequate space management and workroom efficiency with a view toward prompt, economical, accurate deliveries.
5. Efficient use of equipment: scales, postage meters, etc.
6. Setting up work schedules (coordinating with filing department).

CORRESPONDENCE MANAGEMENT

Correspondence (especially letters and memorandums) comprises a significant portion of office records, second only to business forms. The correspondence function is particularly important because it involves the duties of dictating, transcribing, and transmitting of information upon which major business decisions are made. Since most letters and memorandums are personally dictated, considerable cost is involved in their preparation.

The cost of letter preparation has risen considerably. Notice the steady escalation of business-letter costs as compiled by the Dartnell Corporation, Chicago: [21]

Year	Average-Length Letter (250 words) Cost
1960	$1.83
1962	1.97
1964	2.32
1966	2.44
1967	2.49
1968	2.54
1969	2.74
1970	3.05
1971	3.19
1972	3.20
1973	3.31

Other reports show a 1953 letter-cost at $1.17 and a 1972 cost at $3.20 which indicates a two-decade profile of correspondence costs.[22]

To reduce correspondence costs related to *composition*, writing consultants recommend making letters shorter (to promote clarity, conciseness, correctness, and completeness and to require less rewriting) and more personal in style (by which persuasive elements in the message may be enhanced). The effective composition of the message is a difficult task, usually requiring special training.

From the standpoint of *production* of the correspondence, the use of form paragraphs, form letters, central stenographic pools and word-processing departments, greater use of transcribing machines, photocopying machines, automatic typewriters, standard correspondence styles, postage meters, and the like, will reduce correspondence costs and enhance the records management program.

---

[21] Dartnell Corporation, "The Cost of a Business Letter—1971," *Analysis and Staff Report,* 1971, p. 4, and *The Secretary* (March 1973), p. 4.

[22] " 'Average' Business Letter Costs $3.20," *Analysis and Staff Report* (Chicago: The Dartnell Corporation, 1972). According to the Dartnell Corporation, 1973 letter cost is $3.31.

SPACE MANAGEMENT

Most office layouts represent a compromise between *too much* and *too little*—too much furniture and equipment (and too many people) and too little space. With the uncontrolled growth of records has come a critical need to control space for two closely related reasons: (1) to get the maximum amount of productivity at the least possible cost and (2) to arrange the equipment in a manner that promotes worker efficiency and an attractive work environment.

Typical techniques for saving space in records management are open-shelf files, which occupy approximately 50 percent of space required by regular filing cabinets, the use of five-drawer cabinets instead of four-drawer, resulting in a 20 percent increase in filing space as well as microrecording of documents or using commercial records centers. Other suggestions for layout and better management of space may be found in office management texts.[23]

SECTION 5. RECORDS MANAGEMENT IN THE SMALL OFFICE

All across America the majority of offices are small in size, that is, they have fewer than 25 employees. In every county-seat town, for example, there are such prominent offices as the courthouse, the offices of the professional men (doctors, lawyers, and dentists), the city board of education, real estate and insurance establishments, banks, public utilities (telephone, light, and power companies), small industry offices, and the informal part-time office staff in every retail store. In every small office, one key factor is ever present: lack of specialization.

This, however, does not mean that the small office cannot be efficiently administered, for it can adapt many of the controls of the large office to its own advantage. It can, for example, develop an efficient, orderly, systematic, and attractive layout based on the flow of work. It can keep its equipment up to date and in good repair, in keeping with its own needs and resources. Workers, though not specialized, can practice partial specialization, especially in the area of filing.

To manage records in the small office, the suggestions on the next page should be followed.

---

[23] Neuner, Keeling, and Kallaus, op.cit., pp. 82-107.

One person, with widespread office experience, organizing ability, vision, and the interest and aptitude for managing office work, should be assigned the responsibility for managing the paper work. Illustrations of possible duties are:

1. Being responsible for the files, deciding who has access to the files, and training other office workers in good filing techniques.
2. Designing, approving, and ordering all forms.
3. Standardizing the format of all letters, memorandums, and other correspondence and providing instructions for message construction and letter production for all personnel.
4. Developing part-time specialization in mail handling.
5. Developing an overall office operating manual including office operating rules and office policies.
6. Compiling a notebook containing all forms used in the office and keeping it up to date.
7. Maintaining close ties with forms salesmen and analysts, machines vendors, and other specialists who can provide advice at little or no cost, on paperwork efficiency in order to compensate for the lack of specialization.

SECTION 6. THE CHALLENGE OF RECORDS MANAGEMENT

There can no longer be any doubt about human potential to create information (and records). Whole new industries and products attest to this fact as a growing number of business firms, hospitals, and governmental organizations now recognize the vital role that information and records play in their organizations. The ads in this section are typical of the newer worker skills and positions available for broadly trained men and women who can handle the entire scope of information-processing operations, the so-called cradle-to-the-grave cycle of the record.[24]

Looking to his future, the student of records management should consider these key influences and trends in office administration:

1. The key concept is *information* and what it can do for the business firm. Information, and not the record on which it appears, will receive principal emphasis.
2. Management has developed an insatiable demand for information. In an age of intense competition and critical need for reducing costs, the manager with the best information and decision-making skills has the "edge" over his competitors. The records manager and his staff are custodians of this information and occupy a key role in business management.
3. Greater capabilities for processing information exist. The age of machine creation, processing, retrieving, and disposing of information is at hand. The future will see an extension of this trend so that greater education and vision is demanded of the information specialist. Data processing, microrecording, and retrieval skills are now widely sought.
4. The very nature of records is changing. Records are no longer considered as isolated pieces of well-designed paper, but rather as integrated units of information that exist only to serve a useful function in a company-wide information system. The narrow view of records control as effective filing must, therefore, give way to an enlightened, expanded picture of the information system.
5. Better control will be expected over all records, and better design of the records and the system they serve will be demanded. Management over all those phases of records management discussed in this chapter will be increased, and measurement techniques refined to permit greater standardization of work.
6. With a greater appreciation of the importance of records and the development of more sophisticated approaches in managing information, more formal training in records management can be expected. Many colleges today offer filing courses, with probably the greatest growth of collegiate records management courses being at the junior (or community) college level. Other paper-related courses, such as systems analysis, office management, data processing, and management systems, are increasing and usually cover important aspects of the records management problem. Seminars in records management are held periodically for experienced records managers at metropolitan locations such as the Management Institute, New York University.
7. An increasing number of professional associations now offer guidance and direction in records management. Following are some of the most notable examples:

    Administrative Management Society
    American Management Association

---

[24] *Information and Records Management,* Vol. 5, No. 12 (December, 1971), p. 36.

American Records Management Association (developer of correspondence study in records management and publisher of the
Records Management Quarterly)

Association of Records Executives and Administrators (publisher
of the *Records Management Journal*)

Association for Systems Management

International Records Management Federation

National Microfilm Association

National Records Management Council

Society of American Archivists

8. An upgrading of the information-processing personnel, such as the
well-trained secretary, and other office personnel is occurring so that,
in addition to performing their clerical activities, they may also
become working partners in the information system.

It may be, in fact, that the next generation of records management may be renamed "information management," for information
is the lifeblood of all organized business and society. Records management can make notable contributions to the orderly development
of this field at a time when changes in technology and society are
rapid and numerous. To borrow from the prophetic French sage,
Alexis de Tocqueville, in his *Democracy in America*, written 135
years ago,

> "They (Americans) judge that the diffusion of knowledge must neces-
> sarily be advantageous, and the consequences of ignorance fatal. They
> all consider . . . humanity as a changing scene, in which nothing is, or
> ought to be, permanent. And they admit that what appears to them
> today to be good, may be superseded by something better tomorrow." [25]

**For Review
and
Discussion**

1. How does the systems approach help to explain the real-world operation
of a management program such as records management?

2. Discuss the point that the changing office concepts outlined in Chapter
14 represent more than new labels for old ideas but rather are sub-
stantive changes in office work.

3. Why is the usual stress on filing as opposed to other records processing
activities a misplacement of emphasis in the total program of records
control?

4. What differences in philosophy would you expect to find from the following two records control personnel:

   a. a files supervisor who was promoted after long service as a files clerk

   b. a records manager who was college trained in records systems and
   data processing.

---

[25] Walter A. Kleinschrod, Editor, "Three Facets of the Changing Office,"
Administrative Management, Vol. XXVI, No. 1 (January, 1965), p. 23.

5. Compare the differences in responsibilities of a computer tape librarian with those of a "paper" records file clerk.

6. Both governmental and private-business organizations have recently given increasing attention to records management programs. What similarities and differences would you expect these programs to have? Why?

7. "Bootlegging" of forms and other records is a common problem of all offices. Why is this condition so common and what steps can be taken by records managers to reduce its severity?

8. What are some of the main considerations in organizing a records management program? Where (or to whom) would you turn for help in this organizing function?

9. Research the main costs of each of the following records:
   a. a one-page business letter that was dictated by an executive
   b. a one-page business letter that was composed and typed by a secretary
   c. filling in a sales invoice form on a typewriter
   d. handling incoming mail
   e. handling outgoing mail

10. Suggest ways in which the costs outlined in #9 above can be reduced.

11. What significant differences occur between processed forms costs and the physical costs (such as paper and printing) of a business form?

12. Correspondence duties and habits are usually firmly ingrained in both experienced executives and their secretaries. Assume that you have worked for five years for an employer who has held his management position 15 years. What suggestions could you give him which might help to reduce costs of dictating, transcribing, and transmitting of information?

13. Discuss (or outline) in detail the specific steps you should follow in developing a reliable work standard for these filing tasks:
   a. extracting information from a visible card file
   b. sorting 5 x 3 cards in alphabetic sequence
   c. pulling carbon copies from a geographic file

14. What assumptions must be made before either the accuracy ratio or the activity ratio (as measures of filing/finding efficiency) can be used to advantage?

15. From your study of records management, discuss what you consider to be an ideal plan for managing a firm's total record system. Keep in mind both small and large organizations in developing your answer.

Learning Projects

1. To understand clearly the diversity of operating programs in records management, visit several large businesses where paperwork is the predominant product of the firm. Arrange to speak with a key office

executive, such as the office manager, who can provide reliable information about the firm's records system. To develop an interview instrument, use as a guide the chart in Figures 14-1 and 14-2 to help you understand the organization and collect the information you require for this assignment. (Note: Both in-class and out-of-class group work can be used to develop such an interview instrument.)

After you have completed the firm visitations, write a short report in which you outline the nature of these records management programs and your view of the future which such type of work holds for students who study records management.

2. Records managers must be able to design efficient business forms. A handwritten draft of a form (as presented to you by the form author) is shown here and has these characteristics:

   a. It represents a new form.
   b. It will be used and filed by your school as a final record of all students' work in business.
   c. It will be mimeographed on some standard-size sheet (or card).

Graduate Record Card

Name _____ date _____
Address _____ tel # _____
Major _____ Sem Hrs. in Bus. _____
                   Sem Hrs. in Major _____
Date of graduation _____
Age _____ Degree _____
Plans for Future _____
_____
_____
_____
_____

   d. It will be filled in on the typewriter with information provided by a computer printout student transcript.
   e. Approximately 500 such records will be filled out and filed each term.
   f. Reference to the card will be by student name or a student (social security) number.
   g. Before graduation each student will check his form for accuracy.

Study the form, its use, and the information planned for it. Then design the form without deleting any of the information planned but making improvements wherever possible. Suggest an appropriate size for this form and defend the reasons for making this suggestion.

3. Assume that in the future more and more records will be produced by machine and many even retained on machine files (tapes and disks). To understand "machine" filing and finding, collect job descriptions of records personnel such as tape librarians and documentation clerks in computer installations and compare their duties with similar job descriptions which you should obtain from manual filing systems departments. Develop a comparative report in which you analyze the training necessary for both groups of records personnel.

4. When you report for a job interview in a large office, your records management training comes to the attention of the executive interviewing you. In fact, he asks you this question, "What kinds of good practices would you put to work in developing an effective filing system for my office?" To be able to answer this question, develop a highly concise one- or two-page set of evaluative criteria by which a filing system could be judged. Do not ignore the very important factors of cost and convenience.

Index

City State Address Street Alumb